GUIDE TO RURAL ENGLAND

THE NORTH WEST OF ENGLAND

By Peter Long

© Travel Publishing Ltd.

Published by:
Travel Publishing Ltd
7a Apollo House, Calleva Park
Aldermaston, Berks, RG7 8TN
ISBN 1-904-43400-2
© Travel Publishing Ltd

Country Living is a registered trademark of The National
Magazine Company Limited.

First Published: *2003*

COUNTRY LIVING GUIDES:

East Anglia	Scotland
Heart of England	The South of England
Ireland	The South East of England
The North East of England	The West Country
The North West of England	Wales

PLEASE NOTE:

All advertisements in this publication have been accepted in good faith by Travel
Publishing and they have not necessarily been endorsed by *Country Living*
Magazine.

All information is included by the publishers in good faith and is believed to be
correct at the time of going to press. No responsibility can be accepted for errors.

Editor: Peter Long

Printing by: Scotprint, Haddington

Location Maps: © Maps in Minutes ™ (2003)   © Crown Copyright, Ordnance Survey 2003

Walks: Walks have been reproduced from the Jarrold Pathfinder Guides
                 © Jarrold Publishing

Walk Maps: Reproduced from Ordnance Survey mapping on behalf of the
                 Controller of Her Majesty's Stationery Office, © Crown Copyright.
                 Licence Number MC 100035812

Cover Design: Lines & Words, Aldermaston

Cover Photo: Little Langdale, Lake District, Cumbria © www.britainonview.com

Text Photos: Text photos have been kindly supplied by the Britain on View photo library
                 © www.britainonview.com

Contents

LOCATOR MAP

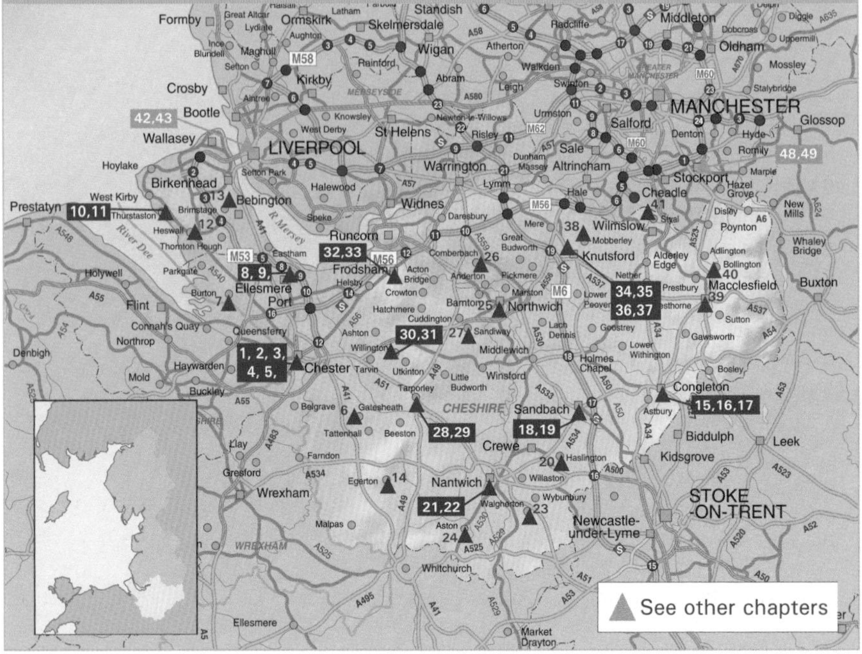

See other chapters

ADVERTISERS AND PLACES OF INTEREST

1 CHESHIRE

The shape of the county of Cheshire has been likened to a teapot: its base is the Staffordshire border, its handle the strip of land running from Stockport up to the Yorkshire border, with the Wirral providing the spout. And, tucked away in the crook of the spout, is the capital of the county, the City of Chester.

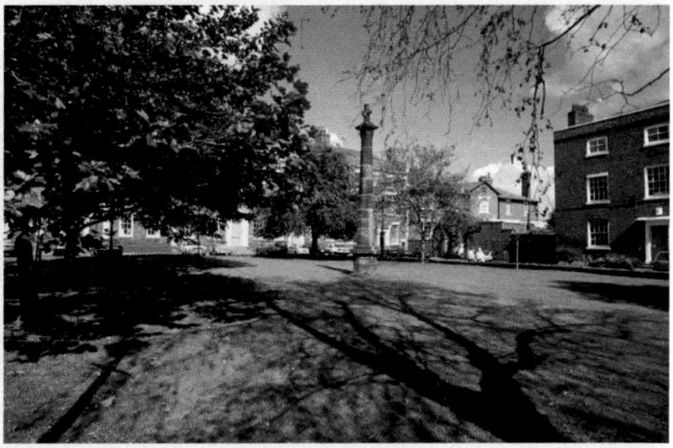

Abbey Square, Chester

There are many aspects to Cheshire: the rural landscape of the Cheshire Plains, the textile towns in the east, the ancient salt towns, the grand stately homes and the charming black and white houses and cottages, and the delightful city of Chester, where in AD 70 the famous 20th legion, the Valeria Victrix, established its headquarters and took full advantage of the strategic position on the River Dee. In the course of his *Tour through the Whole Island of Great Britain*, Daniel Defoe came to Chester by the ferry over the River Dee. He liked the city streets, "very broad and fair"; admired the "very pleasant walk round the city, upon the walls", disliked its cathedral, "built of red, sandy, ill-looking stone", but had

ADVERTISERS AND PLACES OF INTEREST

nothing but praise for its "excellent cheese". Cheshire cheese has been famous for generations. John Speed, the famous Elizabethan map-maker and a Cheshire man himself, noted: "The soil is fat fruitful and rich....the Pastures make the Kine's udders to strout to the pail, from whom the best Cheese of all Europe is made".

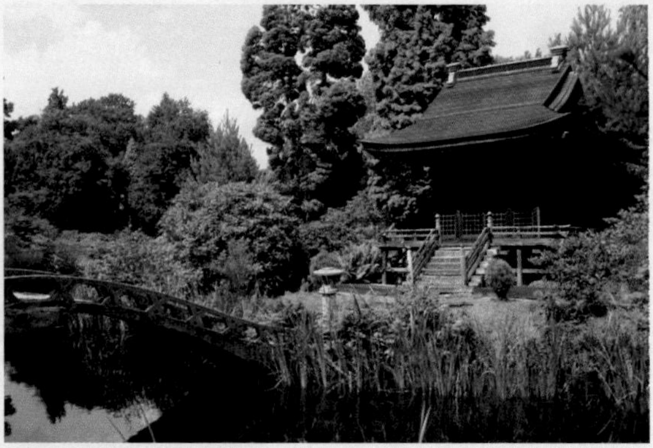

Japanese Temple, Tatton Park

Later, some enthusiasts even promoted the idea that the name Cheshire was actually short for cheese-shire.

One of the county's other major industry was salt, mined here even before the Romans arrived. By the time of the *Domesday Book*, the salt towns, or 'wiches' – Nantwich, Northwich, Middlewich, were firmly established. The process then involved pumping the salt brine to the surface and boiling it to produce granular salt. In 1670, huge deposits of rock salt were discovered and these are still being mined, mostly for use in keeping the country's roads free from ice. Macclesfield was famous as a silk town, while Styal was created as a model village for one of the first cotton mills in the area, Quarry Bank Mill. One thing that visitors don't get to see is the county's best known character, the grinning Cheshire Cat. The expression 'to grin like a Cheshire cat' was in use long before Lewis Carroll adopted it in *Alice in Wonderland*. Carroll spent his childhood in the Cheshire village of Daresbury and would have regularly seen the local cheeses moulded into various animal shapes, one of which was a grinning cat.

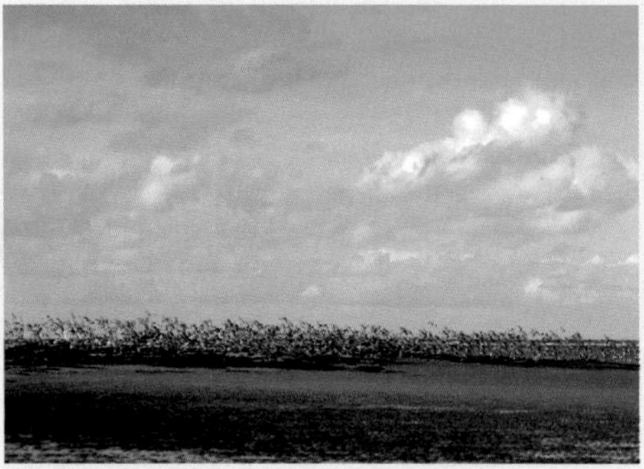

Hilbre Islands

Cheshire boasts a number of very fine churches, some of them built in grand style with money from the salt industry. Of particular note are the churches at Lower Peover, the oldest aisled wooden church in England; at Macclesfield, with superb tombs and monuments and wonderful stained glass; and at Nantwich, with its octagonal tower and medieval stall canopies.

CHESTER

The city's actual position, a strategic site on the River Dee close to the Welsh border, was important even before the Romans arrived in AD 70. They based a large camp here and called it Deva after the Celtic name for the river. It was during this period that the splendid city walls were originally built – two miles round, and the most complete in the country.

In Saxon times 'Ceastre' became the administrative centre of a shire, and was the last major town in England to fall to William the Conqueror during his dreadful Harrowing of the North. William pulled down half of Chester's houses and reinforced the message of Norman domination by building a castle overlooking the Dee.

Old Dee Bridge, Chester

Subsequent Earls of Chester (the present Prince of Wales is the current one) were given a free, firm hand in dealing with the local Saxons and with the still rebellious Welsh, who continued to make a nuisance of themselves right through the Middle Ages. In return for its no-nonsense dealing with these problems Chester received a number of royal privileges: borough status, a licence for a market and, around 1120, the first commission in England for a Sheriff, long before the more famous holder of this position received one.

The problem with the Welsh was finally resolved in 1485 when a Welsh-based family, the Tudors, defeated Richard III at Bosworth Field and Owen Tudor claimed the throne as Henry VII. For more than 150 years Chester enjoyed an unprecedented period of peace and prosperity. Then came the Civil War. Chester supported the King but Charles I had the galling experience of watching from the city walls as his troops were defeated at nearby Rowton Moor. For two

CHESHIRE MILITARY MUSEUM

The Castle, Chester CH1 2DN
Tel: 01244 327617

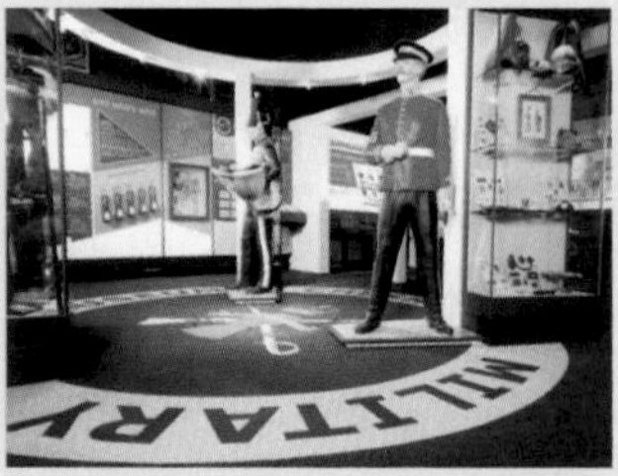

The **Cheshire Military Museum** is a registered museum with stunning displays and collections telling the story of Cheshire's military history. The Soldiers of Cheshire is an interactive exhibition where 300 years of history of the soldier's life is shown through computers, tableaux and hands-on exhibits.

Here you can meet Sergeant Shipp at Bhurtpore and walk a length of trench at Ypres. Enjoy the 'With Love' feature and much more for all the family. Facilities include a small shop, toilet and access for the disabled. Open daily 10am-5pm (last entry 4.30) except for two weeks over Christmas.

long years after that rout, the city was under siege until starvation finally forced its capitulation. **The King Charles Tower** on the wall is now a small museum with displays telling the story of the siege.

James Boswell, Dr Johnson's biographer, visited Chester in the 1770s and wrote "I was quite enchanted at Chester, so that I could with difficulty quit it". He was to return again, declaring that, "Chester pleases my fancy more than any town I ever saw". Modern visitors will almost certainly share his enthusiasm.

Probably the best introduction to this compact little city is to join one of the frequent sightseeing tours conducted by a Blue Badge guide. These take place every day, even Christmas Day, and leave from the **Chester Visitor Centre**. The Centre can also provide a wealth of information about the city, including a full calendar of events that range from the **Chester Regatta**, the oldest rowing races in the world, and Chester Races, the oldest horseraces in Britain, to the Lord Mayor's Show in May and the Festival of Transport, featuring an amazing parade of vintage cars, in August.

Towering above the city centre is **Chester Cathedral**, a majestic building of weathered pink stone which in 1992 celebrated its 900th birthday. It was originally an Abbey and is one of very few to survive Henry VIII's closure of the monasteries in the 1540s. The cloisters are regarded as the finest in England and the monks' refectory is still serving food - although nowadays it is refreshments and lunches for visitors. There's a fine 14th century shrine to St Werbergh, the princess/abbess who founded the first church on this site in Saxon times, and some intricately carved Quire stalls

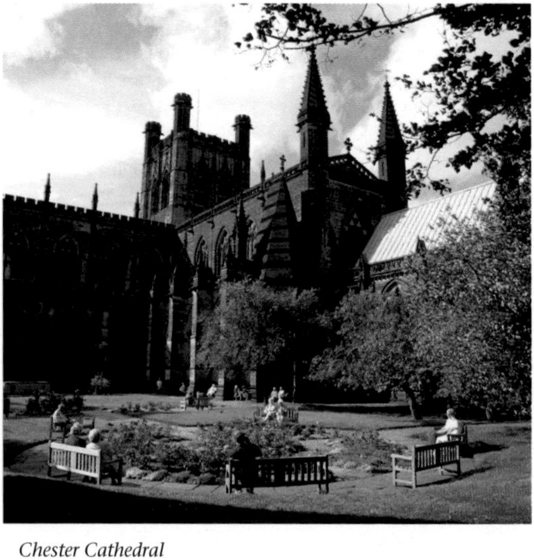

Chester Cathedral

almost 800 years old which are reckoned to be the finest in Britain. It was at Chester Cathedral, in 1742, that George Frederick Handel personally conducted rehearsals of his oratorio *The Messiah* before its first performance in Dublin: a copy of the score with annotations in his own hand is on display.

Chester is famous for its outstanding range of museums. At the **Dewa Roman Experience** visitors can re-live the sights, sounds and even the smells of daily life in Roman Chester. A superb array of artefacts from Chester and elsewhere in the Roman Empire is on display and kids love dressing up in replica suits of Roman armour. In the **Grosvenor Museum** are furnished period rooms, the Timeline Gallery travelling back through

The Rows, Chester

the city's history, the Natural History Gallery, the Silver Gallery featuring the Chester race cups, a gallery of paintings by local contemporary artists, and many more attractions, events and activities that make this a great place for all the family to visit. **On The Air** broadcasting museum chronicles the world of radio

PASTARAZZI RISTORANTE

29 Grosvenor Street, Chester, Cheshire CH1 2DD
Tel: 01244 400029 Fax: 01244 347756
e-mail: info@pastarazzi.com
website: www.pastarazzi.com

Local businessman Stephen Wundke created an Italian restaurant to compete with the best in the country when he opened **Pastarazzi Ristorante** in 1996. The building is Grade II listed, and behind the grand Gothic arched windows and the tall spired clock, there

are panelled walls, panelled floors and the bar top and 17th century church pews in the bar. Fresh produce, both British and international, is the basis of the menu, and the 60 different dishes cooked fresh daily are exceeded by a 70-strong globally sourced wine list. The head chef and his team combine traditional Italian recipes with imaginative, well-considered modern touches. Thus carpaccio, the Italian classic of wafer-thin raw steak, is accompanied by marinated grilled artichokes; calamari are presented with cherry tomatoes and crisp chorizo; mussels are prepared Thai-style with coconut milk, lime leaves and coriander; fillet steak is served on rösti topped with a field mushroom filled with dolcelatte and fresh asparagus.

Nothing succeeds like success, and the thousands of satisfied customers who pass through the doors each week confirm just how inspired a decision Stephen Wundke made back in 1996.

and television from the pioneering days of BBC radio to satellite and digital TV, while the **Chester Toy & Doll Museum** is a nostalgic treasure-house of antique playthings. The **Cheshire Military Museum** (see panel on page 6) recounts the story of the county's military history using computers, tableaux and hands-on exhibits to present the soldier's life through the last 300 years.

Quite apart from its historical attractions, Chester is also one of the major shopping centres for the north west and north Wales. All the familiar High Street names are here, often housed in much more appealing buildings than they usually inhabit, along with a great number of specialist and antique shops. A unique shopping experience is provided by the world-famous, two-tiered galleries of shops under covered walkways known as **The Rows** which line both sides of Bridge Street. The Rows are an architectural one-off: no other medieval town has anything like them. Many of the black and white, half-timbered frontages of The Rows, so typical of Chester and Cheshire, are actually Victorian restorations, but crafted so beautifully and faithfully that even experts can have difficulty distinguishing them from their 13th century originals.

Close by is the **Eastgate Clock**. It was erected in 1897 to celebrate Queen Victoria's Diamond Jubilee, a beautifully ornate construction which is one of the most photographed timepieces in the world.

Chester's famous City Walls were originally built by the Romans to protect the fortress of Deva from attacks by Celtic tribes. Nowadays, the two-mile long circuit – an easy, level promenade - provides thousands of visitors with splendid views of the River Dee, of the city's many glorious buildings and of the

---

CHESTER GATEWAY THEATRE

Hamilton Place, Chester, CH1 2BH
Tel: 01244 340392 Fax: 01244 341296
e-mail: boxoffice@chestergateway.co.uk
website: www.chestergateway.co.uk

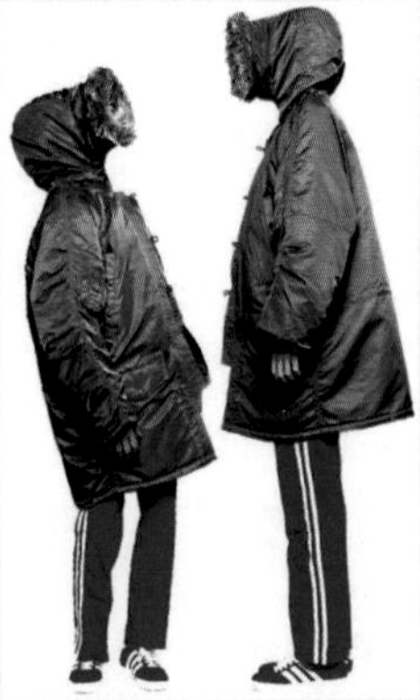

In the city centre, with easy parking near the premises, **Chester Gateway** has a long tradition as a major centre for the performing arts, catering for all tastes and all ages. Plays pre- and post-West End are performed to full houses (the main house has 435 seats), and the first half of 2003 saw productions as diverse as *Dick Whittington*, *A Passionate Woman* by Kay Mellor, *My Life with Kenneth Williams*, written and performed by David Benson, and an evening with the *Big Chris Barber Band*.

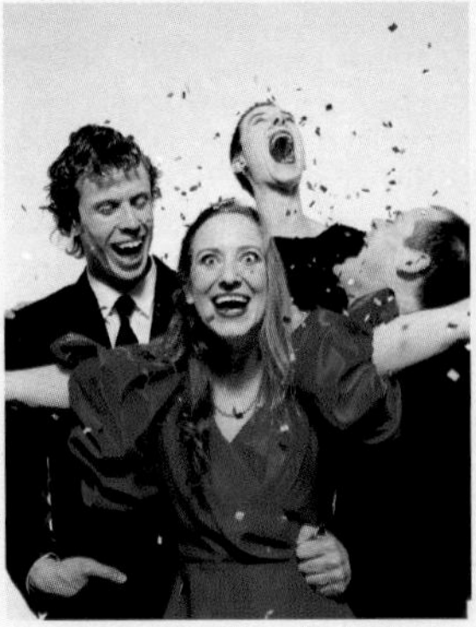

Among the shows scheduled for later in 2003 are *The Banquet*, a new production by Protein Dance; *Men in Coats* - one of the most talked-about comedy duo acts of the year; and *Merlin & Arthur - Discover the Legend*. Other shows are performed in the 110-seat Manweb Studio, where the cast and the audience are on the same level. Chester Gateway is committed to providing a series of events introducing people of all ages to live theatre, and its activities include a youth theatre, summer schools, a playwriting group and education workshops on a wide variety of drama-related subjects.

CLUB GLOBE

10 Steam Mill Street, Chester, Cheshire CH3 5AN
Tel: 01244 340417 Fax: 01244 317969
e-mail: clubglobe@btopenworld.com
website: www.pastarazzi.com/index_clubglobe.htm#

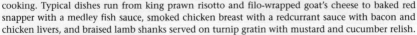

1999 saw the opening of **Club Globe**, a restaurant and bar in a handsomely converted industrial building, serving great food and drink in a lively, relaxed atmosphere. The decor draws its inspiration from the Caribbean and the Far East (a definite touch of Raffles), and the head chef also takes a look round the world for his exciting fusion cooking. Typical dishes run from king prawn risotto and filo-wrapped goat's cheese to baked red snapper with a medley fish sauce, smoked chicken breast with a redcurrant sauce with bacon and chicken livers, and braised lamb shanks served on turnip gratin with mustard and cucumber relish.

Simpler but equally satisfying are the pasta dishes, the salads and the chunky sandwiches overflowing with good things.

In the bar, there's live music every Friday and Saturday, with a mixture that's every bit as eclectic as the decor and the cuisine. For regular diners the management have had the excellent idea of a membership scheme offering discounts and other benefits at Club Globe and Pastarazzi (see separate advertisement). These include free entry for the music nights and watching major sporting events on Saturday on a large screen in the bar, with a sports bar menu to accompany the big match. Club Globe is open Monday to Saturday 11am to midnight.

distant Welsh mountains. Here, during the summer months, Caius Julius Quartus, a Roman Legionary Officer in shining armour, conducts a patrol around the fortress walls and helps to re-create the life and times of a front-line defender of the Empire. At one point, the wall runs alongside St John Street, which has a curious history. In Roman times it was the main thoroughfare between the fortress and the **Amphitheatre**, the largest ever uncovered in Britain, capable of seating 7,000 spectators. During the Middle Ages however this highway was excavated and turned into a defensive ditch. Over the years, the ditch gradually filled up and by Elizabethan times St John Street was a proper street once again.

No visit to Chester would be complete without a trip to **Chester Zoo** on the northern edge of the city. Set in 110 acres of landscaped gardens, and the

brainchild of George Mottershead, it's the largest zoo in Britain, caring for more than 5,000 animals from some 500 different species. The zoo also provides a refuge for many rare and endangered animals which breed freely in near-natural enclosures. What's more, it has the UK's largest elephant facility and is the only successful breeder of Asiatic elephants in this country. The zoo has more than a mile of overhead railway providing a splendid bird's-eye view of the animals and the Roman Garden. Other attractions include the Rare Penguin Breeding Centre with windows enabling visitors to see the birds 'flying' underwater; a Forest Zone with spacious homes for Buffy Headed Capuchin monkeys; and special enclosures for the black rhinos and red pandas (Lushui and Lushan are great favourites with visitors). And in the award-winning Spirit of the Jaguar enclosure the spotted jaguar Sofia

Continued on page 12

WALK 1.

Chester and the River Dee

Start	Chester, The Cross
Distance	5 miles (8km)
Approximate time	2½ hours
Parking	Chester
Refreshments	Pubs and cafés at Chester
Ordnance Survey maps	Explorer 266 (Wirral & Chester), Landranger 117 (Chester & Wrexham)

This flat and easy walk to the south of Chester falls into two distinct halves. Much of the first half is through attractive woodland and the return leg is across meadows bordering the River Dee. The route uses short stretches of Chester's medieval walls and passes some of the city's historic sites. Allow plenty of time for a thorough exploration of one of England's most attractive, historic and fascinating cities.

Throughout its long history Chester has played many roles. Originally the Roman fort of Deva, it has been a major port (until the Dee silted up), both a defensive fortress against the Welsh and a springboard for English invasions of Wales, as well as an administrative centre and cathedral city.

Although none of the original gateways survive, Chester retains its circuit of medieval walls and most of its historic and architectural attractions lie within the walls. Foremost among these are the castle and cathedral. Of Chester's medieval castle, one of the principal fortresses along the Welsh border, only the 13th-century Agricola Tower remains. Most of it was pulled down in the late 18th and early 19th centuries and replaced by imposing classical buildings to serve as barracks and a law court. Chester Cathedral was originally a Benedictine abbey, raised to cathedral status by Henry VIII in 1541 after the dissolution of the monasteries. The cloisters and other monastic buildings on the north side of the church are among its principal assets. Also worth seeing are the superb and intricately-carved 14th century choir stalls, among the

finest in the country. Most of the cathedral dates from the 14th and 15th centuries and it was heavily restored in the Victorian era.

Unique to Chester are the Rows, a series of covered walkways. These are medieval in origin, are found in the four main streets which radiate from The Cross and roughly correspond to the area originally enclosed by the Roman walls. Although their picturesque black and white appearance is more Victorian than Tudor, this in no way detracts from their appeal and attractiveness.

From The Cross, walk down Bridge Street and on down Lower Bridge Street, passing under Bridgegate to reach the Old Dee Bridge. Immediately turn right along Castle Drive and after passing County Hall, you can either continue along the road or take to the medieval walls, passing below the buildings of Chester Castle, to a main road. Cross over, turn left to cross Grosvenor Bridge and then bear right **Ⓐ** through a gap in the railings onto a path which descends through woodland, bending right to meet another path.

Turn left to continue through the trees and the path rises to emerge onto a road at a busy junction. Cross four roads in quick succession, curving left all the time, to reach Wrexham Road. Turn right and then immediately turn left along a tarmac path to a T-junction to the right of ornamental gates and in front of a lodge **B** . Turn right onto an attractive tarmac track which continues through woodland. This is the Chester Approach, a driveway constructed to link the Duke of Westminster's residence of Eaton Hall with Chester. After ¾ mile (1.2km), look out for a ladder stile on the left at the corner of a wood. Do not climb it but a few yards farther on, turn left **C** along a path which keeps by the left inside edge of the wood. At a fork, take the right-hand path which continues through the trees and pass beside a fence onto a road.

Turn sharp right and at a public footpath sign, turn left **D** over a stile and walk along the left edge of a field, descending an embankment to reach the River Dee. Turn left over a stile and follow an attractive riverside path back to Chester, a distance of about 2¼ miles (3.6km). The path keeps along the edge of meadows, via a series of stiles, and follows the river around a left bend. In the corner of the final meadow, go through a kissing-gate and keep ahead along a paved path to a suspension footbridge **E** .

Immediately after going under the bridge, turn left up a flight of steps and turn left at the top to

cross the bridge. There are fine views both up and down the river. On the other side, keep ahead up more steps and walk along a paved path which curves left by the wall of St John's Church on the left. This majestic and partly ruined Norman church briefly served as the cathedral of the Mercian diocese in the late 11th century. Keep ahead along Little St John Street, passing to the right of the Roman amphitheatre, built towards the end of the 1st century AD, and on reaching Newgate climb steps onto the walls.

Cross Newgate and keep along the walls as far as Eastgate, which is surmounted by a distinctive clock tower, erected in 1897 to commemorate Queen Victoria's Diamond Jubilee. Here you descend from the walls, turn right to pass under the gate and walk along Eastgate Street back to the start.

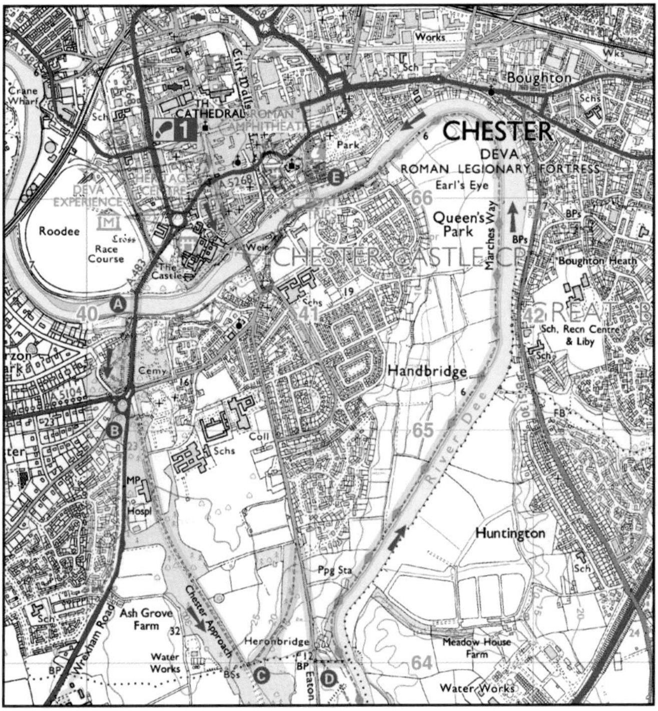

joined Carlos, Salvador and Ebony in 2002. Offering more than enough interest for a full day out, the zoo is open every day of the year except Christmas Day. Children can romp happily in the Fun Ark, and new attractions include A Dragons in Danger exhibit.

AROUND CHESTER

TARVIN
5 miles E of Chester off the A54 or A51

In the *Domesday Book* Tarvin is recorded as one of the larger manors in Cheshire and by the 1300s was the centre of an extensive parish. The present church was begun at this time and boasts the oldest surviving timber roof in Cheshire. The village came to prominence in the Civil War when General Sir William Brereton made it his headquarters during the siege of Chester. In August 1644 there was fighting around the church and bullet marks can still be seen around its west door. One of them even penetrated a brass by the chancel in memory of a former Mayor of Chester and remained there for many years until a Victorian sightseer prised it out and made off with it. Tarvin is about halfway along the **Baker Way**, which runs from Chester Station to Delamere Station at the edge of Delamere Forest Park. The trail follows

the Shropshire Union Canal from Chester to Rowton Bridge, thence to Hockenhull Platts, Tarvin, Ashton, Brines Brow and Delamere Forest.

GATESHEATH
8 miles SE of Chester off the A41

Occupying a Victorian farmhouse in Gatesheath, the **Country Centre** at New Russia Hall is a unique attraction. To begin with, there's the Orchard Paddock, a magnet for children with its appealing collection of farm animals and pets, swings and crazy golf. Anyone interested in flower arranging can watch the staff of the Dried Flower Workshop creating unique arrangements - for sale, or you can buy all the materials to make your own - and painted plant pots, boxes and small pieces of furniture. There is a comprehensive display of greeting cards and gifts, a tea room, and Uncle Peter's Fudge Kitchen where you can try the superbly tasty fudge. The name New Russia Hall has nothing to do with Russia but comes from a corruption of 'rushes' which once grew abundantly in the marshy ground nearby and provided the basic materials for local basketmakers.

TATTENHALL
8 miles SE of Chester off the A41

Tattenhall is a fine old village within

CARRIAGES LICENSED RESTAURANT AND B&B

New Russia Hall, Chester Road, Gatesheath, Tattenhall, Nr Chester, Cheshire CH3 9AH
Tel: 01829 770958

Tracy and Colin Oats took over a handsome redbrick Georgian farmhouse at the end of 2001 and turned it into **Carriages Licensed Restaurant and B&B**. In what was the old cheese-making room, lunches are served every day (traditional roasts on Sunday), along with teas, coffees and evening meals. Small parties can be catered for, and booking is advisable at peak times. The owners also offer bed & breakfast accommodation and a site for caravans.

sight of the twin castles of Beeston and Peckforton perched atop the Peckforton Hills. It has some attractive old houses and a Victorian church with a graveyard which gained notoriety during the 19th century because of the activities of a gang of grave-robbers. They lived in caves in the hills nearby and, once they had disposed of the bodies to medical gentlemen, used the empty coffins to store their booty from more conventional thieving. At that time Tattenhall was a busy little place. The Shropshire Union Canal passes close by and the village was served by two railway stations on different lines. Today, only one railway line survives (and no stations), the canal is used solely by pleasure craft, but the village is enjoying a new lease of life as a desirable community for people commuting to Chester, a short drive away.

Brown tourist signs on the A41 point the way to **Cheshire Ice Cream Farm**, where real dairy ice cream is made in over 30 different flavours, including rhubarb and custard, Cointreau and orange, and a seasonal sherry trifle. Visitors can watch the cows being milked, and a video shows the whole process of making ice cream 'from cow to cone'. Young visitors can romp in the Playbarn, and the farm is home to many rare breed animals (alpacas, miniature donkeys, pygmy goats, Jacob sheep) and rescued birds of prey and hedgehogs.

BELGRAVE

4 miles S of Chester on the B5445

Belgrave is hardly large enough to qualify as a hamlet but it has given its name to the London area known as Belgravia. Both are owned by the Duke of Westminster, Britain's richest landowner, whose family home, Eaton Hall, stands beside the River Dee a couple of miles west of the village.

The Duke's family, the Grosvenors, were well established in Cheshire by the 1300s but it was acquisition by marriage of a large estate to the west of London that brought them huge riches. As London expanded westwards during the 18th and 19th centuries, their once rural estate was developed into elegant squares and broad boulevards, many with names reflecting the Duke's Cheshire connections – Eaton Square, Eccleston Square, Grosvenor Place and Chester Row.

The Grosvenor's vast Victorian mansion suffered badly when it was occupied by the military during the Second World War. In the 1970s it was demolished and replaced by a more modest concrete structure which has divided architectural opinion as to its merits – one writer described it "as modern as a 1970s airline terminal". The house is not open to the public but its gardens occasionally are.

THE WIRRAL (PARTLY IN MERSEYSIDE)

Two Old English words meaning heathland covered with bog myrtle gave The Wirral its name and well into modern times it was a byword for a desolate place. The 14th century author of *Sir Gawayne and the Green Knight* writes of

> "The wilderness of Wirral:
> few lived there
> Who loved with a good heart
> either God or man".

The Wirral's inhabitants were infamous for preying on the ships tossed on to its marshy coastline by gales sweeping off the Irish Sea. The 19th century development of shipbuilding at Birkenhead brought industry on a large scale to the Mersey shore and also an influx of prosperous Liverpool commuters

GORDALE GARDEN CENTRE

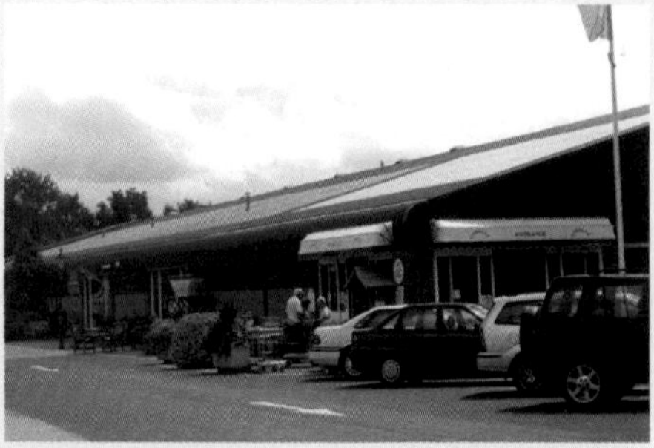

Chester High Road, Burton, South Wirral,
Cheshire CH64 8TF
Tel: 0151 336 2116 Fax: 0151 336 8152
e-mail: jill@gordale.co.uk
website: www.gordale.co.uk

Easy to find on Chester High Road midway between Chester and Heswall, **Gordale Nursery & Garden Centre** has been a leader in its field for more than 50 years. Attention to detail puts Gordale head and shoulders above the rest, and owners Jill and Peter Nicholson never stop looking for ways to make a top-notch business even better. Superbly laid out in extensive purpose-built premises that cover 12 acres, the centre stocks everything connected with gardens, and a great deal more besides, and each department is run by a highly trained manager (some of whom have more than 20 years' service).

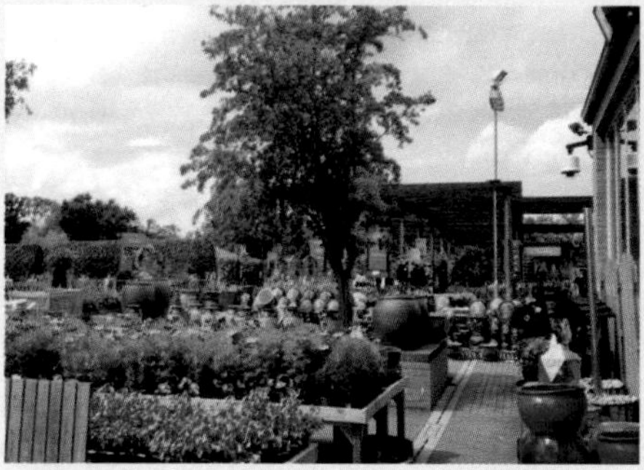

The range of plants for sale is second to none with plants sourced from leading nurseries across Europe. Traditional roses, rhododendrons, azaleas, alpines, heathers, climbers,perennials, fruit and conifers sit alongside the increasingly fashionable tree ferns, bamboos, ferns, palms, citrus and grasses. Bedding and houseplants are kept in climatically controlled greenhouses ensuring the best quality whatever the season and staff are always on hand to provide advice. Also for sale are birdbaths, sundials, traditional and modern sculptures from the stoneware department and wonderful pots.

The range of garden furniture and accessories is as wide as you'll find anywhere, with tables and chairs in wood, resin, metal and glass, indoor cane furniture for conservatories, sunloungers, side tables and footstools, parasols and cushions, garden lighting, gas and charcoal barbecues, and picnic ware in all styles. Other departments provide books, clothes, speciality foods, ceramics, fresh and silk flowers, and a huge selection of gifts for birthdays, weddings and other special occasions as well as the departments you would expect to find in a traditional garden centre such as bulbs, seeds, composts, tools, garden care and watering equipment. The 180 seat coffee shop is open throughout the day for coffees, teas, home made cakes and light meals.

The children's play area, combined with the extensive landscaped grounds, wild fowl, ducks and peacocks make the centre a worthwhile day trip for the entire family, and its regular programme of promotional events including a bulb weekend and the annual summer garden party, provide interest throughout the seasons. But it is at Christmas time when the centre takes on a magical quality. With regular demonstrations by leading florists, late night shopping, Santa's grotto and one of the best Christmas displays in the North West, they have everything you need under one roof to complete your Christmas shopping each and every year.

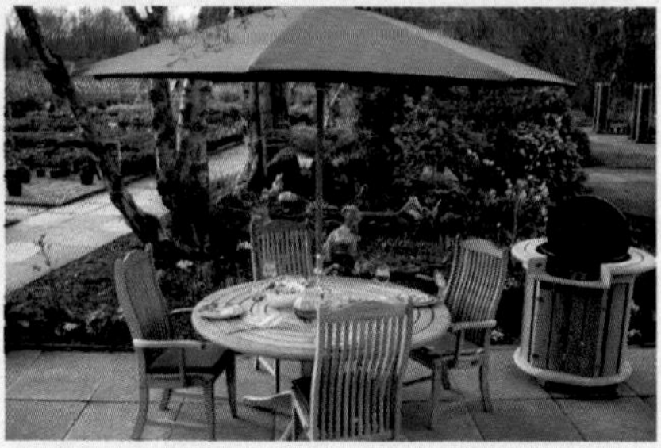

who colonised the villages of the Caldy and Grange Hills and transformed the former wilderness into leafy suburbia. The 1974 Local Government changes handed two thirds of The Wirral to Merseyside, leaving Cheshire with by far the most attractive third, the southern and western parts alongside the River Dee. Tourism officials now refer to The Wirral as the Leisure Peninsula, a fair description of this appealing and comparatively little-known area. One of its major attractions is **Ness Gardens**, a 62-acre tract of superbly landscaped gardens on the banks of the River Dee. Founded in 1898 by Arthur Kilpin Buley, a Liverpool cotton broker, the gardens have been developed into one of the country's leading botanic gardens. Ness is now run by the University of Liverpool as an Environmental and Horticultural Research Station and provides magnificent displays all year round. There are children's play and picnic areas, well-marked interest trails, a visitor centre with weekly summer exhibitions, a gift shop and licensed refreshment rooms.

ELLESMERE PORT

8 miles N of Chester on the A5032

An interesting 8½-mile trail for walkers and cyclists runs along the Shropshire Union Canal between Chester and Ellesmere Port. It passes through communities and countryside, and along its route are 10 sculptures that mark important gateways to the Canal. Local artist Stephen Hitchin designed each sculpture to reflect the character of its location and to provide directions along the route. Among the places of interest on the route are the Backford Gap, marking the southern end of the Wirral Peninsula, and Caughall Bridge, constructed by Thomas Telford. The northern end of the Canal lies within the Mersey Community Forest, a network of

small woodlands with public access. The first part of the Shropshire Union Canal was completed in 1779, linking Chester to Nantwich. The link between Chester and Netherpool (soon to become better known as Ellesmere Port) was opened in 1795, and passengers could take the boat from Chester to Liverpool, changing at Ellesmere Port, for 7½d first class (about 3p). Railways gradually replaced the canals in the 19th century, and the Shropshire Union had more or less ceased its working life by the 1920s. Since the 1960s this and many other canals have found a new role supporting the leisure industry. The history of the Canal can be explored at the **Boat Museum** (see panel below), set in Ellesmere Port's historic dock complex. The Museum has the world's largest floating collection of canal craft, along with working exhibitions of restored steam, diesel and gas engines in the Power Hall and Pump

THE BOAT MUSEUM

South Pier Road, Ellesmere Port CH65 4FW
Tel: 0151 355 5017 Fax: 0151 355 5017

Experience life afloat as you climb aboard the historic narrow boats, or step back in time to the period dockworkers cottages along Porters Row. With exhibitions of working steam diesel engines, colourful displays of canal ware and the fascinating history of canal development, Britain's industrial and social heritage is brought vividly to life at **The Boat Museum.** The 7.5 acre site is right by J9 of the M53, provides a great day out for all the family, and has a gift shop, café and free car park.

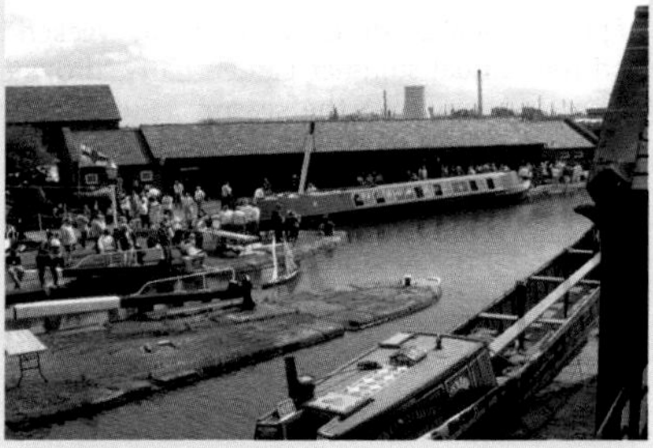

House. Porters Row recreates the dockworkers' cottages of 1840, 1900, 1930 and 1950. Boat trips run most days throughout the summer. Ellesmere Port's other major attraction is **Blue Planet**, (see panel below) billed as Britain's biggest and best aquarium adventure. On the moving walkway that runs through the underwater safari tunnel visitors can see rays, sharks and over 1,000 other fish and marine life at close quarters. The piranha exhibit is one of the largest in Europe, and among the many other attractions are a display of amphibians, shark feeding and regular special events.

EASTHAM

10 miles NW of Chester off the A41

Eastham Woods Country Park is a 76-acre oasis of countryside amidst industrial Merseyside and enjoys considerable status among birdwatchers as one of few northern woodlands with all three species of native woodpecker in residence. Just a mile or so from the Park is Eastham village, another little oasis with a church and old houses grouped around the village green. The yew tree in the churchyard is reputed to be the oldest in England.

BEBINGTON

12 miles NW of Chester off the A41

Much of the Wirral's Merseyside is heavily industrialised but a dramatic exception is **Port Sunlight** near Bebington. This model village was created in 1888 by William Hesketh Lever, later 1st Viscount Leverhulme, to house the workers in his soap factory and was named after his most famous product, Sunlight Soap. Leverhulme wanted to provide 'a new Arcadia, ventilated and drained on the most scientific principles'. Some 30 architects were employed to create the individually designed rows of rustic cottages and the village is now a Conservation Area. The history of the village and its community is explored at the Port Sunlight Heritage Centre, where there are scale models of the village, a Victorian port and Sunlight House, original plans for the building and displays of period advertising and

BLUE PLANET AQUARIUM

Longlooms Road, Ellesmere Port,
Cheshire CH65 9LF
Tel: 0151 357 8804

The award winning **Blue Planet Aquarium** is Britain's largest all weather aquarium attraction and has two floors of interactive displays and exhibits. Take a journey of adventure through the waters of the world, from the misty northern streams to the shark-inhabited waters of the exotic Caribbean. Take a peek at the array of some of the most scary and poisonous creatures in the world. Watch one of the

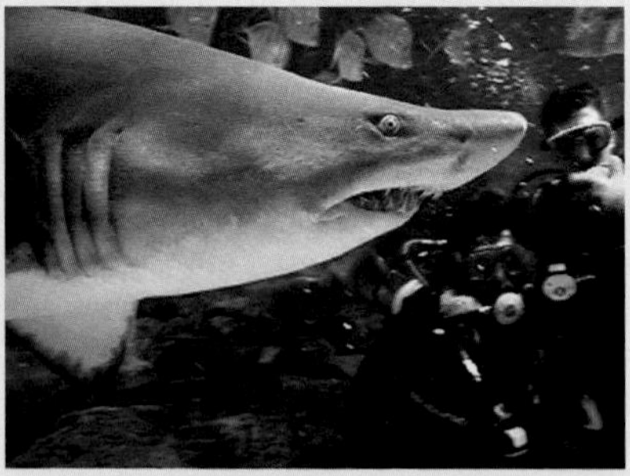

largest collections of sharks in Europe pass inches from your face, as you walk through the breathtaking underwater tunnel, which at 240ft, is one of the longest in the world. An otter enclosure has been carefully constructed to create the perfect environement for its inhabitants and friendly sea creatures can be seen in the Rockpool area, where there are crabs, rays, starfish and lots more.

Tasty meals are available at the Caribbean themed restaurant and fantastic souvenirs can be purchased at the gift shop. For those over 18, there is a chance to dive with the sharks. The fee includes two hours training and safety briefing, equipment hire, a 30 minute dive in the main exhibit with the expert team of divers and a certificate. Qualified divers can also have night dive sessions.

soap packaging. The jewel in the crown of Port Sunlight is the Lady Lever Art Gallery, which houses a magnificent collection of pre-Raphaelite paintings by Millais, Ford Madox Brown and Rosetti, portraits by Gainsborough and Reynolds, dramatic landscapes by Turner and Constable, an impressive Wedgwood collection and some superb pieces of 18th century furniture. The gallery also has a gift shop and a popular tea room, the Lady Lever Café. Lord Leverhulme and his wife are buried in the graveyard of Christ Church.

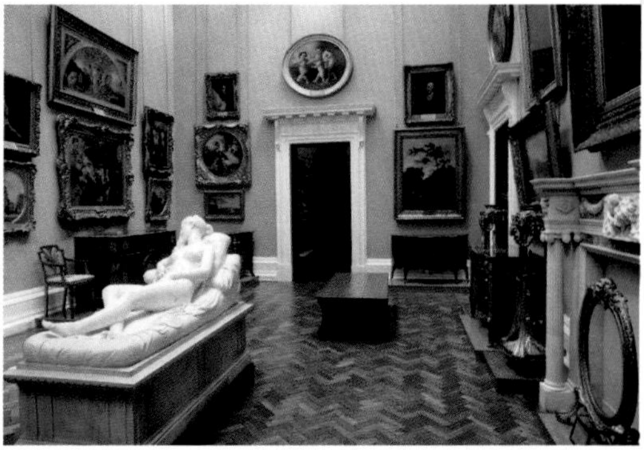
Lady Lever Art Gallery

BIRKENHEAD

20 miles NW of Chester off the M53

If you were asked, "Where is the largest group of Grade I listed buildings in England?", Birkenhead would probably not be your first guess. But you can find these buildings in Hamilton Square where also stands the Town Hall, now **Wirral Museum**. Opened in 1887 by John Laird, this grand building houses an exhibition telling the story of the famous Cammell Laird shipyard, a model of the Woodside area in 1934 when King George V opened the Queensway road tunnel under the Mersey, a collection of delightful Della Robbia pottery and Mayoral and Civic silver. Also within the Town Hall are an art gallery, theatre, cinema and concert hall.

The **Birkenhead Heritage Trail** guides visitors around the town's various attractions and includes trips on a genuine Hong Kong tram and a beautifully restored Birkenhead tram of 1901. The trail takes in the Shore Road Pumping Station with its 'Giant Grasshopper' steam pump. It was one of several used to extract water from the Mersey railway tunnel – Europe's very first underwater rail tunnel. Other attractions along the trail include an Edwardian Street scene display, a unique historic transport collection and the Pacific Road Arts and Exhibition Centre. Just along from Pacific Road is Egerton Bridge, which offers a bird's eye view over the docklands and houses models and information about the Birkenhead Dock system. Moored alongside East Float Dock Road are two historic warships, now museums. Both the frigate *HMS Plymouth* and the submarine *HMS Onyx* served during the Falklands War and are now preserved as they were in the 1980s. *HMS Plymouth* saw action throughout the campaign and while carrying out a lone daylight bombardment was hit by four bombs. *HMS Onyx* was the only non-nuclear submarine to take part in the conflict. She carried 20 men from the SAS and SBS in addition to her own full crew, and was so crowded that she fully deserved her nickname *'The Sardine's Revenge'*. Also on display is a German U-boat, *U534*, whose sinking marked the end of the Battle of the Atlantic in May 1945. The submarine was recovered after lying for 50 years on the seabed. The latest addition to the Birkenhead fleet is *HMS Bronington*, a 'Ton' class minesweeper launched in 1953. The

CHURCH FARM ORGANICS

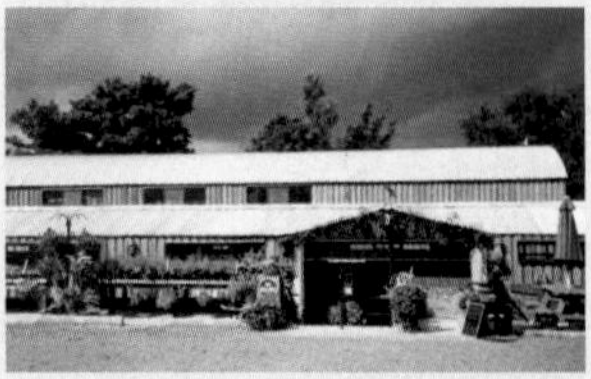

Church Farm, Church Lane, Thurstaston, Wirral,
Cheshire CH61 0HW
Tel: 0151 648 7838 Fax: 0151 648 9644
website: www.churchfarm.org.uk
e-mail: sales@churchfarm.org.uk

Taking over an old cattle farm in 1992, Steve and Brenda Ledsham have created and built up **Church Farm Organics** to be one of the very best sources of organic produce in the whole area. The fruit and vegetables on sale in the farm shop are all organic, and most of them are grown on the 60-acre farm, along with bedding and herbaceous plants. Among hundreds of organic lines, including meat and fish, the owners also sell their own honey and free-range eggs, vital elements in their commitment to selling local food to local people and to contributing to the local community in whatever ways they can.

This ethos manifests itself in many ways: the coffee shop on the premises is a favourite meeting place, and among other services are a box scheme and home delivery service, pick-your-own facilities in season (including a wonderful maze of lavender), a livery yard, a caravan and camping site with full facilities, and a guest room for Bed & (Organic) Breakfast. Children's parties and tractor tours provide an opportunity to tour the farm and meet the animals, and other fun seasonal events include the Haunted Hay Ride (a scary tour around the farm at night), the Santa Christmas Trail, and the Easter Egg Hunt. The shop is closed on Mondays and open Tuesday to Friday 10am-5.30pm, Saturday 9am-5.30pm, and Sunday 11am-5pm.

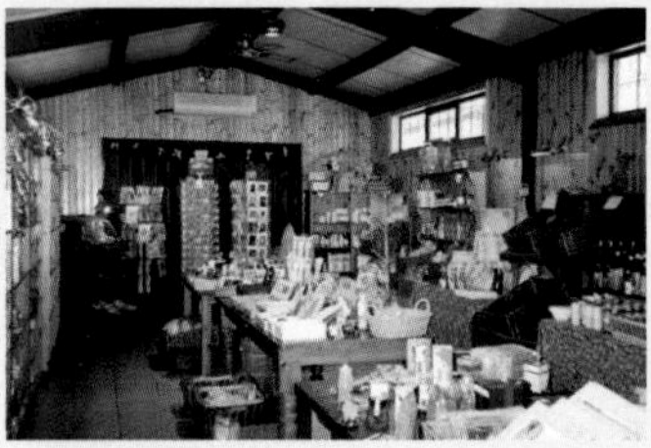

CONIFERS GUEST HOUSE

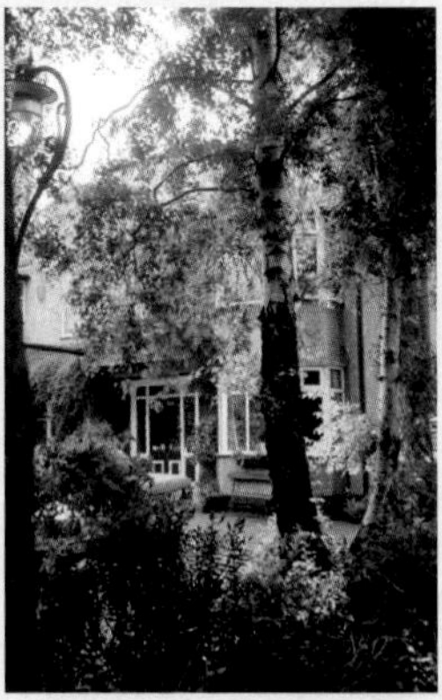

102 Thurstaston Road, Thurstaston, Wirral CH6 0HG
Tel/Fax: 0151 648 0099
website: www.conifersguesthouse.org.uk

The Wirral is full of interesting things to see and do, and for anyone seeking a quiet, comfortable and very civilised base the Colburn family's **Conifers Guest House** fits the bill perfectly. Set back from the road, with ample private parking, the house has three letting bedrooms - two en-suite doubles (one can be used as a family room) and a single with adjacent bathroom, all neat and bright, with tv, video (a wide range of videos is available) and tea/coffee making facilities. A Playstation is guaranteed to keep younger guests amused.

A comfortably furnished lounge is at the disposal of guests, with plenty of books for browsing and patio doors that lead out into the large rear garden. The day starts with a full English or Continental breakfast; individual diets can be catered for with a little notice, and packed lunches can be provided. Rooms are let on a Bed & Breakfast basis, but evening meals are available by arrangement, and the hosts can arrange dinner parties and young children's birthday parties. Conifers, which is open all year round, has a non-smoking policy.

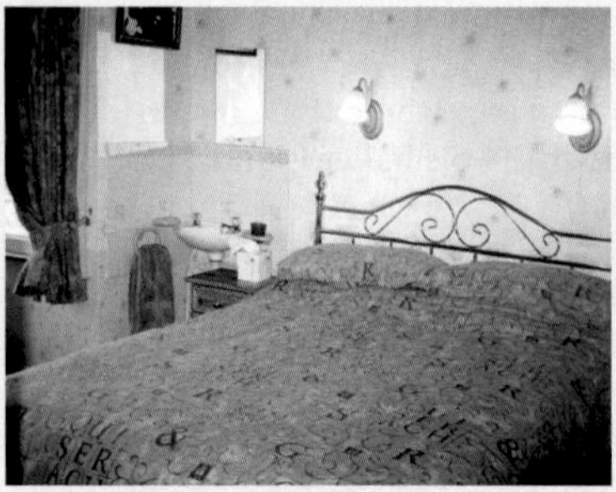

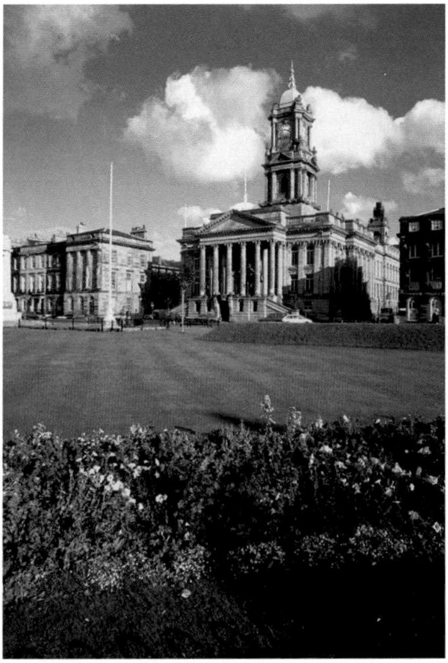

Hamilton Square, Birkenhead

'Tons', the last wooden warships built for the Royal Navy were all named after towns and villages listed in the Domesday Book whose names ended with 'ton'. HRH Prince Charles commanded *HMS Bronington* from February 1976 until December 15th of that year, the final day of his active service in the Royal Navy.

Birkenhead Priory, a Benedictine monastery established around 1150, is the oldest standing building on Merseyside. The site contains museum displays, concert space and a chapel dedicated to *HMS Conway*. A climb up St Mary's is rewarded with magnificent views across Birkenhead to the Welsh Hills and across the Mersey to Liverpool.

Birkenhead Park, to the east of the town centre, is a remarkable example of an early Victorian urban park with two lakes, a rockery, a Swiss bridge and formal gardens. This vast parkland was designed

by Sir Joseph Paxton, architect of London's Crystal Palace, who also designed the spectacular main entrance which is modelled on the Temple of Illysus in Athens. Interestingly, it became the model for an even more famous park – Central Park in New York.

Just out of town is the purpose-built **Williamson Art Gallery & Museum** which exhibits a wealth of local and maritime history, a permanent display of Victorian oil paintings, tapestries by Lee and English watercolours, and also hosts a full programme of temporary exhibitions.

WEST KIRBY

18 miles NW of Chester on the A540

Set beside the Dee estuary and looking across to the Welsh mountains, West Kirby was just a small fishing village until the railway link with Liverpool was established in the 1880s. Today, it's a bustling seaside town with some 28,000 inhabitants. A big attraction here is the **West Kirby Marine Lake**, a 52-acre man-made saltwater lake. With a maximum depth of five feet it offers a degree of safety unobtainable on the open sea. Courses in sailing, windsurfing and canoeing are available at the Wirral Sailing Centre.

West Kirby is well known to birdwatchers and naturalists because of the **Hilbre Islands**, 'part-time' islands that can be reached at low tide across Dee Sands. Permits (free) from the Wirral Borough Council are required to visit the main island, where there is a resident warden. Two smaller islands, Middle Eye and the tiny Little Eye, do not require permits. The latter is notable for its impressive number of wader roosts.

West Kirby is also the starting point for the **Wirral Way**, a 12-mile-long linear nature reserve and country park created mostly from the track bed of the old

GOULD'S

3 Castle Buildings, Heswall, Wirral CH60 7SE
Tel: 0151 342 6022

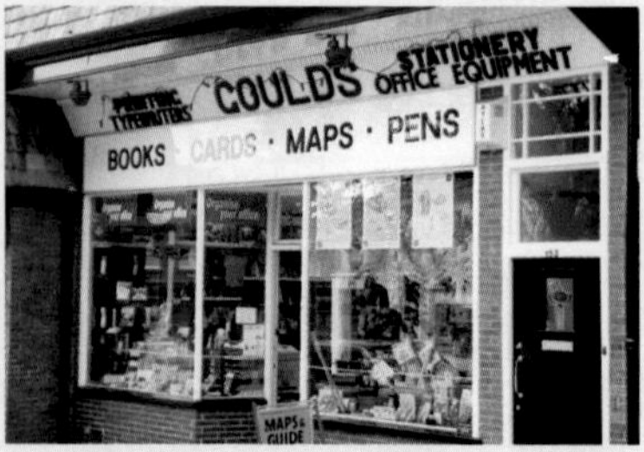

2004 will be a red letter year for printers, stationers and booksellers **Gould's**, marking the centenary of its opening in West Kirby. The Heswall site opened in 1937, and Anne Gould, who took over in 1989, is the fourth generation to run this well-known family business. Behind a traditional shop front in the town's main shopping street, every inch of space is filled with goods for sale, from low-cost disposable pens to bespoke stationery, from BluTack to brief- cases, cards, guide books, giftware, artists' and craft requisites and office and computer accessories of all kinds.

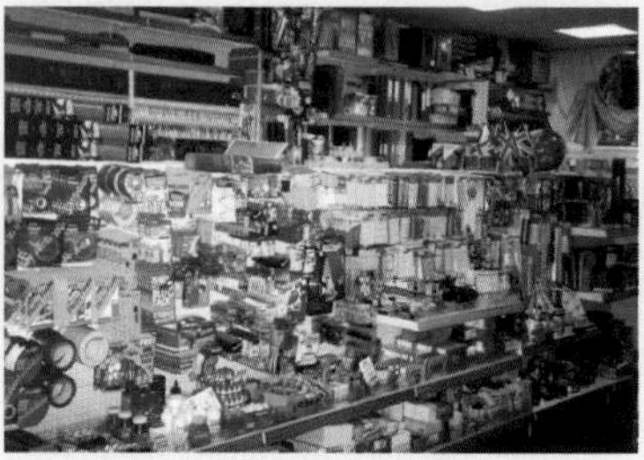

Pens have always been something of a speciality: Anne's great great grandfather was selling pens as long ago as 1888, when George Parker invented the fountain pen, and when the Queen opened a local hospital in 1982 she signed the visitors' book with a pen bought at Gould's. Service to the customer has always been the first aim of Gould's, whether it is selling or repairing a pen or undertaking a major printing job or advertising scheme, and the name of Gould has for a century been one of the most respected in the region.

West Kirby to Hooton railway. When it was opened in 1973 it was one of the first Country Parks in Britain. The local council has also produced a series of circular walks based around the former stations along the line. One of these, **Hadlow Road Station**, a short distance from the centre of Willaston, is especially interesting. The station hasn't seen a train since 1962 but everything here is spick and span, the signal box and ticket office apparently ready for action, a trolley laden with milk churns waiting on the platform. Restored to appear as it would have been on a typical day in 1952, the station's booking office still has a pile of pre-decimal change at the ready, including sixpences, half-crowns and eight-sided threepenny pieces.

HESWALL

14 miles NW of Chester on the A540

Set on a steep hillside, Heswall was an important port before the silting up of

the River Dee. After decades of decline, the town flourished again as a choice retreat for Liverpool commuters following the opening of the railway tunnel under the Mersey in 1888. If you take the road down to the beach from the town centre there are outstanding views across the Dee estuary to the hills of Wales. Heswall's most famous son is the cricketer Ian Botham.

BRIMSTAGE

14 miles NW of Chester via M53 and A5137

The most striking building in this tiny hamlet is **Brimstage Hall**, a medieval pele, or fortified tower. It's not known why such a tower, more appropriate to the lawless border regions, should have been built in peaceful Cheshire, nor when – estimates range from 1175 to 1350 and a raft of human bones found at the bottom of a long-forgotten well in 1957 failed to resolve any of these questions. There is another puzzle too:

Courtyard Crafts

Brimstage Hall, Brimstage, Wirral CH63 6JA
Tel: 0151 342 4216
e-mail: sales@courtyardcraft.co.uk
website: www.courtyardcraft.co.uk

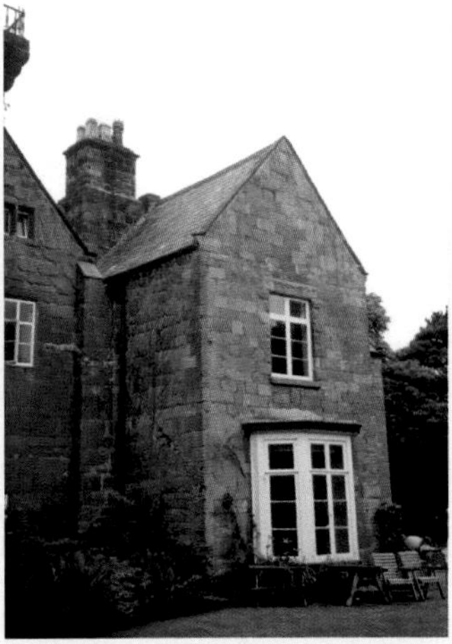

Gillian Stuart spent many years successfully running other people's businesses before setting up **Courtyard Crafts** in 2001 to specialise in the making of beautiful bespoke cards for all occasions. In the heart of the Wirral countryside, it is located in the 17th century courtyard of Brimstage Hall, an atmospheric setting it shares with several other interesting craft-related retail outlets, a café and a restaurant. The business has recently expanded into the ancient Brimstage Hall itself, still in the courtyard but five times bigger than when it first opened.

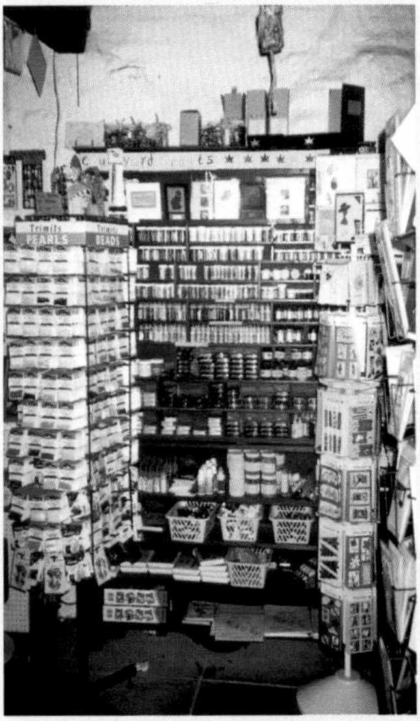

This fascinating building has two floors, which Courtyard Crafts has filled from floor to ceiling with rubber stamps and accessories - everything needed for making cards, together with numerous card display boards to provide inspiration. A wide range of techniques is employed in the making of the cards, and Gill, her husband Steve and their happy, well-informed staff are always searching for new ideas and new products. There's a great deal of skill involved in making cards, and the owners run frequent workshops for adults and children on various linked topics - the Allsorts classes, using bits and bobs from the stock in the shop, are particularly popular. Free monthly demonstrations, evening demo nights and evening stamp clubs are other attractions, and twice a year there is a craft extravaganza.

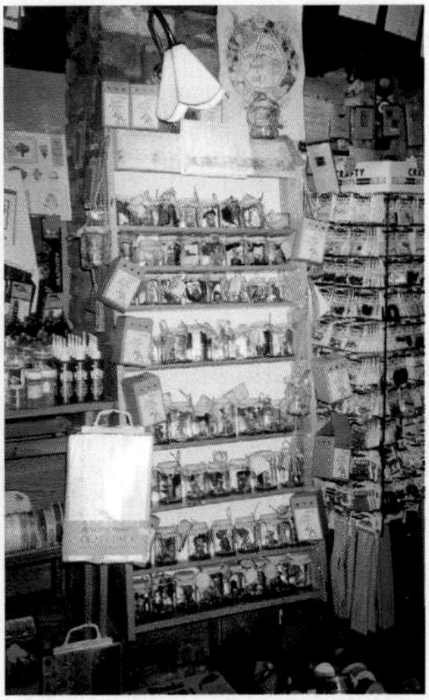

Courtyard Crafts offers much more than a specialist card service and has become a great find for practitioners of all sorts of arts and crafts, including painting, drawing and printing. The setting itself is a great asset, and the beautiful gardens, the children's maze and the other shops are guaranteed to keep visitors happily occupied for hours. The Hall itself, which was built as a pele, or fortified tower, probably as long ago as the 12th century, has many interesting architectural features: one of the most curious is an image, carved into the stonework of the crypt, of a grinning cat - some claim that this is the original of Lewis Carroll's Cheshire Cat.

Courtyard Crafts, which is open from 10am to 5pm Monday to Saturday and from 12pm to 5pm on Sunday, is a short drive from the M53 - leave at Junction 4, follow the large roundabout and look for the sign to Brimstage Hall.

could the stone carving of a smirking domestic cat in the old chapel be the original of Lewis Carroll's Cheshire Cat, which was wont to disappear leaving only its grin behind? Today, the old courtyard is home to a cluster of craft and speciality shops, and an excellent tea room and restaurant.

THORNTON HOUGH

14 miles NW of Chester via the A540 and B5136

The huge village green at Thornton Hough, covering some 14 acres and surrounded by half-timbered black and white houses, was one of the most picturesque spots in Cheshire until it was relocated to Merseyside in 1974. The village boasts two churches, one of which has no fewer than five clocks – the fifth was installed by Joseph Hirst, a Yorkshire mill owner who also built houses here and wished to see a church clock from his bedroom window.

PARKGATE

12 miles NW of Chester via the A540 and B5134

After Neston port became unusable, maritime traffic moved along the Dee Estuary to Parkgate, which, as the new gateway to Ireland, saw some notable visitors. John Wesley, who made regular trips to Ireland, preached here while waiting for a favourable wind, and George Frederick Handel returned via Parkgate after conducting the first public performance of *The Messiah* in Dublin. The great artist JMW Turner came to sketch the lovely view across to the Flintshire hills. A little later, Parkgate enjoyed a brief spell as a fashionable spa. Lord Nelson's mistress, Emma Hamilton (who was born about 1761 at nearby Ness where you can still see the family home, Swan Cottage), took the waters here in an effort to cure an unfortunate skin disease. The daughter of a poor labourer

and baptised Amy, she worked as a nurse girl in Hawarden and then in London, where her beauty captivated many famous men. In 1791 she married Sir William Hamilton, British Ambassador in Naples. She met Lord Nelson in 1793 and again in 1798, and bore him a child in 1801. Another visitor was Mrs Fitzherbert, already secretly married to the Prince Regent, later George IV. When Holyhead developed into the main gateway to Ireland, Parkgate's days as a port and watering-place were numbered. But with fine Georgian houses lining the promenade, this attractive little place still retains the atmosphere of a gracious spa town.

THE WELSH BORDERS

Awake or asleep, the medieval Lords of the Marches made sure their swords were close at hand. At any time, a band of wild-haired Welshmen might rush down from the hills to attack the hated Normans who had dispossessed them of their land. A thousand years earlier their enemies had been the Romans and the centuries-old struggle along the Marches only ended when one of their own people, Henry Tudor, defeated Richard III in 1485 and ascended the throne as Henry VII.

Conflict was to flare up again during the Civil War when the Welsh supported the Royalist forces against mainly Parliamentary Cheshire but nowadays the valley of the Dee is a peaceful and picturesque area, and nowhere more so than around Farndon on the Denbighshire border.

FARNDON

7 miles S of Chester off the B5130

Built on a hillside overlooking the River Dee, Farndon is literally a stone's throw

from Wales. Most travellers agree that the best approach to the principality is by way of this little town and its ancient bridge. Records show that building of the bridge began in 1345 and it is one of only two surviving medieval bridges in the county, the other being in Chester. From Farndon's bridge, riverside walks by the Dee extend almost up to its partner in Chester. During the Civil War, Farndon's strategic position between Royalist North Wales and Parliamentarian Cheshire led to many skirmishes here. Those stirring events are colourfully depicted in a stained glass window in the church, although only the Royalist heroes are included.

One Farndon man who deserves a memorial of some kind but doesn't have one is John Speed, the renowned cartographer, who was born here in 1542. He followed his father's trade as a tailor, married and had 18 children, and was nearly 50 before he was able to devote himself full time to researching and producing his beautifully drawn maps. Fortunately, he lived to the age of 87 and his 54 maps of England and Wales were the first really accurate ones to be published.

Close to Farndon, and well signposted from the A534, stands **Stretton Watermill**, a working corn mill in a lovely peaceful setting.

MALPAS

14 miles S of Chester on the B5069

With its charming black and white cottages and elegant Georgian houses Malpas is one of the most delightful old villages in Cheshire though its Norman-French name implies that it once lay in difficult terrain – "mal passage". Of the Norman castle that once protected this hill-top border town only a grassy mound behind the red sandstone church survives.

MANOR FARM

Egerton, Cholmondeley, Nr Malpas,
Cheshire SY14 8AW
Tel: 01829 720261

In the pleasant surroundings of the gently rolling Cheshire countryside, Janice Dilworth and her son Tim welcome guests to **Manor Farm** with a choice of high-quality accommodation. Built in 1730 and superbly renovated in 1990, the main house has three well-equipped

en suite double bedrooms and a twin with private bathroom let on a Bed & Breakfast basis. One of the rooms is on the ground floor, one has a splendid half-tester bed, and all are decorated and furnished to a very high standard. A full English breakfast starts the day, served in the delightful dining room at a communal table, and guests have the use of a very comfortable lounge where they can watch TV or read a book.

For guests who prefer a self-catering holiday the farm can offer a number of one- and two-bedroom cottages, all with modern kitchens, bathrooms and laundry facilities. Guests can stroll at leisure through the farm's extensive gardens, which include a croquet lawn and a summer house. Among the many local attractions are the walled city of Chester, the gardens of the mock-medieval Cholmondeley Castle (only a mile away), Beeston Castle, Peckforton Castle and the Sandstone Trail.

Approached through 18th century gates attributed to Vanbrugh, **St Oswald's Church** is lavishly decorated with a striking array of gargoyles but is most notable for the splendour of its interior. The nave roof is brilliant with gilded bosses and winged angels, all created around 1480, and there are two magnificent chapels separated from the nave by delicately carved screens. The Brereton chapel dates from 1522 and contains an alabaster effigy of Sir Randal Brereton, in the armour of a medieval knight, together with his lady. Across the aisle, the Cholmondeley chapel commemorates Sir Hugh Cholmondeley, who died in 1605.

The Cholmondeley family owned huge estates around Malpas and it was they who built the town's attractive old almshouses and a school in the 18th century. They lived at Cholmondeley Castle, a few miles to the north-east. The Gothic-style castle is not open to the public but the 800 acres of **Cholmondeley Castle Garden** are. The gardens are planted with a variety of acid-loving plants including rhododendrons, hydrangeas, magnolias, camellias, dogwoods, mahonias and viburnums. There's a lovely Temple Garden with a rockery, lake and islands, and a Silver Garden planted with distinctive silver-leafed plants as a commemoration of Elizabeth II's Silver Jubilee. The paddocks are home to rare breeds of farm animals, including llamas and African pygmy goats.

CHESHIRE PEAKS AND PLAINS

To the east rise the Peak District hills, while westwards gently undulating pastures and woods drop down to the Cheshire Plain. This is an area of sudden and striking contrasts. Within half a mile you can find yourself travelling out of lowland Cheshire into some of the highest and wildest countryside - acres of lonely uplands with rugged gritstone crags, steep valleys watered by moorland streams. Here, too, is the old salt town of Middlewich, and Sandbach with its famous Saxon crosses, along with a host of quiet, attractive villages. The two major towns of South Cheshire are Nantwich, with a history stretching back beyond Roman times, and Crewe, with no history at all until 1837. That was when the Grand Junction Railway arrived and five years later moved all its construction and repair workshops to what had been a greenfield site.

CONGLETON

Some residents have dubbed this thriving old market town the 'Venice of the North' because of the number of nearby man-made lakes such as Astbury Mere and Brereton Country Park, which both offer a wide range of recreational activities. Set in the foothills of the Pennines, Congleton was an inhabited place as long ago as the Stone Age. The remains of a 5,000-year-old chambered tomb known as **The Bridestones** can be seen beside the hill road running eastwards from the town to the A523 road to Leek.

In Elizabethan times, the townspeople of Congleton seem to have had a passion for bear baiting. On one occasion, when the town bear died they handed 16 shillings (80p) to the Bear Warden to acquire another beast. The money had originally been collected to buy a town bible: the disgraceful misappropriation of funds gave rise to the ditty: *"Congleton rare, Congleton rare, sold the bible to buy a bear"*. Known locally as the 'Bear Town', Congleton was the very last town in

England to outlaw the cruel practice of bear baiting, and the town's emblem is still an upright chained bear.

Congleton's impressive Venetian Gothic style **Town Hall**, built in 1864, contains some interesting exhibits recalling the town's long history, including some fine civic regalia. **Congleton Museum** contains displays recording the work of such ancient civic officials as the swine-catcher, the chimney-looker and the ale-taster, and aids to domestic harmony like the 'brank' – a bridle for nagging wives which the town jailer would activate for a small fee: a metal framework was fitted over the 'victim's' head and a metal tongue acted as a gag, making speech almost impossible. Other exhibits include a prehistoric log boat found in 1923 at Ciss Green near Astbury, prehistoric tools and pottery, coin hoards and cannonballs from the Civil War, and more recent acquisitions covering the Industrial Revolution and the Second World War. Congleton did not play a big part in the Civil War (due in part to an outbreak of the plague in 1641) but it was a Congleton man, John Bradshaw, who was president of the court which condemned Charles I to death; his signature was the first, even before Cromwell's, on the death warrant.

During the 18th century Congleton developed as an important textile town with many of its mills involved in silk

Continued on page 29

THE BLACK SWAN GALLERY

7a Swan Bank, Congleton,
Cheshire CW12 1AN
Tel: 01260 290900

Carole Whitehead, a lady of many talents, opened the **Black Swan Gallery** in August 2002 as a natural extension of her work as a painter of acrylic abstracts. In two rooms in a listed 17th century building, with black beams, laminate floors and white walls, her own work and that of other artists is the basis of well-lit, regularly changing displays of paintings in both traditional and contemporary styles in watercolours, oils and acrylic; much of the subject matter is

inspired by local sights and scenery.

The Gallery is much more than a showcase for traditional and contemporary paintings: there are striking black and white and colour photographic images by a talented Lancashire photographer, bronze sculptures of hares, foxes and other creatures, hand-made wooden bowls and vases in all shapes and sizes, glassware and ceramics, hand-painted birds on reclaimed slate tiles, hand-made greetings cards, and rings, brooches, bracelets and necklaces in gold and silver, crystal and stainless steel. Some of the proceeds from the sale of the pictures are donated to a 'Schools for Gambia' project.

WALK 2

Timbersbrook and The Cloud

Start	Timbersbrook Picnic Area, about 2 miles (3.2km) to the east of Congleton
Distance	6 miles (9.6km) Two shorter options of 4 miles (6.4km) and 2½ miles (4km)
Approximate time	3 hours (2 hours and 1½ hours for the two shorter walks)
Parking	Timbersbrook Picnic Area
Refreshments	None
Ordnance Survey maps	Explorer 268 (Wilmslow, Macclesfield & Congleton), Landranger 118 (Stoke-on-Trent & Macclesfield)

A walk across fields and beside the Macclesfield Canal is followed by a steady and relatively easy climb to the summit of The Cloud, 1125 ft (343m) high and a magnificent viewpoint. After the descent the route passes by a prehistoric burial chamber. There are a series of fine and contrasting views, both across the Cheshire plain and the hills and moors of the Peak District. As it is almost a figure-of-eight, the route can be divided into two shorter walks: the 4 mile (6.4 km) walk is basically an ascent of The Cloud; the 2½ mile (4 km) one omits The Cloud but includes the canal.

Timbersbrook is so green and quiet nowadays that it is almost impossible to envisage it as a noisy industrial area, the site of the Silver Springs Bleaching and Dyeing Company works. There is an information board in the car park.

Begin by turning right out of the car park along a lane. Just after crossing a brook, turn left Ⓐ along a track, at a public footpath sign, joining both the Gritstone Trail and the Staffordshire Way.

If doing the 4 mile (6.4 km) walk, continue along the lane and rejoin the full walk at point Ⓓ.

After passing in front of a house, keep ahead along a path beside a factory building and descend steps to cross a footbridge over Timbers Brook. Ascend steps to climb a stile, bear slightly left across a field, climb a stile and keep ahead across the next field, heading down into a dip and up again to another stile. Climb it, turn right along the right edge of a

field and at a Gritstone Trail post, turn left and continue across the field, by a line of trees on the right. Climb a stile, head in the same direction across the next field towards a farm, keep to the right of the farm buildings and on the far side of the field, climb two stiles in quick succession. Turn left along a path which curves right and climb a stone stile onto a lane Ⓑ.

Turn right, at a public footpath sign turn left along a concrete track, go through a gate and continue along an enclosed track. Climb a stone stile, walk along the right edge of a field and in the corner, turn right over a stile. Keep along the left edge of the next field, parallel to a disused railway track on the left, continue along the left edge of the next two fields, finally climbing a stile and descending steps to the Macclesfield Canal.

Turn right beside it and after going through a gate, turn left to cross a canal

bridge. Immediately turn left through a gate, go down steps and turn sharp left to pass under the bridge. Continue beside the canal and just before the next bridge (no 71), turn left up to a T-junction **C** . Turn right to cross the bridge and keep ahead along a path through trees to enter a field. Ahead are superb views of The Cloud. Continue across the undulating field, bearing slightly right and making for the far right corner. Climb a stile, keep ahead along a track and climb another stile onto a lane **D** .

Turn right to return to the start if doing the 2½ mile (4 km) walk.

For the full walk, turn left and at a public footpath sign, turn right beside a gate, here rejoining the Gritstone Trail and Staffordshire Way, and head gently uphill along a tree-lined track (Acorn Lane). The track later heads more steeply uphill to a road. Cross over, continue along the uphill track ahead (Gosberryhole Lane) through trees and follow it around a left bend to a fork. Take the left hand rocky path, passing a National Trust sign 'The Cloud', to a T-junction and turn left. Continue uphill, curving right, pass beside a fence, at a Gritstone Trail waymark, and follow the direction of the waymark – there are several paths here – uphill along a track to emerge from the trees onto heathery moorland.

Follow the winding path uphill through the heather to the triangulation pillar on the summit **E** . This magnificent and contrasting all-round viewpoint includes the hills and moors of the eastern Peak District, the

Cheshire plain, Congleton, Macclesfield and Jodrell Bank. Beyond the summit, the path bears right to continue along the edge, descending gently. After passing through a fence gap, walk along an enclosed path, descend steps to a T-junction and turn left along a track which bends right to a lane **F** .

Turn right and after ¾ mile (1.2km), take the first lane on the right **G** which curves left to a road. Turn right and a short detour along a tarmac track to the right brings you to the prehistoric burial chamber of the Bridestones. Continue along the road to a public footpath sign and turn right **H** through a gate. Climb the stile ahead, bear gradually left across a field, making for the far left corner, keep ahead to pass between redundant gateposts and continue through a shallow valley by Timbers Brook on the left. Bear right away from the brook up to a stile, climb it and keep ahead by the left edge of a field above the sloping wooded valley of the brook.

Where the field ends on a narrow ridge, turn left downhill and cross a footbridge over the brook. Head uphill to climb a stone stile, turn right along a lane and keep ahead at a crossroads to the start. ●

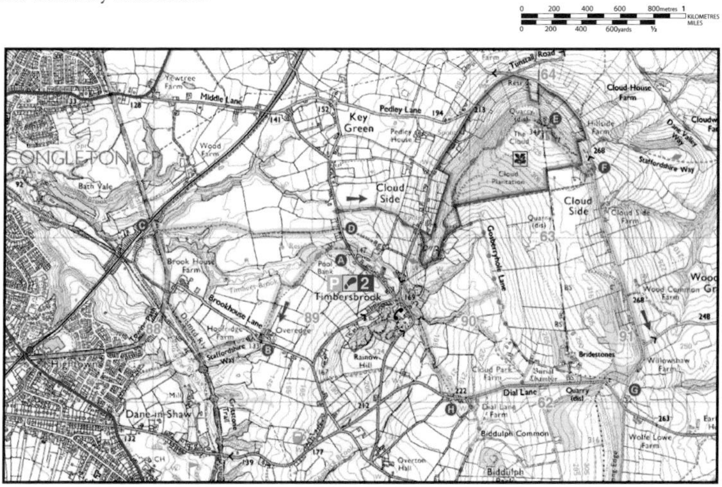

BEEZ

1 West Street, Congleton, Cheshire CW12 1JN
Tel: 01260 291968
e-mail: beeandbeamish@btopenworld.com

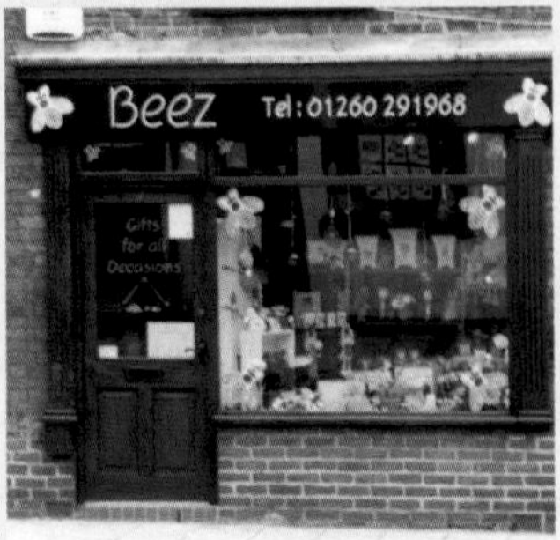

November 2002 saw the opening of **Beez** in a modern brick building a minute's walk from the centre of Congleton. This delightful gift shop is the brainchild of Bridget Stevens and her mother Wendy, both locally born, and anyone looking for

an unusual present will know they are in the right place as soon as they step inside this bright, cheerful little shop. Many of the items in stock are unique to Beez, including brightly painted pendulum clocks, hand-made by Bridget's sister Lorna's local craft company Monkey Business.

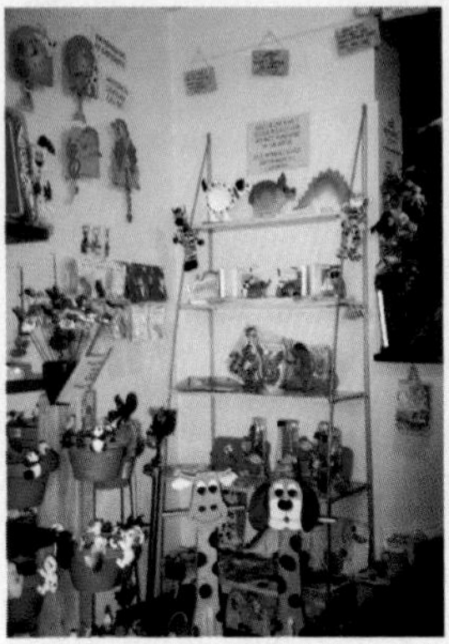

Lorna is also responsible for a wide range of wooden goods and toys, from bookends and CD racks to money boxes and jigsaw puzzles. Brightly coloured animals on springs to hang over cradles or cots, Bad Taste Bears (large, small and keyring size), floating and scented candles, glassware and ceramic kitchen ware are among other items to be found in this Aladdin's Cave, along with perhaps the most intriguing of all – the Double Bubble Scent Ball, based on the Witch Ball traditionally hung in windows to ward off witches and made by hand from lead crystal by Robbie Campbell in Fife.

CAFÉ SYMPHONY

18-20 Rood Hill, Congleton, Cheshire
Tel: 01260 270243

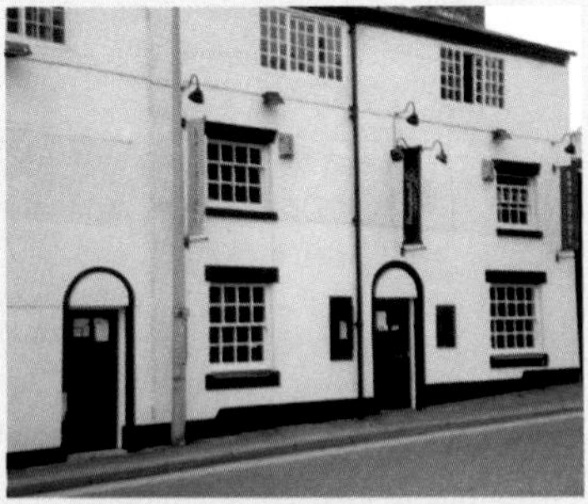

Behind a handsome period frontage in the thriving old market town of Congleton, **Café Symphony** is not only an excellent restaurant but also the town's premier bar. The restaurant, open lunchtime and evening Monday to Friday, Saturday evening and all day Sunday, has a selection of menus to suit all tastes, from light snacks or full meals at lunchtime (with a traditional Roast among the Sunday options) to a great-value early evening menu and the full evening à la carte and chef's specials. When

the sun shines, the wine terrace is the place to be, whether for a meal or just a cool drink.

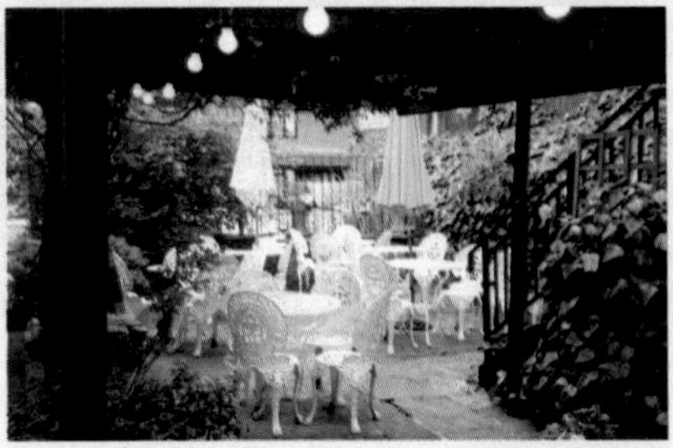

The bar provides a lively yet chilled atmosphere in sophisticated modern surroundings. Drinks promotions and happy hours make it an ideal place to meet after work, whether as individuals or as part of Drinks Clubs available Tuesday to Friday between 6pm and 7pm. With a DJ and jazz, the bar is at its liveliest at the weekend, and any evening it's the perfect place to entertain friends or business clients, with table service and free nibbles. Opening times are from 6pm onwards Tuesday to Saturday and from 5pm to 10.30pm on Sunday.

manufacture, cotton spinning and ribbon weaving. In the Community Garden, a life-size bronze statue has recently been erected to commemorate Congleton's war hero, Sgt George Harold Eardley, who won the Victoria Cross while serving with the King's Shropshire Light Infantry in Holland in October 1944.

AROUND CONGLETON

ASTBURY

2 miles SW of Congleton on the A34

The pretty little village of Astbury, set around a triangular village green, was once more important than neighbouring Congleton which is why it has a much older church, built between 1350 and 1540. Arguably the finest parish church in the county, **St Mary's** is famous for its lofty recessed spire (which rises from a tower almost detached from the nave) and the superb timber work inside: a richly carved ceiling, intricate tracery on the rood screen, and a lovely Jacobean font cover.

Just three miles down the A34 is an even more remarkable building. Black and white half-timbered houses have almost become a symbol for the county of Cheshire and the most stunning example is undoubtedly **Little Moreton Hall** (National Trust), a 'wibbly wobbly' house which provided a memorable location for Granada TV's adaptation of *The Adventures of Moll Flanders*. The only bricks to be seen are in the chimneys, and the hall's huge overhanging gables, slanting walls and great stretches of leaded windows create wonderfully complex patterns,

all magically reflected in the moat. Ralph Moreton began construction in 1480 and the fabric of this magnificent house has changed little since the 16th century. A richly panelled Great Hall, parlour and chapel show off superb Elizabethan plaster and wood work. Free guided tours give visitors a fascinating insight into Tudor life, and there's also a beautifully reconstructed Elizabethan knot garden with clipped box hedges, a period herb garden and a yew tunnel.

About a mile south of Little Moreton Hall is the Rode Hall estate. It was an 18th century owner of the estate, Randle Wilbraham, who built the famous folly of **Mow Cop** (now in the care of the National Trust) to enhance the view from his mansion. This mock ruin stands atop a rocky hill 1,100 feet above sea level, just yards from the Staffordshire border. On a clear day, the views are fantastic: Alderley Edge to the north, the Pennines to the north-east, south to Cannock Chase and Shropshire, and westwards across Cheshire. **Rode Hall** itself, home of the

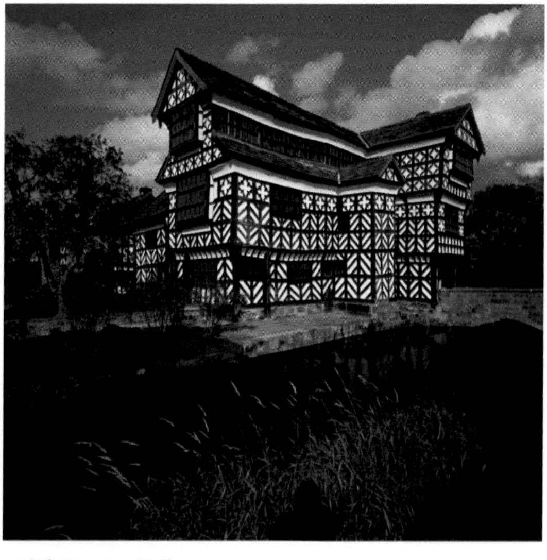

Little Moreton Hall

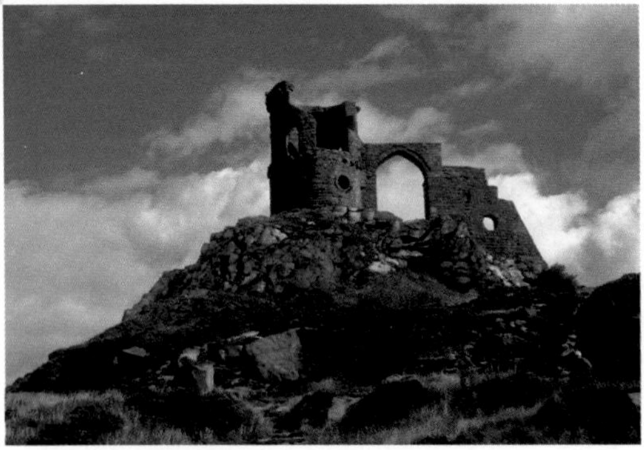

Mow Cop, Nr Astbury

Wilbraham family since 1669, is a fine early 18th century mansion standing within grounds created by three of the most notable landscape designers. Humphry Repton drew up the plans for the landscape and Rood Pool in 1790, and between 1800 and 1810 John Webb constructed the Pool, a 40-acre lake, along with the terraced rock garden and grotto. In 1860 William Nesfield designed the formal garden, which remains much as he planned it to this day.

BIDDULPH

5 miles SE of Congleton on the A527

Biddulph Grange Gardens are imaginatively divided into a series of enclosed areas bounded by massive rock structures, hedges, stumps, roots and moulded banks. A trail leads through a superb Chinese garden to an enchanting Scottish glen while other areas reproduce the magic of Egypt or the tranquillity of rural America. The shop is packed with gardening books, Victorian plants, cards and quality souvenirs, and a pleasant tearoom serves local specialities and home-made cakes.

SANDBACH

6 miles W of Congleton on the A534, 1 mile SW from Junction 17 of the M6

Sandbach's former importance as a stopping place for coaches (both stage and motor) is evident in the attractive old half-timbered inns and houses, some of them thatched, which line the main street. Sandbach's handsome market square is dominated by its two famous stone crosses, 16 and 11 feet tall. These superbly carved crosses (actually only the shafts have survived) were created some time in the 9th century, and the striking scenes are believed to represent the conversion of Mercia to Christianity during the reign of King Penda. A plaque at their base notes that they were restored in 1816 'after destruction by iconoclasts' – namely the Puritans. The restorers had to recover fragments from here and there: some had been used as

CAFÉ SYMPHONY

48 Congleton Road, Sandbach, Cheshire
Tel: 01270 763664

Good food, a pleasant, relaxed atmosphere and friendly staff are among the many attractions of **Café Symphony**, which stands close to the historic centre of the handsome little market town of Sandbach. In stylish surroundings, visitors are welcome to drop in for a leisurely coffee and a browse through the magazines and papers, to enjoy a quick snack or to settle down to a full meal. The menus, both fixed price and à la carte, provide plenty of choice and abundant interest, with a mixture of dishes from home and overseas: traditional British favourites, curries, Tex-Mex and Chinese.

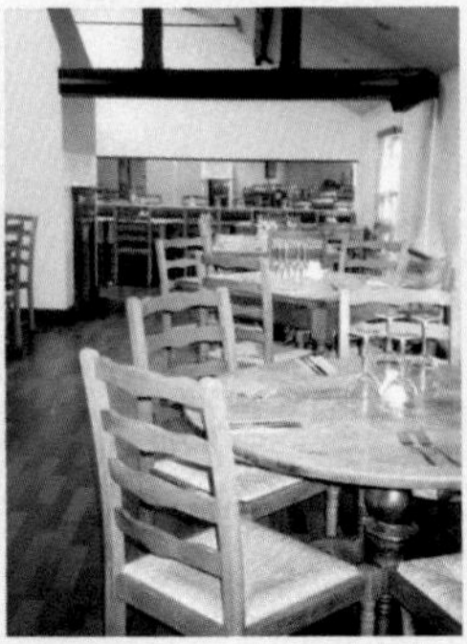

THE WHOLE KIT & CABOODLE

9 The Common, Sandbach, Cheshire CW11 1EG
Tel: 01290 763322

Sue Harrod owns and runs **The Whole Kit & Caboodle**, where visitors will be amazed at the wide range of exclusive country gifts arrayed in the quaint little shop. It's a perfect place for browsing and seeking out a special gift, and the stock includes quilts and cushions, dolls and teddies and fairies, lavender scented goods and pot pourri, pictures, trinket boxes and locally made jugs in all patterns and sizes and colours. At Christmas time, the shop is *the* place for decorations and seasonal gifts.

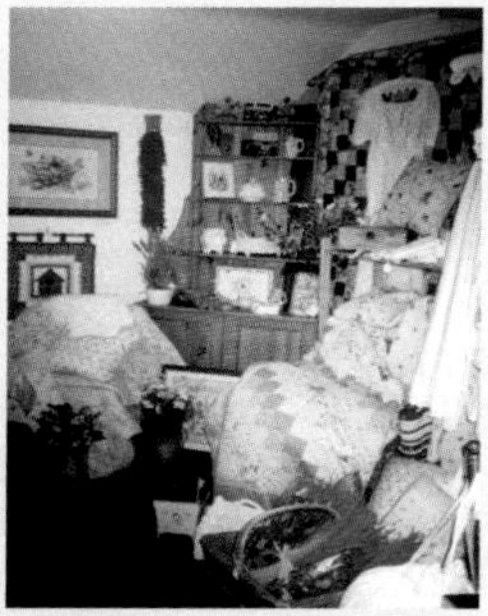

street paving, cottage steps or in the walls of a well. Somehow they fitted the broken stones together, like pieces of a jigsaw, and the result is immensely impressive.

HOLMES CHAPEL

5 miles NW of Congleton on the A50/A54

In the mid 18th century, the little village of Holmes Chapel was stirred by two important events. In 1738, John Wesley came and preached outside St Luke's Church. Fifteen years later, on July 10th 1753, a disastrous fire swept through the village. When the flames were finally quenched, only two buildings had survived the blaze: St Luke's Church and The Old Red Lion alongside.

About three miles southeast of Holmes

Chapel, **Brereton Heath Country Park** is a popular beauty spot where the heath land and flower meadows are criss-crossed by a network of many footpaths. The former sand quarry provides a congenial habitat for a range of species, details of which can be obtained from the park ranger at the Visitor Centre. The lake here is used for angling, canoeing and windsurfing.

GOOSTREY

7 miles NW of Congleton on minor road off the A50/A535

The village of Goostrey is a quiet little place on a minor road just north of Holmes Chapel but famous for its annual gooseberry shows where competitors vie to produce the plumpest berries. The name of the village actually has nothing to do with gooseberries but derives from a personal name, Godhere, and the Saxon word for tree.

LOWER WITHINGTON

7 miles NW of Congleton on the B5392 (off the A34)

Visible from miles around, the huge white dish of the world famous **Jodrell Bank** radio telescope has a good claim to being the most distinctive building in the

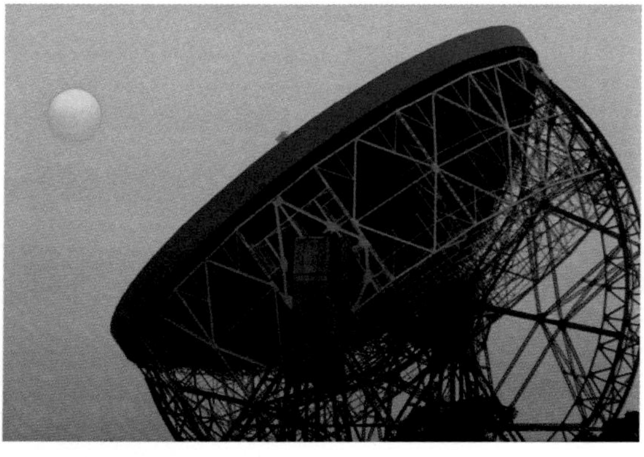

Jodrell Bank

county. The Observatory came into service in 1957 and was used by both the Americans and the Soviets in their exploration of space. Jodrell Bank offers visitors a fascinating guide to exploration of the Universe with its 3D theatre and exhibition centre. Outside, there's a superb 35-acre Arboretum planted with 2,000 species of trees and shrubs, each one helpfully labelled, and an Environment Discovery Centre which explains the importance of trees to the natural environment. The site also contains a picnic area, play area, café and shop. A new development programme is currently underway to include a pathway around the Lovell Radio Telescope and external displays.

MIDDLEWICH

10 miles W of Congleton on the A54, 2 miles W of Junction 18 of the M6

The Romans called their settlement here Salinae, meaning saltworks. Excavations have revealed outlines of their long, narrow, timber workshops, brine pits and even a jar with the word AMYRCA scratched on it (Amurca was the Latin name for brine waste, which was used throughout the Empire as a cleansing agent). Middlewich Town Council publishes an informative leaflet detailing the **Roman Middlewich Trail**, a one-mile circular walk that reveals the history and layout of the Roman town and shows how Middlewich would have looked in those days.

In more recent times it was the need for Cheshire's salt manufacturers to get their cumbersome product to markets in the Midlands and the south that gave a great impetus to the building of canals in the county. Middlewich was particularly well provided for with its own Middlewich Branch Canal linking the town to both the Shropshire Union and the Trent & Mersey Canals. Today, most

of the canal traffic comprises traditional narrow boats, some of which can be hired for holiday trips.

During the Civil War, Middlewich witnessed two of the bloodiest battles fought in the county. In March 1644, Royalists trapped Cromwell's men in the narrow lanes and alleys of the town and slaughtered 200 of them. A few managed to find refuge in **St Michael's Church.** The church has changed greatly since those days but still has some notable old carvings and a curiosity in the form of a carved coat of arms of the Kinderton family of nearby Kinderton Hall. Their crest shows a dragon eating a child, a reference to the occasion on which Baron Kinderton killed a local dragon as it was devouring a child. The incident apparently took place at Moston, near Sandbach, and a lane there is still called Dragon Lane.

CREWE

In 1837 the Grand Junction Railway arrived and five years later moved all its construction and repair workshops to what had been a greenfield site. A workforce of 900 had to be housed so the company rapidly built cottages, each one shared by four of the lowest paid workers, and detached 'mansions' which accommodated four families of the more highly skilled. At one time, seven out of every ten men in Crewe worked on the railways.

Later, in 1887, the railway company also provided the town with one of the most splendid parks in the north of England, **Queens Park**, some 40 acres of lawns and flowerbeds together with an ornamental lake. Rolls Royce's engineering works brought further prosperity to the town, but it is as a railway centre that Crewe is best known. The **Railway Age** museum offers a

LAKEMORE COUNTRY PARK ANIMAL KINGDOM

Lane Ends Farm, Clay Lane, Hasligton, Crewe, Cheshire CW1 5SQ
Tel: 01270 253556

Lakemore Country Park, located in the heart of Cheshire's tranquil countryside, is within easy reach of the M6 motorway. The Park covers 36 acres of which 10 acres are divided up into five wonderful fishing lakes. Experience the nature trail and see the wallabies, llamas, miniature donkeys, owls and many more unusual and rare breeds. Why not see and feed the farm animals and visit the pets corner.

Lakemore Country Park has both indoor and outdoor children's play areas and for a small charge, children's rides and theme Crazy Golf are available. The log cabin coffee shop offers a selection of hot or cold meals ar why not try one of the Farm House ice-creams!

Open Wednesday to Sunday 10am-5.30pm Easter to October. Open daily in school holidays and all Bank Holiday Mondays.

fascinating insight into Crewe's place in railway history with hands-on exhibits, steam locomotive rides, model railway displays and a children's playground. Also worth a visit is the **Lyceum Theatre**, built in 1902 and with its glorious Edwardian opulence undimmed.

A couple of miles north of Crewe, **Lakemore Country Park Animal Kingdom** (see panel above) is home to a wide variety of animals – wallabies, llamas, miniature donkeys, owls and many other unusual and rare breeds. Children can feed the farm animals, visit the pets corner and enjoy both the indoor and outdoor play areas. Within the 36-acre site are five fishing lakes and a log cabin coffee shop. A pleasant country walk using footpaths, towpaths and old drovers' roads starts at Moss Bridge, on the western outskirts, and takes in **Sandbach Flashes**, one of the best places for birdwatching in Cheshire. Waders and wildfowl gather in large numbers in winter, attracting predators such as merlin and sparrowhawks, and the salty conditions resulting from the local industry are ideal for plants usually only found in coastal areas, such as sea club-rush, lesser sea-spurrey and sea aster. Further along the walk, Winterley Pool is

a refuge favoured by mute swans. Nearby Haslington Hall, a fine Tudor house, was built by Admiral Sir Francis Vernon in 1545. Sir Francis had the task of dismantling ships from the Spanish Armada and some say that timbers from these ships were in later extensions to the Hall.

NANTWICH

4 miles SW of Crewe on the A51

Several disasters have befallen Nantwich down the centuries. In the 11th century the town was destroyed except for a single building, and King Henry III destroyed it to prevent the Welsh using it and the amenity of the salt spring. The most disastrous event fully recorded was the Great Fire of 1583 which consumed some 600 of its thatched and timber-framed buildings. Fanned by constant winds, the blaze raged for 20 days and the fire-fighting operations were more than somewhat hampered by the escape of four bears from their cage in the town's bear pit behind the Crown Hotel. (Four bears from Nantwich are mentioned in Shakespeare's comedy *The Merry Wives of Windsor*.) Queen Elizabeth I contributed the huge sum of £1,000 to the cost of rebuilding and ordered her

HENHULL HALL

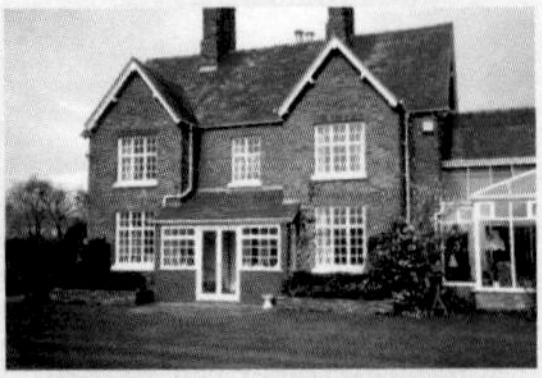

Welshmans Lane, Nantwich, Cheshire CW5 6AD
Tel/Fax: 01270 624158
e-mail: philip.percival@virgin.net

Henhull Hall offers high standards of Bed & Breakfast accommodation in a peaceful garden setting on a 250-acre working dairy farm. Philip and Joyce Percival have a warm welcome for both business and holiday guests, and the three bedrooms, individually decorated and furnished, provide exceptional comfort. The pine-furnished double room has a shower room en suite, while the twin-bedded room and the mahogany-furnished single share a luxury bathroom. The guests' sitting room is a perfect place to relax and the hearty breakfast that starts the day features fresh farm produce.

Privy Council to arrange collections throughout the land to augment the funds; she also donated quantities of timber from Delamere Forest to assist in the building work. A grateful citizen, a builder by the name of Thomas Cleese, commemorated this royal largesse with a plaque on his new house at No. 41 High Street. The plaque is still in place and reads: "God grant our ryal Queen in England longe to raign / For she hath put her helping hand to bild this towne again".

The most striking of the buildings to survive the conflagration, perhaps because it was surrounded by a moat, is the lovely black and white house in Hospital Street known as **Churche's Mansion** after the merchant Richard Churche, who built it in 1577. Astonishingly, when the house was up for sale in 1930, no buyer showed any interest and the building was on the point of being transported brick by brick to America when a public-spirited local doctor stepped in and rescued it. The ground floor is now an antiques centre.

The Great Fire also spared the stone-built 14th century church. This fine building, with an unusual octagonal tower, is sometimes called the **Cathedral of South Cheshire** and dates from the period of the town's greatest prosperity as a salt town and trading centre. Of exceptional interest are the magnificent

chancel and the wonderful carvings in the choir. On the misericords (tip-up seats) are mermaids, foxes (some dressed as monks in a sharp dig at priests), pigs, and the legendary Wyvern, half-dragon, half-bird, whose name is linked with the River Weaver, 'wyvern' being an old pronunciation of Weaver. An ancient tale about the building of the church tells of an old woman who brought ale and food each day from a local inn to the masons working on the site. The masons discovered that the woman was cheating them by keeping back some of the money they put 'in the pot' for their refreshment. They took revenge by making a stone carving showing the old woman being carried away by Old Nick himself, her hand still stuck in a pot. A plaque in the church remembers the Rev Joseph Priestley (1733-1804), who was a minister here. A writer on education, philosophy, government and science, he is best known today as the discoverer of oxygen.

During the Civil War, Nantwich was the only town in Cheshire to support Cromwell's Parliamentary army. The town was frequently besieged by Royalist troops and after a particularly long siege the Royalist forces under Lord Byron were finally defeated on 25th January, 1644. The people of Nantwich celebrated by wearing sprigs of holly in their hair and hats, and the day became known as

'Holly Holy Day'; every year, on the Saturday closest to January 25th, the town welcomes Cromwellian pikemen and battle scenes are re-enacted by members of the Sealed Knot. There are records of the Civil War in the **Nantwich Museum** in Pillory Street, which also has exhibitions about the town and its dairy and cheese-making industries. Just before Nantwich Lake, on the edge of town, is a memorial linked with a later war. First Lieutenant Arthur L Brown, an American pilot, crashed here in 1944, staying with his blazing Thunderbolt fighter to avoid coming down on the town.

It was salt that had once made Nantwich second only in importance to Chester in the county. The Romans had mined salt here for their garrisons at Chester and Stoke where the soldiers received part of their wages in 'sal', or salt. The payment was called a 'salarium', hence the modern word salary. Nantwich remained a salt producing town right up to the 18th century but then it was overtaken by towns like Northwich which enjoyed better communications on the canal system. But a brine spring still supplies Nantwich's outdoor swimming pool.

Within a few miles of the town are two notable gardens. A mile south, off the A51, is **Stapeley Water Gardens**, which attracts nearly 1.5 million visitors each year. The 64-acre site includes the National Collection of Nymphaea (more than 350 varieties of water lilies), a comprehensively equipped garden centre, an angling centre, a pet centre, a restaurant, two cafés and a gift shop. In The Palms Tropical Oasis are a vibrant fountain and koi pool, blue and gold macaws and Amazon parrots. The Zoo room is home to a family of cotton top tamarin monkeys, water dragons, box tortoises, scorpions, tarantulas and a cayman crocodile. There are frogs of all kinds - poison arrow frogs, tree frogs, South American cane toads - in the World of Frogs, while in the tropical house piranhas, catfish and pacus are shaded by the enormous leaves of the Giant Amazon water lily. The stingray pool, the Tunnel of Underwater Life and the blacktip reef sharks are other attractions not to be missed at this brilliant family venue, which is open throughout the year.

About six miles further south along the A51 and straddling the Staffordshire border, **Bridgemere Garden World** provides the location for BBC TV's *Gardeners' Diary*. This is just one of 22 different gardens, among them a French rose garden, a woodland setting, a cottage garden and a rock and water area. The extensive glasshouses contain houseplants of every description and the garden centre is stocked with everything a gardener could possibly need. There's

---

CLASSIC STONE

Units 2-20, Dagfields Craft Centre, Walgherton,
Nr Nantwich, Cheshire CW5 7LG
Tel: 07710 524978 Fax: 01270 811545

Colin Cliffe set up his business **Classic Stone** in 1991, and it has been in the Dagfields Craft Centre longer than any other. This is a must for anyone looking to put the finishing touches to a garden, and the stock runs to over 1,500 items, including an amazing choice of more than 50 fountains, both

pond and self-circulating.

Garden ornaments include animals (meerkats and lions are very popular), birds and gnomes, there are troughs empty or planted, statues, busts, sundials, planters, candle holders, obelisks and plaques, along with rustic furniture that is both practical and attractive: tables and benches, love seats, swing seats, benches, bird tables and much, much more. Classic Stone (opening hours 11am-5pm Monday–Friday; 10am-5.30pm Saturday and Sunday) lies just off the A51 between Stapeley (Water Gardens) and Bridgemere (Garden World); turn off the main road by the Boars Head pub.

THE FIRS POTTERY

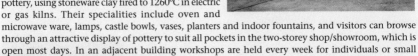

Sheppenhall Lane, Aston, Nr Nantwich,
Cheshire CW5 8DE
Tel: 01270 780345
website: www.firspottery.co.uk

In pretty countryside off the A530 south of Nantwich, **The Firs Pottery** has been built up by Joy and Ken Wild over the past 20 years. They design, throw and hand-build a wide range of functional and decorative pottery, using stoneware clay fired to 1260°C in electric or gas kilns. Their specialities include oven and microwave ware, lamps, castle bowls, vases, planters and indoor fountains, and visitors can browse through an attractive display of pottery to suit all pockets in the two-storey shop/showroom, which is open most days. In an adjacent building workshops are held every week for individuals or small

groups, beginners or advanced, where under the expert guidance of Joy and Ken participants can spend the day working with clay, designing, making and glazing their own pots; handbuilding and wheel work are both included, and the "Making Days", which run from 10am to 4.30pm, include a light lunch, tea and coffee.

Run independently from the pottery but on the same site, Potters Barn is a luxury beamed apartment in a tastefully converted barn that provides excellent self-catering accommodation for two or four guests. No smoking or pets.

also an aquatics house with some splendid fish, a specialist food hall, a flower arrangers' centre, a bookshop, HobbyCraft arts and crafts shop, a restaurant and a coffee shop.

A few miles south of Nantwich, just off the A530 Whitchurch road, is **Hack Green Secret Nuclear Bunker**. For 50 years this vast underground complex remained secret, built as the centre of regional government in the case of a nuclear war, but it was declassified in 1993 and is now a unique attraction open to the public. Visitors pass through the massive blast doors into the chilling world of the Cold War, including the Minister of State's office, life support area, communications centre and decontamination facilities. Cinemas show once secret films, and children can have fun as secret agents, following the Soviet Spy Mouse Trail. A trip can end with a visit to the bunker's NAAFI-style canteen to pick up survival rations, and a browse through the shop for a souvenir.

AROUND NANTWICH

Beeston
8 miles NW of Nantwich on minor road off the A49

A craggy cliff suddenly rising 500 feet from the Cheshire Plain, its summit crowned by the ruins of **Beeston Castle** (English Heritage), Beeston Hill is one of the most dramatic sights in the county. The castle was built around 1220 but didn't see any military action until the Civil War. On one rather ignominious occasion during that conflict, a Royalist captain and just eight musketeers managed to capture the mighty fortress and its garrison of 60 soldiers without firing a shot. A few years later, Cromwell ordered that the castle be 'slighted', or partially destroyed, but this 'Castle in the

Air' is still very imposing with walls 30 feet high and a well 366 feet deep. An old legend asserts that Richard II tipped a hoard of coins, gold and jewels down the well, but no treasure has ever been discovered. The castle hill is a popular place for picnics, and it's worth climbing it just to enjoy the spectacular views which extend across seven counties and over to a 'twin' castle. **Peckforton Castle** looks just as medieval as Beeston but was, in fact, built in 1844 for the first Lord Tollemache who spared no expense in re-creating features such as a vast Great Hall and a keep with towers 60 feet tall. The architect Gilbert Scott later praised Peckforton as "the very height of masquerading". Its authentic medieval appearance has made the castle a favourite location for film and television companies, as well as for conferences and weddings.

Willaston
2 miles E of Nantwich between the A534 and A500

It was in the village of Willaston that one of the most unusual world records was established in 1994. Some 200 competitors had gathered at the Primary School here for the annual **World Worm Charming Championships**. The prize goes to whoever induces the greatest number of worms to poke their heads above a small patch of playing field aided only by a garden fork. Each contestant is allowed half an hour and the fastest have charmed more than 500 out of the ground in the prescribed time. What is their sercret? No one has been able to worm it out of them!

Wybunbury
5 miles S of Crewe on the B5071

South Cheshire's answer to the Leaning Tower of Pisa is the 100ft tower of **St Chad's Church** in Wybunbury. It was

built in 1470 above an unsuspected ancient salt bed. Subsidence has been the reason for the tower's long history of leaning sideways by as much as four feet and then being straightened up, most recently in 1989. Once given the title of 'The Hanging Steeple of Wimberie', it now rests on a reinforced concrete bed and is unlikely to deviate from the vertical again. The tower stands alone, surrounded by a graveyard: the body of the church, once capable of holding a congregation of 1,600, collapsed on no fewer than five occasions. In 1972, the villagers finally decided to abandon it and build a new church on firmer ground. The tower is still used for bell ringing, with a fine set of bells rung on special occasions. In the fields near the church can be seen the remains of two medieval moated houses that were used as 'safe houses' for visiting clergy. In the 15th century the Bishop of Coventry leased two gardens to a hermit called Nicholas Baker on condition that they were kept only by fit priests or honest hermits. A pleasant walk from the tower takes in **Wybunbury Moss National Nature Reserve**, where the mossland habitat is home to rare plants such as sundew, bog asphodel and bog rosemary. The boggy area at the western end of the Moss is what remains of the well that supplied the north end of the village in the Middle Ages. At one time Wybunbury Brook was a source of power for corn milling and iron production.

NORTH WEST CHESHIRE

The northwestern part of the county contains the pleasant rural area known as the Vale Royal, and the more industrial environs of Warrington and Runcorn. It was Prince Edward, later Edward I, who gave the area its name and who founded the great Abbey of Vale Royal in

fulfilment of a solemn vow made in dramatic circumstances. He was returning from the Crusades when his ship was struck by a violent storm. The Prince made a pledge to the Virgin that if his life were spared he would found an Abbey for 100 monks. Lo! the ship was tossed ashore, and the Prince and his companions waded through the surf to safety. In 1277, Edward, now King and with his young wife Eleanor of Castile by his side, honoured his vow by placing the first stone of Vale Royal Abbey. "No monastery," he decreed, "shall be more royal than this one in liberties, wealth and honour, throughout the whole world". Vale Royal Abbey, about three miles south of Northwich, indeed became the largest and most powerful Cistercian Abbey in England, a building reputedly even more glorious than Tintern or Fountains. Unlike those Abbeys, however, barely a stone of Vale Royal now remains in place. The abuse by the medieval Abbots of their vast wealth, and of their unfettered power of life and death over the inhabitants of the Vale, may partly explain why their magnificent building was so quickly and completely destroyed after Henry VIII's closure of the monasteries. Over the centuries, the county has lost many fine buildings unnecessarily, but the deliberate destruction of Vale Royal Abbey must take prime place in the litany of crimes against wonderful architecture.

NORTHWICH

The Vale Royal is now a district borough centred on the old salt town of Northwich. Even before the Romans arrived, Cheshire salt was well known and highly valued. But production on a major scale at Northwich began in 1670 when rock salt was discovered in nearby Marston. Salt may seem an inoffensive

WEAVER GALLERY

45 Castle Street, Northwich, Cheshire CW8 1EY
Tel: 01606 871191

A distinctive red brick building on a corner site in Northwich is home to **Weaver Gallery**, which has acquired a reputation as an Aladdin's Cave for picture lovers. The display runs from 19th century engravings and watercolours to contemporary work both figurative and abstract, and the Gallery also provides an expert in-house framing service. The owner is a man with several strings (literally!) to his bow: as Brian Bailey he paints traditional watercolours, while as Paco Torres he produces vibrant Spanish themes and abstracts and is a professional Flamenco guitarist. Brian/Paco and his friendly staff are always ready with advice for amateur artists.

sort of product, but its extraction from the keuper marl of the Cheshire Plain has produced some quite spectacular side-effects. In Elizabethan times, John Leland recorded that a hill at Combermere suddenly disappeared into underground workings, and Northwich later became notorious for the number of its buildings leaning at crazy angles because of subsidence. Even today, the White Lion Inn in Witton Street lies a complete storey lower than its original height. The arrival in the 19th century of new processes of extraction brought different problems. In 1873, John Brunner and Ludwig Mond set up their salt works at Winnington on the northern edge of the town to manufacture alkali products based on brine. The ammonia process involved cast an appalling stench over the town and devastated vegetation for miles around. On the other hand, Brunner and Mond were model employers: they paid their workforce well, built houses for them and were among the first firms in the country to give their employees annual holidays with pay.

The long involvement of Northwich and Cheshire with salt production is vividly recorded at the **Salt Museum**, the only one of its kind in Britain. It stands about half a mile south of the town centre in London Road (A533) and occupies what used to be the Northwich Workhouse which, like so many of those dreaded institutions, is an exceptionally handsome late-Georgian building, designed by George Latham, the architect of Arley Hall. With its unique collection of traditional working tools, and displays that include working models and videos, the Salt Museum recounts the fascinating story of the county's oldest industry. Not only can ancient remains such as Roman evaporating pans and medieval salt rakes be seen, but there is also much to remind visitors of the vital part that salt plays in the modern chemical industry.

The **Water Heritage Trail** concentrates on the industrial archaeology and water heritage of Northwich, and takes visitors to docks, locks, bridges and warehouses. One of the highlights is the **Dock Road Edwardian Pumping Station**, a fully restored sewage pumping station where the noise and splendour of the working machinery create an atmosphere of power and tradition.

AROUND NORTHWICH

ANDERTON

1 mile N of Northwich on minor road off the A533

One of the most stupendous engineering feats of the canal age was the **Anderton Boat Lift**, built in 1875 and recently

comprehensively restored. This extraordinary construction - known as the 'Cathedral of the Canals' - was designed by Edwin Clark to transfer boats from the Trent and Mersey Canal to the Weaver Navigation 50 feet below. Two barges would enter the upper tank, two the lower, and by pumping water out of the lower tank, the boats would exchange places. Thousands of visitors come every year to marvel at this impressive structure, and to take a trip through the lift on the *Edwin Clark*, converted from a maintenance craft that once worked on the Leeds and Liverpool Canal. Also here are an exhibition centre and operations centre. A six-mile circular trail - the Victorian Trail - visits the Boat Lift, the Lion Salt Works and Great Budworth, providing an insight into the area's industrial heritage and also into its rural character. For nature lovers, another trail runs through **Anderton**

Nature Park. This wildflower trail introduces visitors to the varied plant life that thrives in the prevailing soil conditions (salt, lime, ash clinker), and markers along the trail show the best places to look for particular plants.

About a mile north of Anderton, **Marbury Country Park** (see panel below) was formerly part of a large country estate but the area is now managed by Cheshire County Council whose wardens have created a variety of habitats for plants, trees and animals. The Park lies at the edge of Budworth Mere and there are attractive walks and bridleways around the site, which also has an arboretum, picnic area and garden centre.

SANDIWAY

5 miles SW of Northwich on the A49

A popular attraction at Blakemere Craft Centre on Chester Road is the **Cheshire**

MARBURY COUNTRY PARK

Comberbach, Northwich,
Cheshire CW9 6AT
Tel: 01606 77741

Marbury Country Park was once part of a large country estate whose history dates back to around 1200 AD. Marbury itself means a fortified or stockaded dwelling by the mere or water. The first family took the name Marbury and lived there until 1684. When the last male heir died the estate was bought by Richard Earl Rivers who never lived there. On

his death in 1714 it was bought by his son-in-law James, the 4th Earl of Barrymore. It was the Barry family who shaped the park with extensive landscaping and the building of the hall.

A succession of owners and uses then followed, culminating in the hall being demolished in 1968 due to rot. In 1975, 196 acres was leased from the owners, ICI, by Cheshire County Council and restoration work was begun. Further land was later aquired and today it is managed by the Countryside Management Service to benefit wildlife and visitors.

Each habitat is carefully managed to encourage different plants and animals, so there is always plenty to see at all times of the year. In spring the woodland is covered by a spectacular carpet of wildflowers and willow warblers, chiffchaffs and blackcaps herald the arrival of summer. Autumn shows the colours of the trees off to their best and in winter, the Mere becomes a focus for many birds including goldeneye and greylag geese.

The Potters Wheel

Cherry Lane, Blackmere Craft Centre, Sandiway,
Cheshire CW8 3EB
Tel: 01606 301269

Potter and artist Gill Nicholas owns and runs **The Potters
Wheel**, which has an ever-changing display of ceramics
handmade by British artists. There's always a fine choice
of items for sale, along with a wide range of plaster and
clay models for visitors to paint on site or to take home.
For a small charge you can throw your own pot, which
will be ready for collection after being dried out and 'cooked' in the kiln. Group bookings are welcome
for any of the activities.

Waterlife Aquatic and Falconry Centre.
Falconers fly several different species of
birds of prey, supplying a running
commentary on each bird, and visitors
can also take a guided tour of the aviary
complex - home to several species of rare
owls - and take lessons in bird handling
and falconry. The centre has a pets
corner, with rabbits, guinea pigs,
hamsters and caged birds, and also
houses marine fish and invertebrates, koi
carp and tropical fish.

CUDDINGTON

5 miles SW of Northwich off the A49

Cuddington is at the western end of the
Whitegate Way, a pleasant rural walk of
about five miles which follows the
trackbed of the old railway that used to
carry salt from the Winsford mines.
There is a picnic site and car park at the
former Whitegate Station.

HATCHMERE

8 miles W of Northwich on the B5152

In medieval times the village of
Hatchmere was surrounded by the Forest
of Delamere, the largest of Cheshire's
three woodlands. It stretched from the
Mersey to Nantwich and although there
were small areas of pasture and arable
land, its status as a royal forest meant
that the prime duty of those in charge of
it was the preservation of the 'beasts of

the chase'. It was not until 1812 that
Delamere was officially 'disafforested'
and today Delamere Forest covers little
more than an area about two miles long
and one mile deep. From Hatchmere
attractive trails lead through the woods
and around Hatch Mere, the sizeable lake
that gives the village its name.

CROWTON

4 miles W of Northwich on the B5153

Crowton has many times been voted the
Best Kept Village in Cheshire and its 18th
century hostelry, The Hare and Hounds,
enjoys a particularly scenic position in
this appealing village.

ACTON BRIDGE

4 miles W of Northwich off the A49

The bridge here crosses the River Weaver,
a waterway whose scenic merits have
been largely unsung. The Vale Royal
Council has developed the **Weaver
Valley Way** which allows walkers to
enjoy some lovely stretches, particularly
those between Weaver Bridge and
Saltersford Locks, and the six mile route
from Northwich to Winsford Marina.

During World War I, Acton Bridge
made an unusual contribution to the war
effort. Near the village was a plantation
of hazel pear trees, whose fruit is quite
inedible but whose juice provided the
khaki dye for soldiers' uniforms.

MARSTON

1 mile NE of Northwich on a minor road

In Victorian times, the Old Salt Mine at Marston was a huge tourist attraction. About 360 feet deep and covering 35 acres, it even brought the Tsar of Russia here in 1844. Ten thousand lamps illuminated the huge cavern as the Emperor sat down to dinner with eminent members of the Royal Society. By the end of the century, however, subsidence caused by the mine had made some 40 houses in the village uninhabitable, and one day in 1933 a hole 50 feet wide and 300 feet deep suddenly appeared close to the Trent and Mersey Canal. Happily, the village has now stabilised itself, and at the **Lion Salt Works Museum** volunteer workers keep alive the only surviving open pan salt works in Britain.

GREAT BUDWORTH

3 miles NE of Northwich off the A559

A charming small village nowadays, 'Great' Budworth was accorded that designation at a time when it was the largest ecclesiastical parish in all Cheshire, the administrative centre for some 35 individual communities. The imposing church on the hill, built in the 14th and 15th centuries, reflects its importance during those years. **St Mary and All Saints** attracts many visitors to its host of quaint carvings and odd faces that peer out at unexpected corners: some with staring eyes, others with their tongues poking out. A man near the pulpit appears to be drowsing through some interminable sermon.

Under the roof of the nave you'll find a man with a serpent, another in mid-somersault, and a minstrel playing bagpipes. The distinguished 17th century historian, Sir Peter Leycester, is buried in the Lady Chapel, and the Warburton Chapel has a finely carved Tudor ceiling and 13th century oak stalls – the oldest in Cheshire. During the 19th century, Great Budworth was part of the Arley Hall estate and it is largely due to the energetic Squire Egerton-Warburton, a conservationist well ahead of his time, that so many of the attractive old cottages in the village are still in place.

Cheshire can boast many grand houses and many fine gardens, but at **Arley Hall and Gardens** one of the grandest houses and one of the finest gardens are in perfect harmony. The present Hall was completed in 1845, a few years after Rowland Egerton-Warburton arrived at Arley with his new bride, Mary Brooke. The newly-married couple took possession of a dilapidated old mansion, infested with rats and with antiquated drains from which an unbearable stench drifted through the house. Understandably, Rowland and Mary soon demolished the old hall and in its place rose a sumptuous early-Victorian stately

Arley Hall and Gardens

home complete with (bearing in mind those drains) such state-of-the-art innovations as 'Howden's Patent Atmospheric Air Dispensers'. Rowland and Mary were both ardent gardeners and it was they who master-minded the magnificent panoramas of today's Arley Gardens. Rowland is credited with creating what is believed to be the first herbaceous border in England; his descendant, the present Viscount Ashbrook, has continued that tradition by cultivating The Grove, an informal woodland garden planted with spring bulbs, flowering shrubs and exotic trees, a pleasing contrast to the more formal design of the main gardens.

Other attractions at Arley include a tea room housed in a beautifully converted 16th century barn and a plant nursery offering a wide selection of herbaceous and other plants.

Also within the Arley estate, **Stockley Farm** is a 400-acre organic dairy farm that provides a great family day out. A visit begins with a tractor and trailer ride to the farm where there are always baby animals for children to handle and feed. Adult animals include an 18-hand shire horse, Star, a lovely big pig called Olive, and Kate, the Highland cow. There are miniature tractors to ride, pony rides, an adventure play area, a souvenir shop and a Country Café.

PICKMERE

6 miles NE of Northwich on the B5391

The delightful village of Pickmere commands superb views of the Cheshire Plain, extending from the Dee estuary to the Pennine hills. The nearby **Pick Mere**, from which the village takes its name, is popular with wind surfers and yachtsmen, and boats are available for hire.

LACH DENNIS

4 miles SE of Northwich on the B5082

The small village of Lach Dennis derives its name from the Old English 'laecc', meaning a bog, and the Dennis family which once had an estate here. A mile or so to the east, **Shakerley Mere Nature Reserve** is host to a diverse range of wildlife with Canada Geese, herons, mute swans and mallards a common sight. Cormorants fly here from their breeding grounds on the coast to feast on the fish, and more exotic species arrive at different times of the year.

WINSFORD

6 miles S of Northwich on the A54

Winsford is another of the Cheshire salt towns which expanded greatly during the 19th century, swallowing up the old villages of Over and Wharton on opposite banks of the River Weaver. Two legacies of those boom years should be mentioned. One is Christ Church, which was specifically designed so that it could be jacked up in the event of subsidence. The other is Botton Flash, a sizeable lake caused by subsidence but now a popular water recreation area for the town.

LITTLE BUDWORTH

7 miles SW of Northwich on a minor road off the A49 or A54

Little Budworth Common Country Park is a pleasant area of heathland and woods, ideal for picnics and walking. The nearby village enjoys splendid views over Budworth Pool but will be better known to motor racing enthusiasts for Oulton Park racing circuit a mile or so to the south.

TARPORLEY

12 miles SW of Northwich on the A51/A49

In the days when most of this area was part of Delamere Forest, Tarporley was

THE TARPORLEY GALLERY

64a High Street, Tarporley, Cheshire CW6 0AG
Tel: 01829 730930 Fax: 01829 730073

Angela McAlpine's love of art inspired her to open the
Tarporley Gallery in the spring of 2003. In a Grade II
listed building on a corner site in the main street, the
work of local artists both prominent and lesser known
is on display. In addition to the paintings in oils,
watercolours and acrylic, both traditional and
contemporary, there are sculptures in wood, stone,
bronze, metal, glass and ceramic, along with smaller
items such as bottles and bowls. The Gallery is a great place to browse and well worth a pause on a tour
of Tarporley.

NO. 6 COFFEE SHOP

6 Chestnut Terrace, High Street, Tarporley, Cheshire CW6 0UW

Carol Duncan, language and business graduate, found the
enterprise she was looking for in 1998, in a period brick building
on the main street of Tarporley. In **No. 6 Coffee Shop** friendly
waitresses serve superb home-baked cakes such as lemon drizzle,
date slice and coffee and walnut cake, accompanied by top-quality
coffee and fine leaf teas. On the savoury side the choice runs from
light snacks and salads to doorstop toast topped with cheese, baked
beans or eggs and a full English breakfast. The interior is in comfortable bistro style, with wooden
tables and chairs, and in fine weather tables are set out under sunshades on the patio.

the headquarters of the verderers or
forest wardens. It was from Tarporley in
the early 17th century that John Done,
Chief Forester and Hereditary Bow-bearer
of Delamere, entertained King James to
a hunt. The chase was, he reported, a
great success: *"deer, both red and fallow,
fish and fowl, abounded in the meres"*. A
grateful King rewarded his host with
a knighthood.

UTKINTON

10 miles SW of Northwich off the A49 or A51

During the Middle Ages, the verderers
had their own courts in which they
meted out rough justice to offenders
against the forest laws. One such court
was at Utkinton, and in an old
farmhouse stands a column formed by
an ancient forest tree, its roots still in the

WILLINGTON FRUIT FARM

Hillside Farm, Chapel Lane, Willington, Nr Tarporley,
Cheshire CW6 0PH
Tel: 01829 751216 Fax: 01829 752928
e-mail: info@winsors.co.uk website: www.winsors.co.uk

In a beautiful part of Cheshire, close to Delamere Forest and the Sandstone
Trail, 'Winsors Fruit Farm' is a family run business established over 50 years.
The shop is open from June to January. Home-grown strawberries, raspberries, blackcurrants and
gooseberries as in season from June to October, plus fifteen varieties of apple from September onwards.
Always on sale in the shop is a wide selection of salads and vegetables, locally produced preserves, free
range eggs, pre-packed cheeses, Cheshire Farm Icecream, Welsh farmhouse yogurts, cordials, Home
Pressed Apple Juice and herbs in pots. Visitors may browse around the small herb garden.

WILLINGTON HALL HOTEL

Willington, Nr Tarporley, Cheshire CW6 0NB
Tel: 01829 752321 e-mail: enquiries@willingtonhall.co.uk
Fax: 01829 752596 website: www.willingtonhall.co.uk

Built in 1829 as a grand private house, **Willington Hall** is now a
very comfortable hotel and an ideal base for touring Chester and
North Wales. The interior has retained many handsome period
features, and fine antiques and oil paintings are prominent
throughout. Each of the ten en suite bedrooms has its own individual style and charm, and the hotel's
bars are convivial spots for meeting old friends or making new. Lunch and dinner (non-residents
welcome) are served in the Gainsborough Restaurant. The Hall stands in 17 acres of formal gardens
and parkland, with wonderful views towards the Welsh mountains.

---

ground. When the court was in session,
the wardens would place on this tree the
symbol of their authority, the Hunting
Horn of Delamere. The farmhouse is not
open to the public but the horn, dating
from around 1120, has survived and
can be seen at the Grosvenor Museum
in Chester.

ASHTON

8 miles E of Chester on the B5393

A couple of miles to the northeast of
Ashton stretch the 4,000 acres of
Delamere Forest, a rambler's delight with
a wealth of lovely walks and many picnic
sites, ideal for a peaceful family day out.
In Norman times, a 'forest' was a part-
wooded, part-open area, reserved as a
hunting ground exclusively for royalty or
the nobility. There were savage penalties
for anyone harming the deer, even if the
deer were destroying crops, and
household dogs within the forest had to
be deliberately lamed to ensure that they
could not harass the beasts. By the early
years of the 17th century many of the
great oaks in the forest had already been
felled to provide timber for ship-building
– as well as for Cheshire's familiar black
and white half-timbered houses. Since the
early 1900s, Delamere Forest has been
maintained by the Forestry Commission,
which has undertaken an intensive
programme of tree planting and

woodland management. Delamere is now
both an attractive recreational area and a
working forest, with 90% of the trees
eventually destined for the saw mills.

WARRINGTON

Lying on an important bridging point of
the River Mersey, Warrington claims to
enjoy Britain's most convenient location.
It stands midway between the huge
conurbations and ports of Manchester
and Liverpool and on a pivotal point of
communications close to where the M6,
M62 and M56 motorways intersect, and
where the West Coast main railway line
links London and Scotland.

Warrington is North Cheshire's largest
town – an important industrial centre
since Georgian and Victorian times and
with substantial buildings of those days
to prove it. Its imposing **Town Hall** was
formerly Lord Winmarleigh's country
residence, built in 1750 with all the
appropriate grandeur: windows framed in
painfully expensive copper, and
elaborately designed entrance gates 25
feet high and 54 feet wide. Along with its
park, it provides a dignified focus for the
town centre. A major Victorian
contribution to the town is its excellent
Museum and Art Gallery in Bold Street,
dating from 1857 and one of the earliest
municipal museums. The exhibits are

remarkably varied: among them are shrunken heads, a unique china teapot collection, a scold's bridle, Egyptian mummies, a Roman actor's mask and other Roman artefacts discovered in nearby Wilderspool. There are some fine paintings as well, most of which are Victorian watercolours and oils, and a rare Vanous still life. In the Old Market Square is a granite sculpture by Edwin Russell of the Mad Hatters Tea Party. This statue was unveiled by the Prince and Princess of Wales in 1984 and commemorates the area's connection with Lewis Carroll, who lived in nearby Daresbury. The River of Life in Bridge Street is a memorial to the victims of the 1993 terrorist bomb: artist Stephen Broadbent worked with local children to design 12 bronze plaques, each with an inscription chosen by the children - self-control, joy, peace, forgiveness, encouragement, reconciliation, patience, justice, love, hope, friendship and faithfulness.

Also worth visiting is **St Elphin's Church** with its 14th century chancel and memorials celebrating the Butler and Patten families. The town's premier leisure site is Victoria Park, purchased by the Corporation in 1897 and named to commemorate Queen Victoria's jubilee. The park is a good starting point for exploring the area, following the Mersey Way along the river or joining Black Bear Park and the Trans-Pennine Trail. An interesting curiosity at Bridge Foot nearby is a combined telephone kiosk and letter box. These were common in the early 1900s, but Warrington's is one of the few survivors. Also associated with the town are the television presenter Chris Evans who was born here, and the durable comedian and ukulele player George Formby is buried in the Catholic section of the town's cemetery.

AROUND WARRINGTON

WIDNES
6 miles SW of Warrington on the A557

Described in the 1860s as 'a quiet industrial village', Widnes now has a population of around 60,000. It stands on the north shore of the Mersey, linked to Runcorn by a remarkably elegant road bridge.

A popular attraction is **Spike Island**, which provides a landscaped walk from where the superstructures of ships passing along the Manchester Ship Canal can be seen gliding past. Widnes has a popular family attraction in the Catalyst Science Discovery Centre, where four galleries and over 100 hands-on exhibits make sense of the world of science and technology.

RUNCORN
7 miles SW of Warrington on the A557

Runcorn is one of Britain's best known post-war new towns, developed around a much older town bearing the same name. For 'Inspiration All Year Round' visit **Norton Priory**, just five miles from Junction 11 of the M56. Enjoy a warm welcome and discover the 800 year old priory range, excavated priory remains, purpose built museum, the St Cheistopher statue - one of the great treasures of medieval Europe - exciting sculpture trail and award winning Walled Garden with its National Collection of tree quinces, herbs, roses, vegetables and fruit. All set in 38 acres of tranquil, beautiful woodland gardens, Norton Priory also has a coffee shop, retail area and temporary exhibitions gallery. A programme of exciting events takes place throughout the year with something for everyone from medieval festivals to make your own scarecrow

days.The museum is open every day from noon and the Walled Garden from April to October between 1.30pm and 4.30pm.

LYMM

6 miles E of Warrington on the A56

During the stage coach era, Eagle Brow was notorious, a dangerously steep road that dropped precipitously down the hillside into the village of Lymm. To bypass this hazard, a turnpike was built (now the A56), so preserving the heart of this ancient village with its half-timbered houses and well-preserved village stocks. The Bridgewater Canal flows past nearby and the church is reflected in the waters of Lymm Dam. Popular with anglers and birdwatchers, the dam is a large man-made lake, part of a lovely woodland centre linked to the surrounding countryside and the canal towpath by a network of footpaths and bridleways. The village became an important centre for the fustian cloth (corduroy) trade in the 19th century but is now best known simply as a delightful place to visit.

Lymm stands on the sides of a ravine and its streets have actually been carved out of the sandstone rock. The same rock was used to construct Lymm's best-known landmark, the ancient cross crowned with a huge cupola that stands at the top of the High Street.

DUNHAM MASSEY

4 miles E of Lymm on B5160

Dunham Massey Hall and Park (National Trust) has 250 acres of parkland where fallow deer roam freely and noble trees planted in the late 1700s still flourish. A fully restored 17th century sawmill can be seen in working action, and there are splendid walks in every direction. The Hall, once the home of the Earls of Stamford and Warrington, is a grand Georgian mansion of 1732

with an outstanding collection of furniture, paintings and Huguenot silver. The Hall is open most days from late March to early November, and the Park is open every day.

DARESBURY

5 miles SW of Warrington on the A558

There has been a church at Daresbury since the 12th century and the present church has many interesting features including 17th century carvings, a 16th century font and an 18th century hair picture, a beautifully embroidered picture of the church sewn completely in human hair. The church also has a unique 'Green Man' and a Geoffrey Webb stained glass window in memory of Lewis Carroll who was born in the village in 1832 when his father was vicar there. The window depicts Lewis Carroll and many characters from *Alice in Wonderland*. The church is open daily from 9am to dusk and a small gift stall sells cards and souvenirs.

HELSBY

8 miles NE of Chester on the A56

There are seven Iron Age forts scattered across Cheshire, but only the one at Helsby, maintained by the National Trust, is open to the public. The climb out of the village along pretty woodland paths to the red sandstone summit is quite steep but the views across the marshes to the Mersey Estuary and Liverpool repay the effort.

FRODSHAM

10 miles NE of Chester on the A56

This is an attractive town with a broad main street lined with thatched cottages and substantial Georgian and Victorian houses. During the 18th and early 19th centuries, Frodsham was an important coaching town and several fine coaching

THE RIDGEWAY COUNTRY HOLIDAY PARK

The Ridgeway, Frodsham,
Cheshire WA6 6XQ
Tel/Fax: 01928 734981
e-mail: enquiries@ridgewaypark.com
website: www.ridgewaypark.com

At **The Ridgeway Country Holiday Park**, Sue and David offer luxury lodges and caravans for holiday letting in a very tranquil and attractive part of the Cheshire countryside. Accommodation comprises luxury timber lodges with two bedrooms, fully equipped kitchen/dining areas and verandas with garden furniture. Central heating and double glazing keep things cosy and quiet at all times, and each unit has its own parking space.

The caravans are also available with either two or three bedrooms, and everything needed for a carefree holiday. The Park is surrounded by mature woodland and is an ideal base for those who enjoy walking and wide open spaces – it is bordered on two sides by footpaths, one being the 32-mile Sandstone Trail that stretches from Frodsham to the Shropshire border. Adjoining the Park is the Foxhill Arboretum, a 50-acre country woodland park, and the ancient forest of Delamere is a short distance to the south. With easy access to the major road network (Junction 12 of the M56 is only a ten-minute drive away), it is also an excellent choice as a base for touring the region.

The Ridgeway has plots available where holiday home owners can site their own new units.

FOOD!

27 Church Street, Frodsham, Cheshire WA6 6PN
Tel: 01928 734100 e-mail: enquiries@foodforfood.co.uk
website: www.foodforfood.co.uk

Nick and Jane Harris and manager Dan Redfern have a passion for good food which they share with their customers, and **Food!** is a real boon to the citizens of Frodsham and the surrounding area. To ensure that all the produce on sale is of the best quality and originality, the owners try as far as possible to source products from small, individual manufacturers and traders, both local and from other parts of the UK as well as Europe and even further afield. Apart from the extensive and exciting range on display, the delicatessen offers other services. Sandwiches

with unusual and imaginative fillings in a variety of breads are freshly made to order with ingredients from the deli, and ready made meals and snacks include quiches, pâtés, meats, pasta and cheeses.

Platters for business lunches and meetings can be made up and delivered locally, and the bespoke catering service extends to cocktail parties, private dinners, functions and receptions. There's a gift-wrapping service for items bought as presents, and hampers can be made up to suit individual tastes and budgets. Opening hours are 9.00am to 2pm Monday and Wednesday, 9.00am to 4pm Tuesday, 9.00am to 5.30pm Thursday and Friday and 9.00am to 5pm Saturday.

inns survive. Of the Earl of Chester's Norman castle only fragments remain, but the **Church of St Laurence** (an earlier church here was recorded in the *Domesday Book*) is noted for the fine 17th century panelling in its exquisite north chapel.

The vicar here from 1740 to 1756 was Francis Gastrell, a name that is anathema to all lovers of Shakespeare. Gastrell bought the poet's house, New Place, at Stratford and first incensed the townspeople by cutting down the famous mulberry tree. Then, in order to avoid paying the Corporation poor rate, he pulled the house itself down. The outraged citizens of Stratford hounded him from the town and he returned to the parish at Frodsham that he had neglected for years.

KNUTSFORD

Knutsford and its people were the heroes of one of the most durable of Victorian novels, Elizabeth Gaskell's *Cranford*. This gently humorous, sympathetic but sharply-observed portrait of the little Cheshire town, and the foibles and pre-occupations of its citizens, was first published in 1853 and is still delighting readers today. Elizabeth was scarcely a month old when she came to Knutsford. Her mother had died shortly after her birth and her father sent her here to be brought up by an aunt who lived in a road which has now been re-named Gaskell Avenue. The motherless child grew up to be both strikingly beautiful and exceptionally intelligent. Early on she evinced a lively interest in the town's characters and its history: she was

BELLE EPOQUE BRASSERIE AND HOTEL

King Street, Knutsford, Cheshire WA16 6DT
Tel: 01565 633060/632661 Fax: 01565 634150
e-mail: info@thebelleepoque.com
website: www.thebelleepoque.com

The Mooney family have owned and run **The Belle Epoque** for 30 years, and with brothers Matthew and David at the helm its appeal is as strong as ever. Matthew is the managing director, David the very talented chef, and Mark Walkden, the restaurant manager for 20 years, is an essential element in the success story and virtually part of the family. The building is unique, a shrine to Art Nouveau, with many amazing features, including the 120ft Elizabeth Gaskell Memorial Tower, a Venetian glass mosaic floor, marble pillared alcoves, lavish drapes and antiques from several periods.

In the 60-cover non-smoking brasserie, David, who trained with Marco Pierre White under Raymond Blanc at Le Manoir aux Quat'Saisons, prepares a menu that caters for all tastes, from traditional British to modern worldwide, and the superb food is matched by discreet, personal service. Smoking is allowed in the bar/lounge area, and there are three private dining rooms and a fully enclosed roof garden. The Belle Epoque is also one of the most comfortable hotels for miles around, and the six beautifully refurbished en suite bedrooms (non-smoking), each with its own distinct style, are equipped with TV, telephone and tea/coffee making facilities.

intrigued, for example, to find that in the house next door to her aunt's had once lived a notorious highwayman, Edward Higgins, hanged for his crimes in 1767; she wrote a story about him. Marriage to William Gaskell, a Unitarian pastor in Manchester, took her away from Knutsford, although she returned often and for long periods, and after her death in 1865 she found a resting place in the grounds of the Unitarian Chapel; here, too, lie her husband and two of her four daughters.

The Knutsford that Elizabeth Gaskell knew so well and wrote about so vividly has expanded a great deal since those days of course, but in its compact centre, now designated an outstanding area of conservation, the narrow streets and cobbled alleys still evoke the intimacy of a small Victorian town. Two parallel roads, Toft Street and King Street, form a rectangle surrounding the old town. But

Mrs Gaskell would surely be astonished by the building erected in King Street to her memory by Mr Richard Harding Watt in 1907. A gifted entrepreneur, Mr Watt had made a huge fortune in Manchester as a glove manufacturer, but what really aroused his enthusiasm was the flamboyant architecture he had seen during his travels through Spain, southern Italy and the Near East.

On his return, he spent lavishly on trying to transform Knutsford in Cheshire into Knutsford-on-the-Med. At the north end of the town, he built a laundry complete with Byzantine domes and a minaret. A vaguely Ottoman style of architecture welcomed serious-minded artisans to his Ruskin Reading Rooms. In Legh Road, he erected a series of villas whose south-facing frontages are clearly in need of a really hot sun. And in King Street, as homage to the town's most famous resident, Richard Watt spent

THE CROSS KEYS HOTEL

King Street, Knutsford, Cheshire WA16 6DT
Tel: 01565 750404 Fax: 01565 750510
e-mail: thekeysknutsford@msn.com

The Cross Keys Hotel has long been a distinctive landmark close to the centre of the market town of Knutsford. Andrew and Rachel Burke and their staff provide a warm Cheshire welcome at this splendid 18th century former coaching inn, where the traditional look and atmosphere are combined with all the modern amenities that today's guests expect. Behind the gabled black and white frontage, with flower tubs and hanging baskets adding to the picturesque scene, the hotel has a longstanding reputation for providing good food and drink in relaxed, stylish surroundings, and in the bar connoisseurs of real ale will always find plenty of choice.

Bar meals are served daily, while in the cellar restaurant an extensive à la carte menu supplemented by daily specials and lighter options is complemented by a range of wines from around the world. The bars and restaurant are open to the public as well as hotel guests. The 13 bedrooms, sympathetically converted from the coaching house and stables, all have en suite facilities, TV, radio, telephone, hairdryer and beverage tray. Two of the rooms can easily be converted into meeting rooms, and the hotel offer support services for business guests.

LA BOUTIQUE D'OR

43-45 King Street, Knutsford, Cheshire WA16 6DW
Tel: 01565 634770 Fax: 01565 751076

La Boutique d'Or has been a leading ladies fashion store for 30 years, and since 1992 has been owned and run by Sally-Anne Goodman and her mother Pauline Taylor. In an attractive listed Tudor building in the main street of |Knutsford, the top-quality stock includes extensive ranges by Basler, Jobis, Blue Willis, Lucia and Luisa Cerano. An alteration service is available. Staff are friendly and helpful, paying great attention to customer requirements. Opening hours are 9 to 5 Monday to Saturday.

thousands of Victorian pounds on the Gaskell Memorial Tower. This tall, blank-walled building seems a rather incongruous tribute to the author who was herself so open and so down-to-earth.

But it is eccentrics like Richard Watt who make English architecture as interesting as it is. He was so proud of his contribution to the town's new buildings that, travelling on his coach to the railway station, he would rise to his feet and raise his hat to salute them. As he did so, one day in 1913, his horse suddenly shied, the carriage overturned, and Richard Watt was thrown out and killed. What other changes he might have made to this grand old town, had he lived, we can only imagine.

An unusual exhibition and well worth visiting is the **Penny Farthing Museum**, located in the Courtyard Coffee House off King Street. These bizarre machines were in fashion for barely 20 years before the last model was manufactured in 1892. The collection includes a replica of the famous Starley Giant with a front wheel seven feet in diameter, and a sign outside the coffee house promises a free tea to anyone arriving on a penny-farthing.

Close by, in Tatton Street, is the **Knutsford Heritage Centre.** Knutsford is a town with a long history – Edward I granted the town a Charter in 1262, and at the same time a local landowner, William de Tabley, was given a money-making licence to control the market. The Heritage Centre is housed in a restored 17th century timber-framed building which in Victorian times was a smithy. During the restoration the old forge and bellows were found in a remarkable state of preservation. The wrought-iron gate in front of the centre

CHURCH HILL GALLERY

Church Hill, Knutsford, Cheshire WA16 6DH
Tel: 01565 633636 Fax: 01565 621162
website: www.churchhillgallery.com

Walk up the cobbled street that rises to Knutsford's picturesque church and you'll find **The Church Hill Gallery** set in a beautiful 17th century building. Upstairs the gallery houses a stunning range of pictures by leading contemporary artists including originals and silkscreen prints by J.C.G.Illingworth. A professional framing service offering expertise and advice from experienced framers. Downstairs within the cellars, a stunning range of interesting stationary, handmade gifts, imaginative cards and exquisite wrapping papers all displayed in hand built oak units.

was specially created for the Centre and depicts dancing girls taking part in Knutsford's famous Royal May Day celebrations – Royal because in 1887 the Prince and Princess of Wales honoured the festivities with their presence. Every May Day the town centre streets are closed to all traffic except for the May Queen's procession in which colourful characters such as Jack in Green, Highwayman Higgins and Lord Chamberlain, Morris dancers, Maypole dancers and many others take part. One curious tradition whose origins are unknown is the practice of covering the streets and pavements with ordinary sand and then, using white sand, creating elaborate patterns on top. A colourful Knutsford character was Trumpet Major Smith, who sounded the Charge into the Valley of Death at the Battle of Balaclava. He is buried in the grounds of the Georgian parish church.

AROUND KNUTSFORD

Sweeping up to the very edge of Knutsford are the grounds of **Tatton Park**, 2,000 acres of exquisite parkland landscaped in the 18th century by the celebrated Humphry Repton. This lovely park, where herds of red and fallow deer roam freely, provides a worthy setting for the noble Georgian mansion designed by the equally celebrated architect Samuel Wyatt. The combination of the two men's talents created a house and park that have become one of the National Trust's most visited attractions. Tatton's opulent state rooms, containing paintings by artists such as Canaletto and Van Dyck along with superb collections

of porcelain and furniture, provided the television production of *Brideshead Revisited* with a sumptuous setting for Marchmain House.

More than 200 elegant pieces of furniture were commissioned from the celebrated cabinet-makers, Gillow of Lancaster. Particularly fine are the superb bookcases in the library, constructed to house the Egerton family's collection of more than 8,000 books. By contrast, the stark servants' rooms and cellars give a vivid idea of what life below stairs was really like. The Egerton family built Tatton Park to replace the much earlier **Tudor Old Hall**, which nestles in a wood in the deer park and dates back to around 1520. Here, visitors are given a guided tour through time from the late Middle Ages up to the 1950s. Flickering light from candles reveals the ancient timber roof of the Great Hall, supported by ornate quatrefoils, while underfoot, the floor is strewn with rushes, providing a warm place for the medieval Lord of the Manor and his servants to sleep. There's much more: Home Farm is a working farm, working as it did in the 1930s, complete with vintage machinery. Traditional crafts (including pottery),

Tatton Park

Tatton Park Gardens

(who painted the house several times), Lely, Reynolds, Opie and Martin Danby, along with furniture by Gillow, Bullock and Chippendale, and fascinating family memorabilia spanning three centuries. Through various activities, the Friends of Tabley House raise funds for the restoration and refurbishment of the house; recent undertakings have included the redecoration of the grand entrance hall and the restoration and rehanging of the 18th hall lantern. The 17th century chapel next to the house looks perfectly in place but it was originally built on an island in Tabley Mere and only moved to its present site in 1927.

stables and many farm animals provide a complete picture of rural life some 60 years ago. Tatton's famous gardens include a Victorian maze, an orangery and fernery, a serene Japanese garden, American redwoods, and a splendid Italian terraced garden. There's also a busy programme of educational activities for children, an adventure playground, shops, and a restaurant. You can even get married in the sumptuous mansion and hold your reception either in the house itself, in the Tenants Hall which can cater for parties of up to 430, or in a marquee in the magnificent grounds. With so much on offer it is small wonder that Tatton Park has been described as the most complete historic estate in the country.

Just west of Knutsford, on the A5033, is **Tabley House,** home of the Leicester family from 1272 to 1975. Mrs Gaskell often came to picnic in the grounds of the last of their houses, a stately Georgian mansion designed by John Carr for the first Lord de Tabley in 1761. This Lord de Tabley loved paintings and it was his son's passion for art, and his hunger for others to share it, that led to the creation of London's National Gallery. His personal collection of English pictures, on display in Tabley House, includes works by Turner

Also in Tabley, at the Old School, is the **Tabley Cuckoo Clock Collection.** Brothers Roman and Maz Piekarski are well-known horologists and clock restorers and over the last 25 years they have sought out and renovated some of the rarest and most notable examples of this 300-year-old craft. Also on display are some mid-19th century cuckoo clocks which include complex musical movements to reproduce popular tunes of the day.

MERE

3 miles NW of Knutsford on the A50/A556

One of the **Kilton Inn**'s more notorious guests, back in the 18th century, was Dick Turpin. This intrepid highwayman made the inn the base from which he plundered travellers along the Knutsford to Warrington road (now the comparatively safe A50). After one such robbery (and murder) Turpin, on his famous horse Black Bess, "galloped to the Kilton and, altering the clock, strolled on to the bowling green and proved an alibi by the short time he took to cover the four miles".

MOBBERLEY

2 miles E of Knutsford on the B5085

The main glory of this scattered village is the spectacular woodwork inside the church: massive roof beams with striking winged figures and one of the finest rood screens in the country, dated 1500. The screen is covered with a rich tracery of leaves and fruit, coats-of-arms, and religious symbols. Two generations of the Mallory family held the rectorship here, one of them for 53 years. He is commemorated in the east window. Another window honours his grandson, George Mallory, the mountaineer who perished while making his third attempt to climb Mount Everest in 1924. Just off the B5085 is the **Hillside Bird Oasis**, (see panel below) with a private collection of birds that includes flamingoes (greater, lesser, Chilean and Caribbean), owls, pelicans, penguins, toucans, hornbills, ibis, cranes and kookaburras - over 100 species in all.

At the Whitsun Bank Holiday each year steam traction enthusiasts from all across the country descend on the village for the **Mobberley Steam Party** hosted by the Bull's Head Inn.

LOWER PEOVER

4 miles S of Knutsford on the B5081

The village of Lower Peover (pronounced Peever) is effectively made up of two hamlets. One is grouped around the village green on the B5081, the other is at the end of a cobbled lane. It's a picturesque little group. There's a charming old coaching inn, The Bells of Peover, which during World War II numbered Generals Patton and Eisenhower among its customers. The American flag still flies here alongside the Union Jack. Nearby are a handsome village school founded in 1710, and a lovely black and white timbered church, more than 700 years old, with a massive Perpendicular tower built in 1582. St Oswald's is notable as one of the few timber-framed churches in the country still standing, and probably the oldest. Inside, there is a wealth of carved wood – pews and screens, pulpit and lectern, and a massive medieval chest made from a single log of bog oak. At one time local

HILLSIDE BIRD OASIS

Beech Hill, Mobberley, Nr Knutsford,
Cheshire WA16 7HY
Tel: 01565 873282

The **Hillside Bird Oasis** is a superb private collection, started over 30 years ago as a small collection of wildfowl. It now inludes a vast variety from penguins to parrots.

The pleasant combination of pools, waterfalls, paths and gardens makes an attractive haven for birds and visitors alike. The

most fascinating features here are the five species of penguins which have all bred successfully.

An eyecatching sight are the elegant flamingoes, whilst Owl Wood is home to a vast array of owls from the largest to the smallest. Parrots and pelicans are among the more exotic birds to be found in this beautiful setting, as well as aviaries containing toucans, kookaburras, cranes and pheasants.

Seasonal talks are given throughout the year and there are many seats within the grounds where you can picnic. A gift shop sells a range of 'Birdie' gifts and in the Pelican Pantry drinks, snacks and ice creams are available. Open daily except Thursdays in Summer (April 1st to October 31st) and Wednesdays and Sundays in Winter.

girls who wished to marry a farmer were required to raise its lid with one hand to demonstrate they had the strength to cope with farm life.

About three miles east of Lower Peover is **Peover Hall**, very much hidden away at the end of a winding country road but well worth tracking down. During World War II, General George Patton lived for a while at the Hall, which was conveniently close to his then headquarters at Knutsford. There's a memorial to him in the church nearby, but many more to the Mainwaring family, whose fine monuments crowd beside each other in both the north and south chapels.

MACCLESFIELD

Nestling below the hills of the High Peak, Macclesfield was once an important silk manufacturing town. Charles Roe built the first silk mill here in 1743, beside the River Bollin, and for more than a century and a half, Macclesfield was known as *the* silk town. It's appropriate then that Macclesfield can boast the country's only

Silk Museum (see panel below), where visitors are given a lively introduction to all aspects of the silk industry, from cocoon to loom. The Museum is housed within the Heritage Centre, built in 1813 as a Sunday school to provide education for the children who worked in the silk mills. An award-winning audio-visual programme traces the development of the silk industry in Macclesfield and there are fascinating exhibitions on the Silk Road across Asia, on silk cultivation, fashion and other uses of silk. The Heritage Centre has some interesting displays on Macclesfield's rich and exciting past.

The silk theme continues at nearby **Paradise Mill**. Built in the 1820s and in commercial use until 1981, it is now a working museum demonstrating silk weaving on 26 Jacquard hand looms. Exhibitions and restored workshops and living rooms capture the working conditions and lives of mill workers in the 1930s. It is also possible to buy locally-made silk products here.

In pre-Saxon times, Macclesfield was known as Hameston – the homestead on

---

MACCLESFIELD SILK MUSEUMS

Silk Museum, Park Lane, Macclesfield, Cheshire SK11 6TJ
Tel: 01625 612045 Fax No: 01625 612048
e-mail: postmaster@silk-macc.u-net.com
website: www.silk-macclesfield.org

Macclesfield Silk Museums, based on three listed sites, tells the story of silk with particular reference to Macclesfield, once known as the silk capital of England and associated with silk for 400 years.

The Silk Museum is housed within the Heritage Centre, a former Sunday School built in 1814 to educate the children who worked in the mills. There is an-award winning audio visual programme whilst silk costume and textiles illustrate the importance of silk to fashion and its use for special occasions. The Mulberry Tree coffee shop offers light snacks and a fuller menu. Just a short walk away new displays have been developed in the former School of Art and Design exploring the properties of silk, design education and Macclesfield's diverse textile industries. Archive footage accompany displays of historic textile machinery. Experience what life was like in a typical silk mill by taking a guided tour with one of the museum's knowledgeable and entertaining guides. Exhibitions and room sets illustrate life in the 1930s.

the rock, and on that rock is set the church founded by King Edward I and Queen Eleanor. From the modern town, a walk to the church involves climbing a gruelling flight of 108 steps. **St Michael and All Angels** was extended in the 1890s but its 14th century core remains, notably the Legh Chapel built to receive the body of Piers Legh, who had fought at Agincourt and died at the Siege of Meaux. Another chapel contains the famous Legh Pardon brass, which recalls the medieval practice of selling pardons for sins past, and even more conveniently for sins not yet committed. The inscription on the brass records that in return for saying five Paternosters and five Aves the Legh family received a pardon for 26,000 years and 26 days. The Savage Chapel and other parts of the church contain many memorials to the illustrious Savage family, whose numbers included Sir Thomas, who became Archbishop of York towards the end of the 15th century.

One of the Macclesfield area's most famous sons is Charles Frederick Tunnicliffe, the celebrated bird and wildlife artist, who was born at the nearby village of Langley in 1901. He studied at the Macclesfield School of Art and first came to public attention with his illustrations for Henry Williamson's *Tarka the Otter* in 1927. A frequently changing collection of Tunnicliffe's striking oil paintings, watercolours and etchings can be seen at the **West Park Museum** in a public park on the northwestern edge of town. This purpose-built museum, founded in 1898 by the Brocklehurst family, also includes exhibits of ancient Egyptian artefacts acquired by Marianne Brocklehurst during visits to Egypt between 1873 and 1891. The collection features a mummy case, and the afterlife displays examine the process of mummification and the

objects buried with the dead. Incidentally, the park boasts what is thought to be the largest bowling green in England.

A less well-known figure is William Buckley, who was born in Macclesfield around 1780 and later became a soldier. He took part in a mutiny at Gibraltar against the Rock's commanding officer, the Duke of York, father-to-be of Queen Victoria. The mutiny failed and Buckley was transported to Australia. There he escaped into the outback and became the leader of an aboriginal tribe who took this giant of a man, some six feet six inches tall, as the reincarnation of a dead chief. For 32 years Buckley never saw a white man or heard a word of English. When the explorer John Bateman, on his way to what is now Melbourne, discovered him, Buckley had virtually forgotten his mother tongue. He was pardoned, given a pension and died at Hobart at the age of 76.

AROUND MACCLESFIELD

PRESTBURY

3 miles N of Macclesfield via the A523/A538

A regular winner of the Best Kept Village title, Prestbury is a charming village where a tree-lined main street runs down to a bridge over the River Bollin, ancient stocks stand against the church wall, and old coaching inns and black and white buildings mingle with the mellow red brickwork of later Georgian houses. The Church of St Peter, dating from the 13th century, still maintains a tradition which began in 1577. Every autumn and winter evening at 8pm a curfew bell is rung, with the number of chimes corresponding to the date of the month. Close by is a building known as the **Norman Chapel** with a striking frontage carved with the characteristic Norman

zig-zags and beaked heads. Even older are the carved fragments of an 8th century Saxon cross preserved under glass in the graveyard. Opposite the church is a remarkable magpie timber-framed house which is now a bank but used to be the vicarage. During the Commonwealth, the rightful incumbent was debarred from preaching in the church by the Puritans. Undaunted, the priest addressed his parishioners from the tiny balcony of his vicarage.

ADLINGTON

4 miles N of Macclesfield off the A523

Adlington boasts a fine old house, **Adlington Hall**, which has been the home of the Legh family since 1315 and is now one of the county's most popular attractions. Quadrangular in shape, this magnificent manor house has two distinctive styles of architecture: black and white half-timbered buildings on two sides, later Georgian additions in warm red brick on the others. There is much to see on a tour of the Hall, with beautifully polished wooden floors and lovely antique furnishings enhancing the air of elegance and grandeur. The Great Hall is a breathtaking sight, a vast room of lofty proportions that set off perfectly the exquisitely painted walls. The beautifully preserved 17th century organ here has responded to the touch of many maestros, none more famous than George Frederick Handel, who visited the Hall in the 1740s.

BOLLINGTON

4 miles NE of Macclesfield on the B5091

In its 19th century heyday, there were 13 cotton mills working away at Bollington, a little town perched on the foothills of the High Peak. Two of the largest mills,

HIGHER INGERSLEY BARN

Oakenbank Lane, Bollington, Nr Macclesfield, Cheshire SK10 5RP
Tel: 01625 572245 Fax: 01625 574231
e-mail: bw.peacock@ntlworld.com
website: www.higheringersleybarn.co.uk

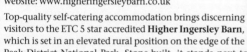

Top-quality self-catering accommodation brings discerning visitors to the ETC 5 star accredited **Higher Ingersley Barn**, which is set in an elevated rural position on the edge of the Peak District National Park. Stone-built, it stands next to owners Brian and Chris Peacock's 17th century farmhouse, with its own private garden and patio, sitting-out area, parking for four cars and superb views in all directions. The Barn, which is centrally heated, has accommodation for six in three double bedrooms, all with en suite shower and toilet plus a bath in the master bedroom. The first-floor lounge, which can seat up to nine in comfort, is equipped with TV, video recorder/player and hi-fi music centre and two more people can be accommodated in a sofa bed.

The dining room is bright, spacious and very stylish, with French doors opening to the patio and garden, and the kitchen is fitted with everything that guests could need. The accommodation is completed by a cloakroom and a utility room with washing machine, tumble drier and plenty of storage space. In keeping with the original character of the barn, several of the rooms boast impressive exposed oak beams. The barn's water supply is natural water from the farm's own spring. There are excellent walks in all directions from the doorstep, varied sporting and leisure activities within easy reach, and many places of scenic and historic interest in the locality.

the Clarence and the Adelphi, still stand, although now adapted to other purposes. The Victorian shops and cottages around Water Street and the High Street recall those busy days. A striking feature of the town is the splendid 20-arched viaduct which once carried the railway over the River Dean. It is now part of the **Middlewood Way**, a ten-mile, traffic-free country trail that follows a scenic route from Macclesfield to Marple. The Way is open to walkers, cyclists and horse riders and during the season cycles are available for hire, complete with child seats if required. Just as remarkable as the viaduct, although in a different way, is **White Nancy.** This sugarloaf-shaped, whitewashed round tower stands on Kerridge Hill, more than 900 feet above sea level. It was erected in 1817 to commemorate the Battle of Waterloo and offers sweeping views in all directions.

SUTTON

2 miles S of Macclesfield on minor road off the A523

This small village, close to the Macclesfield Canal, is honoured by scholars as the birthplace of Raphael Holinshed, whose famous *Chronicles of England, Scotland & Ireland* (1577) provided the source material for no fewer than 14 of Shakespeare's plays. As well as drawing heavily on the facts in the Chronicles, the Bard wasn't above adopting some of Holinshed's happier turns of phrase.

BOSLEY

6 miles S of Macclesfield on the A523

To the east of Bosley town centre runs the **Macclesfield Canal**, one of the highest waterways in England, running for much of its length at more than 500 feet above sea level. Thomas Telford was the surveyor of the 26-mile route,

opened in 1831, which links the Trent and Mersey and the Peak Forest canals. Between Macclesfield and Congleton, the canal descends over 100 feet in a spectacular series of 12 locks at Bosley, before crossing the River Dane via Telford's handsome iron viaduct. Other unusual features of this superbly engineered canal are the two 'roving bridges' south of Congleton. These swing from one bank to the other where the towpath changes sides and so enabled horses to cross over without having the tow-rope having to be unhitched.

GAWSWORTH

3 miles SW of Macclesfield off the A536

Gawsworth Hall is a captivating sight with its dazzling black and white half-timbered walls and lofty three-decker Tudor windows. The Hall was built in 1480 by the Fitton family, one of whose descendants, the celebrated beauty Mary Fitton, is believed by some to be the Dark Lady of Shakespeare's sonnets. The Bard would no doubt approve of Gawsworth's famous open-air theatre, where performances range from his own plays to Gilbert and Sullivan operas, with the Hall serving as a lovely backdrop. Surrounded by a huge park, Gawsworth, to quote its owner Timothy Richards, is "the epitome of a lived-in historic house". Every room that visitors see (which is virtually every room in the house) is in daily use by him and his family. And what wonderful rooms they are! Myriad windows bathe the rooms in light, the low ceilings and modest dimensions radiate calm, and even the richly-carved main staircase is conceived on a human scale. The beautifully sited church, and the lake nearby, add still more to the appeal of this magical place. The Hall was the scene - in 1712 - of a famous duel when Lord Mohun and the

Duke of Hamilton fought over the estates; both were killed. The country's last professional jester, a certain Samuel Johnson, lived in the house and is buried in a nearby spinney.

CAPESTHORNE HALL

5 miles W of Macclesfield on the A34

The home of the Bromley-Davenport family for generations, Capesthorne Hall dates back to 1719, when it was designed by the Smiths of Warwick. It was altered in 1837 by Blore, and following a fire in 1861 it was remodelled and extended by the celebrated architect Anthony Salvin. The present building presents a magnificent medley of Elizabethan-style turrets and towers, domes and cupolas, while inside the house is a wealth of portraits and artefacts collected by family members during the course of their Grand Tours throughout Europe, America and the Far East. The Queen Anne Room features a monumental fireplace, while the Box Room has a fascinating collection that ranges from a Victorian oak letterbox to antique hat boxes and cigar boxes. In medieval times the head of the Bromley-Davenport family held the post of Chief Forester of Macclesfield Forest, which gave him authority to mete out summary justice to anyone who transgressed the savage forestry laws. As a reminder of their power, the family crest includes the severed head of a felon. One of these crests, on the main staircase built in the 1860s, was commissioned by the staunchly Conservative Bromley-Davenport of the time and the felon's head is instantly recognisable as the Liberal leader of the day, William Ewart Gladstone. In the grounds, near the Georgian family chapel, the 18th century Italian gates open on to lakeside gardens.

NETHER ALDERLEY

6 miles NW of Macclesfield on the A34

Nether Alderley Mill is a delightful 15th century watermill that has been restored by the National Trust. The red sandstone walls are almost hidden under the huge sweep of its stone tiled roof. Inside is the original Elizabethan woodwork and Victorian mill machinery which is still in working order, with two tandem overshot wheels powering the mill. The 14th century church of St Mary is almost a private mausoleum for the Alderley branch of the Stanley family: monuments to dead Stanleys are everywhere. Living members of the family were provided with an unusual richly carved pew, set up on the wall like an opera box and reached by a flight of steps outside.

ALDERLEY EDGE

6 miles NW of Macclesfield on the A34

Alderley Edge takes its name from the long, wooded escarpment, nearly two miles long, that rises 600 feet above sea

Alderley Edge

level and culminates in sandy crags overlooking the Cheshire Plain. In Victorian times, this spectacular area was the private preserve of the Stanley family and it was only under great pressure that they grudgingly allowed the 'Cottentots' of Manchester access on occasional summer weekends. Nowadays, walkers can roam freely along the many footpaths through the woods, one of which will take them to **Hare Hill Gardens**, one of the lesser-known National Trust properties. These Victorian gardens include fine woodland, a walled garden themed in blue, white and yellow flowers, and huge banks of rhododendrons.

WILMSLOW

6 miles NW of Macclesfield off the A34

The oldest building in Wilmslow is St Bartholomew's Church, built between 1517 and 1537, and notable for its magnificent ceiling, some striking effigies, and for the fact that Prime Minister-to-be Gladstone worshipped here as a boy. A hamlet in medieval times, Wilmslow mushroomed as a mill

town in the 18th and 19th centuries, and is now a busy commuter town offering a good choice of inns, hotels and restaurants.

STYAL

7 miles NW of Macclesfield, on a minor road off the B5166

Cared for by the National Trust, **Styal Country Park** is set in 250 acres of the beautifully wooded valley of the River Bollin and offers many woodland and riverside walks. The Park is open to the public from dawn to dusk throughout the year and is a wonderful place for picnics. Lying within the Park is **Quarry Bank Mill** (see panel below), a grand old building erected in 1784 and one of the first generation of cotton mills. It was powered by a huge iron waterwheel fed by the River Bollin. Visitors follow the history of the mill through various galleries and displays within the museum, including weaving and spinning demonstrations, and can experience for themselves, with the help of guides dressed in period costume, what life was like for the 100 girls and boys who once

QUARRY BANK MILL & STYAL ESTATE

Styal, Cheshire SK9 4LA
Tel: 01625 527468
e-mail: quarrybankmill@ntrust.org.uk
website: www.quarrybankmill.org.uk

Run by the National Trust, **Quarry Bank Mill** is a historic working water powered Cotton Mill. Here you can see cotton production from the plant to the cloth, as well as hand and power spinning and weaving demonstrations every day. There are hands on workshops and plenty of 'have a go' activities.

Go back in time and experience life in the 19th century Apprentice House or take a stroll to the Factory Village in the beautiful setting of the woodland, fields and river of the Bollin Valley. An exciting day out for all the family, there are events and activities for all ages including the children's adventure playground.

A unique range of gifts, clothing, books and genuine Styal calico products are on sale in the shop and refreshments are available in the Mill Kitchen restaurant. The Mill is open daily March to September and daily except Mondays the rest of the year. Phone for details.

lived in the Apprentice House. The Mill stages a full programme of events throughout the year. Also within the park is the delightful **Styal Village**, which was established by the mill's original owner, Samuel Greg, a philanthropist and pioneer of the factory system. He took children from the slums of Manchester to work in his mill, and in return for their labour provided them with food, clothing, housing, education and a place of worship.

Lyme Park

DISLEY

8 miles SE of Stockport on the A6

The small town of Disley lies close to the Macclesfield Canal and little more than half a mile from **Lyme Park Country Park**. At the heart of the spectacular 1,400-acre moorland park where red and fallow deer roam freely stands Lyme Park (National Trust), home of the Legh family for more than 600 years. The elegant Palladian exterior of this great house encloses a superb Elizabethan mansion. Among the many treasures on show are carvings by Grinling Gibbons, tapestries from Mortlake, and a unique collection of English clocks. The house featured many times in the BBC's 1995 production of *Pride and Prejudice* when it represented the exterior of Pemberley, the home of Elizabeth Bennett's curmudgeonly lover, Mr Darcy. It also appeared in Granada's *The Forsyte Saga*, and some of the costumes from that production are on display.

Amenities at the park include two shops, a restaurant, a tea room and a children's play area. From Easter to October, Lyme Park hosts a varied programme of events, from plant fairs and outdoor performances of plays to art exhibitions and a Morris Minor Owners Club Rally.

LOCATOR MAP

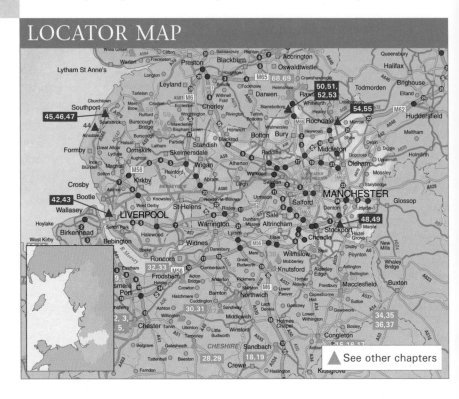

See other chapters

ADVERTISERS AND PLACES OF INTEREST

2 MERSEYSIDE AND GREATER MANCHESTER

The Local Government Act of 1972 (effective 1974) involved the creation of Merseyside and Greater Manchester. Greater Manchester took a major chunk from Lancashire and a smaller part from Cheshire, while Merseyside took another section of Lancashire and the northern part of The Wirral from Cheshire.

The metropolitan county of **Merseyside** comprises the districts of Liverpool, Knowsley, St Helens, Sefton and The Wirral (places of interest in The Wirral will be found in the Cheshire chapter). Merseyside is centred round Liverpool, one of the country's leading cities, and recently announced as the European City of Culture for 2008. After decades of neglect and under-investment the city has been transformed and has become one of the most vibrant and exciting in the land. Liverpool first began to show a different face to the world at the time of the Merseybeat Era in the 1960s.

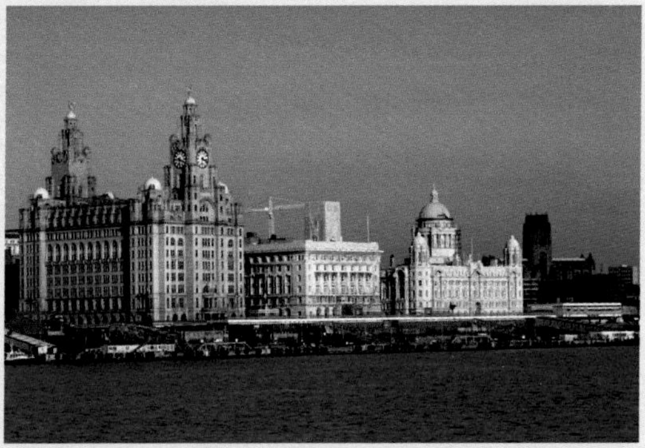

Liver Building across the Mersey

It was The Beatles who really put the city on the map, and the Fab Four are still responsible for a large proportion of the millions of tourists who now flock here each year. The annual Beatle Week is by far the busiest time to visit Liverpool, and 2003 saw its 20th anniversary. The Beatles Story is a permanent exhibition in the regenerated Albert Dock, and two of the Beatles' former homes are in the care of the National Trust and open for visits. Albert Dock's many other visitor attractions include the Merseyside Maritime Museum dealing with many aspects of Liverpool's links with the sea, and the impressive Tate Liverpool, the largest gallery of modern and contemporary art outside London.

Liverpool has two magnificent cathedrals, both of which should be on the itinerary of any visitor to the city. Football fans will be sure to visit the grounds of Liverpool or Everton. There are many organised walks and tours covering all aspects of city life, and the Mersey ferry is a favourite way of admiring the city's transformed waterfront. Aintree is the home of the

world's most famous steeplechase, the Grand National, and Merseyside has another major racecourse in Haydock Park at Newton-le-Willows.

Outside the city, Merseyside has its share of grand houses and rural attractions. Notable among these are Croxteth Hall & Country Park, Knowsley Safari Park and the National Trust's Speke Hall. The Trust also has the care of a stretch of coast at Formby, an internationally important site for wildlife and home of the famous Formby red squirrels. The whole stretch of coastline from the Mersey Estuary to north of Southport, is a haven for birdwatchers. Southport itself is a delightful spot that combines Victorian elegance with all the amenities of a popular seaside resort and a generous supply of culture. Its many places of interest include the Atkinson Art Gallery and the unique British Lawnmower Museum.

The metropolitan county of **Greater Manchester** comprises the districts of Bolton, Bury, Manchester, Oldham, Rochdale, Salford, Stockport, Tameside, Trafford and Wigan.

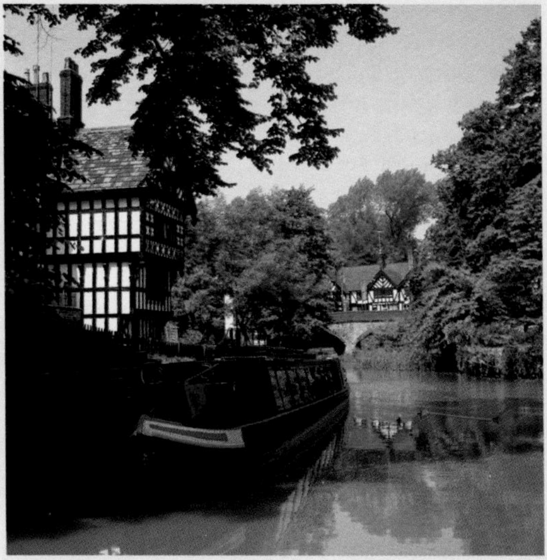

Bridgewater Canal, Worsley

Manchester, which has been transformed over the past few years, is notable for many fine buildings; some, like the Town Hall and the Cathedral, have long been city landmarks, while the new generation of buildings include Trinity Bridge and the City of Manchester Stadium. Manchester's museums and galleries are the most numerous and diverse outside the capital, ranging from the Museum of Science & Industry to the John Rylands Library and the Whitworth Gallery. And even in the post-Beckham era, the Manchester United Museum in Trafford is a magnet for football fans from all over the world. In Salford, the Lowry is a stunning cultural complex overlooking the Manchester Ship Canal.

Visitors to Manchester do not have to travel far to be in the country: Tameside, for example, offers country parks, woodland, moorland and reservoirs. It was the 3rd Duke of Bridgewater who commissioned the first canal in the country, linking his coal mines with Manchester and Liverpool.

By 1850, 4,000 miles of canals transported 30 million tonnes of freight throughout the country each year. They have long since ceased to fulfil their original role, but many stretches have been restored to become a splendid leisure amenity. Several canals run through Greater Manchester, including the Ashton Canal, the Bridgewater Canal, the Leeds & Liverpool Canal, the Rochdale Canal and the Manchester Ship Canal.

The main towns of Greater Manchester - Bolton, Bury, Oldham, Rochdale, Stockport, Wigan - have all retained a great sense of history with restored old industrial buildings and a variety of museums, and careful, public-spirited planning has ensured that they all offer plenty of green spaces for walking and leisure activities. Among the finest of the attractions outside the towns are Bramall Hall, a wonderful old 'magpie' house near Cheadle Hulme, Haigh Hall & Country Park near Wigan, and Hall I' th' Wood near Bolton.

LIVERPOOL

Liverpool, which has been completely transformed in recent years, was recently announced as the European City of Culture for 2008. The title is awarded by the European Union to celebrate the cultural identity of Europe's greatest cities and alternates annually among the member states. The most striking example of this transformation is **Albert Dock**, a painstakingly restored masterpiece of Victorian architecture. Designed by Jesse Hartley and built to hold the biggest sailing ships of the day,

it was opened by Prince Albert in 1846. By the end of the 19th century steam had largely replaced sail and the Dock was in decline. It finally closed in 1972 and stood derelict for some years. 1984 saw the start of its rebirth, and now the Dock is among the country's most popular heritage attractions, with some 4 million visitors a year. Behind the giant cast-iron columns and huge brick facades are dozens of visitor attractions, shops and retail outlets, restaurants, cafés, offices, television studios and luxury apartments.

Tate Liverpool is the largest British gallery of modern art outside London, showing modern and contemporary art from 1900 to the present day. Spread over four floors, it is one of four Tates, the others being Tate Britain and Tate Modern in London and Tate St Ives in Cornwall. Tate Liverpool hosts regular special exhibitions and has a year-round programme of tours, informal gallery talks, study days and Sunday family events.

Merseyside Maritime Museum is three museums in

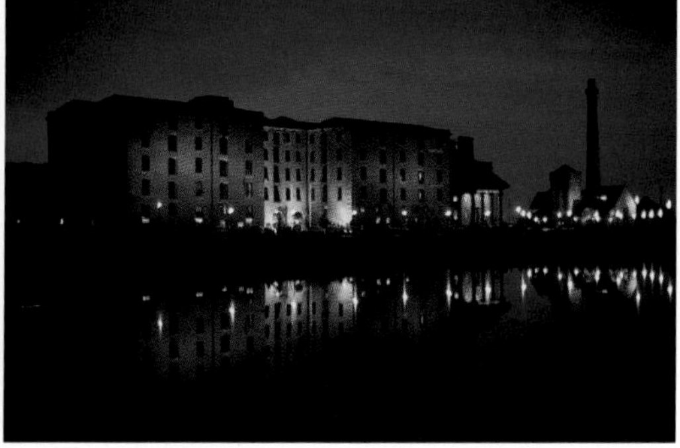

Albert Dock at Night

BLUECOAT DISPLAY CENTRE

Bluecoat Chambers, School Lane,
Liverpool L1 3BX
Tel: 0151 709 4014 Fax: 0151 707 8106
e-mail: crafts@bluecoatdisplaycentre.com
website: http://bluecoatdisplaycentre.com

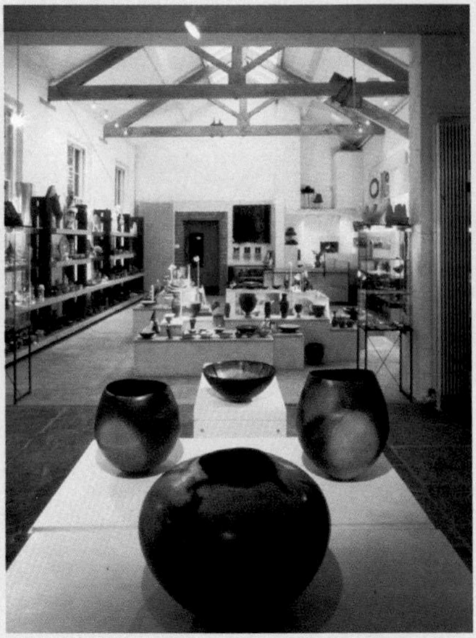

Set in the tranquil walled garden of a beautiful
Queen Anne building in the heart of the city, the
Bluecoat Display Centre is a haven for buyers of
everything exquisite in the field of arts and crafts,
from cutting edge to classic collector's pieces. This
nationally recognised contemporary craft and
design gallery has built up a fine reputation in the
40 years since it was established, supporting,
promoting, exhibiting and selling work by 400
innovative and exciting professional craft makers
whose work can range from the classically cool to
the highly humorous; they work in many media
and their output includes hand-made glass,
ceramics, studio pottery, jewellery, wood and
textiles. Maureen Bampton, a director here for
several years, and her friendly specialist team are

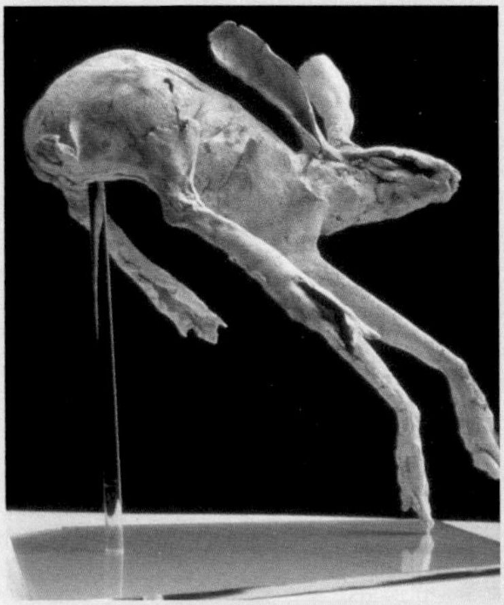

by Emma Rodgers

always happy to offer help and advice to ensure that
whether as an individual or representing an institution,
visitors will find the right piece of work to celebrate a
special occasion or to enhance a location.

The centre's services include assistance and advice
with wedding gifts and jewellery, along with specialist
advice for one-off commissions for pieces to complement
architectural situations or personalised pieces organised
for presentations. Thousands of pieces of applied art are
on display and for sale, and the challenging, ever
changing exhibition programme reflects both emerging
talent and established craftsmanship. The exhibitions
cover a very varied range of crafts, typified by the

successful summer 2003 'Tracing Paper' featuring
woven and sculptural works in paper. Bluecoat's
computer-aided study centre allows access to a
database of makers and archive of its exhibitions
as an education resource or commissioning aid.
A recent refurbishment project has led to many
new and improved facilities at the centre, which
is open from 10 to 5.30 Monday to Saturday.

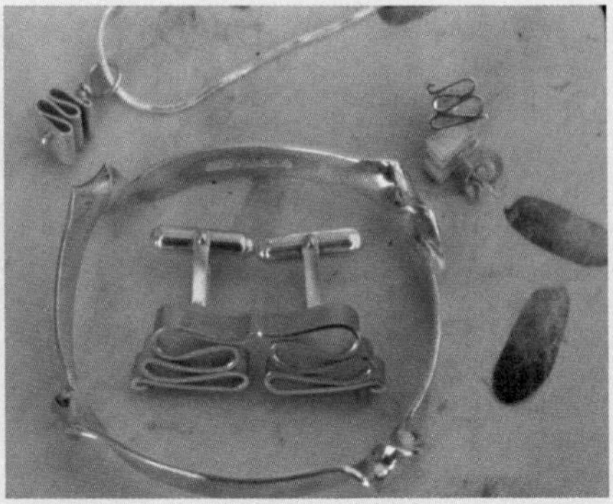

by Anthony Wong

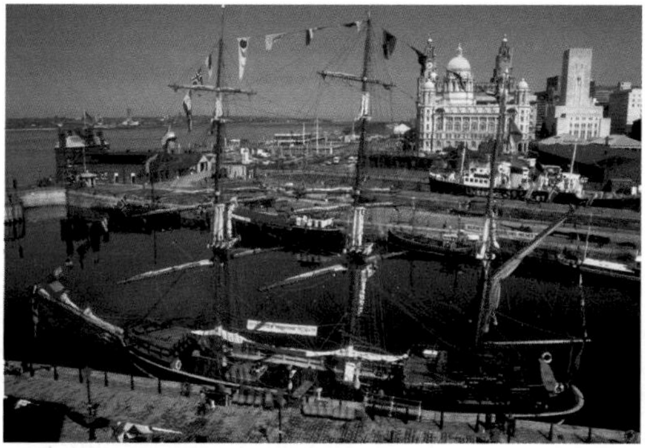

Maritime Museum

one - the Maritime Museum with its Transatlantic Slavery Gallery, the Museum of Liverpool Life and HM Customs & Excise National Museum. **The Beatles Story** is the city's major tribute to its four most famous sons, a walk-through experience that recreates the sights and sounds of the Merseybeat era.

The National Trust is responsible for two of the Beatles' homes. **Mendips** was the childhood home of John Lennon, where he lived with his Aunt Mimi and Uncle George, while **20 Forthlin Road** was the terraced home of Paul McCartney during the early years of the Beatles. Here they composed and rehearsed their earliest songs. Visits to these houses start from Albert Dock or Speke Hall (see below).

Liverpool has many other notable architectural gems apart from Albert Dock. Among these are **Liverpool Museum**, whose collections cover archaeology, ethnology and the natural and physical sciences; the **Walker**, with 600 years of art including masterpieces by Rubens, Rembrandt, Poussin,

Gainsborough and Hogarth; and St George's Hall, one of the finest neo-classical buildings in the world.

Liverpool has two spectacular Cathedrals, one Anglican, the other Roman Catholic. **Liverpool Cathedral** is an amazing 20th century Gothic-style masterpiece, begun in 1904 when the foundation stone was laid by King Edward VII and completed in 1978, when Queen Elizabeth II attended the celebrations. Even through two world wars, work never ceased, and, though the city was assailed repeatedly by enemy bombs, the Cathedral escaped serious damage. Designed by Giles Gilbert Scott and built mainly of locally quarried sandstone, the Cathedral abounds in superlatives: the largest Anglican Cathedral in Europe; the largest church organ in the world, with 9,765 pipes; the highest and heaviest ringing peal of bells in the world.

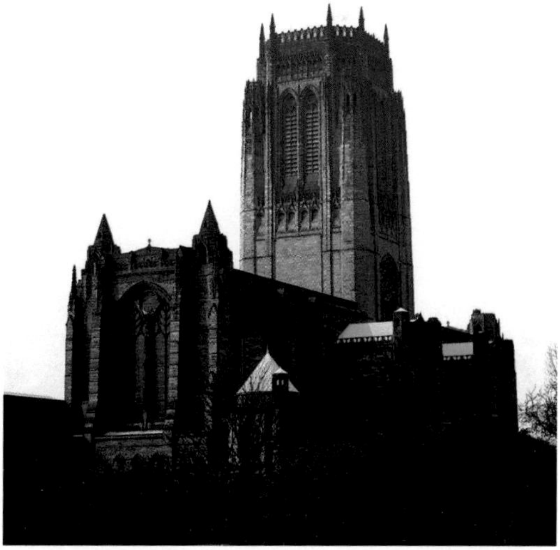

Liverpool Cathedral

Roman Catholic Cathedral

The Metropolitan Cathedral of Christ the King is a dramatic modern masterpiece, its focal point being a circular nave of glass and concrete, the work of Sir Frederick Gibberd. The Lantern Tower of the nave contains the world's largest stained-glass window, designed by John Piper and Patrick Reyntiens. This Cathedral was completed in 1967, but in the previous century there was a scheme to build a Cathedral second only in size to St Peter's. Only the crypt was built, and that can be visited on a guided tour.

The Liverpool Football Club Museum & Tour Centre celebrates all things Liverpool, past, present and future, including a re-creation of the standing Kop. The tour takes in the dressing room, the team dug-out and the tunnel, and displays in the museum cover the whole history of the club. Fans of The Toffees will make for Goodison Park for a tour of **Everton Football Club**.

DOMINO GALLERY

11 Upper Newington (off Renshaw Street), Liverpool L1 2SR
Tel: 0151 707 0764
e-mail: felicity.wren@fsbdial.co.uk

Felicity Wren, a vivacious and very sociable local lady who teaches art full time, opened **Domino Gallery** in 1991, since when it has been a popular and successful showcase for the works of numerous artists. Among those whose works have adorned the Gallery are Jason Jones and Claire Chinnery, painters of abstract studies; Michael Pace Sigge, photographer; Kate Lloyd, painter of local scenes; and Valerie Culpan, maker of craft pieces including bags. A small collection of Adrian Hill drawings from the 1960s is a notable feature, and among other artists whose work has been displayed and sold are George Jardine, Adrian Henri and John Bratby.

The Gallery shares its space with the **Green Fish Café**, which is open during gallery hours for teas, coffees and light meals. Works of art hang around the eating area, with display cabinets for specialist showings. Exhibitions are arranged on a regular basis, featuring both local artists and higher profile names. One of the most popular recent shows was A Night at the Theatre, an exhibition of works for sale by Rachel Merriman. The Gallery and Café, which are open from 10 to 5 Monday to Saturday, are situated off Renshaw Street, close to The Adelphi Theatre, the Roman Catholic Cathedral and Central Station.

AROUND LIVERPOOL

SEFTON PARK

3 miles SE of Liverpool City Centre

The beautifully restored centrepiece of the park is the **Palm House**, opened in 1896 and rescued from a dilapidated state in the early 1990s. Re-opened in 2002, The Grade II* listed octagonal three-tiered structure houses plants from around the world in the Liverpool Botanical Collection and stages a year-round programme of events and concerts.

SPEKE

8 miles SE of Liverpool City Centre off the A561

Dating from 1490, **Speke Hall** is one of the greatest half-timbered houses in the country, set in splendid gardens and woodland that belie its location in the Liverpool suburbs close to the airport. The interior spans the centuries, from the Tudor Great Hall to Jacobean plasterwork and the Victorian oak parlour and kitchens. Other attractions include the restored Home Farm building, a children's play area and a giant maize maze. The Hall also hosts a programme of events from Easter onwards.

KNOWSLEY

5 miles E of Liverpool City Centre off the A580

Easily reached from the city, the A580 and the M57 (Junction 2), **Knowsley Safari Park** brings visitors face to face with the great outdoors and creatures of the wild. A five-mile safari drive gets close to baboons, lions, tigers, zebras, elephants, rhinos, bison, ostriches, camels, wildebeest and many other creatures. In the walkabout area are a reptile house, children's lake farm, otter pools, giraffes and meerkats, performing sea lions and parrots, as well as a restaurant and snack bar and over 20 rides, including dodgems, a pirate ship and a mini railway.

ST HELENS

12 miles E of Liverpool City Centre

St Helens was once a centre of the glass industry, a heritage that is illustrated in the fascinating displays in the **World of Glass**. Here, visitors can learn about the history and the techniques, both through interactive displays and through regular demonstrations by the resident glass artists.

NEWTON-LE-WILLOWS

15 miles E of Liverpool on the A580

One mile from Junction 23 of the M6, Haydock Park is the region's premier year-round racecourse, with 30 days racing on the Flat and over the jumps. Highlights of the year include the Peter Marsh Chase and Swinton Hurdle under National Hunt rules and the Stanley Leisure Sprint Cup on the Flat. Newton-le-Willows was the site of the first fatal railway accident. William Huskisson, MP for Liverpool, alighted from a carriage on the opening day of the Manchester & Liverpool Railway and was struck by a train hauled by George Stephenson's *Rocket*.

WEST DERBY

4 miles NE of Liverpool City Centre close to the M57/A580 junction

Croxteth Hall & Country Park is the Edwardian country estate of the Earl of Sefton, a place with many attractions for all ages. The Hall itself - elegant, opulent and beautifully maintained - stands in a 500-acre estate that includes a working farm, a lovely walled garden and a country park with woodland, wildlife, an adventure playground and a riding centre. Special events staged throughout the year include flower shows, family-fun days and murder mystery nights.

AINTREE

3 miles N of Liverpool City Centre on the A59

One of the most popular sporting attractions around Liverpool is the **Grand National Experience** at Aintree racecourse. The tours, which take place at 11am and 2pm on Tuesday and Friday, take in the museum and picture gallery, the weighing room, parade ring, stables, stewards room, a simulated race of champions, a virtual reality ride, Red Rum's statue, Red Rum's grave, a tour of the actual racecourse, souvenir shop, coffee shop and picnic area. Red Rum's record in the world's greatest steeplechase is one that will probably never be equalled: three times a winner (1973, 1974 & 1977) and twice runner-up (1975 & 1976).

Year by year, the facilities for spectators at the Grand National are improving, and there are other meetings apart from the three-day Grand National fixture: Ladies night May evening meeting, Family Day meeting in October, Becher Chase Day in November. The Visitor Centre at the course is open Tuesday to Friday late May to late October, and at other times by appointment.

Aintree is on the A59, 6 miles from Liverpool City Centre, a mile from the M57 and M58, with links to the M6 and M62.

SEFTON

5 miles N of Liverpool off the A59

This quiet old village stands at the edge of a rich and fertile plain of farmland that lies just behind the West Lancashire coast. It formed part of the estate of the Earls of Sefton (descendants of the Molyneux family) right up until 1972. The village has a pub, a 16th century corn mill and a delightful church, **St Helen's**, with a 14th century spire. Inside, there's a beautifully restored ceiling with bosses and moulded beams, 16th century screens, well-preserved box pews, two medieval effigies of knights, and an elaborately carved pulpit of 1635. A series of brasses recounts the history of the Molyneux family from their arrival in Britain with William the Conqueror.

Though this is a small village, its name has also been given to the large metropolitan district of north Merseyside which stretches from Bootle to Southport.

INCE BLUNDELL

6 miles N of Liverpool off the A565

The village takes part of its name from the Blundell family who have for centuries exerted much influence on the village and surrounding area. Ince comes from the Celtic word 'Ynes' which means an island within a watery meadow and it would have perfectly described the village's situation before the surrounding land was drained.

The annual candlelight service at the village **Church of the Holy Family** is an ancient custom that appears to be unique to this country. The people of

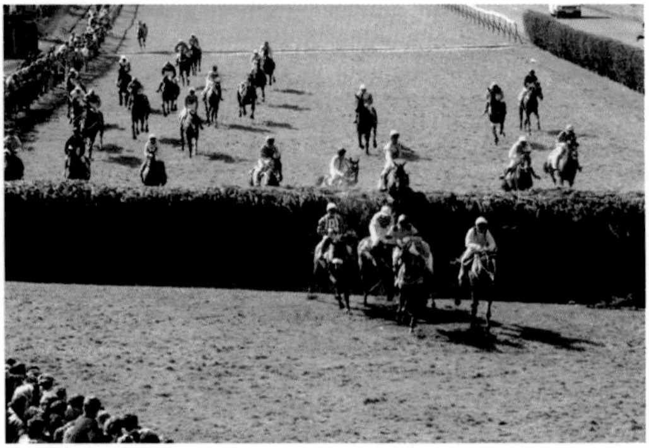

Grand National

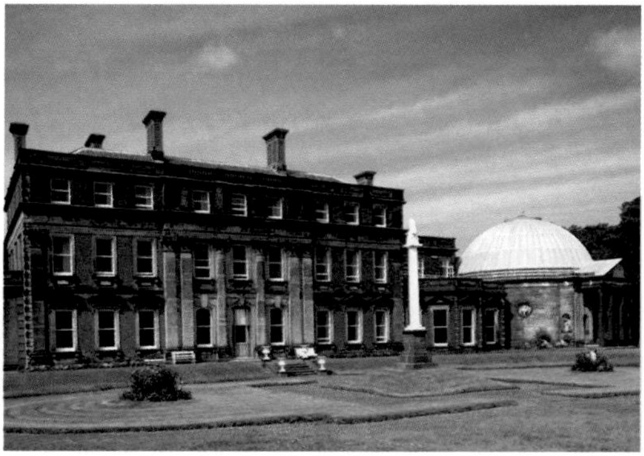

Ince Blundell Hall

the parish decorate the graves in the cemetery with flowers and candles before holding a service there. Common in Belgium, this custom was brought to the village at the beginning of the 20th century.

LYDIATE

7 miles N of Liverpool on the A5147

This is another pleasant old village bordering the flat open farmland created from the West Lancashire mosses. Lydiate itself means an enclosure with a gate to stop cattle roaming and, though the age of the settlement here is uncertain, the now ruined **St Katharine's Chapel** dates from the 15th century. However, the most frequented building in the village is **The Scotch Piper**, a lovely cruck-framed house with a thatched roof that has the reputation for being the oldest pub in the region.

FORMBY

12 miles N of Liverpool off the A565

Like Ormskirk, Formby has a connection with potatoes. It's said that sailors who had travelled with Sir Walter Raleigh to Virginia brought back potatoes with them and grew them in the fields around what was then a small village. There are still many acres of potato fields being cultivated in the area. To the west of the town, **Formby Point** and Ainsdale National Nature Reserve form the most extensive dune system in Britain, 450 acres of wood and duneland. Formby Point was the site of Britain's first lifeboat station, built in 1776 and still to be seen.

The origins of this small coastal town lie in the time of the Vikings and the name Formby comes from the Norse Fornebei meaning Forni's town. Between the Norman Conquest and the time of the Dissolution in 1536, there were a succession of landowners but, by the mid-16th century, the Formby and Blundell families emerged as the chief owners. Formby Hall, built for William Formby in 1523, occupies a site that was first developed in the 1100s.

Today, Formby is perhaps better known as a quiet and desirable residential area and also the home of an important red squirrel sanctuary at the National Trust **Freshfield Nature Reserve** and pine forest. From the shoreline there are magnificent views over the Mersey estuary and, on a clear day, the hills of Wales and of Lakeland are also visible. The whole stretch of this coastline is filled with birding sites, from Seaforth Nature Reserve on the Mersey Estuary to Marshside RSPB Reserve north of Southport.

AINSDALE

17 miles N of Liverpool on the A565

Towards the sea, from the centre of the village, lies what was Ainsdale-on-Sea with its old Lido and the more modern Pontin's holiday village. Between here and Formby, further down the coast, the

Continued on page 74

WALK 3

Formby Point

Start	Formby Point, Lifeboat Road car park and picnic site
Distance	4 miles (6.4km)
Approximate time	2 hours
Parking	Formby Point
Refreshments	None
Ordnance Survey maps	Landranger 108 (Liverpool, Southport & Wigan), Explorer 285 (Southport & Chorley)

The first part of the walk is through or along the edge of woodland which fringes the dunes of Formby Point on the Merseyside coast. It continues over the dunes to the beach and this is followed by an exhilarating 1½ mile (2.4km) walk along the broad, firm sands. Finally, you head back over the dunes of the Raven Meols Hills to the start. The combination of woods, dunes and beach is most attractive and the contrasting and extensive views take in the skyline of Liverpool and the hills of North Wales.

The dunes, woods, meadows and marshy slacks around Formby Point are the home of several rare creatures, including the red squirrel and natterjack toad. Much of the area comprises nature reserves and the whole of the coastline between Southport and Liverpool is one of the most extensive areas of sand dune in the country.

Start in front of the information board and, with your back to it, walk along the tarmac drive ahead which bends right to exit from the car park. Turn left along Lifeboat Road and, at a T-junction, turn

right **A** along a broad, tree-lined track, part of the Sefton Coastal Footpath. Keep in more or less a straight line for the next ¾ mile (1.2km) – along first a tarmac track, then a rough track and finally sandy and grassy paths – to a crossroads. Continue ahead along a fence-lined path by the edge of the Cabin Hill Nature Reserve and, in front of the Altcar Rifle Ranges, follow the path to the right **B** in the beach direction.

Head over the dunes to the beach. Ahead, the hills of North Wales are on the horizon and, to the left, the Wirral and the buildings of Liverpool can be

seen. Turn right **C** along the wide, sandy beach as far as the marker post 'Car Park, Information'. Just before reaching it, you pass the foundations of what is said to be the earliest lifeboat station in Britain. After becoming redundant, it served for a while as a tearoom.

At the marker post, turn right **D** onto a path which heads over the dunes again, passing an observation platform – a superb viewpoint – before returning to the start.

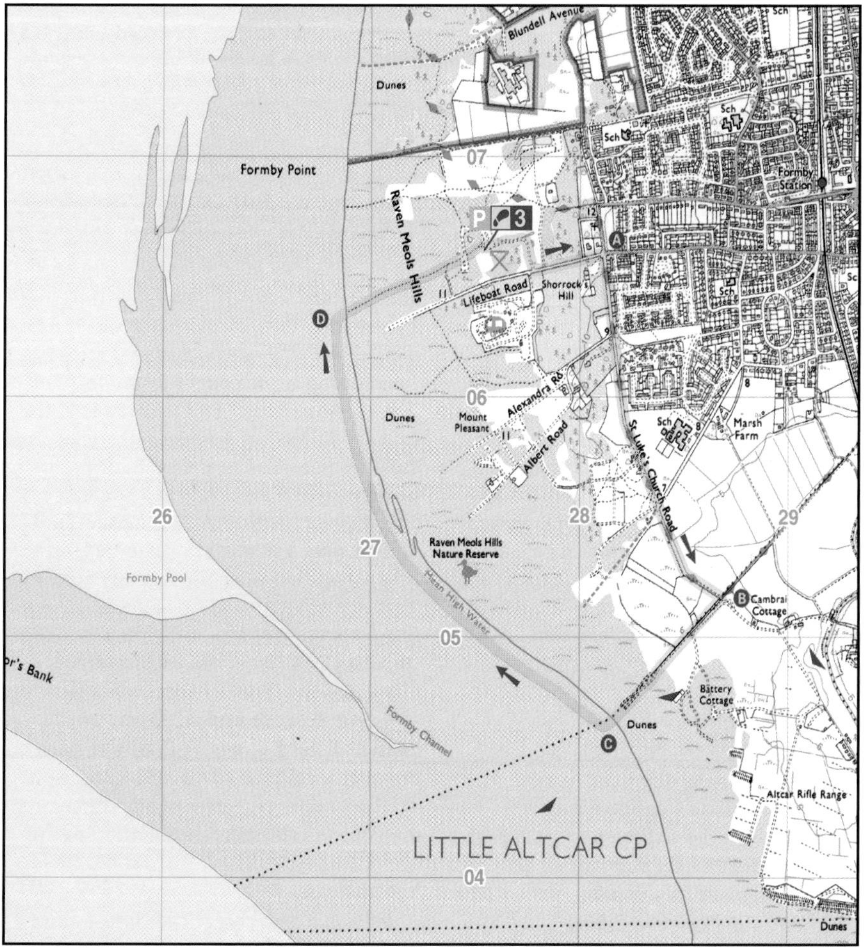

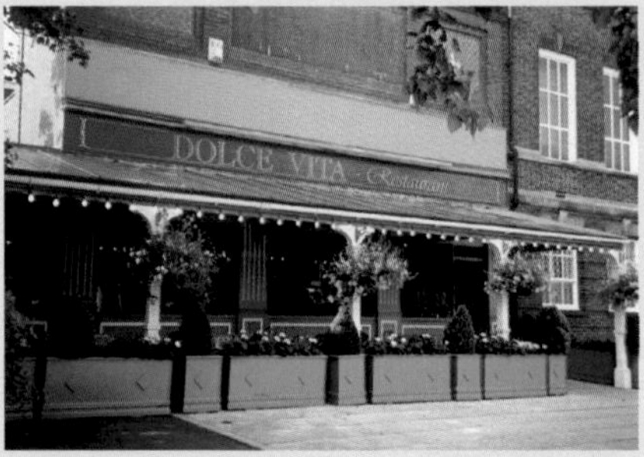

DOLCE VITA

90 Station Road, Ainsdale, Nr Southport,
Merseyside PR8 3HW
Tel: 01704 575535

Mario Cardillo came to the region with his wife Clare to enjoy the excellent facilities for golfers. They liked it so much that they moved here permanently and set up a business in the village of Ainsdale just south of Southport. That was 20 years ago, since when their friendly restaurant **Dolce Vita** has become one of the most popular in the area. The restaurant's attractive frontage is adorned with hanging baskets and tubs of flowers and shrubs, while inside, the owners have created the look and feel of Italy with prints of Italian scenes and racks of Italian wines.

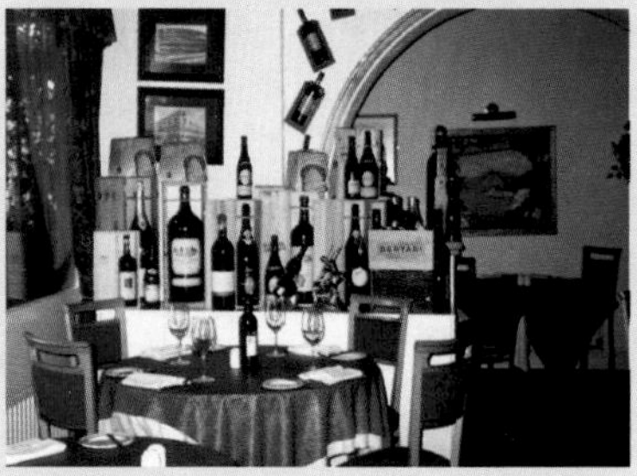

A comfortable bar with sofas and easy chairs is a pleasant spot to enjoy an aperitif before moving into the pastel decorated, carpeted dining area to enjoy classic Italian dishes prepared with skill and flair. Mussels marinara, garlicky king prawns or parma ham with melon might start the meal, followed perhaps by pizza, pasta, scampi, grilled sea bass or one of the many chicken or meat dishes, with a classic dessert to finish. A sister establishment, Via Veneto, is at 25-31 Old Hall Street, Liverpool, Tel: 0151 258 1878.

sand dunes form part of the **Ainsdale National Nature Reserve**, one of the most extensive dune systems in the country. It's also one of the few remaining habitats of the endangered natterjack toad which breeds in the shallow pools that form in the sand dunes. This quirky creature is the only species of toad that walks rather than hops. As well as supporting the toads, the salt pools are the natural habitat for a variety of rare dune plants, including Dune Helleborine, Grass of Parnassus and round-leaved wintergreen.

SOUTHPORT

Besides offering a step back in time, the broad promenades of Southport, its elegant tree-lined streets, and its superb shopping still makes this one of the most visited towns in this region.

The fashion for sea-bathing is usually reckoned to have originated with George III's regular dips at Weymouth in the late 1700s, but at Southport they'd already been doing it for generations. Only once a year though, on St Cuthbert's Eve, the Sunday following August 20th. The holiday became known as 'Bathing Sunday, when folk travelled some distance to throw off their clothes and frolick naked in the sea'. The tradition was associated with the legend, or fact, that St Cuthbert had once been shipwrecked but had miraculously been able to swim to the shore and safety.

Southport's history as an all-year, rather than a one-day-a-year resort began in 1792 when its first hotel was built. A local man, 'Duke' Sutton, went to the beach, gathered all the driftwood he could find, nailed it together, put in the minimum of furniture, and opened for business.

Within a few years other houses and

Southport Pier

environmentally-friendly hotel, in stone. Over-confident as it turned out. The following year he was thrown into Lancaster gaol for debt and later died a pauper.

Southport though continued to thrive and by the 1860s was by far the most popular seaside resort in Lancashire. The town's only problem was that its main attraction, the sea, was getting further and further away as silt from the Ribble estuary clogged the beach. The town council's response was to build the second-longest pier in the country, complete with a miniature railway which is still operating, create numerous parks and gardens, and construct elegant boulevards such as Lord Street. All that activity in Victorian times imbued the town with an appealingly genteel atmosphere which, happily, it still retains.

hotels had sprung up among the dunes and by 1802 'Duke' Sutton felt confident enough to rebuild his makeshift, if

PHILLIP GODFREY
DESIGNER GOLDSMITH

6 Bold Street, Southport, Merseyside PR9 0DD
Tel: 01704 544817
e-mail: godfreyphillip@hotmail.com
website: www.phillipgodfrey.biz

Designer and goldsmith **Phillip Godfrey** and his wife Elizabeth run their eponymous shop in smart premises just off Lord Street- the main shopping street of Southport. Apprenticed as a goldsmith in 1973 in

his native Birmingham, Phillip became a master of his profession, building a lofty reputation for superb design and craftsmanship in precious metals.

The shop, which he opened 15 years ago, has attractive window displays and a ground floor showroom. An ever-changing 'off-the-shelf' selection of jewellery is available from £10 to £10,000 and combines well with his own designer range. Phillip has built up a large clientele, who regularly travel from London and beyond to seek out his unusual designs. He is much in demand for his bespoke and commission work, and advises clients to make an appointment to discuss their individual requirements. The shop is open from 10 to 5pm Tuesday to Saturday.

THE EMPORIUM & DRAGONFLY CRAFTS

45a Wayfarers Arcade, Lord Street, Southport,
Merseyside PR8 1NT
Tel: 01704 512234
e-mail: andrea@andreawright.co.uk
website: www.andreawright.co.uk

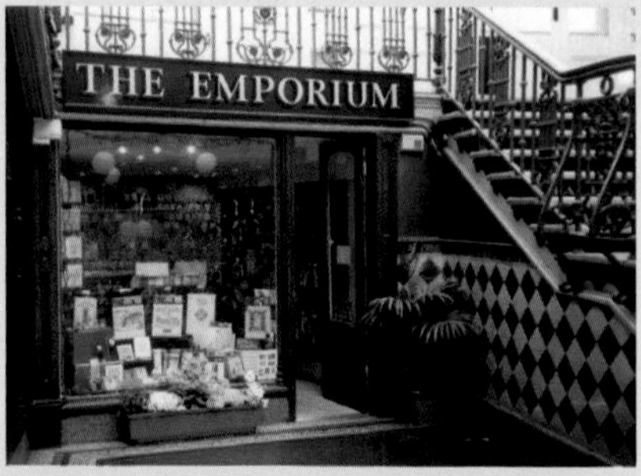

Sisters Andrea and Fiona Wright pooled their application, their enterprise and their imagination, and came up with **The Emporium & Dragonfly Crafts.** Cross-stitch hand-embroidered cards, hand-made jewellery and embroidery kits are among the items for which they have become best known, and the stock in their shop includes Andrea's lovely cards and embroidered samplers, both of which can be made to the individual requirements of their customers to produce a unique keepsake for a special occasion such as a wedding or the arrival of a baby.

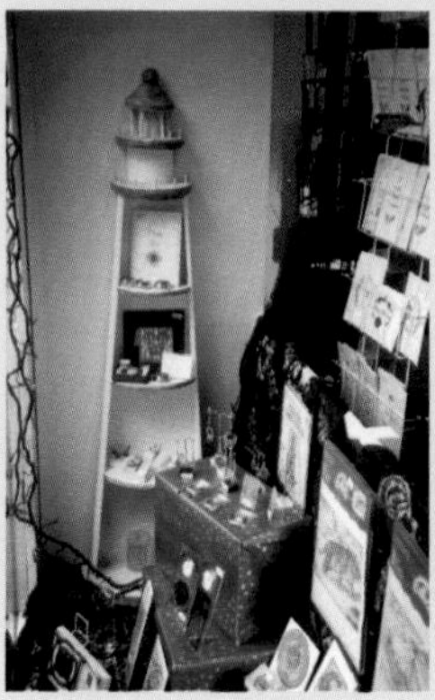

The jewellery, some of it in a delightfully quirky and very personal style, includes bracelets, necklaces and earrings. The shop has a predominately Celtic theme and as well as the jewellery and cards you'll find glassware, pottery, pewter and even mousemats! The sisters initially set out their stall (literally!) in this busy retail shopping arcade before taking a permanent shop space in the summer of 2002. Opening hours are 10 to 5 Tuesday to Saturday and 11 to 4.30 on Sunday.

The town's central, main boulevard, **Lord Street**, is a mile long road that was built along the boundary bordering the lands of the two neighbouring lords of the manor. A superb shopping street today, the exceptionally wide pavements, with gardens along one side and an elegant glass-topped canopy along most of the other side, make this one of the most pleasant places to shop in the country. Many of the town's classical style buildings are found along its length and it has been designated a conservation area. Off Lord Street, there is one of the town's several covered arcades – **Wayfarers Arcade**, built in 1898 and a fine example of these popular shopping malls. The modest entrance opens out into a beautiful cast-iron and glass conservatory with a first floor gallery and splendid central dome. Originally named the Leyland Arcade after the town's Member of Parliament, it took its present name in 1976 after the arcade's most successful leaseholder.

In a central position along Lord Street stands Southport's rather modest Town Hall. Built in 1852 and of a classical design, its facade includes a beautiful carving in bold relief of the figures of Justice, Mercy, and Truth picked out in white against a Wedgwood blue background. Further along, the Atkinson Central Library was built in 1879 as the premises of the Southport and West Lancashire Bank. The original ceiling of the banking hall can still be seen as can its fireplace. On the first floor is the **Atkinson Art Gallery**, which contains collections of British art and Chinese porcelain. In Shakespeare Street, the **British Lawnmower Museum** (see panel opposite) is a tribute to the gardening machinery industry, with an unrivalled collection of machines, many from the Victorian and Edwardian eras. The

Museum is open every day except Sunday and Bank Holidays.

Not all the notable buildings in Southport are Victorian and the Top Rank Bingo Club, originally called the Garrick Theatre, was held to be the finest theatre when it was opened in 1932. With much of its exterior as it would have appeared when it first opened, it is a wonderful example of the Art Deco style. Finally, Lord Street is also home to the town's war memorial, **The Monument**. Opened on Remembrance Day 1923 by the Earl of Derby, this is a large and grand memorial that remains the town's focal point. Its design was the subject of a competition and the winning entry was submitted by Garyson and Barnish, designers of the famous Royal Liver Building in Liverpool. The central obelisk is flanked by twin colonnades on which the names of the town's more than 1,000 dead are inscribed.

As every Victorian resort had a **Promenade**, so does Southport and this is a typical example: flanked by grand hotels on the land side and a series of formal gardens on the other. As the silting up of the Ribble estuary progressed unchecked the **Marine Lake** was constructed at the northern end of the promenade. At over 86 acres, this man-made lake is the largest in Britain and as well as being an attractive site and a place for the pursuit of all manner of watersports it is also host to an annual 24-hour yacht race.

From the centre of the promenade extends Southport's **Pier** which, at 1,460

BRITISH LAWNMOWER MUSEUM

106-114 Shakespeare Street, Southport, Lancashire
Tel: 01704 501336 Fax: 01704 500564

The **British Lawnmower Museum** located in the picturesque Victorian seaside holiday resort of Southport, Lancashire, houses a private collection of over 200 pristine exhibits of special interest (part of 400) built up over a period of 50 years and is now a tribute to the garden machinery industry which has developed over the past 170 years from the Industrial Revolution, when modern technology was not available, to the present day. Many of the machines have been rescued from the scrap yard and restored to their present very high standard. In addition to early grass cutting and garden machines dating from the 1830's, the exhibition houses the largest collection of vintage toy lawnmowers and games in the world.

The lawnmower was invented in 1830 by Edwin Budding of Gloucester, thought of as a madman testing the strange contraption at night. Originally designed to trim the nap from cloth, the cylinder machine he devised has not changed in principle since that date and has been the only traditional lawnmower for formal lawns used throughout Great Britain, although somewhat unique in so far as every other country in the world use the more recently introduced (circa 1930) rotary grass cutter.

The museum has now become one of the world's leading authorities on vintage lawnmowers and is now the largest specialists in antique garden machinery, supplying parts, archive conservation of manuscript materials including 500 original patents from 1799, and valuing machines from all over the world. The museum retains a character not often seen in these modern times.

Included in this unique national collection are manufacturers not normally associated with the garden industry, names such as Rolls Royce, Royal Enfield, Daimler, Hawker Sidley, Perkins Diesel, British Leyland and many more. A lot of the exhibits memorabilia and industrial artifacts are from the Victorian and Edwardian era and have been restored and keep a small part of British engineering heritage alive.

yards long was the longest pier in the country until 1897. Following a fire in 1933 it was shortened but it remains the second longest in the country. Looking at the pier today it is hard to imagine that at the end of the last century pleasure steamers were able to depart from here to Barrow in Cumbria, Bangor, Wales, and the Isle of Man. Along the shore line, and opened in the spring of 1998, the new sea wall and **Marine Drive** is a wonderful modern construction, the length of Southport's sea front, that blends well with the town's Victorian heritage.

The normal attractions of a seaside resort have not been forgotten and **Pleasureland** is the obvious choice for those seeking thrills and hair-raising rides; the 100+ rides and attractions include the country's tallest, fastest looping coaster, go-karts, kids' quad bikes and bumper boats. Keen gardeners will know Southport for its splendid annual Flower Show, second only to Chelsea, and golfers will be familiar with the name of Royal Birkdale Golf Course, just south of the town centre. Southport has one more sporting association of which it is justly proud. From behind a car show room in the 1970s, Ginger McCain trained Red Rum on the sands of Southport to a record breaking three magnificent wins in the Grand National run at Aintree. A statue of the great horse can be seen in Wayfarers Arcade.

AROUND SOUTHPORT

CHURCHTOWN
1 mile NE of Southport on the A5267

This charming village, now a small part of Southport, has retained much of its village feel and is certainly worthy of exploration in its own right. Considerably predating the seaside

resort, Churchtown is, as its name suggests, centred around its church. Since it is dedicated to St Cuthbert, it is possible that while fleeing from the Danes, the monks of Lindisfarne rested here with the remains of their famous saint.

However, it is likely that the village was, for many years, known by the name of North Meols and a chapel of Mele is mentioned in the *Domesday Book*. Derived from the Norse word 'melr' meaning sand dune, there was certainly a thriving fishing village here in the early 1100s. In 1224, Robert de Coudrey granted the village the right to hold a market, the likely place for which is the cross standing opposite the church in the heart of the village.

As the settlement lay on a crossroads and at the start of a route over the sands of the Ribble estuary, it was a place of considerable importance. It was also here that the tradition of sea bathing in this area began, when, in 1219 St Cuthbert's Eve was declared a fair day, which later became known as Bathing Sunday.

There is still plenty to see in this small village. The present **Meols Hall** dates from the 17th century but its appearance today is largely thanks to the work carried out by the late Colonel Roger Fleetwood Hesketh in the 1960s. When the colonel took over the house in the late 1930s, the older and larger part of the hall had been demolished in 1733 and the remaining building was rather nondescript. Taking the gabled bay of the late 17th century, extensions were added to give the house a varied roofline and a three dimensional frontage.

The hall is the last home of the Hesketh family who at one time had owned most of the coastal area between Southport and Heysham. Originally, the manor had been granted to Robert de Coudrey, coming into the Hesketh family

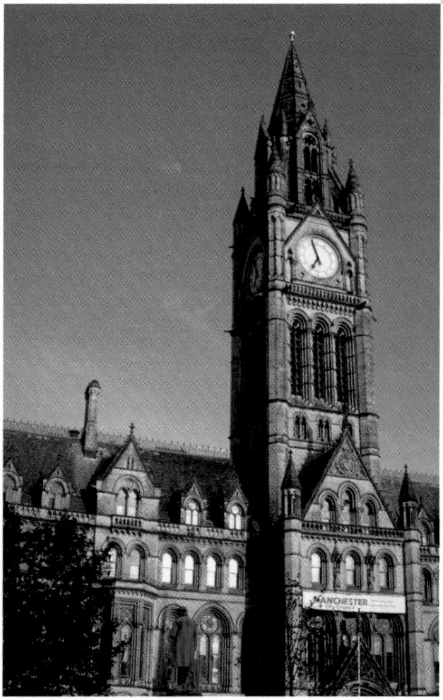

by marriage in the late 16th century. There has been a house on this site since the 13th century. Occasionally open to visitors, the hall has a fine art collection and, in the entrance hall, are three carved chairs that were used in Westminster Abbey during the coronation of Charles II. During World War I, Moels Hall was used as a military hospital.

Planned on the site of the old Churchtown Strawberry Gardens in 1874, the **Botanic Gardens**, restored in 1937, are beautifully maintained and present a superb example of classic Victorian garden design. With magnificent floral displays, a boating lake, wide, twisting paths, and a fernery, little has changed here since the day the gardens were first opened by the Rev Charles Hesketh. Built in 1938, following the gardens' restoration, the **Botanic Bowling Pavilion** mimics the style of the late Regency architect Decimus Burton. Here, too, is the Botanic Gardens Museum, with its fine exhibition on local history and its gallery of Victoriana.

MANCHESTER

Like Liverpool, Manchester has seen an urban renaissance as new buildings and open spaces have been developed, transforming the face of the city. Santiago Calatrava's Trinity Bridge, Bridgewater Hall, home of the Hallé Orchestra, and the City of Manchester Stadium take their places as landmarks alongside the splendid Town Hall, the Cathedral and the Baroque Church of St Ann with its rare glass by William Peckitt of York. The Victorian **Town Hall**, perhaps the finest in the country, is the work of Alfred Waterhouse; its many treasures include a wealth of stained glass and mosaic, and Ford Madox

Manchester Town Hall

Brown's murals in the Great Hall.

Manchester's museums and art galleries are the most impressive and diverse outside London. All repay lengthy visits, and in particular the **Museum of Science & Industry**, telling the story of the world's first major industrial city; the **Jewish Museum** housed in the city's oldest purpose-built synagogue; **Manchester Museum** in the University, famed for its Egyptian collections; the ultra-modern **Urbis** with interactive displays exploring life in different cities of the world; the **Manchester United Museum** in Trafford; the **City Art Gallery**; the **Whitworth Gallery**, best known for its British watercolours; and the **John Rylands Library**, built by Basil Champneys to house the library of the cotton magnate.

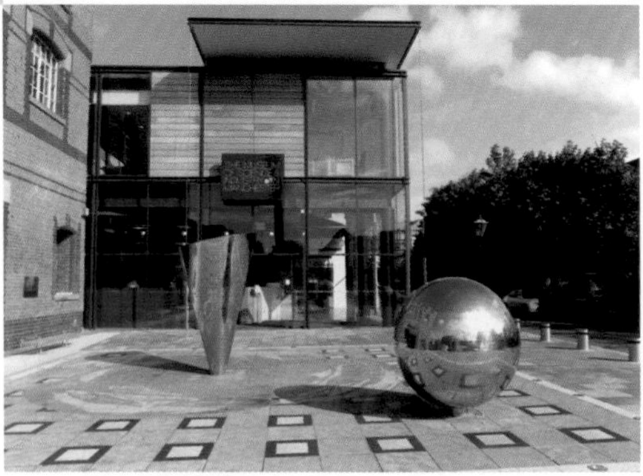

Museum of Science & Industry

associated with Manchester United. A footbridge to the Trafford side of the canal leads from The Lowry to the Imperial War Museum North, a fantastic aluminium-clad building whose three metal 'shards' represent conflict on air, sea and land.

AROUND MANCHESTER

ALTRINCHAM
8 miles SW of Manchester on the A560

The writer Thomas de Quincey visited Altrincham in the early 1800s and thought its bustling market "the gayest scene he ever saw". The market was established by Royal Charter in 1290 is still very active, although the old houses that de Quincey also noted have sadly gone. The market is now centred on a Victorian hall opened in 1880, and the range of stalls is splendidly diverse (though the goods for sale do not now run to wives - it is recorded that in 1823 a man sold his wife by auction for the equivalent of 7½p!). A modern bustling town, Altrincham nevertheless has a long history, with clear evidence that there was a settlement beside the River

Seven miles to the east of Manchester is the district of **Tameside**, much of which is open land comprising moorland, country parks, reservoirs and woodland. At Portland Basin, where three canals meet, is a new heritage centre that hosts special events throughout the year, including the Tameside Canals Festival.

On the western edge is the district of **Salford**, where the attractions include The Lowry, located in the fashionable Salford Quays, and Clifton Country Park. **The Lowry**, a stunning modern complex overlooking the Manchester Ship Canal, houses two theatres and an exciting children's activity gallery as well as the eponymous Lowry collection. L S (Laurence Stephen) Lowry, noted for his distinctive paintings of Northern industrial landscapes, spent some time as a rent collector. He was granted the freedom of Salford in 1965 and is buried in Manchester Southern Cemetery, which is also the final resting place of Sir Matt Busby, for 50 years intimately

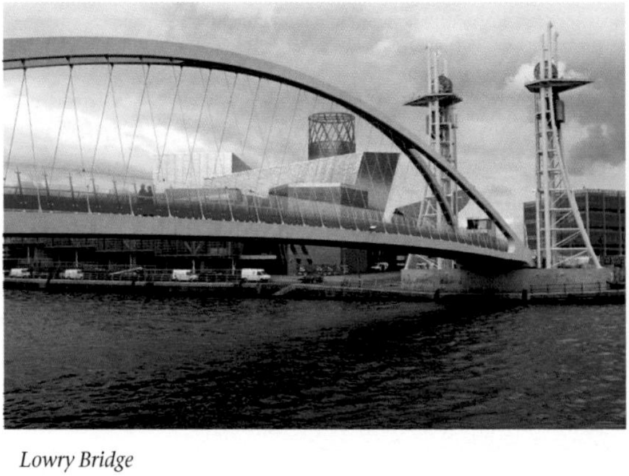

Lowry Bridge

Bollin some 6,000 years ago. Even older than that is the prehistoric body preserved in peat discovered on Lindow Common nearby. From Victorian times, Altrincham has been a favoured retreat for Manchester businessmen and the town is well supplied with inns and restaurants.

STOCKPORT

6 miles SE of Manchester on the A6

Nearly 50 percent of the borough is green space, so visitors will find plenty of opportunities for walking and enjoying the countryside. One of the town's most fascinating attractions is the **Hat Works**, located in the restored Wellington Mill. It is the country's first and only museum dedicated to hats and hat-making, and visitors can learn about Stockport's historic links with hatting (over 4,500 people were employed in the industry here at the end of the 19th century), see the original machinery and enjoy an amazing display of hats of all shapes and sizes, from miniature hats made by apprentices to the world's tallest topper. Close by are Stockport Museum, the delightful Victorian Vernon Park, and the **Air Raid Shelters** (see panel below), which provide a trip back in time to the Second World War, when tunnels were built into the red sandstone rock to accommodate thousands of people seeking refuge from air raids.

CHEADLE HULME

7 miles S of Manchester on the A34

Developed in Victorian times as a commuter town for better-off workers in Manchester, Cheadle Hulme is a busy place with a fine park on its eastern edge in which stands one of the grandest old 'magpie' houses in Cheshire, **Bramall Hall** (see panel on page 82). This eyecatching, rambling perfection of black and white timbered buildings overlooks some 62 acres of exquisitely landscaped woods, lakes and formal gardens. The oldest parts of the Hall date from the 14th century: for five of the next six centuries it was owned by the same family, the Davenports. Over the years, the Davenport family continually altered and extended the originally quite modest manor house. But whenever they added a new Banqueting Hall, 'Withdrawing Room', or even a Chapel, they took pains to ensure that its design harmonised happily with its more ancient neighbours. Along with Little Moreton Hall and Gawsworth Hall, Bramall represents the fullest flowering of a lovely architectural style whose most distinctive examples are all to be found in Cheshire.

STOCKPORT AIR RAID SHELTERS

Stockport, Cheshire
Tel: 0161 474 1940

Stockport's unique **Air Raid Shelters** have been carved into the natural sandstone cliffs in Stockport Town Centre and are the largest purpose built Second World War civilian underground air raid shelters. They were boarded up after the war and rediscovered a few years ago, since when they have been imaginatively restored to give visitors the feel of wartime Britain.

Visitors can explore the labyrinth of underground passages and wander through the reconstructed Warden's post, Toilets, First Aid Room, Canteen Tool Stores, Benches and Bunkers that once housed over five thousand people during a night in the Blitz.

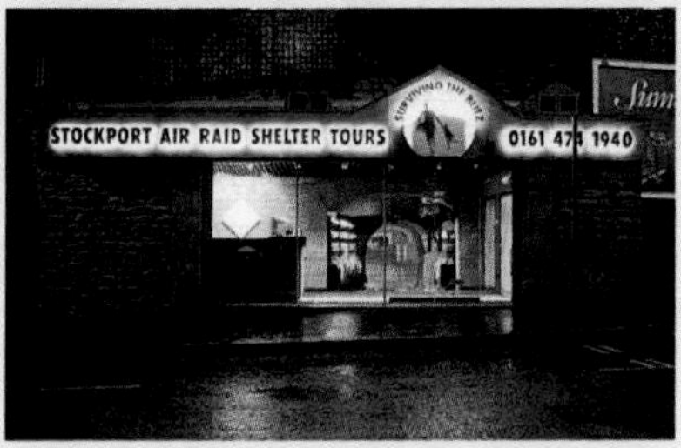

BRAMALL HALL

Stockport, Cheshire
Tel: 0161 485 3708

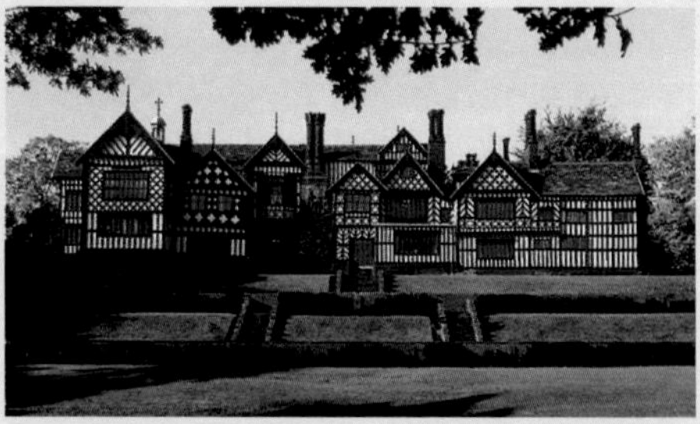

Bramall Hall is known as one of "England's treasures". It is a magnificent black and white Tudor manor house with Victorian additions set in 70 acres of beautiful parkland, which is landscaped in the style of Capability Brown. Take a tour of this beautiful house and you'll discover the spectacular Tudor plaster pendant ceiling, a wonderful 16th century embroidered table carpet and the wonderful wall paintings discovered by the Victorian owner.

The new costumed interpretation will give you a feel of the household in Bramall in 1890, with glimpses of the family from upstairs and the staff from downstairs. After a tour around this beautiful house, relax in the tearoom or restaurant and be tempted by delicious cakes, scrumptious light refreshments or a three-course lunch. Bramall Hall provides a pleasurable learning experience with a fascinating day out.

THE PANHANDLE

The narrow finger of land pointing up to West Yorkshire was chopped off from Cheshire in the 1974 Local Government redrawing of boundaries and put into Greater Manchester, but almost 30 years on most of its population still consider themselves Cheshire folk. At its northern end lie Longdendale and Featherbed Moss, Pennine scenery quite unlike anywhere else in the region.

MARPLE

10 miles SE of Manchester on the A626

Marple's most famous son is probably the poet and novelist Christopher Isherwood, who was born at Marple Hall in 1904 and could have inherited it from his grandfather had he so wished. Instead, the author of *Mr Norris Changes Trains* and *Sally Bowles* (the source material for the musical *Cabaret*) renounced the life of a country squire for the more sybaritic attractions of California. But Marple made a great impression on him as is evident from his book *Kathleen and Frank,* based on the letters and diaries of his parents. Isherwood revels in the wildness of the

Goyt Valley, not just its scenery but also its weather - "it never really dries out," Isherwood wrote.

Marple is also famous for its flight of 16 locks on the Peak Forest Canal and the mighty three-arched aqueduct that carries the canal over the River Goyt. At Marple, the Peak Forest Canal is joined by the Macclesfield Canal and there are some attractive towpath walks in both directions.

STALYBRIDGE

6 miles E of Manchester on the A57

Set beside the River Tame and with the North Pennine moors stretching for miles to the east, Stalybridge was one of the earliest cotton towns and its mill workers among the most radical and militant during the Chartist troubles of the 1840s. Oddly, one of their leaders was a former Methodist minister, the Rev. Joseph Rayner Stephens, who had broken away from the Wesleyan ministry and established his own 'Stephensite' chapels – one in King Street, Stalybridge, the other in the sister town across the Tame, Ashton under Lyme. He campaigned tirelessly against the long hours worked in the factories and the

policy, introduced in 1834, of refusing poor relief outside the workhouse.

When in 1842 the mill-owners tried to impose reductions in pay, the workers' embryonic trade union closed all the mills in north Cheshire and south Lancashire. Stephens was tried and sentenced to 18 months in Chester gaol. On his release, he continued his efforts to improve the workers' pay and conditions for another 38 years. His funeral was attended by thousands and the workers erected a granite obelisk to his memory in Stalybridge's attractive Stamford Park. On it is inscribed a quotation from the speech he delivered at his trial: "The only true foundation of Society is the safety, the security and the happiness of the poor, from whom all other orders of Society arise".

NORTH AND WEST OF MANCHESTER

The area that was the eastern part of Lancashire was, before the Industrial Revolution, a sparsely populated region of remote hillside farms and cottages that relied, chiefly, on sheep farming and the wool trade. Many of the settlements date back to before the Norman Conquest and although little may have survived the rapid building of the 19th century there are three surprisingly wonderful ancient houses to be seen here: Smithills Hall and Hall-i'-th'-Wood at Bolton and Turton Tower, just to the north.

However, there is no escaping the textile industry. The climate was ideal for cotton spinning and weaving – damp so that the yarn does not break – so it was the obvious choice for the building of the mills. There are numerous valleys with fast flowing rivers and streams and then the development of the extensive

coalfields around Wigan supplied the fuel to feed the power hungry machinery. Finally, there was a plentiful supply of labour as families moved from the hill top sheep farms into the expanding towns and villages to work the looms and turn the wheels of industry.

In a very short time, smoke and soot filled the air and the once clear streams and rivers became lifeless valleys of polluted squalor. There are many illustrations in the region of the harsh working conditions the labourers had to endure and the dirt and filth that covered much of the area. Now that much of this has been cleaned up, the rivers running once again fast, clear, and supporting wildlife, the lasting legacy of those days is the splendid Victorian architecture of which every town has at least one example.

WIGAN

The American travel writer, Bill Bryson, visited Wigan in the mid 1990s and wrote, "Such is Wigan's perennially poor reputation that I was truly astounded to find it has a handsome and well maintained town centre".

Although to many this town is a product of the industrial age, Wigan is one of the oldest places in the region. As far back as the 1st century AD there was a Celtic Brigantes settlement here that was taken over by the Romans who built a small town called Coccium. Little remains of those far off days but during the construction of a gasworks in the mid 19th century various burial urns were unearthed during the excavation work. By the end of the 13th century, the town had not only been granted a market charter but was also sending two members to Parliament. A staunchly

Catholic town, Wigan fared badly during the Civil War. The Earl of Derby, whose home, Lathom House, lay on the outskirts of the town, was a favourite with the King and this was where Charles I made his base for his attacks on Roundhead Bolton. The bitter attacks on Wigan by the Cromwellian troops saw the fortifications destroyed and both the parish church and the moot hall were looted. The Battle of Wigan Lane, the last encounter between the warring forces in Lancashire, is commemorated by a monument which stands on the place where a key member of the Earl of Derby's forces was killed.

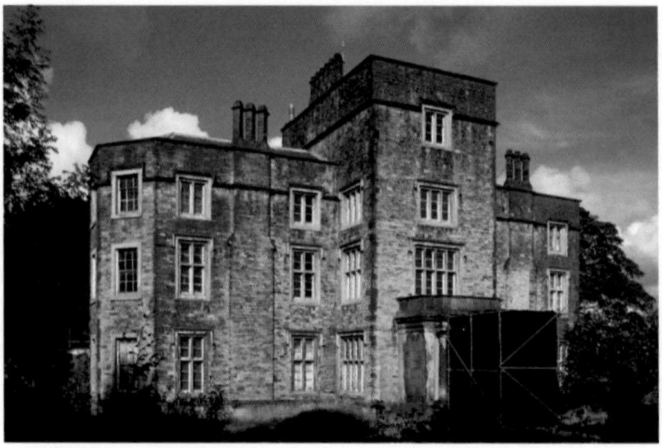

Winstanley Hall, Wigan

Wigan's development as an industrial town centred around coal mining, which began as early as 1450. By the 19th century, there were more than 1,000 pit shafts in operation in the surrounding area, supplying the fuel for Lancashire's expanding textile industry. The Leeds and Liverpool Canal, which runs through the town, was a key means of transporting the coal to the cotton mills of Lancashire and **Wigan Pier**, the major loading bay, remains one of the most substantial and interesting features of the waterway. A well-known musical hall joke, first referred to by George Formby senior as he told of the virtues of his home town over Blackpool, it was the 1930s novel by George Orwell, *The Road to Wigan Pier*, that really put the old wharf on the map. Today, the pier has been beautifully restored and it is now a key attraction in the area. Visitors can see what locals did on holiday during the traditional Wakes Week break; witness a colliery disaster; sing along in the Palace of Varieties Music Hall, or experience the rigours of a Victorian schoolroom. There's also a superb exhibition, The Way

We Were, based on local social history and with costumed actors playing the part of the townsfolk of the 19th century. A short journey along the canal in a bateau mouche-style Waterbus is **Trencherfield Mill** where the star of the show is the largest working mill steam engine in the world; also on display is a collection of old textile machines and other engines. The Mill is also home to the award-winning **Opie's Museum of Memories**, a fascinating collection of actual products and brands, fashions, advertising and furniture from the last century. Incidentally, it was in Wigan that Michael Mark and Thomas Spencer first joined forces in 1894 and for three years the town was the headquarters of Marks & Spencer. Over the past few years, an interesting art trial has been developed, taking in points of interest both old and new. Among them are Sir Giles Gilbert Scott's War Memorial of 1925, the Market Cross Floor Mosaic by Sebastian Boyesen (1998), a cast bronze rugby football in Central Park (Joanne Risley, 2001) and Wigan Warp and Weft, a plate steel remembrance of Wigan's textile heritage (Adrian Moakes, 2001).

As well as having a modern town centre with all the usual amenities, including a theatre and art gallery,

Wigan has some fine countryside on its doorstep, some of which can be explored by following the **Douglas Valley Trail** along the banks of the River Douglas. Even the town's coal mining past has interesting links with the natural world: **Pennington Flash** is a large lake formed by mining subsidence that is now a wildlife reserve and a country park. To the north of the town lies **Haigh Hall and Country Park**, one of the first to be designated in England and formed from the estate of the Earls of Crawford. With its 250 acres of lush and picturesque woodlands are a 15-inch gauge miniature railway; a very well-equipped children's playground; a crazy golf course; a model village and an art and craft centre in the original stables block. There are walks along the towpath of the Leeds to Liverpool canal which bisects the park or around the rose-filled Walled Gardens.

BOLTON

Synonymous with the Lancashire textile industry, Bolton is also an ancient town that predates its expansion due to cotton by many centuries. First settled during the Bronze Age, by the time of the Civil War, this was a market town supporting the surrounding villages. The town saw one of the bloodiest episodes of the war when James Stanley, Earl of Derby, was brought back here by Cromwell's troops after the Royalists had been defeated. In a savage act of revenge for the massacre his army had brought on the town early in the troubles, Stanley was executed and his severed head and body, in separate caskets, were taken back to the family burial place at Ormskirk. Whilst in captivity in the town, Stanley was kept prisoner at Ye Olde Man and Scythe Inn which, dating from 1251, is still standing in Churchgate today and is the town's oldest building.

Bolton is fortunate in having two particularly fine old mansions, both on the northern edge of town. **Hall-i'-th'-Wood** is a delightful part-timbered medieval merchant's house dating from 1530 to 1648. A fine example of its kind, it was saved from dereliction by Lord Leverhulme in 1900 and has been restored and furnished with displays of fine 17'h and 18th century furniture along with interesting items of local importance. The hall has a second claim to fame: for a number of years one of several tenants was Samuel Crompton, the inventor in 1799 of the spinning mule. Naturally, the hall has a replica of Crompton's mule on display.

Bolton's second grand house, **Smithills Hall**, stands on an easily defended hill and was built in the 1300s as a pele, or fortified dwelling. It was extended over the years and this superb

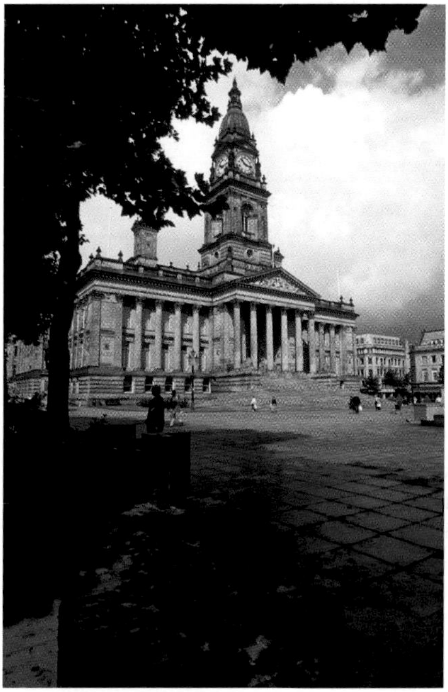

Albert Hall, Bolton

Grade I listed building now boasts some of the best examples of medieval, Tudor and Victorian Arts & Crafts architecture in the region. The hall was bought by Bolton Corporation in the late 1930s and has been beautifully restored. In addition to the impressive collection of furniture and artefacts on display, the hall also hosts changing exhibitions throughout the year. As well as seeing one of the oldest and best preserved fortified manor houses in the county, visitors can also wander along the hall's wooded nature trail.

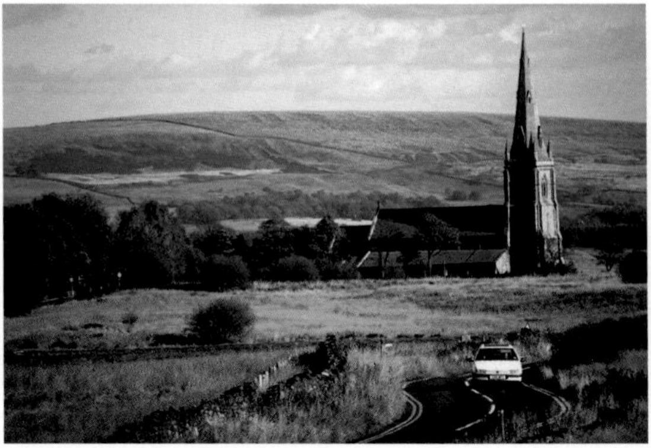

Moors North of Bolton

Close to Smithills Hall, in Moss Bank Park, is **Animal World & Butterfly House**, which provides a safe habitat for a variety of animals and birds ranging from farm animals to chipmunks, wildfowl and tropical birds. In the tropical atmosphere of the Butterfly House are free-flying butterflies and moths as well as insects, spiders, reptiles and tropical plants.

The centre of Bolton is a lasting tribute to the wealth and prosperity generated by the spinning of high quality yarn for which the town was famous. The monumental **Town Hall**, opened in 1873, is typical of the classical style of buildings that the Victorian town fathers favoured – tours are available. The hall is still the town's central point and it is now surrounded by the recently refurbished pedestrianised shopping malls, market hall, and the celebrated Octagon Theatre. The town's excellent **Museum, Art Gallery & Aquarium** is one of the largest regional galleries in the northwest with excellent collections of fine and decorative art, including examples of British sculpture and contemporary ceramics. There are collections of natural history, geology, and Egyptian antiques here as well as some fine 18th and 19th century English watercolours and some contemporary British paintings and graphics. One of Bolton's most recent major attractions is the state-of-the-art **Reebok Stadium**, home of Bolton Wanderers, one of the world's oldest football clubs. Visitors can take a look behind the scenes at one of Europe's finest stadiums, seeing everything from the players' changing rooms to the bird's eye vantage point of the Press Box.

On the northwestern edge of the town is **Barrow Bridge Village**, a small model village built during the Industrial Revolution to house workers at the two 6-storey mills that used to operate here. Small bridges cross a picturesque stream and a flight of 63 steps leads up the hillside to the moors. Barrow Bridge village was the inspiration for Benjamin Disraeli's novel *Coningsby*. In the south of Bolton, where the Rivers Croal and Irwell meet, Moses Gate Country Park is a 750-acre site of urban fringe countryside offering quiet country walks, fishing and more active pursuits such as cycling and orienteering.

Turton Tower

AROUND BOLTON

TURTON BOTTOMS
4 miles N of Bolton off the B6391

Turton Tower near Bolton was built both for defensive purposes and as a residence. In 1400, William Orrell erected his sturdy, four-square pele (fortified dwelling) in search of safety during those lawless and dangerous years. Some 200 years later, in more settled times, a lovely, half-timbered Elizabethan mansion was added. Successive owners made further additions in a charming motley of architectural styles. Quite apart from its enchanting appearance, Turton is well worth visiting to see its display of old weapons and a superb collection of vintage furniture, outstanding among which is the sumptuously carved Courtenay Bed of 1593.

RAMSBOTTOM
6 miles NE of Bolton on the A676

One of the stops along the East Lancashire Railway, this picturesque village, overlooking the Irwell Valley,

THE BAZAAR

37 Bolton Street, Ramsbottom, Lancashire
Tel: 01706 828722

Sheila Byrne has a lifetime's experience in the field of antiques and collectables, and **The Bazaar**, her shop in the centre of town, is filled with all manner of unusual items which she describes as 'original reproduction'. In the double-fronted, single-storey premises, the

stock on attractive display on walls, on the floor and on shelves includes pictures, posters, small items of furniture, luggage, baskets and buckets, pots and jugs, photo frames, vases and figurines, magazine racks and a great deal more besides.

Tourists stream from the railway at the bottom of town, and those in the know make tracks for The Bazaar to spend a happy hour browsing and seeking out a special gift, Sheila's shop is definitely a place to be visited on any trip to the market town on Ramsbottom, which overlooks the Irwell Valley. Among the other attractions are the preserved East Lancashire Railway and the Peel Tower, which commemorates the town's most famous son, Sir Robert Peel.

CLARK CRAFTS

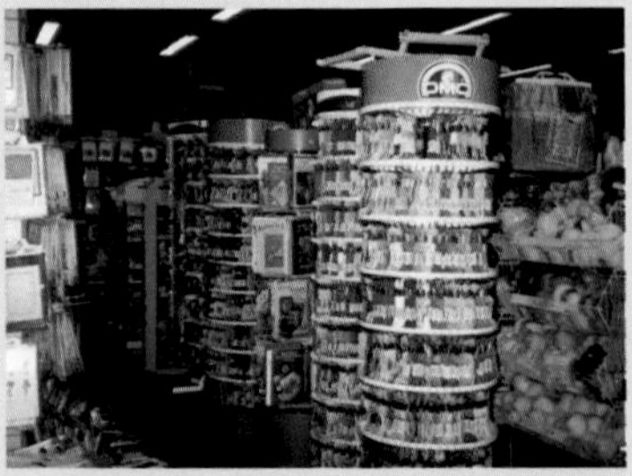

Empire Works, Railway Street, Ramsbottom, Lancashire,
BL0 9AL
Tel: 01706 826479 Fax: 01706 825603
e-mail: crafts@clarkcraft.co.uk
website: www.clarkcraft.co.uk

John and Sheila Clark spent many years in manufacturing
and sales of footwear before embarking on **Clark Crafts**,
an enterprise that they have been running with great
success for more than 20 years. It started in a small way,
but has gradually expanded into a display area of 6,000
square feet and a stock of requirements for artists and craftspeople that runs into tens of thousands of
lines. Apart from all the top names in the fields of papers and paints and brushes, there's also a full

range of supplies for cross stitch, tapestry, embroidery,
knitting and fabric painting.

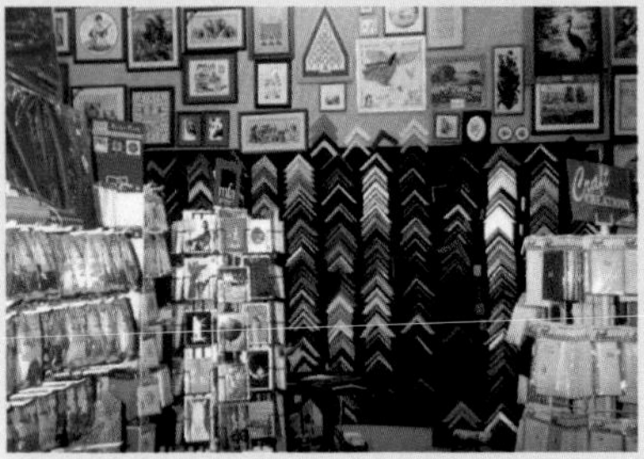

Other items in the impressive stock include picture
frames, card making and wedding stationery. The
Clarks and their friendly staff are true experts in their
field and are always ready with helpful advice for
customers. They also impart their skills more formally
in classes for watercolour, rubber stamping, parchment
craft and other techniques, all are held on a regular
weekly basis on the premises. Clark Crafts lies at the
southern end of the town, opposite the railway that
brings so many visitors to Ramsbottom.

RAMSONS

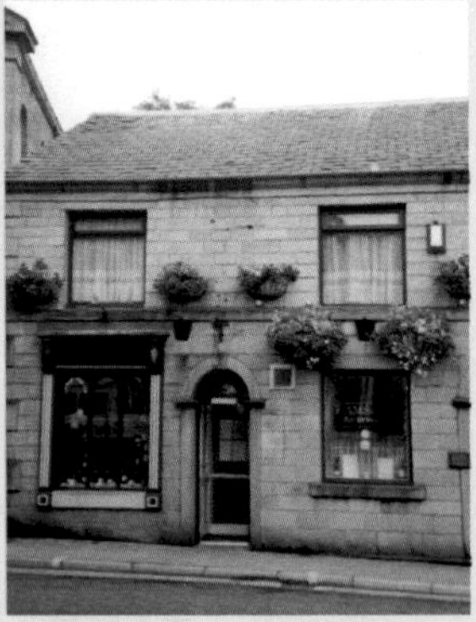

18 Market Place, Ramsbottom, Lancashire BL0 9HT
Tel: 01706 8250707 Fax: 01706 822005
e-mail: chris@ramsons.org.uk website: www.ramsons.org.uk

Chris Johnson, a scientist by training and a perfectionist by nature,
ate his way round rural Italy, assimilating the culture, the quality
and the love of life that he discovered there. That experience
provided the inspiration for **Ramsons**, which he designed as a
typical Italian small town eating place. Twenty years on, his
restaurant has never stopped winning the plaudits of diners and
critics alike. The stone building has many attractive features, with
hanging baskets outside, a handsome stone fireplace and pretty
floral fabrics. Much of the produce used in the dishes comes direct

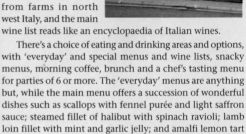

from farms in north
west Italy, and the main
wine list reads like an encyclopaedia of Italian wines.

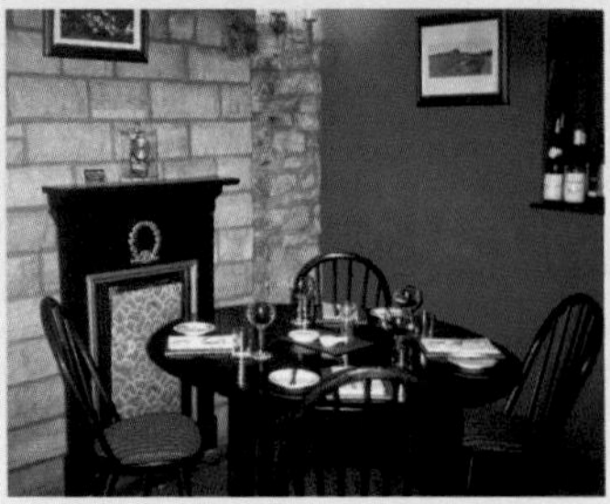

There's a choice of eating and drinking areas and options,
with 'everyday' and special menus and wine lists, snacky
menus, morning coffee, brunch and a chef's tasting menu
for parties of 6 or more. The 'everyday' menus are anything
but, while the main menu offers a succession of wonderful
dishes such as scallops with fennel purée and light saffron
sauce; steamed fillet of halibut with spinach ravioli; lamb
loin fillet with mint and garlic jelly; and amalfi lemon tart
with fruit coulis. Just terrific – an experience not to be missed!

is well worth visiting. One of the best views of the village and, indeed, the surrounding area can be found from **Peel Tower,** which dominates the skyline. Erected in 1852 to commemorate the life of the area's most famous son, Sir Robert Peel, the tower is some 128 feet high. Now restored, the tower itself is occasionally open to the public.

BURY

6 miles E of Bolton on the A58

There was a settlement at Bury in Bronze Age times, but as late as 1770 it was still just a small market town, surrounded by green fields. That was the year a man named Robert Peel established his Ground Calico Printing Works, the first of many mills that would follow. The opening of the works along with the subsequent mills, print and bleach works so dominated this part of the Irwell Valley that not only did they transform the landscape but also heavily polluted the river. At the height of the valley's production it was said that anyone falling into the river would dissolve before they had a chance to drown. Today, thankfully, the valley towns are once again clean and the river clear and fast flowing.

With the family fortune gleaned from those prosperous mills, Robert Peel junior, born in the town in 1788, was able to fund his illustrious career in politics, rising to become Prime Minister in 1841. Famous for the repeal of the Corn Laws, Robert Peel was also at the forefront of the setting up of the modern police force – hence their nickname 'Bobbies'. A statue of Bury's most distinguished son stands in the Market Square and there's an even grander memorial near the village of Holcombe, a few miles to the north.

Another of Bury's famous sons was John Kay, inventor of the Flying Shuttle. Sadly, Kay neglected to patent his invention. He moved to France where he died a pauper and is buried in an unmarked grave. The people of Bury, however, remembered him. In his memory, they created the delightful Kay Gardens in the town centre and erected a splendidly ornate clock-house tower.

A short walk from Kay Gardens, **The Met** is a lively arts centre which puts on performances to suit all tastes, from theatre and children's shows to rock nights and world music. The Met also organises Bury's Streets Ahead Festival each May, a colourful street carnival which attracts performers from around the world.

This part of town has become known as the 'Culture Quarter', since Bury's **Art Gallery & Museum** is also located here. The Gallery has a fine collection of paintings, including works by Turner, Constable and Landseer, and the outstanding Thomas Wrighley collection of Victorian oil paintings. Downstairs, visitors can stroll

Black Pudding Stall, Bury Market

EAST LANCASHIRE RAILWAY

Bury - Ramsbottom - Rawtenstall
Tel: 0161 764 7790

The **East Lancashire Railway** offers visitors an opportunity to
step back in time to the age of steam and travel along this
delightful stretch of track. Your journey can be broken at
Ramsbottom or Irwell Vale stations where you could enjoy a
lineside picnic.

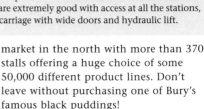

On Platform 2 at Bury Bolton Street Station, the period
tearooms offer views of the locomotives arriving or departing
from the station, while you enjoy a meal in the pleasant
surroundings. Snacks and meals are available and the rooms
can be pre-booked for special occasions.

A wide variety of events take place throughout the year,
including Santa Specials, a Day out with Thomas and Friends,
1940's Wartime weekend and Steam Enthusiasts Weekend - ring for current details. Adults can actually
drive a steam or deisel locomotive on the 'Footplate Experience' or an entire train can be hired for a
special occasion or event. Facilities for the disabled are extremely good with access at all the stations,
toilets at the main stations and a specially adapted carriage with wide doors and hydraulic lift.

along 'Paradise Street', a fascinating re-
creation of Bury as it was in the 1950s.

The town has a real treat for those who
thrill to the sight, sound and smell of
steam locomotives. Bolton Street Station
is the southern terminus of the **East
Lancashire Railway** (see panel above)
which operates regular services along a
nine mile scenic route through the lovely
Irwell Valley to Rawtenstall. Serious
devotees of transport history will want to
explore the **Bury Transport Museum**,
just across the road from the station. The
museum houses a wonderful collection
of vintage road and rail vehicles, ranging
from a 19th century steam road-roller to
a "Stop Me and Buy One" ice-cream
vendor's tricycle.

Another museum of interest is the
Lancashire Fusiliers Museum which
tells the story of Lancashire's famous
regiment from its foundation in 1688
and has an outstanding collection of
medals and period uniforms.

A major shopping centre for the
northwest, Bury is also proud of its
ancient **Market** which has been
operating since 1440. It's now the largest

market in the north with more than 370
stalls offering a huge choice of some
50,000 different product lines. Don't
leave without purchasing one of Bury's
famous black puddings!

Looking at Bury today it seems hard to
imagine that at one time this typical
Lancashire mill town had a castle. A
settlement probably existed here in the
Bronze Age and there is certainly
evidence that the Romans passed
through this area. By the 12th century
the town was the manor of the Norman
de Bury family and, in the mid-14th
century, the land came under the
ownership of the Pilkingtons. It was
dismantled following the Battle of
Bosworth in 1485 at which Henry VII
defeated Richard III. Unlucky Thomas
Pilkington had backed the wrong side.
The foundations of the castle have
recently been excavated and form the
centrepiece of Castle Square.

On the outskirts of the town lies **Burrs
Country Park** which, as well as offering
a wide range of activities, also has an
interesting industrial trail around this
historic mill site.

WALMERSLEY

2 miles NE of Bolton on the A56

Hidden away in the village of Walmersley, just north of Bury, is **Hark to Dandler**, an attractive pub dating from the mid-19th century that is thought to have originally been a vicarage. During a recent refurbishment a very old child's coffin was found, full of early 19th century artefacts, behind the cellar walls and, along with the two resident ghosts, this certainly adds an air of mystery to the pub. The name though is more easily explained as it is named after a lead dog of the local hunt.

OLDHAM

Oldham was once a centre of the textile industry, and many of the magnificent mill buildings that made it one of the world's leading cotton spinning towns still stand. There are other interesting buildings, too, including the Town Hall, where Winston Churchill delivered his first acceptance speech after being elected Member of Parliament for the town in 1900. Gallery Oldham has an impressive collection of paintings by such luminaries as Constable, Turner, Lowry and the Pre-Raphaelites.

AROUND OLDHAM

DELPH

4 miles NE of Oldham on the A6052

Taking its name from the old English for quarry, this is probably a reference to the bakestone quarries found to the north of the village. Also close by, high on a hill above the village, lies **Castleshaw**, one of a series of forts the Romans built on their military road between Chester and York. The banks and ditches give visitors an excellent indication of the scale of the fort and many of the items found during recent excavations are on show in the Saddleworth Museum.

DOBCROSS

4 miles E of Oldham off the A6052

This attractive Pennine village, once the commercial heart of the district of Saddleworth, retains many of its original weavers' cottages, clothiers, and merchants' houses, and little has changed around the village square in the last 200 years. Used as the location for the film *Yanks*, Dobcross is also notable as the birthplace of the giant Platt Brothers Textile Machinery business which was, in the latter part of the 19th century, the largest such machine manufacturing firm in the world.

UPPERMILL

5 miles E of Oldham on the A62

Of the 14 villages that make up Saddleworth parish, Uppermill is the most central. It is certainly home to the area's oldest building, **Saddleworth Parish Church** which was originally built in the 12th century by the Stapletons as their family chapel. Extended over the years, it has several

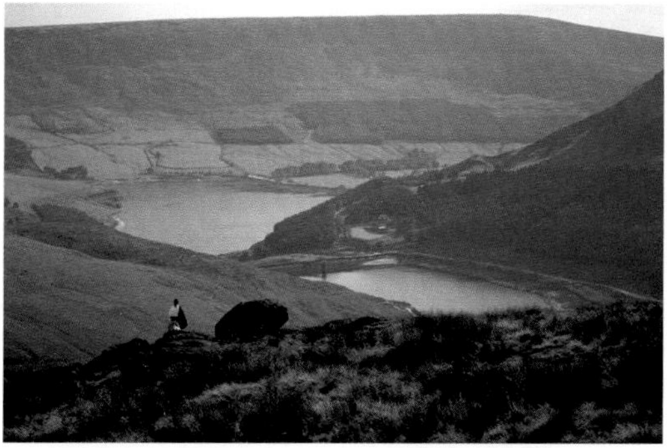

Saddleworth Moor

interesting features including a gravestone to commemorate the Bill's o'Jack's murders. In 1832, the people of Saddleworth were stunned to learn that the landlord of the Bill's o'Jack's Inn and his son had been bludgeoned to death. Several thousand people turned out for the funeral but the case was never solved. The tombstone relates the whole story.

The story of this once isolated area is illustrated at the **Saddleworth Museum**, housed in an old mill building on the banks of the Huddersfield Canal. There is a reconstruction of an 18th century weaver's cottage as well as a collection of textile machinery, local history gallery and local art exhibitions.

Also in Uppermill is the **Brownhill Visitor Centre**, which not only has information on the northern section of the Tame Valley but also exhibitions on local wildlife and the area's history.

DIGGLE

6 miles E of Oldham off the A62

Above the village, on **Diggle Moor** lies Brun Clough Farm where, it is said, the cries of child slaves who were ill treated in the early days of the textile mills can still be heard coming from the outhouses. Part of the **Oldham Way** footpath, a 40-mile scenic circular walk through the countryside on the edge of the Peak District National Park, crosses the moorland. Much of the village itself is a conservation area, where the pre-industrial weaving community has been preserved along with some of the traditional skills. However, Diggle Mill, which used to operate the second largest waterwheel in the country, no longer exists.

The Huddersfield Narrow Canal, completed in 1811, is one of the three canals that crossed the difficult terrain of the Pennines and linked Lancashire with Yorkshire. The entrance to the **Standedge Canal Tunnel**, the longest (over 3 miles) and highest (645 feet above sea level) canal tunnel in Britain, lies in the village. The last cargo boat passed through the tunnel in 1921 and following a long period of closure, it has now been re-opened.

ROCHDALE PIONEERS MUSEUM

31 Toad Lane, Rochdale OL12 ONU
Tel: 01706 524920
e-mail: museum@co-op.ac.uk
website: www.co-op.ac.uk/toad lane

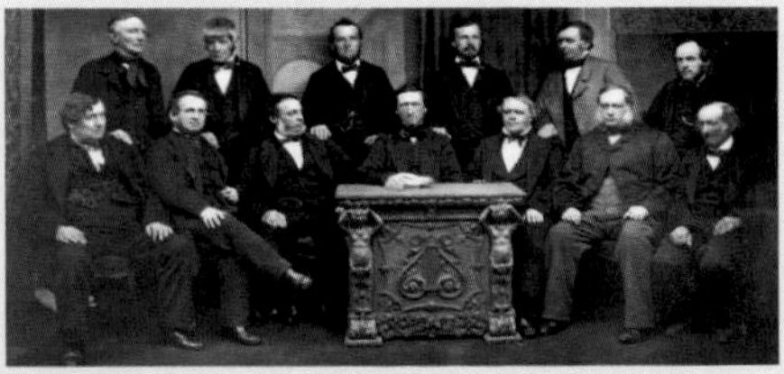

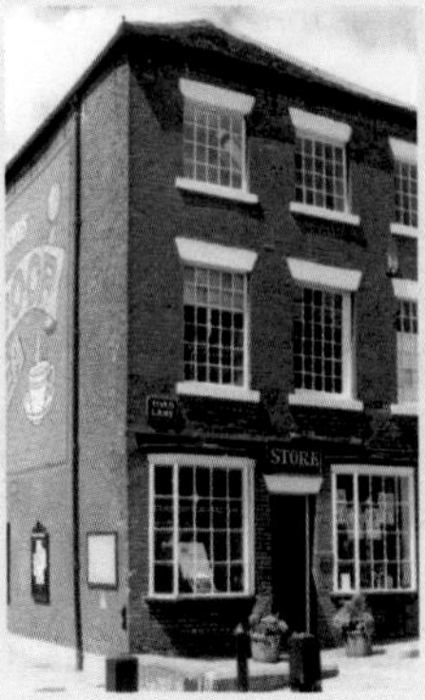

The Rochdale Pioneers Museum is regarded as the home of the world wide co-operative movement. It's the perfect place to come and see how your ancestors did their shopping.

In Toad Lane on December 21 1844 the Rochdale Equitable Pioneers Society opened their store selling pure food at fair prices and honest weights and measures, starting a revolution in retailing.

See the recreation of the original shop with its rudimentary furniture and scales. Here the basic needs of daily life such as butter, sugar, flour and oatmeal first went on sale over 150 years ago.

Journey back in time with early advertising, packaging and retailing artifacts, Co-operative postage stamps, commemorative china and rare dividend coins and commodity tokens. See the development of 'dividend' and the Co-op's success.

ROCHDALE

Lying in a shallow valley formed by the little River Roch, the town is surrounded, to the north and east, by the slopes of the Pennines that are often snow covered in winter. With its origins in medieval times, the town, like so many others in the area, expanded with the booming cotton industry and its magnificent Victorian **Town Hall** (1871) rivals that of Manchester in style if not in size.

However, it is not textiles for which Rochdale is famous but for its role as the birthplace of the Co-Operative Movement. In carefully restored Toad Lane, to the north of the town centre, is the world's first Co-Op shop, now the **Rochdale Pioneers Museum** (see panel opposite). Today, the Co-Op movement represents a staggering 700 million members in 90 countries around the world and the celebration of its 150th anniversary in 1994 focused attention on Rochdale. The story of the Rochdale Pioneers and other aspects of the town's heritage are vividly displayed in the new Arts & Heritage Centre, **Touchstones**. The restored Grade II listed building of 1884 was originally a library but now contains an interactive high-tech museum and exhibitions, four art galleries, the Tourist Information Centre, a local studies centre, café/bar, bookshop and performance studio.

Rochdale Town Hall

As well as the Pioneers, Rochdale was home to several other famous sons and daughters, among them the celebrated singer Gracie Fields, Cyril Smith, Rochdale's former Liberal Member of Parliament, and the 19th century political thinker, John Bright.

The town's most distinctive church is **St John the Baptist Catholic Church**, which has a beautiful dome modelled on

AFTER EIGHT RESTAURANT

2 Edenfield Road, Rochdale, Lancashire OL11 5AA
Tel/Fax: 01706 646432 website: www.aftereightuk.com

In a dignified early 19th century house with a delightfully relaxed, civilised ambience, Geoff and Anne Taylor run one of the very best restaurants in the region. **After Eight** has earned widespread praise from critics and diners alike for Geoff's modern British cuisine, which matches faultless classical technique with contemporary influences. Brill with a herb and brioche crust and Welsh lamb with a minted mash are just two typical dishes,  and Anne's puddings and ice creams round off a memorable meal. There's a separate menu for vegetarians, and the food is complemented by an acclaimed wine list. No smoking except in the bar.

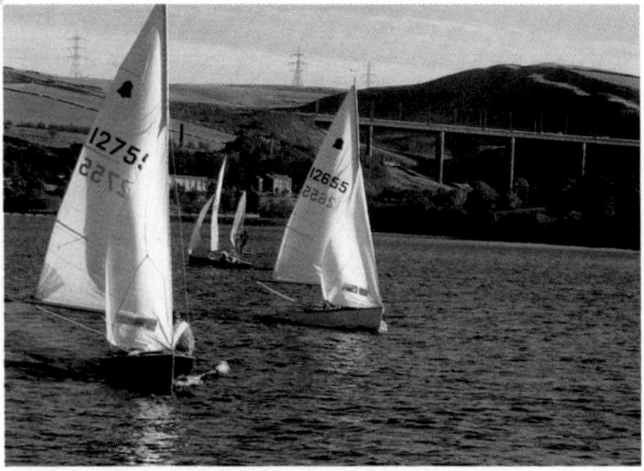

Hollingworth Lake Country Park

AROUND ROCHDALE

HEALEY
2 mile N of Rochdale on the A671

Lying in the valley of the River Spodden, this old village, now almost engulfed by the outer reaches of Rochdale, is an area rich in wildlife as well as folklore. Nearby is Robin Hood's Well, one of a number of springs feeding the river. Here, it is said, sometime in the 12th century the Earl of Huntingdon was lured to the well by a witch pretending to be his nursemaid. Once at the well, the witch told the young man that he would never inherit his earldom unless he had her magic ring as a means of identification. Gazing into the well, Robin got such a fright that he fainted and the witch took off on her broomstick. Emerging from the well the King of the Fairies gave the lad his own ring and told him to go up into Healey Dell and interrupt the witches whilst they were hatching their next spell. Doing as he was instructed Robin entered the coven and threw the ring into their cauldron whereupon there was a great flash of light and the witches were reduced to evil-looking fairies destined to live forever in the Fairy chapel.

Opened in 1972, **Healey Dell Nature Reserve** does not promise visitors sightings of either witches or fairies but there is a wealth of wildlife to be discovered along the nature trails.

This is an ancient area which has only been invaded by the construction of the commercially non-viable Rochdale to Bacup railway in the late 19th century. The oak and birch woodland on the northern river bank is all that remains of a prehistoric forest and, whilst the owners of Healey Hall made some

the Byzantine Santa Sofya in Istanbul. The church is unique in England because of its huge mosaic of Italian marble depicting the Resurrection of Christ.

Running from the southeast corner of the town, the **Rochdale Canal** is a brave piece of early-19th century civil engineering that traversed the Pennines to link the River Mersey with the Calder and Hebble Navigation. Some 32 miles in length and with 91 locks, it must be one of toughest canals ever built and, though the towpath can still be walked, the last commercial boat passed through the locks in 1937. The canal was officially abandoned in 1952, but exactly half a century later the entire length has been re-opened to full navigation. Together with the newly restored Huddersfield Narrow Canal it allows a complete circuit of the South Pennine Ring.

Between Rochdale and Littleborough lies Hollingworth Lake, originally built as a supply reservoir for the canal, but for many years a popular area for recreation known colloquially as the 'Weavers' Seaport', as cotton workers unable to afford a trip to the seaside came here. Now part of the **Hollingworth Lake Country Park** and with a fine visitor centre, there are a number of pleasant walks around its shores.

impact, little has changed here for centuries.

LITTLEBOROUGH

3 miles NE of Rochdale on the A58

This small town lies beside the River Roch and on the main route between Lancashire and Yorkshire first laid down by the Romans. Known as the Roman Causey, it was an impressive structure 16 feet 6 inches wide, cambered and with gutters at each side. In the middle of the road is a shallow groove which has been the subject of endless controversy – no-one has yet come up with a satisfactory explanation of its purpose. The road cuts across the bleak Pennine moors by way of **Blackstone Edge** where some of the best preserved parts of the Roman structure can still be seen. At the summit is a medieval cross, the **Aigin Stone**, which offers spectacular views right to the coast.

To the south of Littleborough, **Hollingworth Lake Water Activity Centre** offers sailing, canoeing, windsurfing, rowing and, during the summer months, lake trips on the *Lady Alice*.

MILNROW

2 miles E of Rochdale on the A640

It was to this small industrial town in the foothills of the Pennines that John Collier came as the schoolmaster in 1729. Then a woollen handloom weaving village, Collier is perhaps better known as Tim Bobbin, the first of the Lancashire dialect poets. Collier remained in Milnrow for the rest of his life and, drinking rather more than he should, he earned extra money by selling his verse and painting pub signs. The local pub, which dates back to the early 1800s is, appropriately, named after him. On the banks of the River Beal, the Ellenroad Cotton Mill, which produced fine cotton yarn from 1892, was demolished in 1985, but the mighty 3,000 horse power engines Victoria and Alexandra, the boiler house and the 220ft chimney were saved. These great engines are usually in steam on the first Sunday of each month except January, and visitors are welcome between noon and 4 o'clock.

SHAW

3 miles SE of Rochdale on the A633

A typical mill town, founded on the wealth of the cotton trade, this was also a market town for the surrounding area. Closed since 1932, **Jubilee Colliery**, to the northeast of the town centre, has been reclaimed as a nature reserve and it is now an attractive haven for wildlife in the Beal Valley.

HEYWOOD

4 miles SW of Rochdale on the A58

Heywood has an attraction that will revive childhood memories in many a grown-up. **The Corgi Heritage Centre** tells the story of Corgi die-cast model vehicles and the Corgi company from its early days as Mettoy, to the introduction of the Corgi name in the mid-50s right up to the present day. Displays include vintage Corgi models, Corgi catalogues, previews of future models and the full range of Corgi Classics Original Omnibus vehicles in a special setting designed by Hornby Railways.

LOCATOR MAP

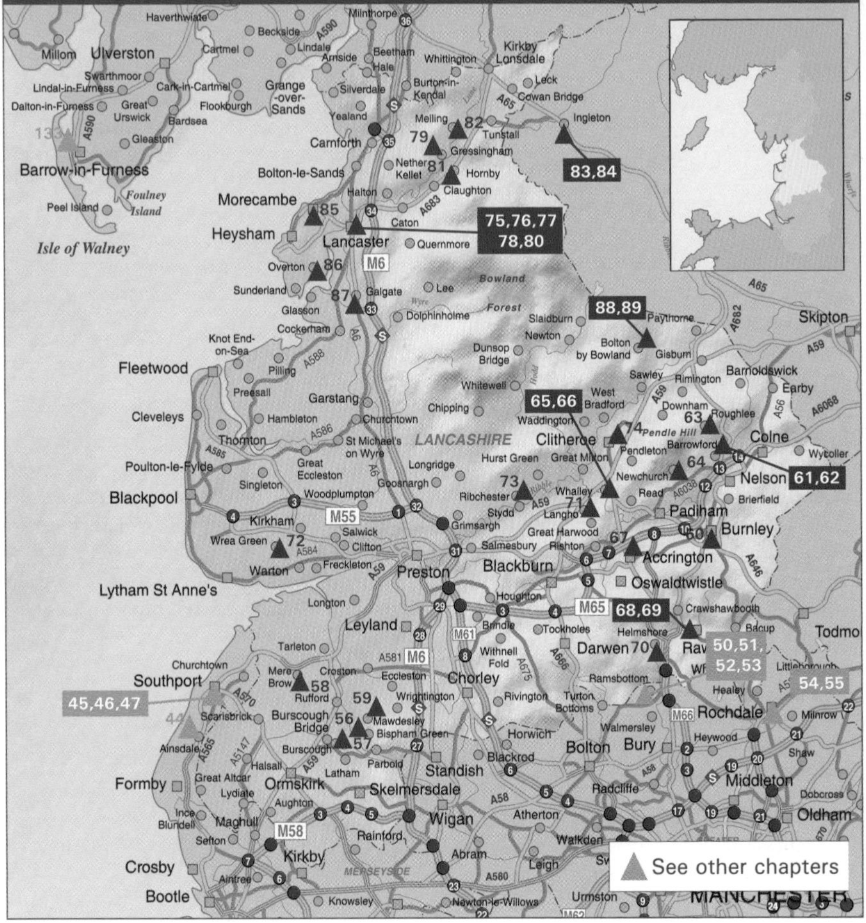

See other chapters

ADVERTISERS AND PLACES OF INTEREST

3 LANCASHIRE

The county of Lancashire is known to many people but, perhaps, more than any other area in the country, it has suffered from clichéd images of its landscape and people: the harsh life of the mill towns and the brashness of Blackpool. Before the reorganisation of the county boundaries in 1974, this large area also included Liverpool and Manchester in the south

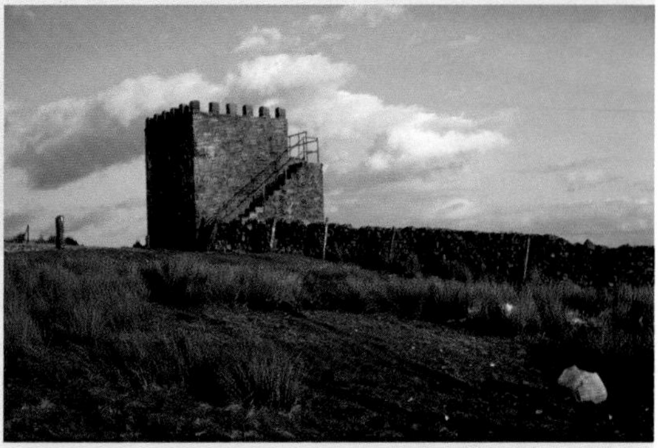

Jubilee Tower, Abbeystead

and the Furness Peninsula to the north. Though each, with its own distinctive character, was lost, the 'Red Rose' county, which has put many a king on the throne of England, still has much to offer.

ADVERTISERS AND PLACES OF INTEREST

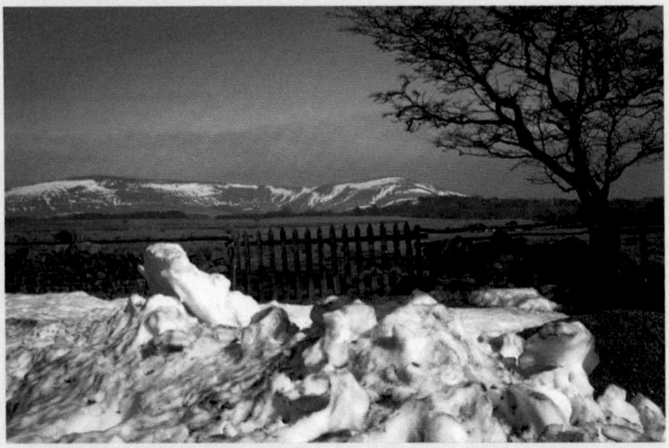

Bleasdale Fells

To the west of Lancashire lies Morecambe Bay, a treacherous place where, over the centuries, many walkers have lost their lives in an attempt to make the journey to the Furness Peninsula in Cumbria considerably shorter. Walks across the sands, at low tide, should only be undertaken with the aid of one of the highly knowledgeable and experienced guides. However, despite its grim history, the bay offers superb views, including glorious sunsets, as well as being an important habitat for a wide variety of birds.

Extending across much of the north of the county is the Forest of Bowland, an ancient royal hunting ground that is dotted with small, isolated villages. With no major roads passing through the area, it has remained little changed and, with so many splendid walks and fine countryside, it is also relatively quiet even during the busiest summer weeks.

The ancient county town of Lancaster, in the north, has a variety of museums and a wealth of interesting buildings, mapping out the life of Lancastrians through the ages.

To the northeast lies Leck Fell, just south of Kirkby Lonsdale and Cumbria. It is easy for the visitor to mistake this for the Yorkshire Dales as there is a typical craggy limestone gorge along the little valley of Leck Beck, as well as one of the most extensive cave systems in the British Isles for the experienced potholer to explore. A natural route from Kirkby Lonsdale back to the county town is marked by the River Lune. For those who like walking, the best way to enjoy this wonderful green and hilly area of Lancashire is to follow the path of the Lune Valley through woodland, meadows, and along the riverside itself.

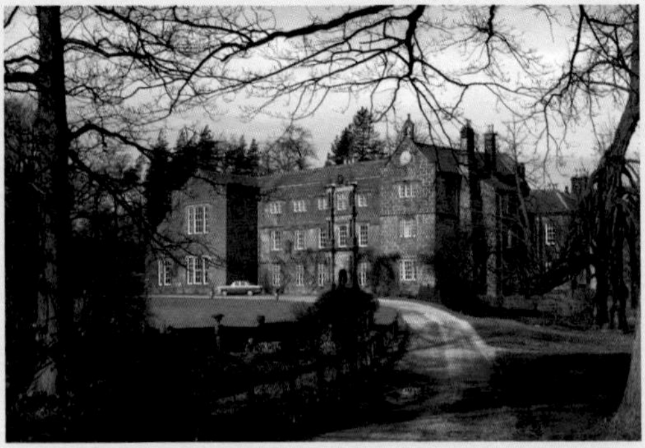

Browsholme Hall, Bashall Eaves

WEST LANCASHIRE

This area of Lancashire, with its sandy coastline and flat fertile farmland, is home to some elegant seaside resorts and ancient market towns. Following the reorganisation of the county boundaries in the 1970s and the creation of Merseyside, much of the coast and the southwestern area of Lancashire became part of the new county, and the towns of Southport, Crosby and Formby and their neighbours and hinterlands will be considered in the Merseyside chapter.

Behind the coast, the flat lands of the West Lancashire plain were once under water. Now with an extensive network of ditches, drainage has provided the old towns and quaint villages with rich fertile land that now produces a wealth of produce all year round and roadside farm shops are very much a feature of the area.

Although there are several rivers flowing across the land, the chief waterway, which is hard to miss, is the Leeds to Liverpool Canal. Linking the port of Liverpool with industrial Leeds and the many textile villages and towns in between, this major navigation changed the lives of many of the people living along its length. The section through West Lancashire, passing rural villages, is perhaps one of the more pleasant stretches. There are plenty of charming canal side pubs in the area and walks along the towpath, through the unspoilt countryside, have been popular for many years.

CHORLEY

A bustling and friendly place, Chorley is a charming town that is locally famous for its market that dates back to 1498. Today, there are two markets – the covered market and the open, 'flat iron'

market. This peculiar and intriguing name stems from the ancient practice of trading by displaying goods on the grounds without the use of stalls.

Dating back to 1360 and standing on the site of a Saxon chapel, the **Church of St Lawrence** is the town's oldest building. The church is said to contain the remains of St Lawrence, brought back from Normandy by Sir Richard Standish, and whether they are his relics or not, during the Middle Ages the saint's shrine certainly brought pilgrims to the parish.

The Civil War also brought visitors to the town, albeit less welcome ones. Following defeat at the nearby Battle of Preston, Royalist troops were twice engaged in battle here by Cromwell's victorious forces. Though not a happy time for both the Royalists and the town, the skirmishes did place Chorley on the historical map of England.

Chorley was the birthplace, in 1819, of Henry Tate. The son of a Unitarian minister, Henry was apprenticed in 1832 to the grocery trade in Liverpool and by 1855 he had not only set up his own business but also opened a chain of six shops. Selling the shops, Henry entered into the world of the competitive sugar trade and founded the world famous business of **Tate and Lyle**. Opening a new sugar refinery equipped with the latest machinery from France, Henry cornered the refining business in Britain and amassed a huge fortune. A great benefactor, Henry not only gave away vast sums of money to worthy causes but also to the London art gallery, which now bears his name.

The jewel in Chorley's crown is undoubtedly **Astley Hall**. Built in the late 16th century and set within some beautiful parkland, the hall is a fine example of an Elizabethan mansion. A notable feature is its south wing – described as "more glass than wall".

Inside, the moulded ceilings of the main hall and the drawing room are quite remarkable, as are the painted panels dating from the 1620s and representing a range of heroes that include Elizabeth I, Philip II of Spain and the Islamic warrior Tamerlane.

Extended in 1666, and again in 1825, this is truly a house of history and the rooms, which reflect the passing of the centuries, contain superb items of furniture from 1600 to the Edwardian period. Whether or not Cromwell stayed at the hall following the Battle of Preston is open to debate but his boots are here on display.

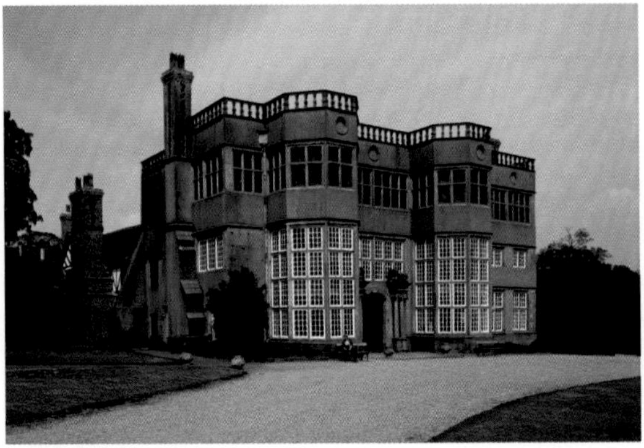

Astley Hall, Chorley

The hall was given to the borough in 1922 by Reginald Tatton and it was he who insisted that the building should incorporate a memorial to those who had died in World War I. As a result, a small room has been devoted to the local men who fought and died for their country. Along with the display of photographs, there is a Book of Remembrance.

AROUND CHORLEY

LEYLAND
4 miles NW of Chorley on the B5253

The town is probably best known for its associations with the manufacture of cars and lorries, and the **British Commercial Vehicle Museum**, the largest such museum in Europe, is well worth a visit. It stands on the site of the former Leyland South Works, where commercial vehicles were produced for many years. On display are many restored vans, fire engines and lorries

along with exhibits ranging from the horsedrawn era, through steam-powered wagons right up to present day vans and lorries. Perhaps the most famous vehicle here is the one used by the Pope and popularly known as the Popemobile.

Leyland is, however, an ancient settlement and documentary evidence has been found which suggests that the town was a Crown possession in Saxon times, owned by Edward the Confessor. The village cross marks the centre of the old settlement around which the town expanded and it is in this area of Leyland that the older buildings can be seen. Founded in the 11th century, much of the present **St Andrew's Church** dates from 1220 although there was some restoration work undertaken in the 1400s. The Eagle and Child Inn is almost as old, said to date from around 1230, and it served the needs of travellers journeying along the ancient highway which passed through the town.

The 16th century Grammar School is today home to the town's **Heritage Museum**, a fascinating place that describes, through interesting displays and exhibits, the history of this ancient market town.

TARLETON

8 miles W of Chorley off the A59

This pleasant rural village, now by-passed by the main road to Preston, is home to **St Mary's Church**, one of the finest buildings in Lancashire. Built in 1719, it is constructed from brick except for the cut-stone belfry. No longer the village church (it was replaced in the late 19th century by a larger building), it is still maintained and its churchyard has remained in use.

CROSTON

6 miles W of Chorley on the A581

This historic village in the heart of rural West Lancashire has been a centre for local farmers since it was granted a weekly market charter in 1283. Set beside the banks of the River Yarrow, a tributary of the River Douglas, much of the village, including the 17th century almshouses and the lovely 15th century church, is a designated conservation area. Church Street is a fine example of an 18th century Lancashire street, some of the houses bearing the date 1704; even older is the charming packhorse bridge dated 1682. The strong links with agriculture are still apparent in this area and the open farmland actually extends right into the village centre.

On **Coffee Day** the village turns out with decorated farm horses and carts to take part in a procession led by a band and morris dancers. The name is derived from the former 'Feoffing Day' when tenants paid their fees, or rents, to the squire.

ORMSKIRK

In the days when Liverpool was just a small fishing village, the main town in

---

SCHOOL OF STITCHED TEXTILES

Eccles Farm Needlecraft Centre, Eccles Lane, Bispham Green,
Nr Ormskirk, Lancashire L40 3SD
Tel: +44(0)1257 463163/463113
e-mail: enquiries@schoolofstitchedtextiles.com
website: www.schoolofstitchedtextiles.com

Gail Cowley, young, enthusiastic and very talented, runs the **School of Stitched Textiles**, which offers a variety of on site, residential and distance-learning courses in patchwork and embroidery as well as many other textile related topics. Gail and her team of highly trained tutors have been extremely successful with their flexible home study City & Guilds programmes and have students all over the world studying with them. They plan to increase their range of courses even further and also to include a distance learning degree specialising in textiles in the near future.

The considerable expertise of the in house tutors has been brought together to launch a completely new and totally different range of kits. These are young, modern designs that are intended for complete beginners to either hand or machine techniques in embroidery or patchwork. Fabrics that are hand dyed at Eccles Farm with names such as Juicy Grape and superb instructions really make these kits unique. The sleek opaque carry-case packaging with its secret box for storing thread, scissors etc. is also top of the range and they make superb gifts. Each kit takes the beginner through at least 4 different techniques and, when the student has finished, they will really be well on the way to proficiency. They are situated in a converted barn just outside Bispham Green, only a 10-minute drive from Junction 27 of the M6. Brochures are available, please contact them for more details.

this area was Ormskirk, founded around 840 AD by a Viking leader called Orme. Surrounded by rich agricultural land, the town has always been an important market centre with the locally-grown potatoes, 'Ormskirks', a firm favourite right across the north-west. The market is still flourishing, held every day except Wednesday and Sunday. In late Victorian times one of the traders in Ormskirk market was a certain Joseph Beecham who did a roaring trade selling his medicinal 'Little Liver Pills'. Joseph became a millionaire through the sales of his little pills; his son, the conductor Sir Thomas, went on to become the most popular and flamboyant figure of English musical life during the first half of the 20th century.

The town received its first market charter from Edward I in 1286 and today the market is still a key event in the region. The partial drainage of Martin Mere in the late 18th century, to provide more rich, fertile agricultural land, as well as the growth of nearby Liverpool, increased the prosperity of the town. Ormskirk was also touched by the Industrial Revolution and, while the traditional farming activities continued, cotton spinning and silk weaving also became important sources of local income. Today, the town has reverted to its traditional past.

The **Church of St Peter and St Paul**, in the centre of the town, unusually has both a steeple and a tower. The tower, added in the 16th century, was constructed to take the bells of Burscough Priory after the religious community had been disbanded by Henry VIII. However, the oldest feature found in the church is a stone carving on the outer face of the chancel's east wall that was probably the work of Saxon craftsmen.

NORTH OF ORMSKIRK

BURSCOUGH
2 miles NE of Ormskirk on the A59

Situated on the banks of the Leeds and Liverpool Canal, the village's Parish Church was one of the Million, or Waterloo, Churches built as a thanks to God after the final defeat of Napoleon in 1815. A later addition to the church is the Memorial Window to those of the parish who died for their country during the First World War.

Little remains of **Burscough Priory**, founded in the early 1100s by the Black Canons. Receiving lavish endowments from the local inhabitants, the priory was at one time one of the most influential religious houses in Lancashire.

RUFFORD
5 miles NE of Ormskirk on the B5246

This attractive village of pretty houses is notable for its church and its beautiful old hall. Built in 1869, the church is a splendid example of the Gothic revival period and its tall spire dominates the skyline.

Rufford Old Hall (National Trust) is an enchanting building. Its medieval part is constructed of richly decorated black-and-white timbering enclosing a glorious Great Hall where angels bearing colourful heraldic shields float from massive hammer-beam trusses. The Hall's 17th century additions are less spectacular but still very attractive and contain displays of historic costumes as well as an interesting local folk museum.

Generally regarded as one of the finest timber-framed halls in the country, the hall was the ancestral home of the Hesketh family, who lived at this site from the 1200s until Baron Hesketh gave

The Martin Inn

Martin Lane, Burscough,
Lancashire L40 0RT
Tel: 01704 892302/895788
Fax: 01704 895735

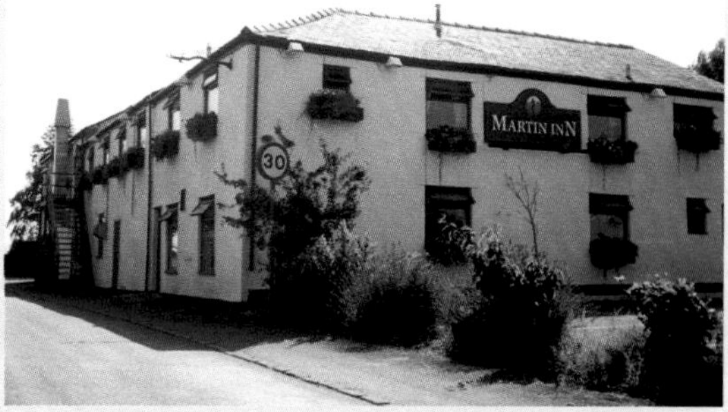

High standards of hospitality, food, drink and accommodation are guaranteed by new owners Jim and Celia Murphy at the **Martin Inn**, a substantial 200-year-old former coaching inn set in countryside on the outskirts of the village of Burscough. Looking a picture inside and out after a top-to-toe programme of refurbishment, the inn is a real delight to visit, whether for a drink, a meal or an overnight stay. Hanging baskets adorn the long frontage, while inside the scene is set by beams, flagstone floors, exposed brickwork and dried flower arrangements.

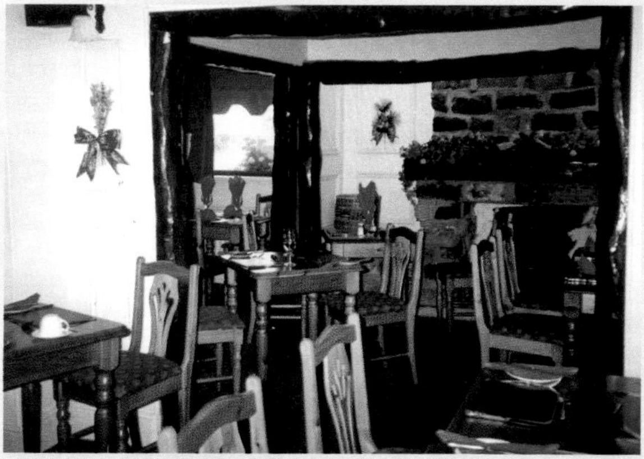

Jim, an ex-Ford man, and his wife have made an immediate impression in their first few weeks, and locals and passing visitors can be assured of the warmest of welcomes. A full range of drinks is served at the bar of this free house, and the choice of food is equally impressive. Bar snacks and meals are served in the comfortable lounge bar every lunchtime and evening and all day Sunday, while the 50-cover à la carte restaurant is open from 5.30 to 10 Monday to Saturday. The choice runs from sandwiches to full-scale feasts, and the all-day Sunday carvery is guaranteed to bring in the crowds.

Daily specials chalked up on a board in the bar widen the already excellent choice, offering such temptations as a tower of black pudding with a four peppercorn sauce and parma ham; grilled cod topped with mushroom duxelles, tomato concassé and a grain mustard sauce; and (among a very good choice for vegetarians) spinach and ricotta cannelloni, Thai vegetable curry or caramelised onion tart served with four cheeses. With a function room that can hold 100 in comfort, the inn is a popular choice for private party, conference or special occasion.

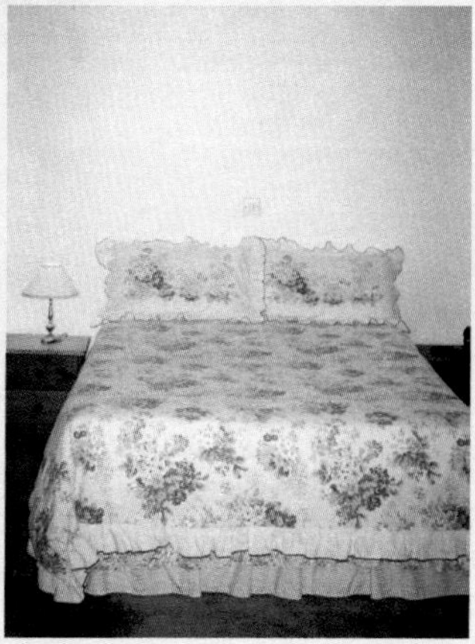

For visitors staying overnight, the inn has 12 en suite bedrooms with tv and beverage tray. Rooms are let on a Bed & Breakfast basis, with discounts for longer stays. The Martin Inn has a large car park and a garden with a barbecue area.

the hall to the National Trust in 1936. From the superb, intricately carved movable wooden screen to the solid oak chests and long refectory table, the atmosphere here is definitely one of wealth and position.

Later additions to the house were made in the 1660s and again in 1821. Parts of these are now devoted to the **Philip Ashcroft Museum of Rural Life** with its unique collection of items illustrating village life in pre-industrial Lancashire. Another attraction here is the spacious garden alongside the canal.

MERE BROW

7 miles N of Ormskirk on the B5246

Just to the south of the village lies the Wildfowl and Wetlands Trust at **Martin Mere** (see panel below), over 350 acres of reclaimed marshland which was established in 1976 as a refuge for thousands of wintering wildfowl. Until Martin Mere was drained in the 1600s to provide rich, fertile farmland, the lake was one of the largest in England. Many devotees of the Arthurian legends believe that the pool into which the dying king's sword Excalibur was thrown (to be received by a woman's arm *'clothed in white samite, mystic, wonderful'*), was actually Martin Mere.

Today, the stretches of water, mudbanks and grassland provide homes for many species of birds and, with a network of hides, visitors can observe shy birds such as the ruff, black-tailed godwit and little ringed plover in their natural habitats. There are also a series of pens, near to the visitors centre, where

WWT MARTIN MERE

Nr Rufford, Lancashire

WWT Martin Mere is one of nine Wildfowl & Wetlands Centres run by the Wildfowl & Wetlands Trust (WWT), a UK registered charity. Visit WWT Martin Mere and come in close contact with wetlands and their wildlife. You can feed some of the birds straight from your hand. Special events and exhibitions help to give an insight into the wonder of wetlands and the vital need for their conservation.

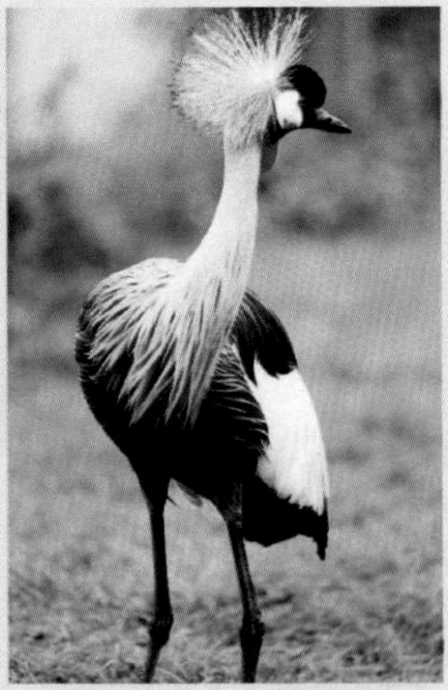

People of all ages and abilities will enjoy exploring the carefully planned pathways. You can go on a journey around the world, from the Australian Riverway, through the South American Lake, to the Oriental Pen with its Japanese gateway, observing a multitude of exotic ducks, geese, swans and flamingos along the way. In winter, WWT Martin Mere plays host to thousands of Pink-footed Geese, Whooper and Bewick's

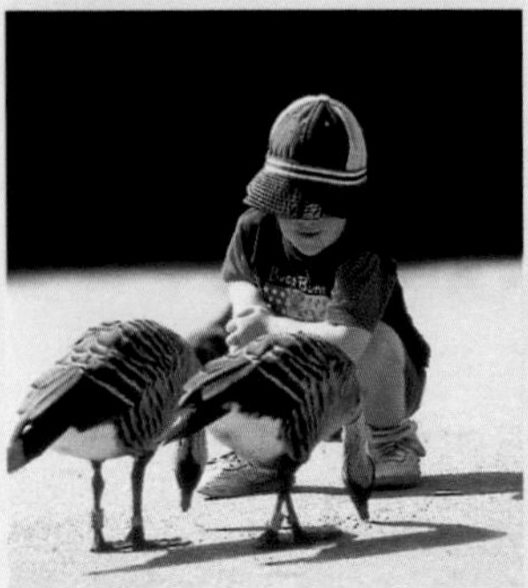

Swans and much more. Visitors can see swans under floodlight most winter evenings.

Covering 150 hectares, the reserve (one of Britain's most important wetland sites) is designated a Ramsar Site and SSSI for its wealth of rare wetland plants.

The Wildfowl & Wetlands Trust is the largest international wetland conservation charity in the UK. WWT's mission is to conserve wetlands and their biodiversity. These are vitally important for the quality and maintenance of all life. WWT operates nine visitor centres in the UK, bringing people closer to wildlife and providing a fun day out for all the family.

many other birds can be seen all year round at closer quarters. The mere is particularly famous for the vast numbers of pink-footed geese that winter here, their number often approaching 20,000. Although winter is a busy time at Martin Mere, a visit in any season is sure to be rewarded. The visitor centre caters for everyone and, as well as the shop and café, there is a theatre and a wealth of information regarding the birds found here and the work of the Trust.

SCARISBRICK

3 miles NW of Ormskirk on the A570

Scarisbrick, which is part of the largest parish in Lancashire, lies in the heart of rich agricultural land that is intensively cultivated for vegetables, including carrots, Brussels sprouts, cabbages, and early potatoes. A feature of this area is the large number of farm shops by the

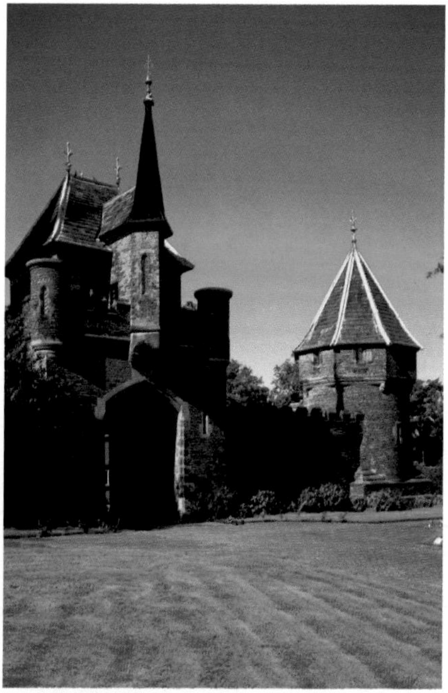

The Stables, Scarisbrick Hall

side of the road selling the produce fresh from the fields.

The first **Scarisbrick Hall** was built in the reign of King Stephen but in the middle of the 19th century the hall, which is screened from the road by thick woodland, was extensively remodelled by the Victorian architect Augustus Welby Pugin for Charles Scarisbrick.

HALSALL

4 miles W of Ormskirk on the A5147

This is a charming unspoilt village lying in the heart of fertile West Lancashire and close to the Leeds and Liverpool Canal – the longest canal in Britain with a mainline of 127.25 miles and 92 locks. **St Cuthbert's Church**, which dates from the middle of the 13th century, is one of the oldest churches in the diocese of Liverpool and it remains one of the prettiest in the county. The distinctive spire, which was added around 1400, rises from a tower that has octagonal upper stages.

SOUTH AND EAST OF ORMSKIRK

GREAT ALTCAR

6 miles SW of Ormskirk on the B5195

Standing on the banks of the River Alt, this old farming village is famous as the venue for the Liverpool Cup, an annual hare coursing event. In the churchyard of the present church, erected by the Earl of Sefton in 1879, are a pedestal font and a stoup which came from the earlier churches that occupied this site.

AUGHTON

3 miles SW of Ormskirk off the A59

This picturesque village, surrounded by agricultural land, is dominated by the spire of St Michael's Church. An ancient

CEDAR FARM GALLERIES

Back Lane, Mawdesley, Nr Ormskirk, Lancashire L40 3SY
Tel: 01704 822038
e-mail: info@cedarfarm.net
website: www.cedarfarm.net

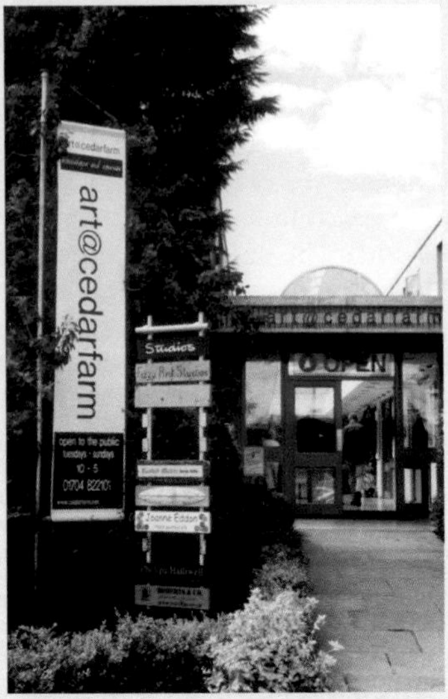

Originally a working farm, Cedar Farm Galleries opened in 1987 as a small but innovative arts centre dedicated to promoting the very best of the UK's crafts. It was an instant success and has grown into the large complex it is today, with a wealth of attractions to entertain all ages. There are now six large shops, a large cafe, and most recently a glass topped arts centre which provides studios for a number of artists who practice a wide range of skills, glass blowing, basket making, photography, silk screen printing, card making and many more. The arts centre is also home to a

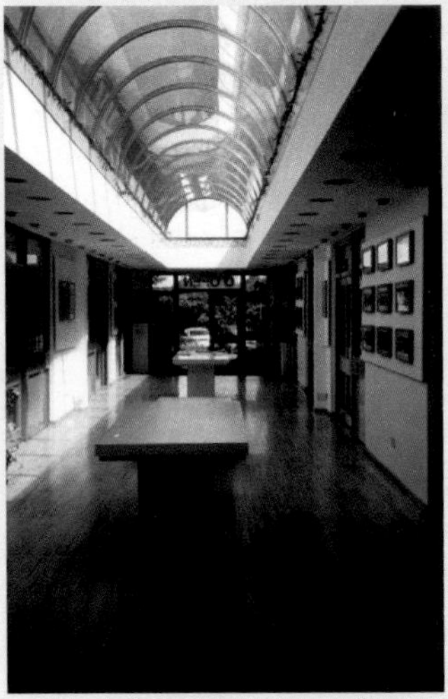

coffee roastery where visitors can relax, drink coffee and inhale the delicious aroma whilst enjoying the featured exhibition.

The original shop, The Gallery has an established reputation for showcasing high-quality British craftwork, and the adjoining shop, the Frame Shop stocks a wide range of artists' materials, prints, etchings and originals; it also offers a bespoke picture framing service with an excellent selection of mounts and mouldings. Other shops include the ladies

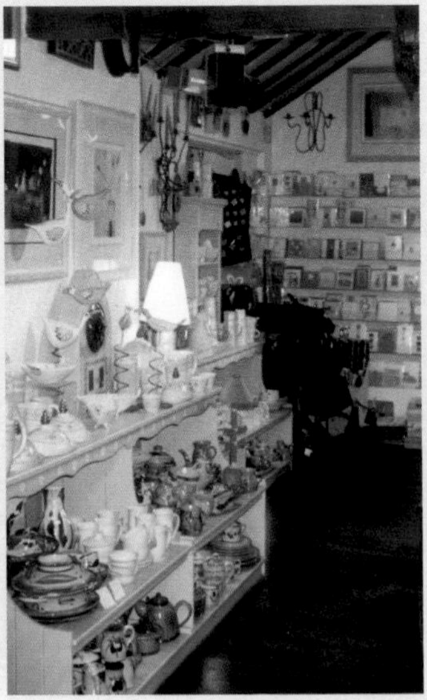

clothing shop Etcetera which predominatly sells the well known German labels but which is also a treasure trove of bags, jewellery, scarves and other accessories.Little Pixies specialises in designers clothes for 0-16 years old, and oriental art, jewellery and clothing are to be found in the ethnic shop, Anise. While Cedar Farm's very own tasty food shop sells delicious pates, salads, pies and puddings.

This is very much a place for a day out for all the family. In addition to the shops and art centre the lively Cafe serves home cooked snacks and light , mainly vegetarian meals, there is a safe play ground for children, and special area with a selection of farm animals who are always happy to be fed. To add to the appeal courses are run in the arts centre and pot painting classes are held most Sundays, and at the Midsummer weekend in June Cedar Farm plays host to the Mawdesley Midsummer Festival which features live music, sideshows and childrens workshops.

place, it was mentioned in the *Domesday Book*; the register of church rectors goes back to 1246 and much of the building's medieval framework remains though it was restored in 1914.

Close by is Aughton Old Hall (private) which stands on a site that has been occupied since Saxon times. The ruins of a 15th century pele tower are visible in the garden and the house is reputed to have been Cromwell's base while he was active in the area.

LATHOM
3 miles NE of Ormskirk off the A5209

The stretch of the famous Leeds and Liverpool Canal which passes through this village is well worth a visit and it includes the **Top Locks** area, a particularly interesting part of this major canal route.

To the south of the village, in Lathom Park, is Lathom House (private), formerly home of Lord Stanley, Earl of Derby, a Royalist who was executed during the Civil War. Only one wing of the original house remains but within the grounds are the ancient **Chapel of St John the Divine**, consecrated in 1509, and ten adjoining almshouses built for the chapel bedesmen. It's a charming cluster of buildings in an attractive setting and visitors are welcome at the services held in the chapel every Sunday.

PARBOLD
5 miles NE of Ormskirk off the A5209

This is a charming village of pretty stone cottages as well as grand, late-Victorian houses built by wealthy Manchester cotton brokers. The village houses extend up the slopes of **Parbold Hill**, one of the highest points for miles around and from which there are superb views of the West Lancashire plain. At the summit stands a rough hewn monument, erected to commemorate the Reform Act of 1832,

that is known locally, due to its shape, as Parbold Bottle.

Ashurst Beacon, another local landmark, was re-erected on Ashurst Hill by Lord Skelmersdale in 1798 when the threat of a French invasion was thought to be imminent.

MAWDESLEY
6 miles NE of Ormskirk off the B5246

A past winner of the Best Kept Village of Lancashire award, Mawdesley lies in rich farming country and was once associated with a thriving basket making industry.

The village has a surprising number of old buildings. Mawdesley Hall (private), originally built in the 1500s and altered in the late 18th century, was for many generations the home of the Mawdesley family.

At the other end of the village is Lane Ends House, built in 1590, which was occupied by a Catholic family and has a chapel in one of its attics. Other venerable buildings include Ambrose House (1577), Barret House Farm (1695), Back House Farm (1690) and Jay Bank Cottage (1692). By contrast, the oldest of the village's three churches dates back only to 1840.

WRIGHTINGTON
8 miles NE of Ormskirk on the B5250

Bypassed by most people as they travel up and down the nearby M6 and overshadowed by the delights of the **Camelot Theme Park** at nearby Charnock Richard, this is another pleasant, rural Lancashire village.

RIVINGTON
13 miles E of Ormskirk off the A673

One of the county's prettiest villages, Rivington is surrounded by moorland of outstanding natural beauty that forms the western border of the Forest of

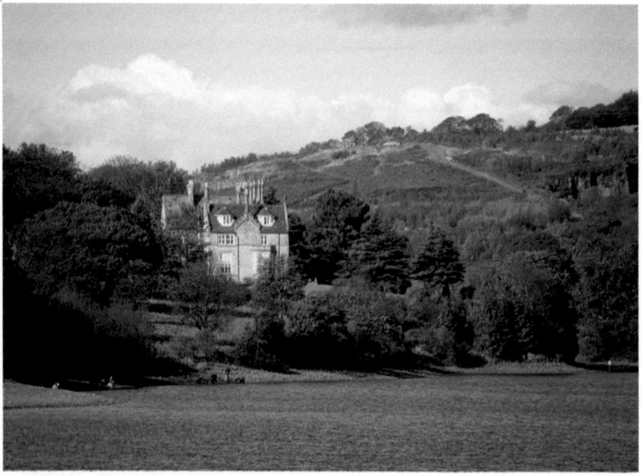

Rivington Reservoirs

importance of the town in the late 1500s, the building stands on the site of a church that was certainly here at the beginning of the 13th century. A look around the interior of the church will provide a potted history of the area: there are tombs and memorials to all the important local families including the Wrightingtons, Shevingtons, and the Standish family themselves.

Rossendale. Overlooking the village and with splendid views over West Lancashire, **Rivington Pike**, at 1,191 feet, is one of the area's high spots. It was once a site of one of the country's chain of signal beacons.

Just to the south of the village, on the lower slopes of Rivington Moor, lies **Lever Park**, which was made over to the public in 1902 by William Hesketh Lever, who later became Lord Leverhulme. The park comprises an awe-inspiring pot pourri of ornamental, landscaped gardens, tree-lined avenues, ancient cruck-framed barns, a Georgian hall, and a treasure trove of natural history within its 400 acres. The park's moorland setting, elevated position, and adjoining reservoirs provide scenery on a memorably grand scale.

STANDISH

9 miles E of Ormskirk on the A49

This historic old market town has several reminders of its past, not least of which is the splendid **St Wilfrid's Church**. Built in a size and style that befitted the

THE FORESTS OF PENDLE & ROSSENDALE

The Pennine Hills, the backbone of England, are such a well known geographical feature that it comes as something of a surprise to find that the name was created as recently as 1750 by a fraudulent professor. Charles Bertram claimed to have discovered a medieval chronicle describing Britain as it was in Roman times. In this non-existent tome, he said, the Romans had named this range of hills 'Alps Penina' because they resembled the Apennine Hills of central Italy. The professor's fake chronicle was soon discredited but his spurious name, the 'Pennines', was universally adopted.

In the 1720s, Daniel Defoe travelled on horseback through the area and wrote it off as "a howling wilderness....the English Andes". A century later the wild, poverty stricken area Defoe had passed through was throbbing with the sound of churning mill wheels, its sky murky

with the smoke of thousands of coal fuelled factories. That sooty, industrial image lingers on despite the fact that this area of Lancashire has re-invented itself in the past few decades. The waste from coalpits has been transformed into smoothly landscaped country parks and energetic local councils are also striving to make the most of the region's natural attractions: swooping hills, stark moorlands and contrasting wooded valleys.

But the area still takes pride in its industrial past, now recognised by its designation as an official Heritage Area. Bacup, for example, as well as being the highest town in Lancashire at 827 feet above sea level, is also acknowledged by English Heritage as the best preserved cotton town in Britain. And the Queen Street Mill at Haile Syke near Burnley is the only surviving steam-powered cotton mill in the country. Here, more than 300 deafening Lancashire looms clatter away in the imposing weaving shed where hundreds of metres of cotton cloth are produced weekly. In Burnley itself, the Weavers Triangle is one of the finest examples of a Victorian industrial townscape still in existence.

Southeast Lancashire also possesses some grand buildings from an earlier era. Gawthorpe Hall at Padiham is a Jacobean gem; Towneley Hall, dating back to the 1400s, houses Burnley's excellent Museum & Art Gallery; and Turton Tower, north of Bolton, is a lovely old building which began as a medieval pele. Set in nine acres of woodland, the tower houses several collections, including furniture, portraits, arms, ceramics and contemporary crafts.

Despite its industrial history, the southern border of Lancashire boasts some attractive villages.

BURNLEY

This cotton town is rich in history as well as being the largest town in this area of East Lancashire. Incorporating some 50 square miles, the town offers visitors a wealth of contrasts, from some of the best preserved industrial landscapes in Britain to the magnificent, untouched moorlands just to the east.

With the Industrial Revolution and the building of the Leeds and Liverpool Canal, Burnley not only expanded but grew in stature until, by the end of the 19th century, it was the world's leading producer of cotton cloth. Burnley's fine Victorian **Town Hall** of 1888 is one of many monumental public buildings in the area erected during that period of unparalleled English prosperity.

A walk along the towpath of the canal, through an area known as the **Weavers' Triangle** is like taking a step back in time. This is an area of spinning mills and weaving sheds; foundries where steam engines and looms were made; canal-side warehouses; domestic buildings, including a unique row of workers' cottages; and a Victorian school house. The Weavers' Triangle Visitors Centre is housed in the former wharfmaster's house and canal toll office. A short walk from the Visitors' Centre is **Oak Mount Mill** engine house. The splendid old steam, originally installed in 1887, has recently been restored and is now operated by an electric motor.

Even more impressive is the **Queen Street Mill**, the only surviving steam-powered cotton mill in Britain. A visit here provides a unique insight into Victorian factory life as the 300 looms boom away, powered by the magnificent steam engine, Peace.

The history of Burnley can also be

TOWNELEY HALL ART GALLERY & MUSEUMS

Burnley, Lancashire BB11 3RQ
Tel: 01282 424213
website: www.towneleyhall.org.uk

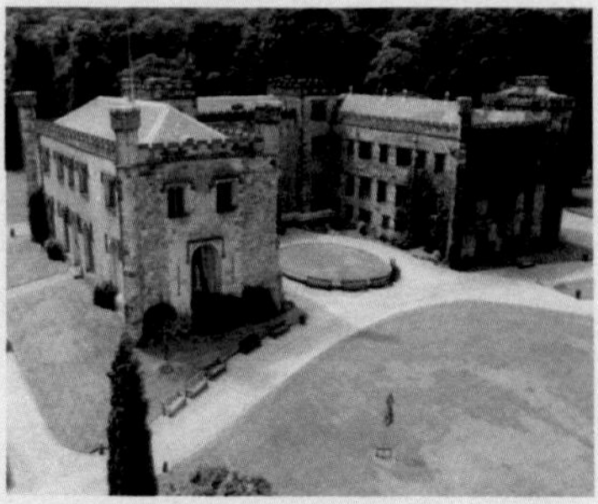

Towneley Hall offers the perfect day out for all the family
- a country house, a museum and an art gallery all in one.
Towneley Hall was the home of the Towneley family from
the 14th century until 1902. Charles (1737-1805) was
one of the 18th century's best known collectors of antique
sculpture and gems. His portrait can be seen in the gallery.
Today visitors can still catch a glimpse of how the family
lived. Original period rooms include the Elizabthan long
gallery and the Regency rooms. See how they compare with life below stairs in the Victorian kitchen
and the servants dining room.

The museum's collections surround you - glass, ceramics and 17th century Lancashire oak furniture.
Pictures by many favourite Victorian artists can be seen in the art galleries, including works by Sir
Edward Coley Burne-Jones, John William Waterhouse and Sir Edwin Landseer. The Whalley Abbey
vestments are another highlight. Embroidered in silk and silver thread on cloth of gold, they were
brought to Towneley in the 16th century and are now extremely rare. A programme of temporary
exhibitions ensures something new to see on every visit. Open daily except Fridays - check for
opening times.

---

explored by boat along the Leeds and
Liverpool Canal. This famous waterway
leaves the Weavers' Triangle via a huge
embankment which carries the canal
across the town. Known as the 'straight
mile', it is in fact less than that but no
less exciting and, at 60 feet above the
ground, it is one of the most impressive
features of the canal's length.

Situated on the Todmorden Road on
the outskirts of Burnley is the **Towneley
Hall Art Gallery and Museum** (see panel
above). The home of the Towneley
family since the 14th century, right up
until 1902, parts of the present building
date from the 15th century. Visitors can
view the art collections, the Whalley
Abbey Vestments, and the museum of
local crafts and industries, and also take
in a tour of the house. A recent
extension contains a lecture theatre,
shop, toilets and a lift.

The grounds too are open to visitors
and contain a traditional Victorian
flower garden, woodland nature trails,
and a fascinating series of sculptures

hewn from the trees around. Subjects
include a giant magpie, a crocodile
emerging from the water, and a huge
cricket. The grounds also include a
natural history centre, a **Museum of
Local Crafts and Industries** and
facilities for golf, tennis, bowls, and
other outdoor pursuits.

Another interesting places to visit is
**The Horses and Ponies Protection
Association**, situated at Shore Heys
Farm, Briercliffe. A must for horse lovers,
this is a haven for rescued and neglected
horses, ponies, and donkeys. Open daily
except Monday and Thursday 1pm-4pm.

NORTH OF BURNLEY

BRIERFIELD
2 miles N of Burnley on the A682

This industrial town has magnificent
views of Pendle Hill as it lies on a steep
slope at the bottom of which is an
attractive **Quaker Bridge** over
Pendle Water.

At the beginning of the 19th century, coal was discovered in the area. Within a few years three pits had opened, thus sealing Brierfield's fate as a place of industry. The laying of turnpike roads, followed by the opening of the Leeds and Liverpool Canal, gave the growing village a further boost and by 1833 a handloom weaving business was also flourishing here.

The humid climate and expanding transport system made Brierfield an ideal place for the burgeoning cotton industry, which had become the main source of employment here by the end of the 19th century.

NELSON

3 miles N of Burnley on the A56

This town, along with its neighbours Colne and Burnley, are now inseparable as they share the same valley running along the length of Colne Water. Nelson is a modern textile town which takes its name from the hotel, The Lord Nelson, which stands by the railway line running along the valley bottom. Although the town itself might have been the product of the Industrial Age, two of its suburbs, Little and Great Marsden, have been here for centuries. Here, above Nelson, lies **Marsden Park**, and once Marsden Hall, the home of the de Walton family until their line died out in 1912. Acquired by the local authority, much of the hall was demolished while the parkland was developed.

COLNE

5 miles N of Burnley on the A56

Before the Industrial Revolution turned this area into a valley devoted to the production of cotton cloth, Colne was a small market town that specialised in wool. Unfortunately, there are few reminders of the days before industrialisation but **St Batholomew's Church**, founded in 1122, is still here and contains some interesting interior decorations and furnishings. In the centre of the town, next to the War Memorial, is another memorial. The statue is of Wallace Hartley, the bandmaster on the ill-fated *Titanic* who, heroically, stayed at his post with his musicians and played *Nearer my God to Thee* as the liner sank beneath the waves of the icy Atlantic in 1912. His body was brought back to Colne to be buried in the cemetery. Another son of Colne was another Hartley, William Pickles Hartley, who founded the mighty Hartley's jam empire and who was a great benefactor of the town.

Colne is also the unlikely home of the **British in India Museum**, where exhibits covering many aspects of the British rule over the subcontinent, from the 17th century until 1947 can be seen. The collection includes coins, medals, uniforms, model soldiers and a working model of the railway from Kalka to Simla. Also on display is a collection of clothes that belonged to EM Forster, author of *A Passage to India*.

Collectors of curiosities will enjoy the unique form of punishment devised for minor malefactors in Colne and preserved in the **Town Museum.** Stocks and pillories enjoyed a long history as a way of humiliating offenders and providing innocent amusement for bystanders. But many of Colne's busy citizens could not spare the time to leave their work and make their way to wherever the stocks were fixed. So a movable cart was constructed, capable of seating three offenders side by side, and the Town Beadle would wheel it around the town so that everyone could join in the fun.

Just north of Colne is the village of **Foulridge**, site of the Foulridge, or Mile

Tunnel. This tunnel on the Leeds and Liverpool Canal took five years to complete and cost the lives of many navvies. There was no towpath through the tunnel, so the horse-drawn barges had to be 'legged': leggers lay on planks fixed to the boats and 'walked' along the tunnel walls, pulling the boat with them. One day in 1912 a cow fell into the canal at the Barrowford end and swam all the way through. She was revived by alcohol and briefly became a celebrity; a picture of the event hangs in a pub in Foulridge.

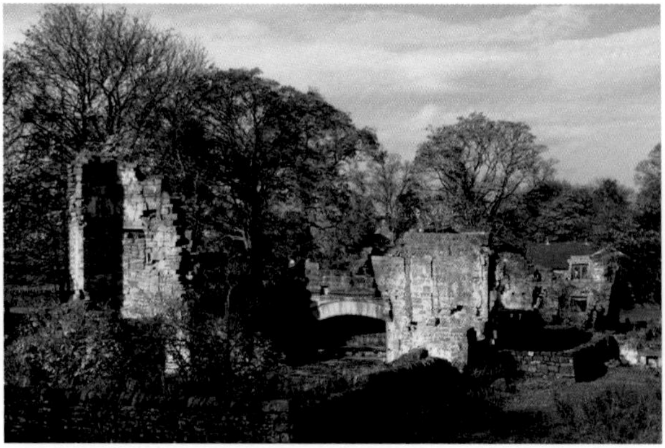

Wycoller Hall

WYCOLLER
6 miles NE of Burnley off the B6250

This hamlet lies amidst the moorlands that rise to the east of the textile towns of the Colne valley and up to the bleak summits of the Pennines. Now almost deserted, this was once a thriving place as an important centre for the wool trade and as a handloom weavers' settlement, but it lost most of its inhabitants to the new factories in the west.

Fortunately, the place has been saved by the creation of a **Wycoller Country Park**, surrounding the village, and many of the buildings have been restored. There is also a delightful old hump-backed packhorse bridge crossing a stream and, above the village, a single slab gritstone bridge, **Clam Bridge**, that is thought to date from the Iron Age. Now a ruin, **Wycoller Hall** was the inspiration for Ferndean Manor in Charlotte Brontë's *Jane Eyre*: Wycoller was one of the villages to which the sisters walked from their house at Haworth and is now a point on the

Brontë Way, which crosses from Lancashire into Yorkshire over moorland featured in *Wuthering Heights*.

EARBY
10 miles NE of Burnley on the A56

In this town almost on the county border with Yorkshire is the **Museum of Yorkshire Dales Lead Mining**, housed in the old Grammar School building. With the largest collection of lead mining tools and equipment used in the Yorkshire Dales on display, there is much to see, including examples of the minerals extracted, a lead crushing mill, and other working models.

PENDLE HILL AND BARROWFORD
5 miles N of Burnley off the A6068

Dominating the landscape here is the great whale-backed mass of Pendle Hill, rising to nearly 1,900 feet above sea-level. The hill became notorious in the early 1600s as the location where the **Pendle Witches** supposedly practised their black arts. It has a more uplifting association, though, since it was from the summit of Pendle Hill in 1625 that George Fox saw a vision which inspired him to found the Society of Friends, or Quakers.

COFFEE CULTURE

Park Mill, Halstead Lane, Barrowford, Nr Nelson, Lancashire BB9 6HJ
Tel: 01282 617200 Fax: 01282 831441
e-mail: k.stevenson1@btinternet.com

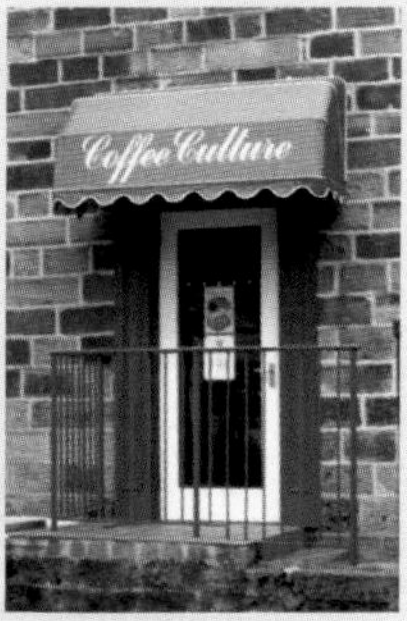

Owner Karen Stevenson has seen a successful first year of trading at **Coffee Culture**, which is located on the first floor above an old restored mill that is open to the public. Behind a cheerful red awning the coffee shop is bright and stylish, a great place to relax over a superb cup of coffee (Drury is the main supplier) and something to eat. Paninis, served grilled with a side salad and home-made coleslaw, are the most popular order, while other options include jacket potatoes, tortilla wraps and salads. Closed Mondays.

Pendle Hill lies at the heart of Lancashire's 'Witch Country', so called because of the events of 1612. On the 18th March of that year, a Halifax pedlar named John Law refused to give some pins to a beggar, Alison Device. She spat out the usual beggar's curse on him and he died almost immediately of a heart attack. The effect of a curse or just a coincidence? The early 1600s were the years of the great witch-hunts, so the authorities had little difficulty in attributing John Law's sudden death to Alison Device's supernatural powers.

Alison was arrested. Under torture, she incriminated eight other 'witches'. All of them were then charged with communing with the Devil and committing a total of sixteen murders. They were tried, found guilty and hanged at Lancaster Castle on August 20th, 1612. All except one: Old Mother

Continued on page 116

INDIGO ROOMS

137 Gisburn Road, Barrowford, Nr Nelson,
Lancashire BB9 6EP
Tel: 01282 603746
e-mail: diane@indigorooms.com
website: www.indigorooms.com

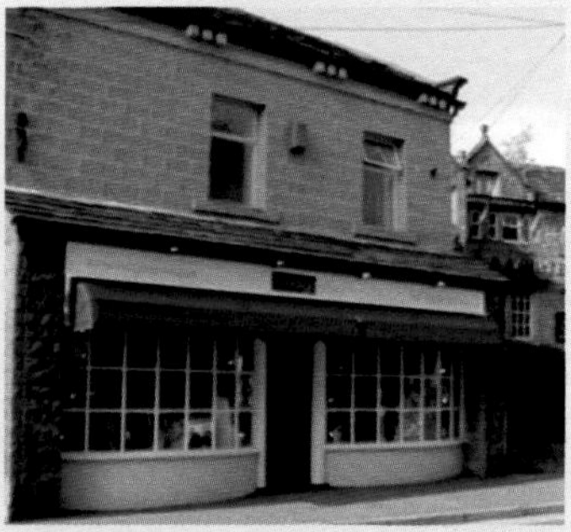

Diane Nowell, her husband Mark, and business partner Janet Robinson run **Indigo Rooms**, a traditional double-fronted shop on the outskirts of Barrowford. The extensive stock covers many aspects of home furnishings, and the items on display in the two attractively laid-out rooms ooze quality and individuality. The range runs from coffee tables, stools and other small items of furniture to designer fabrics

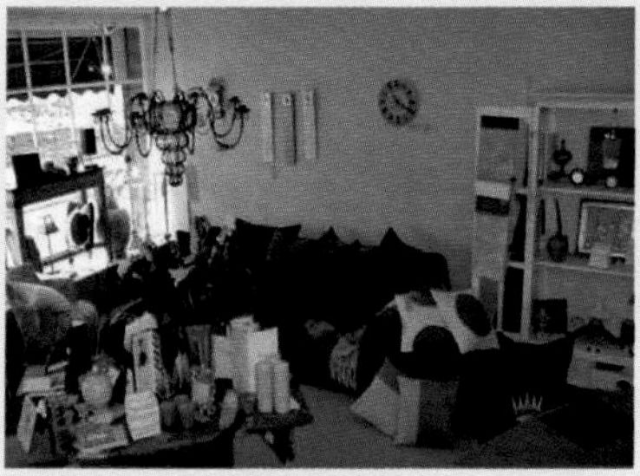

from some of the top names in the business, drapes, rugs, cushions, mirrors, lamps and shades, glassware, table ornaments, clocks and unusual artwork.

The partners in this well-run enterprise are expert professionals, very well aware of the various needs and demands of their customers, and of trends in an ever-changing market place. Apart from the stock of goods for sale, Indigo Rooms offer a measuring, making and fitting service, and can also undertake home consultations. Free parking is available close to the shop, which stands on its own just away from the local high street.

WALK 4

Barrowford and Roughlee

Start	Barrowford, Pendle Heritage Centre
Distance	4 miles (6.4km)
Approximate time	2 hours
Parking	Pendle Heritage Centre
Refreshments	Pubs at Barrowford, café at Pendle Heritage Centre, pub at Roughlee
Ordnance Survey maps	Landranger 103 (Blackburn & Burnley), Outdoor Leisure 41 (Forest of Bowland & Ribblesdale) or 21 (South Pennines)

Much of the first part of the route is through the valley of Pendle Water. A brief climb out of the valley is followed by a descent into Roughlee, a village which has associations with the Pendle Witches. After crossing stepping stones, the return to Barrowford is mainly along tracks and field paths, with a final section through Barrowford Park. The many fine views are dominated by Pendle Hill and Blacko Tower and extend to the edge of the Brontë moors.

The Pendle Heritage Centre, on the opposite side of the road from the car park, is housed in a 16th century manor house and comprises a museum, shop, cafe and tourist information centre. There is also a cruck barn and walled garden.

Go through a gate in the car park, at a Pendle Way sign, and walk along a path beside Pendle Water on the left to emerge onto a road at the side of Higherford Old Bridge. Turn left over the bridge and turn right **A** along a lane called Foreside - now with Pendle Water on the right - passing an old pack-horse bridge. The route continues along an attractive, tree-lined path beside the stream, going through two gates, to reach a T-junction. Turn right over a bridge and turn left over a stile to walk along the other bank.

Turn left to cross a tributary stream (Blacko Water) at the next footbridge, turn right and head uphill across a field, bearing slightly left away from the stream,

to a stile. Climb it, keep ahead to climb another one and walk along the right edge of a field. Climb a stile, keep ahead along the right field edge, climb another stile to the left of a farm, walk along an enclosed path and go through a gate onto a road **B** .

Cross over, take the uphill track ahead to Bank End Farm and climb a stile to the left of a cattle grid. Continue uphill across a field, veering left away from the field edge. Climb a stile, cross a track and continue walking up to climb a stone stile. Turn left along a path through conifers, which passes to the right of the farm, and then climb a stone stile into woodland. Bear left and head downhill through this beautiful woodland, looking out for where you climb another stone stile at its bottom edge.

Walk along the right edge of a field, turn right over a stone stile just before reaching the corner and turn left along a

left field edge, veering away from it to go through a gate. Keep ahead across the next field and, on the far side, turn right to continue along its left edge to a gate. Go through, walk along a tarmac drive, passing to the right of a cottage, go through another gate and turn left between farm buildings.

Head gently downhill along a tarmac track and, at a fork, take the right hand track to pass in front of Roughlee Old Hall. This fine 17th-century building, now divided into a number of separate cottages, was the alleged home of Alice Nutter, one of the Pendle Witches, hanged at Lancaster Castle in 1612. Where the track ends, continue along an enclosed path in front of cottages which bears left to reach the road in Roughlee. Turn left and, at a Pendle Way sign, turn right over a stile **C**, descend a bank and cross stepping stones over Pendle Water.

Head up the bank on the other side, making for a footpath post, and bear right across a field and over a brow to a stile. Climb it, walk along the right edge of the next two fields, heading steadily downhill, and go through a gate in the bottom corner of the second field. Turn left over a stile, pass to the left of a barn, climb another

stile and keep ahead along a hedge-lined path which continues along the left edge of a field. In the bottom corner of the field, cross a footbridge, turn left along a fence-lined path, climb a stile and turn right along a tarmac track.

Head downhill along the track to a road by Pasture Gate House and turn left steeply downhill into Barrowford, bending right to a T-junction. Cross the footbridge almost opposite into Barrowford Park **D** and turn left onto a tarmac path beside Pendle Water again. The park was laid out for local people in the 1920s by two cotton manufacturers. The path leads back to the Pendle Heritage Centre and the start of the route. ●

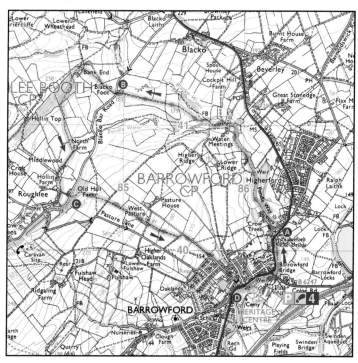

Demdike, eighty years old and half-blind, escaped the gallows by dying in jail. During their trial, the 'Pendle Witches' seem to have taken pride in implicating each other. In effect, they hanged themselves by their fanciful tales of spells, potions, and the coven's naked caperings, fuelling the popular imagination that there really were witches who could affect the lives of other people. The infamous witches were, in the main, old women who dabbled with plants and herbs, knowing which could heal and which, when ingested, would spell certain death.

The Victorian novelist WH Ainsworth was inspired to write a colourful melodrama based on the trial, *The Lancashire Witches – A Romance of Pendle Forest*, and although it's doubtful that 'witchcraft' was any more prevalent around Pendle Hill than anywhere else in the country at that time, the legend has proved very durable. Every year now, on the evening of October 31st, Halloween, Pendle Hill is flecked with the dark figures of masked, black-cloaked figures making their way to its summit.

Something of the old, dark tragedy still broods over Pendle and many memories and places which hark back to those grim days remain. Those interested in finding out more about the trials should visit the **Pendle Heritage Centre** at Barrowford, a linear village situated to the north of Nelson on the A682. The Centre is housed in Park Hill, a collection of buildings centred on a sturdy old farmhouse built by the Bannister family, one of whose descendants was Roger Bannister, the first man to run a mile in less than four minutes. The centre also houses an art gallery, a cruck barn with animals, an 18th century walled garden and a pleasant woodland walk. The **East Lancashire Towel Company** is a working mill where visitors can see the traditional method of weaving terry towels. Historically, witches aside, the hill was one of the many beacon hills throughout the country that formed a country-wide chain and were lit in times of national crisis, such as the sighting of the Spanish Armada. Today, Pendle Hill is one of the best locations in the whole country for paragliding, and recreational pilots regularly achieve altitudes of 4,000 feet above sea level. Barrowford is the start point of the Pendle Way, a 45-mile circular walk that takes in some of the area's most attractive scenery; the way is marked by signs of a witch on a broomstick.

To the west of the hill's summit lies **Apronfull Hill**, a Bronze Age burial site,

THORNEYHOLME FARM COTTAGE

Barley New Road, Roughlee, Forest of Bowland,
Lancashire BB12 9LH
Tel: 01282 612452

A warm welcome awaits visitors to **Thorneyholme Farm Cottage**, a lovely Georgian farmhouse in a beautiful setting close to Pendle Water and the Pendle Way. Janet Taylor offers Bed & Breakfast accommodation in a twin room and a double room with its own lounge. Both are on the ground floor, with en suite facilities, central heating, tv, tea trays and hairdryers. Free-range eggs and excellent local bacon and sausages are part of a superb breakfast that will set guests up for a day's walking or sightseeing. A self-catering option is also available. Thorneyholme Farm Cottage is a non-smoking establishment.

WITCHES GALORE

Newchurch-in-Pendle, Nr Burnley, Lancashire BB12 9JR
Tel: 01282 613111
website: www.witchesgalore.co.uk

The only shop in a pretty hillside village, **Witches Galore**
rightly calls itself 'a little shop with a big reputation'. A coven
of witches sits outside the shop, inviting visitors to 'drop in
for a spell', and owner Maureen Stopford, here for almost a
quarter of a century, stocks hundreds of souvenirs of the
famous Pendle Witches, including puppet witches, china

figures, T-shirts, books, postcards, posters - even broomsticks, all representing the lighter, less spooky
side of witchcraft. Huge fun, and a must on the trail of the Pendle Witches.

that is said to be the place from which
the Devil threw stones at Clitheroe
Castle, creating what is known as the
Devil's Window.

NEWCHURCH

4 miles N of Burnley off the A6068

This charming Pendle village was named
following the consecration of a new
church in 1544 by John Bird, Bishop of
Chester. Earlier, during the Middle Ages,
Newchurch was a cow and deer rearing
centre, as well as part of the old hunting
forest of Pendle but by the reign of
Elizabeth I the area was becoming de-
forested and farming was beginning
to take over as the primary source
of income.

Newchurch did not escape from stories
of witchcraft that surrounded the
notorious Pendle witches trial in the
17th century, and many ghostly tales
and shadowy traditions are said to be
associated with the village. Though those
times were a frightening experience for
anyone living in the area, by the 18th
century, the witch hunts were over and
the village grew rapidly as part of the
expanding textile industry, first with
handloom weavers and then with the
construction of a factory for washing
and dyeing wool.

An old tradition continues here – the
Annual Rushbearing, when dry rushes

are scattered on the church floor and in
the pews. Originally this was to keep
parishioners warm and although the
advent of central heating makes it no
longer necessary the villagers still process
through the village carrying rushes and
singing hymns accompanied by a brass
band. A Rushbearing Queen is crowned
and after a short service in the church
everyone repairs to the school for a slap-
up tea.

PADIHAM

2 miles W of Burnley on the A646

This charming small town of narrow
winding lanes and cobbled alleyways still
retains characteristics typical of the early
days of the Industrial Revolution.
However, there was a settlement here
long before the Norman Conquest and
Padiham was also the market town for
the western slopes of Pendle. A market is
still held here every Wednesday
and Friday.

One of Lancashire's most impressive
stately homes is **Gawthorpe Hall**
(National Trust), which stands on the
bank of the River Calder, surrounded
by gardens and woodland. The
Shuttleworth family have lived at
Gawthorpe since the early 1400s but the
present house is a gracious 17th century
mansion, restored and extended in the
1850s by Sir Charles Barry. This was the

no expense was spared on the opulent decorations and furnishings. The Hall has many pictures on loan from the National Portrait Gallery which add extra lustre to the already notable collection. Open to the public between Easter and October, the house has beautiful period furnishings, ornately decorated ceilings and the original wood panelled walls and is also home to the nationally important Kay-Shuttleworth collection of fine needlework and lace.

Read

5 miles W of Burnley on the A671

Gawthorpe Hall

era of High Victorian extravagance and

Situated on the banks of the River Calder it was during a skirmish near **Read Old Bridge** in April

---

Holts Jewellers

68 King Street, Whalley, Lancashire BB7 9SW
Tel: 01254 824424

Traditional and contemporary jewellery is the stock in trade of **Holts Jewellers**, which was located in Blackburn when it first opened in 1878. In June 2003 the business relocated to Whalley, where it is run by three sisters – Sue Entwhistle, Diane Cooke and Lynne Deney – who are the grandchildren of the founder. The sisters' father took over from the founder and when he retired they came to Whalley to a smaller shop for the three of them to run.

The shop is neat and compact, with a well-lit display area; it is located within an exclusive ladies fashion shop. Gold and silver jewellery, rings set with diamonds and other precious stones, and some lovely pewter ware are set on attractive display, and anyone browsing among the cabinets for a gift is certain to find something really special and original. Holts also undertakes valuations of jewellery and offers a repair service. It is literally a little gem of a place, and is well worth a visit along with Whalley's historic Abbey, which was founded in the 13th century, and its even more venerable parish church.

1643 that the Royalist cause in Lancashire was lost.

Read Hall, privately owned and no longer in the hands of the original family, was the home of one of Lancashire's most famous families, the Nowells. It was Roger Nowell, in 1612, who committed the Pendle witches to trial. The Nowells left the hall in 1772 and in 1799 the house was completely rebuilt in the Georgian style seen today.

WHALLEY

7 miles W of Burnley on the B6246

One of Lancashire's most attractive villages, Whalley grew up around a crossing of the River Calder, between Pendle Hill and the Nab. There are old cottages and Tudor and Georgian houses, and three out of the four inns at the crossroads date from the 1700s. Soaring above the village is the **Whalley Viaduct**, an impressive 48-arched

structure built in 1850 to carry the Blackburn to Clitheroe railway line across the broad valley of the Calder. Rather touchingly, where the viaduct crosses the lane leading to **Whalley Abbey** the arches have added Gothic details that harmonise with the nearby 14th century gatehouse to the abbey.

The abbey was the last to be built in Lancashire, started in the early 1300s, but for the Cistercian monks whose work it was, Whalley was not their first choice. They had already established a religious house at Stanlow, on the banks of the River Mersey and now under a huge oil refinery, in 1172.

Seeking somewhere less harsh and more fertile land, the monks moved to Whalley in 1296 but their attempts to build were hampered as Sawley Abbey felt threatened by the competition for the donations of land and goods expected from the local population.

OASIS

43 King Street, Whalley, Lancashire BB7 9SP
Tel: 01254 824282 Fax: 01254 824705

After many years in financial services partners Danielle Garritt and Phil Critchley launched the exciting new concept of **'Oasis'** in January 2003. Situated on the main street of the picturesque Ribble Valley Village of Whalley the recently` refurbished premises combines two distinctly different activities.

On the ground floor the florist shop provides both traditional and contemporary design in all aspects of floristry, while the first floor accommodates the sale of striking designs in contemporary glass furniture and exclusive ranges of glassware and pottery.

Many of the pieces are unique, designed and created by Oasis, and the owners also offer a bespoke design and manufacture service. Oasis stands close to the River Calder and just two minutes away from the imposing ruins of Whalley Abbey, built by the Cistercian order in the 13th century. Other sights not to be missed are the even older parish church and the famous 48-arched redbrick railway viaduct, but Oasis is reason enough to pause in this interesting village.

Building finally began in 1310 and by 1400 the imposing and impressive abbey had taken shape. The demise of the abbey came, as it did to all religious houses, under Henry VIII but Whalley's abbot, joining forces with the abbot of Sawley, took part in the Pilgrimage of Grace in an attempt to save their houses. This failed and the abbots were both executed.

Now owned and cared for by the Diocese of Blackburn, Whalley Abbey is one of the best preserved such places in the country and its future secure as it also acts as a conference centre.

Whalley's **Parish Church** is almost a century older than the abbey, its oldest parts dating back to 1206. Built on the site of an even older place of worship, the churchyard is home to three ancient crosses and the church itself contains a set of some of the finest choir stalls anywhere. They were brought here from the abbey after the Dissolution and though they are not elaborate there are some intriguing carvings on the lower portions. Even more intriguing are the puzzling tombstones in the churchyard, each one inscribed with impossible dates such as April 31st 1752 and February 30th 1839.

PENDLETON
6 miles NW of Burnley off the A59

Recorded in the *Domesday Book* when the village was part of the vast parish of Whalley, this small settlement of cottages and working farms has retained much of its traditional air – only seven new houses have been built here in the last 100 years. A beck runs through the middle of the village which was designated a Conservation Area in 1968. The discovery of a Bronze Age burial urn in the village in 1969 would indicate that there were settlers here as long ago as 1600 BC.

From the village there is a steep road, to the southeast, that climbs up to the **Nick of Pendle**, from where there are magnificent views.

RISHTON
7 miles W of Burnley on the A678

Originally a Saxon settlement, the name means the fortified village or dwelling place amid the rushes, and, during the Middle Ages, the village grew in importance as an early textile centre with the operation of its fulling mill. By the 17th century, Rishton had gained a name for the manufacture of linen cloth and, in 1766, it became the first village to weave calico. As the Industrial Revolution advanced, the industry moved from the weavers' homes into newly built mills.

OSWALDTWISTLE
7 miles W of Burnley on the A679

This typical Lancashire textile town has produced many miles of cotton cloth over the years. You can still hear the deafening clatter of looms at **Oswaldtwistle Mills** in Collier Street, one of the last working cotton mills in the country. Cotton has been woven here for more than 200 years under the watchful eyes of just two owners – the Walmsleys and the Tattersall/Hargreaves family. The town can justifiably be considered the heart of the industry since it was while staying here, at what is now Stanhill Post Office, that James Hargreaves invented his famous 'Spinning Jenny' in 1764. Although he was forced to leave the area after sometimes violent opposition to his machine from local hand spinners, the town's prosperity is largely due to textiles and, in particular, calico printing. However, Oswaldtwistle is a much older settlement than its rows of Victorian terraced houses would suggest as the

name means the boundary of the kingdom of Oswald, who was a 7th century Northumbrian king. Oswaldtwistle Mills is a family attraction with a variety of shops, a sweet factory, a garden centre and two coffee shops as well as the Textile Museum, which includes a 1700 weaver's cottage and the fastest Jacquard Air Jet looms in the world.

Stanhill, near Oswaldtwistle, is the start point of the Clog Long Distance Walk, which passes through dramatic and varied countryside and offers many spectacular views. The circular walk is 33 miles, but is broken down into seven easy stages.

Great Harwood

6 miles W of Burnley on the B6535

Before the Industrial Revolution, this was a quiet village of farms and cottages nestling between two streams. Famous for its fine woollen cloth, at the beginning of the 19th century cotton handloom weaving and then, by the 1850s, the introduction of the factory system and the cotton mills took over. Today only one mill remains but at the industry's height the town supported 22 mills. Not surprisingly, Great Harwood's most famous son was very much linked with cotton. In 1850, John Mercer, an industrial chemist, developed the technique of processing cotton to give it a sheen and the technique, mercerisation, is still used today. The free-standing clock tower in the Town Square was erected in 1903 to commemorate Mercer's contribution to the life of his home town.

Accrington

5 miles SW of Burnley on the A680

This attractive Victorian market town, as is typical in this area, expanded as a result

Greenwoods

24 Market Hall, Accrington, Lancashire BB5 1ER
Tel: 01254 395027

Having spent most of her working life here, Christine Grayson took over **Greenwoods** ten years ago and now runs it with two very friendly and cheerful helpers. Since 1935 the premises, in the bustling indoor town market, had been run by the Greenwood family, and the reputation they built up as suppliers of fine Lancashire cheeses lives on under Christine. The stock of cheeses from Singleton's Dairy and other local producers is

unbeatable in its variety, from familiar classics to speciality cheeses with garlic, with herbs, with pepper, with apple and cinnamon......even one with the flavour of pickled onions!

And as well as the cheeses greenwoods sells a variety of other tempting goodies, including hotplate potato cakes, breads and biscuits, baps and crumpets, scones, preserves and yoghurts. The stalls in Accrington's market sell a vast range of things, but none make the mouth water quite as much as Greenwoods. The market is definitely a place to make tracks for when visiting Accrington, and another is the famous Haworth Art Gallery in a beautiful parkland setting.

of the boom in the textile industry of the 18th and 19th centuries. Of all Lancashire's indoor markets, Accrington enjoys the grandest surroundings, housed in a magnificent **Market Hall** built in 1868. Accrington is also the place to visit for a real flavour of the old Lancashire: in April it hosts the Lancashire Food Festival, followed in May by the annual Clog Dancing Festival.

The town is the home of the **Haworth Art Gallery**, one of the most appealing galleries in the country – a charming Jacobean-style house built in 1909 and set in beautiful parkland. The gallery owns the largest collection of Tiffany glass – there are over 140 pieces – in Europe.

The collection was presented to the town by Joseph Briggs, an Accrington man, who emigrated to New York and worked with Louis Tiffany for nearly 40 years. Briggs joined the studio in 1890 and rose through the company ranks to become the manager of the Mosaic department before finally becoming Tiffany's personal assistant.

After the First World War, the fashion for Tiffany glassware waned and during the economic depression of the 1920s Briggs was given the sad job of selling off the remainder of the Tiffany stock. Returning to his native Accrington in 1933 with his collection of glass, Briggs gave half to the town and distributed the remainder among his family.

To the west of the town centre, the **Accrington Railway Viaduct** is another magnificent monument to Victorian builders. Erected for the former East Lancashire Railway it sweeps across the River Hyndburn in a graceful curve of 19 arches sixty feet high. Also worth a visit are the imposing **Town Hall** with its Corinthian portico and the elegant glass-roofed Arcade of 1880.

BACUP
7 miles S of Burnley on the A671

At 827 feet the highest town in Lancashire, Bacup was built in the 19th century for the sole purpose of cotton manufacture. It remains one of the best examples of a textile town in England even though the town suffered more than most when the mills began to close. A stroll through the town centre will reveal carefully restored shops and houses, with the grander homes of the mill owners and the elegant civic buildings acting as a reminder of the town's more prosperous times. Also, look out for what is claimed to be the shortest street in the world – Elgin Street off the Market Place is just 17 feet long.

An excellent time to visit the town is during the Easter weekend when the town's famous troop of Morris dancers take to the streets. Known as the **Coconut Dancers**, their costume is unique and involves wearing polished wooden discs strapped to their knees and blackening their faces. Maintaining that the correct name is Moorish not Morris Dancers, the tradition is thought to go back to the times of the Crusades.

RAWTENSTALL
7 miles S of Burnley on the A682

The town first developed as a centre of the woollen cloth trade with the work being undertaken by hand workers in their own homes before steam-powered mills were introduced in the early 19th century. The introduction of the cotton industry to the town happened at around the same time. Lower Mill, now a ruin, was opened in 1840 by the Whitehead brothers who were some of the area's first manufacturing pioneers. The **Weaver's Cottage**, purpose-built for a home weaver, is one of the last buildings remaining of its kind and is open to visitors at

weekends during the summer.

Also in the town, and housed in a former Victorian mill owner's house called Oakhill, is the **Rossendale Museum** (see panel opposite). Naturally, the area's industrial heritage is given a prominent position but collections of the region's natural history, fine art and furniture, and ceramics are on display too.

At one end of the town stands a new railway station which marks the end of a very old railway line – the **East Lancashire Railway**. Opened in 1846 and run commercially until 1980, when the last coal train drew into Rawtenstall, the line is now in the hands of the East Lancashire Railway Preservation Society. Running a passenger service (at weekends with additional summer services), the steam trains offer an enthralling 23 mile round trip along the River Irwell between Rawtenstall and

ROSSENDALE MUSEUM

Whitaker Park, Haslingden Road, Rawtenstall, Rossendale, Lancashire BB4 6RE
Tel: 01706 217777/244682
Fax: 01706 250037

Rossendale Museum is a former 19th century mill owner's house set in Whitaker Park. Displays include a Victorian drawing room, fine and decorative art, local and natural history, and costume. Temporary exhibitions held throughout the year. Disabled access to ground floor. Audio and large print guides available. Admission is free.

LAVANDULA QUALITY CRAFTS

88 Bank Street, Rawtenstall, Lancashire BB4 8EG
Tel: 01706 830718
e-mail: enquiries@lavandula.com
website: www.lavandulauk.com

Attractive corner premises in the centre of town are the home of **Lavandula Quality Crafts**, providing one more reason for visiting this interesting old cotton town. Shirley Brayford and her daughter-in-law Lisa, both with a fine natural artistic talent, represent two generations of the spectrum of arts and crafts; Shirley is well known throughout the UK and has been in the 'making' business for many years. Much of the top-quality giftware, produced by hand in their own workshop, uses lavender as its base, and the range includes sleep pillows and pomanders, bags and bell-pulls, cushions and lavender bunches.

Also on display in the glass cabinets, on the pine dressers, on the counters and on the walls are branded contemporary gifts such as jewellery, pewter and bridal arrangements. The owners are particularly friendly and helpful, and the aromas of oils and lavender that pervade the shop area make it an even more pleasant and civilised place for browsing. Even the gift-wrapping materials are made on the premises, and anyone lucky enough to receive a gift from Lavandula actually has two gifts - the present and the wrapping are both works of art!

Heywood via Bury and Ramsbottom. The railway also operates regular Red Rose Diner trains with Pullman style dining cars offering travellers a gourmet meal and an evening of pure nostalgia.

Rawtenstall itself is noted for having whay could be the only remaining temperance bar in Britain – Herbal Health on Bank Street which serves traditional drinks such as sarsaparilla or dandelion & burdock.

At Rawtenstall, you can join the **Irwell Sculpture Trail**, the largest public art trail in the United Kingdom. New sculptures are appearing all the time and more than 50 regional, national and international artists are being commissioned to produce sculptures

---

HELMSHORE TEXTILE MUSEUM

Holcombe Road, Rossendale,
Lancashire BB4 4NP
Tel: 01706 226459

An 18th Century water powered fulling mill and a Victorian cotton spinning mill, both in working order on one site. Newly designated as a museum with a collection of outstanding national importance, this museum has recently developed an interactive gallery for families on the history of the Lancashire cotton industry. Spinning mules, water wheel, an original Arkwright's Water Frame and other machinery dating from the Industrial Revolution can also be seen. Easily reached from Junction 5 of M65 (Haslingden) or from end of M66. Open from Easter to October every afternoon, closed Saturdays.

---

with an environmental theme. The Trail follows a well-established 30-mile footpath stretching from Salford Quays through Bury into Rossendale and on up to the Pennine Moors.

HELMSHORE

8 miles S of Burnley on the B6214

This small town still retains much evidence of the early Lancashire cotton industry and, housed in an old cotton mill, are the **Helmshore Textile Museums** (see panel opposite). The building dates from 1789 and was one of the first fulling mills to be built in the Rossendale area. The two working mills are packed with national textile treasures, and in the new 'Revolution' Gallery visitors can have fun with fibres and fabrics, follow the lives of the Weaver family, trace the history of Lancashire's textile industry and meet the great Lancashire inventors - Arkwright, Kay, Hargreaves and Crompton.

CRAWSHAWBOOTH

5 miles SW of Burnley on the A682

Once an important settlement in the old hunting forest of Rossendale, the village's oldest house, Swinshaw Hall (now privately owned), is said to have played a part in the destruction of the last wild boar in England. The influence of non-conformists can also still be seen in the village, where a number made their home, in the old **Quaker Meeting House** dating from 1716.

BLACKBURN

The largest town in East Lancashire, Blackburn is notable for its modern shopping malls, its celebrated three-day market, its modern cathedral, and Thwaites Brewery, one of the biggest

NORTHCOTE MANOR

Northcote Road, Langho, Nr Blackburn,
Lancashire BB6 8BE
Tel: 01254 240555 Fax: 01254 246568
e-mail: sales@northcotemanor.com
website: www.northcotemanor.com

1983 saw the arrival of Craig Bancroft and Nigel Haworth at **Northcote Manor**, and 20 years on their late Victorian country house hotel in the lovely Ribble Valley remains top of the tree as a place to stay and as a fine dining destination. Fourteen spacious, beautifully furnished en suite bedrooms, each with its own style and personality, display the obvious pride and attention to detail which have always been behind the owners' philosophy of warm, friendly and sincere hospitality.

That attention to detail is very much to the fore in the Manor's kitchen, where multi-award winning Nigel Haworth and his brigade bring skill, finesse and innovation to top-quality Lancashire ingredients to produce meals that are never less than superb. Nigel's memorable Lancashire hotpot uses heather-fed free-range Bowland lamb, slow-cooked in the Aga and served with oyster fritters, pickled red cabbage and glazed carrots. Black pudding and buttered pink trout with a mustard and watercress sauce, and apple crumble with a Lancashire cheese parfait are other locally inspired dishes, while inspiration comes from further afield in delights such as sushi-style smoked salmon or Italian-style air-dried bresaola. Craig's passion is wine, and his worldwide 400-bin list includes a fabulous range of half-bottles. The Terrace Room is a superb venue for private fine dining or corporate entertainment.

independent brewers of real ale in the north of England. Hard though it may be to imagine today, at the height of the textile industry, Blackburn was the biggest weaving town in the world. At that time there were 120 mills in operation, their multiple chimneys belching out soot and smoke.

In 1931, the town received arguably its most influential visitor when Mahatma Gandhi toured the area on a study trip of Lancashire's textile manufacture. Examples of the early machines, including James Hargreaves' Spinning Jenny and his carding machine, invented in 1760, can be seen at the **Lewis Textile Museum**, which is dedicated to the industry. The town's **Museum and Art Gallery** has, among its treasures, several paintings by Turner, the Hart collection of medieval manuscripts, and the finest collection of Eastern European icons in Britain.

Much of the town seen today was built on the prosperity brought by the cotton trade, a fact symbolized on the dome of **St John's Church** (1789) where there's a weathervane in the shape of a weaving shuttle.

The town's old manor house, Witton House, has long since been demolished but the grounds have been turned into an excellent local amenity. The 480 acres of **Witton Country Park** contain nature trails through woodlands up on to heather covered hill tops. The Visitor Centre, in the restored stable block, includes the British Small Mammal Collection and a tea room. Closer to the town centre, the 60-acre **Corporation**

Park is one of the county's most attractive urban parks.

AROUND BLACKBURN

HOGHTON
4 miles W of Blackburn on the A675

Originally a collection of hamlets with handloom weavers' cottages, the village was, during the 17th century, a place where Roman Catholics still practiced their faith in defiance of the law. It was at **Arrowsmith House** that Edmund Arrowsmith said his last mass before being captured and sentenced to death for being a Catholic priest and a Jesuit.

It is however, today, best known as the home of Lancashire's only true baronial residence **Hoghton Tower** which dates from 1565. The de Hoghton family have owned the land in this area since the time of the Norman Conquest and the house was built in a style in keeping with their social position and importance. The famous banqueting hall, on the ground floor, is where James I is said to have knighted the Sir Loin of Beef in 1617. Another famous visitor was William Shakespeare, who came to

perform with William Hoghton's troupe of players. The grounds, too, are well worth a visit as they are as perfectly preserved as the house.

BRINDLE
5 miles SW of Blackburn on the B6256

An ancient village itself, Brindle's **St James' Church** celebrated its 800th anniversary in 1990. The church was originally dedicated to St Helen, the patron saint of wells. 'Bryn' is the Old English word for a spring and there are still numerous springs in the village.

WITHNELL FOLD
5 miles SW of Blackburn off the A674

A short walk from Brindle, crossing the Leeds and Liverpool Canal, is the village of Withnell Fold whose name comes from 'withy knool' – a wooded hill. It was developed as a model village in the 1840s with 35 terraced cottages, each with its own garden.

The whole village was owned by the Parke family who also owned the cotton mills and paper mill for whose workers the houses were provided. The mills have long since closed but the old mill chimney still towers above the village.

Withnell Fold does have a small claim to fame: the paper mill, built in 1844 overlooking the canal, was once the world's biggest exporter of high-quality banknote paper.

TOCKHOLES
3 miles SW of Blackburn off the A666

This interesting textile village was once an isolated centre of nonconformism. Standing next to a row of

Hoghton Tower

cottages is the **United Reformed Chapel**, founded in 1662, though it has been rebuilt twice, in 1710 and in 1880. The **Parish Church** also has some unusual features. As well as the unique lance-shaped windows, there is an outdoor pulpit dating from the days when the whole congregation could not fit inside the building. Close to the pulpit is the grave of John Osbaldeston, the inventor of the weft fork, a gadget that allowed power looms to weave intricate patterns.

Just to the south of the village lies **Roddlesworth Nature Trail**, a path that follows the line of an old coach drive. Along the trail, for which details can be obtained at the information centre, can be found the ruins of **Hollinshead Hall**, built in the 18th century and once very grand. The ruins were tidied up in the early 1990s but, fortunately, the wishing well has withstood the ravages of time and neglect. Reminiscent of a small Georgian chapel, the well inside dates back to medieval times when its waters were thought to cure eye complaints.

DARWEN

3 miles S of Blackburn on the A666

Dominating the town from the west and situated high on Darwen Moor stands **Darwen Tower**, built to commemorate the Diamond Jubilee of Queen Victoria in 1897. The view from the top of the tower, which is always open, is enhanced by the height of the hill on which it stands (1,225 feet) and with the help of the plaques at the top much of the Lancashire landscape, and beyond, can be identified.

A striking landmark, very visible from the tower, and standing in the heart of Darwen is the chimney of the **India Mill**. Constructed out of hand-made bricks, it was built to resemble the campanile in St

Mark's Square, Venice.

To the west of Darwen lies **Sunnyhurst Wood** and visitor centre in the valley of a gentle brook that originates on Darwen Moor to the south. Acquired by public subscription in 1902 to commemorate the coronation of Edward VII this area of woodland, covering some 85 acres, is rich in both bird and plant life.

THE RIBBLE VALLEY

A dramatic contrast of stark fellsides flecked with woolly sheep, and valleys green with woodland and lush pastures grazed by obviously contented sheep. It's not the conventional image of Lancashire as half Blackpool, half industrial, because the Ribble Valley is the county's best-kept secret – 150 square miles of peaceful countryside, almost two-thirds of it designated as Areas of Outstanding Natural Beauty.

The best overview of this beautiful area can be enjoyed by walking or driving along **Longridge Fell**. Within the space of a few miles, huge vistas unfold, not just of the Ribble Valley from Pendle Hill to Preston but also of the Fylde Plain, the Loud and Hodder valleys, and the Forest of Bowland. This is captivating countryside so it's no wonder that, according to one of her biographers, the Queen herself has divulged that she would like to retire to this region of rural Lancashire.

Flowing between the Forest of Bowland in the north and the hill country of Pendle in the south, the River Ribble cuts a pleasant and green course along a narrow valley. The **Ribble Way** middle-distance footpath follows the full 70 miles of the river, from its source at Ribblehead in North Yorkshire to the flat, tidal marshes of its estuary west of Preston.

A beautiful, unspoilt yet small area, the

Ribble Valley has long been a favourite with the people of Lancashire. Not only is it easily accessible but there are numerous gentle walks in the sheltered valley and a wealth of wildlife is supported by the lush countryside. It is also a place of pretty villages which, even in the 21st century, remain almost unspoilt.

The central point of the valley is Clitheroe, a typical ancient Lancashire market town that clusters around one of the smallest Norman castles in the country. The Normans were not the first invaders to built a fortification in the valley: further down stream lies Ribchester and the Roman fort of Bremetannacum. Up river from Clitheroe lies Sawley and another interesting ruin. The Cistercian monks of Fountains Abbey founded the religious house here in the 13th century and their influence in the area of agriculture can still be seen in the surrounding fields.

The valley is also home to two great houses. The first, Stonyhurst, was originally the home of the Shireburn family and is now the world famous Roman Catholic public school. The second, on the outskirts of Preston, is Salmesbury Hall, a wonderful 14th century house that is now a Mecca for antiques collectors.

Finally, at the mouth of the river lies Preston, the county's administrative centre and a town with more to offer than first appearances would suggest.

PRESTON

'Proud Preston' is the largest city in the county and its administrative centre. It's 'Proud' because it was the first town in the county to receive a borough charter (in 1179), the first borough in which every male over 21 had a vote in parliamentary elections (1798), the first town outside London to light its streets with gas lamps (1816), and in 1958 the Preston bypass was the first stretch of motorway to be built in Britain. Civic pride was fostered even more by Preston's elevation in 2002 to the status of a city, one of only six in the UK so honoured to mark the Queen's Diamond Jubilee. Around the same time, multi-million pound plans were announced to redevelop the City Centre.

During the 19th century, Preston became a 'town of spires' as the evenly-split Protestant and Roman Catholic communities vied to build the most splendid churches. The palm is usually awarded to the Catholic St Walburge's Church whose slender 300ft steeple is the third tallest in England.

In Victorian times, Preston was a major cotton-weaving centre. The mill owners' ruthless exploitation of the cotton workers provoked a major strike in 1854 and the bitter confrontation attracted the attention of Charles Dickens. He had already started to write a novel

Preston School of Art

highlighting the degrading conditions and pitiful wages imposed on industrial workers by outrageously wealthy mill owners. He came to Preston, staying at the Bull and Royal Hotel in Church Street, and his first-hand observations of the unacceptable face of Victorian capitalism displayed in that conflict were embodied in the grimmest novel he ever wrote, *Hard Times*. Many of Preston's old red-brick mills still stand, although now converted to a variety of imaginative uses.

Lancaster may enjoy the distinction of being the elegant county town, but Preston revels in its role as Lancashire's administrative centre – always busy, enterprising, forward-looking but still proud of a historical legacy that stretches back to Roman times. The port activity may have declined but the dockland area, now called Riversway, has become an area of regeneration with a marina

catering for pleasure craft, yachts, and windsurfers. The complex forms part of the recently opened **Millennium Ribble Link** which forms a 3 mile long linear waterpark providing opportunities for walking, angling, cycling and boating as well as a newly commissioned sculpture trail. The Link is an important area for birds and insects and a natural habitat for a wide variety of fish, including roach, perch, flounders and eels. Also in Riversway and due to open in 2004 is the **Ribble Steam Railway Museum.**

A popular annual event is the Easter Egg Rolling event held in **Avenham Park**, one of the city's two splendid Victorian parks; its many attractive features include the riverside Ribble Walk and a Japanese garden with many unusual ornamental plants. The other is the adjacent **Miller Park**, noted for its impressive floral displays and an elaborately designed fountain with four

DIZZY DUCKS

1 Station Road, Wrea Green, Preston,
Lancashire PR4 2PH
Tel: 01772 468675

In the 1950's this was a bakery and tea room, then a grocer's store, and in 2002 along came two enthusiastic ladies and hey presto! **Dizzy Ducks** restaurant was born. The outside of the stone building is adorned with flowers, and inside the scene is set by attractive wooden furniture (some pieces are for sale) and the works of local photographers and artists (also for sale). The main menu

offers soup, jacket potatoes, omelettes, panini, super sandwiches and savoury tarts, and a blackboard lists daily changing specials such as ciabatta melt, chicken pie and a goat's cheese and basil quiche.

To accompany the fresh, tasty food are teas, coffees, cold drinks, house wines and Stella Artois. Theme evenings – French, Italian, Oriental, Pudding Club – are a regular feature, and Dizzy Ducks also provides takeaway and catering services. Why Dizzy Ducks? Marie Gaskell and Wendy McPherson are both bright, bubbly blondes and Dizzy was a name given to them by their husbands. Ducks, from the inhabitants of the nearby village pond. Dizzy Ducks, a non-smoking establishment, is located just off the main square in the centre of the village, which lies just south of the main A583 in countryside between Blackpool and Preston.

figures emblematic of Earth, Air, Fire and Water. Standing watch over the park is an imposing statue of Edward Stanley, 14th Earl of Derby, unveiled in 1873 before a crowd of over 40,000.

Preston featured in the *Domesday Book* although at that time it was known as Priest-town and, in the 1260s, the Greyfriars settled here. The Catholic traditions of Preston continued, as they did elsewhere in the county, and this has, along with the associated loyalty to the crown, had a great part to play in the town's history. During the Civil War it was the Battle of Preston in 1648 which confirmed the eventual defeat of the supporters of Charles I. Later, at the time of the 1745 Jacobite rebellion, Preston played host to Prince Charles Edward, Bonnie Prince Charlie.

The many public buildings of Preston all reflect the prosperity of the town during the Victorian age. This wealth was built upon the textile industry helped by the general location of the town: midway between London and Glasgow, on a major railway route, and with extensive docks. Though the town's prosperity was built on cotton, textiles were not new to Preston as linen had been produced here from as far back as Tudor times. Preston was also the place where, in 1768, the single most important machine of the textile industry was invented: Richard Arkwright's water-frame cotton spinning machine. Almost overnight, the cottage industries of spinning and handloom weaving were moved from the workers' homes into factories and the entrepreneurs of Preston were quicker than most to catch on. One gentleman in particular, John Horrocks, saw the potential of combining the spinning and weaving operations under the same roof and so he was able to take raw cotton in

and produce the finished article on delivery. His firm became the largest of its kind in the world, further adding to the town's prosperity.

Looking at the city now it is hard to imagine those hectic days and may be even hard to believe that when the docks were completed here in 1892, Preston was the second largest container handling port in Britain. In 1900, 1,285 vessels carrying nearly half a million tons of cargo entered and left the port. Unfortunately, the battle of keeping the channel open and free of silt became too expensive, particularly as trade was lost to other, non-tidal ports, and the docks eventually closed.

One of the best places to start any exploration of the city is the **Harris Museum and Art Gallery**. Housed in a magnificent neoclassical building, which dominates the Market Square, the museum and art gallery were opened in 1893. Funded by a successful local businessman and reminiscent of the British Museum, as well as the fine collection of paintings and watercolours by major 19th century British artists, there is an excellent exhibition of the story of Preston. **The Queen's Lancashire Regiment Museum** tells the compelling story of the Lancashire soldier through displays, archives, documents and regimental collections. The museum incorporates the collections and archives of the East Lancashire Regiment, the South Lancashire Regiment, the Loyal Regiment, the Lancashire Regiment, Militia, Volunteers and Territorials. Items in the Fulwood Barracks, which were built in 1848 of Longridge stone, include the famous silver mounted Maida Tortoise, items connected with General Wolfe, souvenirs from the Crimea War, and artefacts from the Defence of Kimberley, the diamond

town in South Africa, which the 1st Battalion the Loyals defended without assistance from any other troops.

Preston's Guild Hall, built in 1972 to celebrate that year's Guild, is known, or at least its interior is, to many snooker and bowls fans since it is the venue for the UK Snooker and the World Indoor Bowls Championships. Another building, less well-known but still a distinctive landmark is **Preston Prison**. Built in 1789, it replaced the town's first House of Correction. In an interesting move to provide the inmates with work, during the 19th century looms were installed in the prison and the prisoners were paid for their labour. Industrial unrest in the area soon followed and, in 1837, it was only the threat of a cannon which saved the prison from invasion by an angry mob intent on destroying the machines. Although the prison was closed in 1931, it re-opened in 1948 and remains so.

As might be expected for a city on the banks of a river, there are many bridges, but two crossings are particularly worthy of note. **Penwortham Old Bridge** is perhaps the most attractive in Lancashire; slightly hump-backed and built of a mixture of stone. Constructed chiefly of buff gritstone and pink sandstone in 1756, it replaced a bridge that had collapsed. By 1912 traffic had increased to such an extent that its use by motor cars and heavy carts was prohibited. For over 150 years, the bridge was the lowest crossing of the River Ribble. By contrast, the **Ribble Viaduct** is a completely different structure. One of the oldest works of railway engineering in the area and a construction of great elegance and dignity, it was built in 1838 and brought the railway from Wigan to the centre of Preston. The Preston Junction Local Nature Reserve, a section of the former Walton Junction-Preston line of the Lancashire & Yorkshire Railway, is now a haven for wildlife, with habitats for butterflies, birds and other creatures, as well as many plants and flowers.

Located on the northern outskirts of the city is one of Preston's most popular visitor attractions, the **National Football Museum**. This contains a huge variety of football-related items, including the official FIFA collection, films and several lively interactive displays. One of the displays gives the visitor access to every League ground in the England.

AROUND PRESTON

SALMESBURY
4 miles E of Preston on the A59

To the east of the village, close to the busy A59, lies **Salmesbury Hall**, built by

Salmesbury Hall

the Southworth family. The hall seen today, an attractive black and white timbered manor house, is actually the second house they built since their original hall was burned to the ground by Robert the Bruce in the early 14th century. Thinking that the original position, close to a crossing of the River Ribble was too vulnerable to attack, the family built their subsequent home in what was then an isolated location.

More peaceful times followed and the hall, surrounded by a moat and with a drawbridge, was a reflection of the family's wealth. A staunchly Catholic family, their 15th century chapel contains a Gothic mullion window that was rescued from Whalley Abbey after the Dissolution in the 1530s. However, it was the loyalty to their faith that finally saw

the demise of the Southworth family. Their continued practice of Catholicism saw Sir John Southworth imprisoned in Manchester in the late 16th century and, by the time of his death a few years later, the family, having kept their faith, had seen their fortune dwindle away.

The hall was sold to the Braddyll family who, having a house near Ulverston, simply stripped Salmesbury Hall of its assets. Somehow the hall survived but by the 1870s it was in a shocking state of repair. First, Joseph Harrison stepped in and began a successful restoration programme, to the point where he was able to entertain the likes of Charles Dickens. However, the building work took all his money and, facing ruin, Harrison committed suicide. By 1925, the hall was once again in a

Nora's Tearooms

27 Church Street, Ribchester, Lancashire PR3 3YE
Tel: 01254 878397

Nora's Tearooms are located in an attractive period building in the picturesque village of Ribchester. The interior is a charming mix of cottagey and Edwardian, and soft music adds to the very civilised atmosphere in which to enjoy excellent home baking and hot and cold light snacks accompanied by coffee or speciality teas. The walls of the tearooms are adorned with old family photographs and paintings by local artists, and many local craft items are on display and for sale. Tables are set outside in fine weather, and ice creams are sold from a separate little stone building.

What is now Nora's was originally the family home of Simon and his mother Nora Livesley. Simon recently

opened the house as a tearoom and craft shop and runs it along with his wife Cheryl and son Robert. The tearooms are open from 10.30 to 5 Tuesday to Sunday and also on Bank Holidays, and they provide a pleasant and refreshing interlude in a visit to Ribchester, a village on the banks of the River Ribble that is best known for its Roman fort.

dilapidated condition and was only saved from demolition by a timber merchant by the efforts of the Salmesbury Hall Trust, a group that is still managing the property today. The hall's unusual history is only equalled by the unconventional manner in which it, quite literally, earns its keep. With no assets left, after being stripped by the Braddylls, the hall is once again full of antiques but these are all for sale. As salerooms go, this has to be one of the most atmospheric in the country.

RIBCHESTER
8 miles NE of Preston on the B5269

Situated on the banks of the River Ribble, the village is famous for its **Roman Fort**, Bremetannacum, on the northern river bank. It was the Roman governor, Gnaeus Julius Agricola, in AD 79, who first established a fort here at the junction of the two important roads between Manchester and Carlisle, and York and the west coast. Although little of the fort's walls remain, the granary or storehouse, with its hypocaust (underfloor heating), has been excavated and has revealed some interesting coins, pottery, sculptures, and inscriptions.

The fort's **Roman Museum** is designed to transport visitors back to the days of the Roman occupation and it offers an excellent insight into those times. Unfortunately, the finest artefact found on the site, an ornate cavalry parade helmet, is not on display here (though they do have a replica) – the original can be seen in the British Museum in London. The Museum, which opened in 1914 to house the Roman finds from Ribchester, has recently been improved with the introduction of exciting new interactive displays.

Back in the village proper, the discovery of some pre Norman Conquest crosses in and around **St Wilfrid's Church** would suggest that this 13th century building occupies the site of a Saxon church. The church is named after the first Bishop of Ripon, who in the 7th century took a prominent role in the Synod of Whitby. This would seem to confirm the earlier buildings existence in the absence of any direct evidence.

CLITHEROE

Perhaps the most appealing little market town in Lancashire, Clitheroe nestles around its miniature Norman castle. The town has a reputation for high quality specialist shops acclaimed for their

Edisford Bridge, Clitheroe

individuality, some of which have gained international recognition: establishments such as Cowman's Sausage Shop in Castle Street which offers 58 different varieties of sausage, among them Welsh pork & leek, venison and wild boar. Fifty-nine varieties if you count his special Christmas sausage, only available during the festive season and containing exotic ingredients such as port, juniper berries and ground almonds. As with the French, traditional Lancashire meat cuisine wastes no part of the animal. Black pudding, tripe and onions, chitterlings, lamb's fry and sweetbreads are dishes that can still be found here although, apart from the first they are rarely seen in southern England.

The **Platform Gallery**, housed in a refurbished railway station of 1870, is well worth a visit. The Gallery presents a regularly changing programme of visual art exhibitions – paintings and prints, textiles, glassware, ceramics, jewellery, papier maché and baskets, with the majority of the work on show produced by regionally based artists. Clitheroe has a sculpture trail leading from Brungerley Bridge to Crosshill Quarry. It was begun in 1993 by Thompson Dagnall, who worked on this commission in the Ribble Valley for seven months. His main sculpture, *Saving Sheep*, portrays a shepherd rescuing a sheep from the swelling river's current. It stands on the site of Victorian bathing huts.

Clitheroe received its first charter in 1147 and ever since then has served the surrounding villages of the Ribble Valley as their market town. Like Lancaster, it too is dominated by an 800-year-old **Castle**. Today only the Keep remains, the second smallest in England and one of the oldest stone structures in Lancashire. According to local legend, the large hole in the keep's east wall was the work of

the Devil who threw a large boulder from the summit of nearby Pendle Hill. Boring historians say it was Oliver Cromwell's troops who inflicted the damage.

Standing close to the castle is **Clitheroe Castle Museum**, home to many exhibits and displays reflecting the history and geology of the Ribble Valley area. Archaeological finds illustrate life in the valley from the earliest days and in this section too can be seen the famous Hacking ferryboat now restored to its former glory. Closer to the present day is the re-creation of an Edwardian kitchen, complete with its unique sound system that brings this turn of the century room to life.

A short walk from the Castle Museum stands the parish **Church of St Mary Magdalen** which, though it was rebuilt by the Victorians, was founded in the 13th century. At that time the town also had a school; however, the present Royal Grammar School was not established until 1554. The school's official charter, granted by Mary Tudor but lost for many years, was eventually found in the vaults of a local solicitor's office in 1990.

The town's narrow, winding streets are full of character and charm and amidst the ancient buildings is the rather incongruous 'The Grand' cinema. Built in the 1920s, this unspoilt monument to the golden days of the silver screen is still lined with plush velvet, has retained its grand piano that was used to accompany the silent films, and remains the town's cinema.

Just outside the town can be found **Edisford Picnic Area**, a popular place for family outings that stands on the site of a battle ground where the Scots fought the Normans. Also near Clitheroe, at **Brungerley**, are a set of stepping stones across the river that are said to be haunted. Apparently the evil

spirit living in the water drags a traveller to his watery death every seven years.

There are few grand houses in the Ribble Valley open to the public, but **Browsholme Hall** near Clitheroe is open at certain times in the summer. Dating back to the early 1500s, the Hall has been the family home of the Parkers for 600 years and there's a special pleasure in being shown around the house by a member of the family. The Parkers took their name from the family's hereditary role in medieval times as keepers of the deer park in the royal hunting ground of the Forest of Bowland.

AROUND CLITHEROE

WEST BRADFORD
1 mile N of Clitheroe off the B6478

This tucked away village, just south of the Forest of Bowland, was mentioned in the *Domesday Book* and there are records of some villagers paying the first poll tax levied by Richard II in 1379. The old part of the village is set around a green bordering the River Ribble. It's a pleasant spot with a stream running alongside the road through the bottom half of West Bradford and access to the houses bordering the beck is made by crossing a quaint stone bridge.

DOWNHAM
3 miles NE of Clitheroe off the A59

Some 40-odd villages are sprinkled along the banks of the Ribble Valley, all of them built in the appealing local stone. One of the prettiest is Downham, renowned as the setting for the cinema classic *Whistle Down the Wind*. The village also provides location scenes for BBC-TV's period drama series *Born & Bred*. Thanks for Downham's unspoilt appearance must go to the Assheton family, which has owned the whole

Downham Village

Although during the reigns Edward I and II the abbots of Sawley were called to the House of Lords, none of the abbots were men of note except, perhaps, William Trafford, the last head of the community. With his colleague and neighbour, the last Abbot of Whalley, Trafford took part in the Pilgrimage of Grace in 1536 and, for his part in the failed uprising, was taken prisoner. Tried for treason at Lancaster in 1537, Trafford, with others like him, was found guilty and executed.

Although little of the abbey remains – much of the stone was cannibalised for village buildings – the site is wonderfully quiet and peaceful and well worth a visit.

village since 1558 – the same year in which they acquired Whalley Abbey. It was the present Lord Clitheroe's grandfather who paid for the electricity supply cables to be laid underground back in the 1930s and the present squire, Lord Clitheroe of Downham still refuses to permit the skyline to be spoilt by television aerials, satellite dishes, and even dormer windows.

SAWLEY
4 miles N of Clitheroe off the A59

At the centre of this historic village, easily missed as the main road by-passes it, are the slight remains of **Sawley Abbey**, founded in the 13th century by the Cistercian monks of Fountains Abbey. As well as building their religious house, the monks had great influence over the whole of the surrounding area. Clearing their immediate surroundings, the monks cultivated the land and their ridge and furrow patterns can still be made out in the fields.

RIMINGTON
5 miles NE of Clitheroe off the A59

This small hillside village has twice won Lancashire's Best Kept Village competition. Its name means 'farmstead on the boundary' and as the Lancashire/Yorkshire boundary has changed over the years the village has been transferred from one county to the other. The most recent transfer was made in 1974 when people who had been Yorkshire born and bred suddenly found themselves Lancastrians. This pleasant rural village was the home of Francis Duckworth, the distinguished composer of hymn tunes, including one he named *Rimington*. His parents ran the village post office and shop next door to the Methodist chapel and a plaque on the chapel, now a private house, commemorates him.

GISBURN

7 miles NE of Clitheroe on the A59

Like Rimington, this village was also once in Yorkshire and, as many locals would like to believe, still is! One of the Ribble Valley's most pleasant and picturesque villages, Gisburn's history is dominated by the Lister family who, from humble beginnings rose to become the Lords of Ribblesdale. Their house, built in the early 17th century in Gisburn Park, is still standing though it is now a private hospital. Over the years, many people were given shelter by the family and, in 1648, Cromwell is said to have rested at the house while on his way to fight at Preston.

PAYTHORNE

10 miles NE of Clitheroe off the A682

Although the source of the River Ribble lies to the north in Yorkshire, near the famous Three Peaks of Whernside, Ingleborough, and Pen-y-ghent, this village is the first on its banks on this side of the county boundary. It also marks the end of the river's journey through the rugged limestone scenery of moorlands and the start of its picturesque course through a lush green valley.

BARNOLDSWICK

10 miles NE of Clitheroe on the B6251

If you approach this former cotton town from the south, off the A56, you may wonder why the road is so straight. The answer is that it was specially constructed in the 1930s to service the new Rolls Royce factory in the town. The B in the names of jet engines such as the RB211 stands for Barnoldswick.

At the western end of the town is **Bancroft Mill Engine Museum**. The mill was the last weaving shed to be built in Lancashire and started cotton weaving in 1920. The mill closed in 1978 but the

grand 600hp cross-compound steam engine was preserved and there are regular demonstrations of it in action. The museum also displays tools and documents connected with the weaving industry. This is the highest point of the Leeds/Liverpool Canal and features three locks at Greenberfield Locks.

WADDINGTON

2 miles NW of Clitheroe on the B6478

This is one of the area's best known villages – its attractive Coronation Gardens have appeared on many postcards and even on biscuit tin lids. King Henry VI spent a whole year here in 1464/5, not because he particularly appreciated its charms but because he was hiding at Waddington Hall from the Yorkists who had defeated him at the Battle of Hexham. When his hiding place was discovered he escaped by a secret tunnel that led from the Hall's dining room but he was quickly captured at Brungerley Bridge, down river near Clitheroe, then imprisoned in the Tower of London where he died in 1471.

Waddington has several times won first prize in Lancashire's Best Kept Village competition and it's easy to see why. Waddington Brook splashes the length of the village and 18th century almshouses cluster around the green.

About ten years ago Waddington's villagers enjoyed a certain amount of fame when, for the sake of a television series, they agreed to renounce their TVs for a whole month. This cold turkey treatment proved too much for some and they had to be resuscitated by having their sets returned.

GREAT MITTON

3 miles SW of Clitheroe on the B6246

Standing opposite the Three Fishes Hotel, which takes its name from the

three fishes on the Whalley Abbey coat of arms, is the attractive **All Hallows' Church**. Housing some of the finest relics to be seen in any British church, this is most certainly worth a visit. Built in around 1270, though undoubtedly there was a wooden Saxon structure hereabouts, little has been done to the building since, although a tower was added in 1438 and the pews are Jacobean. However, it is the Shireburn Chapel that draws most visitors to the church. It was added in 1440 by the Shireburn family of Stonyhurst who claimed to be the direct descendants of the first rector, Ralph the Red of Mytton. The family tombs here are regarded as the best in the county. One of the earliest is the fine alabaster tomb of Sir Richard Shireburn (who died in 1594) and his wife Maude who is dressed in capacious petticoats. The latest is of another Richard who died in 1702 at the age of 9 after eating poisonous berries. Following the fashion of the time the monument displays copious macabre items – a skull, hour glass, sickle, more bones than seem necessary and, emerging from the ground, two skeletal hands.

HURST GREEN
5 miles SW of Clitheroe on the B6243

This pretty village of stone-built cottages nestling in the Ribble Valley is best known for its nearby public school. **Stonyhurst College**, the world famous Roman Catholic school, began life as the residence of the local lords of the manor. The present building, begun in around 1523, was the work of Hugh Shireburn although additions were made in 1592 by Sir Richard Shireburn. The core of this imposing building set beside a lake is late-Elizabethan but there have been major additions almost every century, all of them blending remarkably well with their predecessors.

Sir Richard Shireburn was an ambitious man who served the Tudor monarchy well. As well as being the Chief Forester of Bowland he was also one of Henry VIII's commissioners studying the state of the monasteries. He was an eager participant in the suppression of Whalley Abbey. Though the family publicly adopted the new Protestant religion under Elizabeth I, it was with little enthusiasm and in a short time the Shireburn family, like many other Lancashire families, returned to their Catholic faith. It seems strange then that Cromwell, on his way to and from the Battle of Preston, should take shelter at Stonyhurst although rumour has it that the ardent Puritan slept with a pistol at his side and his guards around him.

In 1794, after the house had been left for some considerable time and had fallen into a state of disrepair, the owner, Thomas Weld, offered the property to the Jesuits who had set up an English Catholic School in Flanders. Unwelcome in France following the revolution, the Jesuits gladly accepted and after restoring the original building they extended it during the 19th century. Their finest addition must be the replica of King's College in Cambridge: **St Peter's Church** was built in 1835 and contains many treasures including a 7th century copy of St John's Gospel and a cope of Henry II that was used by Henry VIII at the battle of the Field of the Cloth of Gold. One of the college's most famous sons was Sir Arthur Conan Doyle, the creator of Sherlock Holmes, and the Conan Doyle desk (into which he carved his name) is one of many artefacts on show when the college is open for tours on some days in the summer holidays. Visitors have the opportunity to see the chapels and historic room including the Great Hall with portraits of the seven former pupils

awarded the Victoria Cross, and the table on which Oliver Cromwell is reputed to have slept on the eve of the Battle of Preston in 1648. The Gardens enjoy scenic views over the Ribble Valley countryside.

STYDD

7 miles SW of Clitheroe off the B6245

Just to the north of Ribchester lies the small hamlet of Stydd. All that remains of the monastery founded here by the Knights Hospitallers of St John of Jerusalem is the Norman **Chapel**, standing alone surrounded by meadows. It contains effigies of some of the knights. A crusading and military order established in 1113, the Knights Hospitallers provided help and assistance to pilgrims travelling to the Holy Land. Their commandery, as their religious houses were called, at Stydd was dissolved by the mid 14th century and, although at one time there were over 50 of their small monasteries in the country, only 15 survived to the 1530s.

LONGRIDGE

10 miles SW of Clitheroe on the B6243

After Clitheroe, bustling Longridge is the only other town of any size in the area. Like Clitheroe it offers a good selection of independently owned shops along with a range of antique galleries, and is widely known for its Lancashire Cheese Dairies.

The village lies at the foot of **Longridge Fell** from whose 1,150ft elevation, especially at Jeffrey Hill or Kemple End, there are superb views northwards over the Loud Valley to Chipping (see later in this chapter): to the south the land drops away towards the River Ribble. For many years this area was an important source of building stone and several of Preston's civic

buildings, including the Harris Library and Museum, and the docks at Liverpool were constructed with Longridge stone.

In the 1790s the stone was also used to build a row of 20 terraced cottages in Longridge – numbers 4 to 44 Higher Road, which now have listed building status. Known as **Club Row**, these mutually funded cottages are the earliest known example of properties built on the principles of a Building Society and have earned themselves an entry in the *Guinness Book of Records*.

GOOSNARGH

12 miles SW of Clitheroe on the B5269

Just to the west of the village lies **Chingle Hall**, a small moated manor house that was built in 1260 by Adam de Singleton. A Catholic family, the Singletons are said to have a chapel with three priest hides and, so the story goes, Cromwell once climbed down one of the hall's chimneys to spy on the Royalists below. As well as being the birthplace of St John Wall, one of the last priests to die for his faith, in 1620, it enjoys the reputation of being one of the most haunted houses in Britain and, as such, the hall has featured on countless television and radio programmes.

GRIMSARGH

11 miles W of Clitheroe on the B6243

As well as having one of the largest village greens in Lancashire, covering some 12 acres, Grimsargh is also home to **Tun Brook Wood**. Following the line of the brook until it meets the River Ribble, this is one of the largest areas of deciduous woodland in the country.

THE FYLDE

The Fylde derives its name from the Anglo-Saxon word 'gefilde' meaning

level, green fields, an apt description of this low-lying area that extends from Fleetwood in the north to Lytham St Annes in the south. It was once known as Windmill Land but nowadays windmills are few and far between. A notable exception is the striking example on the waterfront at Lytham. It was built in 1805, worked until 1929, and now houses a small museum.

This historic area of coastal Lancashire is known to many as the home of Blackpool: the brash, seaside resort that has been entertaining holidaymakers for generations. To the south lies another resort, Lytham St Annes, which is not only somewhat more genteel but also the home of one of the country's most well known golf courses and host to the British Open Championships. Both places grew up as a result of the expansion of the railway system in the Victorian age, when they were popular destinations for the mill workers of Lancashire and Yorkshire.

However, the Fylde is also an ancient region that was known to both the Saxons and the Romans. To the north of this region, around the Wyre estuary, the salt marshes have been exploited for over 2,000 years. Fishing and shipping, too, have been important sources of revenue here. Fleetwood is still a port though smaller than it was while, surprisingly though it might seem today, Lytham was also an important port along the Ribble Estuary.

Inland, the fertile, flat plain has been farmed for many centuries and, with few major roads, the quiet rural communities lie undisturbed and little changed by the 21st century. A haven for wildlife, and particularly birds and plants, the two estuaries, of the Ribble and the Wyre, provide habitats that abound with rare and endangered species of plants and birds. A relatively undiscovered region, the Fylde has much more to offer than a white knuckle ride and candy floss and is well worth taking the time to explore.

BLACKPOOL

Blackpool is unique to England just as Las Vegas is to the United States. Everyone is familiar with Blackpool's brash, warm-hearted attractions.

Today, Blackpool is the largest town in the present county of Lancashire. Little more than a fishing village among the sand dunes of the Fylde coast 150 years ago, Blackpool's huge expansion followed the arrival of the railway. Up until then, travel to and from the village involved considerable discomfort, taking a day from Manchester and two days from York. The great Victorian railway companies put Blackpool well and truly

Blackpool Tower

on the map by laying the railway lines right to the coast and building the grand stations – the town had three. The quiet fishing village was quickly transformed into a vibrant resort as day-trippers from the mill towns of Lancashire and Yorkshire took advantage of the cheap excursion rail fares. Local developers enthusiastically began creating new attractions for their visitors. The first pier was constructed in 1863, followed by two more over the next thirty years. A glass-domed Winter Gardens opened in 1878, and seven years later the town's electric tram system began operating, the first in the world. The Pleasure Beach with its permanent fairground rides and amusements arrived in 1896 with the aim of providing 'an American-style amusement park where adults could feel like children again'.

But the developers' real master-stroke was the construction of the world-famous **Blackpool Tower**. Modelled on the Eiffel Tower and completed in 1894, the Tower stands some 518 feet high, incorporates a Ballroom and Circus, both of which are decorated in a wonderfully over-the-top rococo style. The **Tower Ballroom** is a much loved institution where tea dances are still a regular feature. It was, for many years from the 1960s to the 1980s, the venue for BBC-TV's enormously popular *Come Dancing* competition. The Tower's centenary celebrations in 1994 were numerous and extravagant and included painting the Tower gold.

The introduction of the **Blackpool Illuminations** helped extend the summer season into autumn, and the late 20th century saw yet more visitor attractions added to the mix. **The Pleasure Beach** is an attraction that continues to be extended and improved. However, some of its delights are

Blackpool Pier

certainly not for the fainthearted. It not only boasts its own railway station, but also the tallest and fastest roller-coaster ride in Europe. In the summer of 2002 yet another seafront attraction was installed - the world's largest mirror ball. Weighing four and a half tons and 18 feet across, it is made up of 47,000 different pieces.

The Sandcastle is an all-weather indoor complex where visitors can enjoy waterslides, wave pools and water flumes in sub-tropical temperatures; and **The Sea Life Centre** provides close-up views of a wide range of marine creatures.

The **North Pier,** designed by Eugenius Birch, was opened at the beginning of the 1863 season. It soon became the place to promenade and is now a listed building. Eugenius Birch (1818-1884) was the most famous of all the pier

engineers; he was also a talented artist and mechanic and worked on railways and bridges in Britain and in India. The Blackpool pier was one of many Birch piers; others included Margate, Aberystwyth, Brighton West, Eastbourne, Hastings, Lytham and Plymouth - the last, opened in the year of his death.

Despite its reputation as a brash and lively resort, Blackpool also has its quiet, secluded corners where visitors can escape the hustle of the crowds. There are seven miles of sea front, from the North Shore down as far as Squire's Gate, where the pace of life is gentler and the beaches are quieter. **Blackpool Tramways** have provided a most enjoyable way of exploring these less busy sides of the town and its environs for many years. And it should also be remembered that the world's first electric street tram system opened here in 1885. The route was extended along the Lytham road in 1895 and later connecting with other routes in nearby Lytham and St Annes.

Still a popular means of transport here today, many of the tramcars date from the 1930s or 1950s and the managing company has a special selection of vintage cars which they run throughout the season. The now annual **Illuminations** which, following a ceremonial lighting much like that of the Christmas lights in London, is a splendid end to the season. An eagerly awaited free show, running the full length of the promenade, the lights have, over the years, provided many spectacular shows and incorporated many themes.

Blackpool offers more than seaside attractions: the Blackpool Countryside Experience is a series of nature walks from Stanley Park with its Italian garden and pleasure lake through the Woodland Gardens, around Heron's Reach and linking to **Marton Mere** bird sanctuary. This 10-acre lake is the year-round home for many geese, swans and ducks, and a temporary resting place for many more. Next to Stanley Park is **Blackpool Zoo**, home to over 400 animals from all round the world, including lions, tigers, elephants, gorillas, lemurs, exotic birds and creepie-crawlies.

AROUND BLACKPOOL

A short drive out of Blackpool, at Peel just off the A583, is **Penny Farm**, a recovery and rehabilitation centre run by the International League for the Protection of Horses. The site includes stabling for up to 28 horses, open-fronted barns where visitors can make friends with the horses, an exercise area and a visitor centre with a coffee shop and gift shop. Also run by the ILPH is a caravan and camping site adjacent to the farm.

THORNTON
5 miles N of Blackpool on the B5268

Situated in the west bank of the Wyre estuary, this small town is dominated by **Marsh Mill**, which stands over 100 feet high and was constructed in 1794. The grinding of corn ceased here soon after World War I but the building has been restored and it is now a tourist attraction.

At this point the Wyre estuary is wide and provides shelter for shipping, an advantage that was utilised by both the Romans and the Scandinavians. The **Wyre Estuary Country Park**, taking the whole estuary from Fleetwood up river as far as Shard Bridge, is an excellent place from which to discover the area. An initial stop at the **Wyreside Ecology Centre**, which provides all manner of

Marsh Mill

hardly surprising as the town began to grow after an architectural competition, organised in 1906, in which Sir Edwin Lutyens, the designer of modern Whitehall, London, was involved.

FLEETWOOD
8 miles N of Blackpool on the A587

Cleveleys in turn links up with Fleetwood which until 1836 was just a small fishing village. Local landowner Sir Peter Hesketh-Fleetwood decided to develop the area as a seaside resort and employed the leading architect, Decimus Burton, who had designed London's Regent Street as well as large parts of St Leonards on Sea and Hove.

Prior to the commencement of the building work in 1836, Fleetwood was a small settlement of a few fishermen's cottages. The opening of the railway extension from Preston to Fleetwood was a key player in the town's development and the impressive North Euston Hotel, which opened in 1842, reflects those railway links. Queen Victoria used Fleetwood as she travelled to Scotland for her annual holiday. However, this was all before the railway companies managed to lay a railway over Shap fell

information about the estuary, is a sensible starting point. From here a number of footpaths take in many of the places along the river as well as leading visitors through important areas of salt marsh which contain a wide range of plants, insects, and birds.

CLEVELEYS
5 miles N of Blackpool on the A584

This popular seaside resort is less boisterous than its neighbour, Blackpool, to the south and it is altogether more attractive – architecturally. This is

Fleetwood Harbour

in Cumbria in 1847 and thus provide a direct rail link to Scotland. Sir Peter was bankrupted but the town itself continued to flourish as a port and seaside resort.

The town's **Museum**, overlooking the River Wyre, illustrates the town's links with the fishing industry which suffered greatly from the Icelandic cod wars of the 1970s.

The town's most famous product is known around the world. In 1865, a local chemist named James Lofthouse created a compound of liquorice, capsicum, eucalyptus and methanol designed to relieve the sore throats and bronchial troubles endured by fishermen at sea. He called the mixture **Fisherman's Friend** and it was remarkably successful. The only problem was that the bottles in which it was sold frequently shattered in the rough Atlantic seas. So Lofthouse transformed the liquid into a lozenge which is still produced by his descendants and has enormous sales world-wide.

PREESALL
8 miles N of Blackpool on the B5270

The village's original name, Pressoude, as it was mentioned in the *Domesday Book*, is thought to mean a salt farm near the sea and certainly in 1872 rock salt deposits were discovered beneath the village. From then on, for around 30 years, Preesall became a centre for salt mining and in 1883 the Fleetwood Salt Company was established to develop the field. The bulk of the salt was extracted in the form of brine and by the end of 1891 there was a reliable pipeline pumping the salt under the River Wyre to Fleetwood. However, as much of the salt was extracted from underneath the expanding village, subsidence soon became a problem. In 1923 this led to the opening up of a huge pit, known locally as 'Bottomless' to the west of the village.

KNOTT END-ON-SEA
8 miles N of Blackpool on the B5270

This small coastal resort on the River Wyre estuary grew into a substantial fishing settlement in the 17th and 18th centuries. It was also a pilot base for the upstream ports of Wardleys and Skippool and later developed into a ferry port. Today its broad flat sands and bracing sea air, along with the decline in the fishing industry, have turned the town into a small, quiet holiday resort that is also favoured by those who have retired.

Looking out to sea, at low tide, a rocky outcrop can be seen which, some historians have suggested, is the remains of the masonry of a Roman harbour. Whether this is the port that in the 2nd century Ptolemy marked on a map as Portus Setantiorum is certainly in doubt but it is undeniable that such a building existed as the Romans were planning an invasion of Ireland from this stretch of coast.

PILLING
10 miles N of Blackpool off the A588

This quiet scattered village, on the edge of rich, fertile marshland, was for many years linked to the market town of Garstang by a little, winding, single-track railway known affectionately as the Pilling Pig because the train's whistle sounded like a pig having its throat cut. The last passengers were carried in 1930; the last goods train ran in 1950.

Said to be the second largest village in Britain, Pilling boasts no fewer than five churches. One of them, **Old St John's** is notable as a 'time-warp' church, virtually unchanged since its completion in 1717. Flagged floors, pews and box-pews of unvarnished oak, and a three-decker pulpit have all survived unscathed thanks to the building of a new church in the village in 1887.

There has been a watermill at Pilling since 1242. The present windmill dates back to 1808 and was built on a raft of brushwood. It is now a private residence.

Another building of interest is The Olde Ship Inn, built in 1782 by George Dickson, a slave trader. Now a listed building, the inn is reputed to be haunted by a lady dressed in Georgian attire wandering around with a pale and worried look on her face.

GARSTANG
12 miles N of Blackpool on the A6

This is an ancient, picturesque town whose market dates back to the time of Edward II and is still held every Thursday in the central square with its handsome former Town Hall of 1755. A bell is rung at 10am to signify the opening of trading. Another long-standing institution is the Garstang Agricultural Show, which was founded in 1809 and is held on the first Saturday in August.

The town is also home to an excellent **Discovery Centre**, which deals with a variety of aspects of the region, including the history of the nearby Forest of Bowland and the natural history of the surrounding countryside.

Just to the east of the town, on the top of a grassy knoll, are the remains of **Greenhalgh Castle**, built in 1490 by Thomas Stanley, the first Earl of Derby. Severely damaged during a siege by Cromwell's troops in 1645-46, the castle was one of the last strongholds in Lancashire to have held out and only surrendered when its Governor died.

A little to the north of Garstang, on the B6430, are the remains of a stone-built **Toll House** which probably dates from the 1820s when parts of the turnpike from Garstang to Lancaster were realigned. Although a ruin, the toll house is more than usually interesting as

the posts for the toll gates can still be seen on either side of the road. This stretch of road also features some of the finest **Turnpike Milestones** in the county. To the south of Garstang they are round-faced stones with cursive lettering dating from the 1750s but to the north the stones are triangular, with Roman lettering, and date from the time of the turnpike's realignment in the early 19th century.

HAMBLETON
6 miles NE of Blackpool on the A588

A centre for ship building in medieval times, Hambleton is now a quiet village set around a bend of the River Wyre. A network of narrow lanes radiate from the village and wind through the charming north Fylde countryside.

The village stands on one of the narrowest parts of the river and there was certainly a ford in Roman times, as relics have been found here. However, it is probable that the ford goes back even further, to the Iron Age around 500 BC. On the site of the ford now stands the 325-yard **Shard Bridge**, built in 1864 and still operating as a toll bridge.

POULTON-LE-FYLDE
4 miles E of Blackpool on the A586

This is one of the oldest towns in the ancient area known as Amounderness. The Romans were known to have been in the area and it was probably their handiwork that constructed the **Danes Pad**, an ancient trackway. The town developed as a commercial centre for the surrounding agricultural communities and its Market Place remains its focal point. In 1732, a great fire, started by sparks from the torches of a funeral procession, destroyed most of the thatched cottages that surrounded the market square in those days and a

nationwide appeal was launched to help meet the rebuilding costs. Consequently, little of old Poulton can be seen in the centre of the town.

The present **Church of St Chad** dates from the early 17th century, though the majority of the building is Georgian, and it stands on the site of the original Norman church. Inside there's a splendid Georgian nave from which a magnificent staircase leads to typically Georgian galleries running around three sides. As Poulton was a key town in the area for centuries, it is not surprising that there are several magnificent memorials to the local Fleetwood-Hesketh family also to be found here. Fire seems to have played an important role in the life of the town and one ancient custom still kept is **Teanlay Night**, which involves the lighting of bonfires on Hallowe'en. Each bonfire is encircled with white-coloured stones which are then thrown into the flames by the onlookers and left until the next day. The successful retrieval of one's own stone is considered a good omen for future prosperity.

Strolling around Poulton-le-Fylde now, it is hard to imagine that the town was once a seaport. But, until relatively recently ships sailed up the River Wyre to **Skippool Creek**. Today, the creek is home to the Blackpool and Fleetwood Yacht Club and from here the ocean-going yachts compete in major races around Britain.

The town had a rail link long before Blackpool and it was here that the early holidaymakers alighted from their trains to take a horse and trap the remaining few miles. Fortunately for Poulton, in 1846, the railway reached Blackpool and the town could, once again, return to a more peaceful existence. It is this quiet and charm, as well as sensitive approaches to planning, that have led it

to become, in recent years, a much sought after residential area for businessmen now able to travel the M55 to Manchester and Liverpool.

Incidentally, Poulton's 'le-Fylde' tag was added to distinguish the town from Poulton-le-Sands – nowadays better known as Morecambe.

Singleton
5 miles E of Blackpool on the B5260

Singleton's most famous son is Robert Gillow, who lived here in the first half of the 18th century. He left to become an apprentice joiner at Lancaster and later founded the cabinet making business that became Waring & Gillow of Lancaster.

The village Gillow knew was completely demolished in 1853 after it was bought for £70,000 by Alderman Thomas Miller, a cotton manufacturer from Preston. He then rebuilt it as a model village complete with a church, school, public house – *The Millers Arms*, naturally - and an ornate black-and-white shed for the village fire engine - that building is now an electricity sub-station.

The parish church of this quiet little Fylde village, **St Anne's Church**, was built as part of Miller's model village in 1860. In the sanctuary is a black oak chair which bears the inscription "John Milton, author of Paradise Lost and Paradise Regained 1671" but no-one seems to know where the chair came from and whether the great author did indeed use it.

Great Eccleston
8 miles NE of Blackpool off the A586

This quiet traditional agricultural community on the banks of the River Wyre was once known locally as Little London because it was the social centre for the surrounding area. This was probably directly linked to the generous

number of public houses and inns in the village at that time.

Every Wednesday, a bustling open air market is held in the charming village square. However, unlike most markets Great Eccleston's first took place in 1974 following a campaign started by the parish council a few years previously. The wide variety of stalls attract visitors from not only the immediate surroundings but also coaches from outside the rural area.

St Michael's on Wyre

10 miles NE of Blackpool on the A586

The River Wyre at this point is still tidal and for centuries the inhabitants of St Michael's and other villages in the area have suffered the threat of flooding. An old flood bank has been constructed from the village bridge and below, beyond the overgrown banks, are the fertile fields of the flood plain.

Mentioned in the *Domesday Book* as Michelscherche, is it likely that the first church in the village was founded in the 7th century. As well as many memorials to the Butler family the church also contains a splendid 14th century mural that was only discovered in 1956 when repair work was being undertaken in the sanctuary.

The Butler family, whose home – Rawcliffe Hall – lies a few miles down river, are known to have been in this area for 800 years and their house is built on the site of a Saxon dwelling. Another of the staunchly Catholic Lancashire families, the Butlers finally lost their house and the influence that they had in the area. The house is now part of a private country club.

Churchtown

12 miles NE of Blackpool on the A586

This delightful village has many buildings of both architectural and historic interest and none more so than the **Church of St Helen**, which dates back to the days of the Norman Conquest. Featuring architectural styles from almost every period since the 11th century, this church is well worth exploring. The oldest parts of the building are the circular pillars near the nave which date from around 1200. The roof is the original Tudor structure. Built on the site of a Saxon church, St Helen's is dedicated to the mother of Emperor Constantine and the circular churchyard is typical of the Saxon period.

Known as the Cathedral of the Fylde, the church has been subjected to flooding by the River Wyre and in 1746 such was the damage caused by the rising waters that the rebuilding of the church looked necessary. However, the builder brought in to survey the scene, suggested that moving the river would be a cheaper option and this method of preserving the church was undertaken. The original course of the river can be seen by taking the footpath from the churchyard in the direction of the new river course.

Woodplumpton

12 miles E of Blackpool off the B5269

This charming little village, centred around its church still has its well preserved village stocks behind which is a mounting block that is now designated as a historic monument.

St Anne's Church is also a building of historic note and the keen-eyed will be quick to spot the octagonal cupola shape of tower that is reminiscent of the architecture of Christopher Wren. Completed in 1748, the tower was built to house a new timepiece, a clock, which replaced the sundial that for many years adorned the old tower. Bearing the date 1637, this can now be found in the churchyard.

CLIFTON AND SALWICK

11 miles SE of Blackpool off the A583

Both Salwick and its neighbour, Clifton, were formed from part of the old Clifton estate. As well as the pleasant walks along the banks of the canal, visitors can also enjoy the delights of The Windmill pub which, unlike most pubs of that name, is actually housed in a converted windmill.

KIRKHAM

8 miles SE of Blackpool off the A583

Mentioned in the *Domesday Book*, there was a settlement here in Saxon times, known as Ciric-ham, and before that the Romans had a fort though it is now lost under a modern housing estate. Kirkham was first granted a charter to hold a weekly market in 1287 and since then it has been serving the needs of the surrounding farming communities. Some fine Georgian inns and houses reflect the town's importance in stagecoach days and steep main street contains a number of old-fashioned family-run shops. In the cobbled market square, used for markets and fairs since 1296, The Fishstones are still to be seen – flat stone slabs set on stone uprights to form a broken circle and were the counters from which fish was sold.

FRECKLETON

9 miles SE of Blackpool on the A584

This is the largest village in the Fylde, with a population of more than 7,000. The name is derived from the Anglo-Saxon *Frecheltun* meaning 'an enclosed area' and this is how it featured in the *Domesday Book*. Situated on the northern banks of the River Ribble, the long straggling village was, until the river was canalised, surrounded by marshland.

During World War II the village suffered an appalling tragedy. On a sweltering, thundery day in August 1944 an American Liberator plane took off from nearby Warton aerodrome but because of the adverse weather, the pilot decided to turn back. As it descended over Freckleton it clipped some trees and crashed into the village school. Thirty-six children and 36 adults perished. A disaster fund was set up but villagers bitterly disagreed about how it should be spent. It wasn't until 33 years later that the money was used to build the village's Memorial Hall.

LYTHAM ST ANNES

4 miles S of Blackpool on the A584

Located on the northern bank of the Ribble Estuary, Lytham St Annes is based on a much older community, already well established by the time of the Norman Conquest. It has a short pier, a gracious Victorian Promenade, and an attractive grassy expanse called the Green. Here stands a handsome white-

Sunset at Lytham St Annes

Royal Lytham and St Annes Golf Course

washed windmill, one of very few to have survived from the days when the flat plain of the Fylde was dotted with hundreds of them.

There are actually two towns here: Lytham, which is mentioned in the *Domesday Book*, and St Annes, which was largely developed in the 1870s as a rather upmarket resort. Before the development of the resort, in the Victorian age, Lytham was an important port on the Ribble estuary and was home to the first fishing company on this stretch of the northwest coast. Shipbuilding also continued here until the 1950s when the last vessel constructed in the shipyards was the Windermere Car Ferry. During the 1940s, parts of the famous Mulberry harbour were constructed in secret here in preparation for the invasion of Normandy in 1944.

The arrival of the railway linking Lytham with Preston prompted a group of Lancashire businessmen to plan the construction of a health resort between the old established port and the rapidly expanding town of Blackpool to the north. There was scarcely a cottage on their chosen site when the work began in 1875 but the growth of the carefully planned town was spectacular. In just 30 years the population increased from 1,000 to 17,000 inhabitants.

The **Promenade**, running the full length of the seafront from St Annes to Lytham was constructed in 1875 and on the landward side there are several fine examples of Victorian and Edwardian seaside villas. Beyond the attractive Promenade Gardens, laid out by a local character, Henry Gregson, is **St Annes Pier**. Opened in 1885, the elegant pier was built in a mock Tudor style and up until 1897 fishing smacks and pleasure boats were able to tie up at the end of the jetty. Lytham also had a pier, built in 1865, but during a gale in 1903 two sand barges dragged their anchors and sliced the structure in two. Undeterred, and with the Pavilion still standing at the far end, the pier was rebuilt, only to be almost entirely destroyed by fire in 1928.

In fact, the town has had its fair share of disasters associated with the sea. By far the worst of these occurred in 1886 and it is still Britain's greatest lifeboat disaster. The crew of the St Annes lifeboat, with the help of the Southport lifeboat, set out to answer a distress signal put up by a German ship, the *Mexico*. The sea was so rough that 15 members of the lifeboat crew were lost. The tragedy led to the improvement of lifeboat design. In the **Alpine Garden** on the Promenade is a monument which pays tribute to the men who lost their lives. The statue features the stone figure of a coxswain looking out to sea with a rope in one hand and a lifebelt in the other.

As well as being an elegant place full of

fine Victorian and Edwardian architecture, Lytham St Annes also contains some reminders to the more distant past. **Lytham Hall** started life as a farming cell of the Durham cathedral in 1190. After the Reformation, the estate changed hands several times, until in 1606 it became the property of Sir Cuthbert Clifton, the first squire of Lytham. The fine Georgian hall standing today was the building that John Carr of York built for Thomas Clifton between 1757 and 1764. The extensive grounds, once part of the estate, are now **Lytham Hall Country Park**, where visitors can follow several nature trails to discover the birds and wildlife living here which includes three species of woodpecker, the lesser whitethroat, and the hawfinch.

There has been a **Windmill** at Lytham for more than 800 years though the present structure dates from 1805. A well known landmark along the coast, the building has a solid white tower with a cap that looks rather like an upturned boat. In 1929 the wind set the four sails turning the wrong way, ruining the machinery and firing the mill, which has never worked since. Now renovated, the windmill is home to a permanent exhibition on the building's history and on the process of breadmaking. Adjacent to the windmill, and the original home of the Lytham lifeboat, Old Lifeboat House is home to the **Lifeboat Museum**.

For those interested in discovering more about the abundant wildlife of the dune system here, a visit to **Lytham St Annes Nature Reserve** is a must. Established in 1968, the reserve is an important scientific site as well as being just a small part of what was once a very extensive sand dune system. As well as the rich plant life, the dunes are home to several rare species of migrating birds including osprey, black redstart, and Lapland buntings.

No description of Lytham St Annes is complete without a mention of the **Royal Lytham and St Annes Golf Course**. The club originated after a meeting held in 1886 when a group of 19 keen golfers sought to furnish themselves with suitable facilities. The course opened in 1898 and it is still considered by many to be one of the finest golf links in the country and is a regular host of the British Open.

LANCASTER AND THE FOREST OF BOWLAND

The ancient county town of Lancaster has a wealth of interesting buildings and a variety of museums, and also has the advantage of being slightly off the general tourist routes. To the northeast lie the Lune Valley and Leck fell; to the west are Morecambe and Heysham, while extending across much of the northern part of the county is the Forest of Bowland, an ancient royal hunting ground that offers peace and scenic beauty in abundance.

LANCASTER

An architecturally pleasing city, Lancaster is one of the most appealing of English county capitals. Most of the county's administrative offices are now based in Preston so Lancaster enjoys all the prestige of being the capital without the burden of housing the accompanying bureaucrats. The city also takes pride in the fact that the Duke of Lancaster is the only duke in the kingdom who is a woman – no less a personage than Her Majesty the Queen, for whom the dukedom is one of many subsidiary titles.

Lancaster's story begins some 2,000 years ago when the Romans built a fort

on a hill overlooking a sweep of the River Lune, a site now occupied by the unspoiled 15th century **Priory Church of St Mary**. Right up until the Industrial Revolution, Lancashire was one of the poorest counties in England, lacking the wealth to endow glorious cathedrals or magnificent parish churches. St Mary's is a notable exception, the finest medieval church in the county. It stands on the site of Lancashire's first monastery which was closed not, like most others, by Henry VIII, but by Henry V in 1413. Henry was at war with France, the monastery's mother abbey was at Sées in Normandy, so the 'alien priory' in Lancaster had to be dissolved. The present church contains treasures rescued from the closed priory such as the sumptuously carved wooden choir stalls from around 1345.

Each stall is covered by a superb canopy, lavishly carved with around a hundred small heads and faces surrounded by abundant foliage. Also of note are the fragments of Anglo-Saxon crosses and some very fine needlework. The **Priory Tower**, also on the hilltop, was rebuilt in 1759 as a landmark for ships navigating their way into the River Lune. Nearby is one of Lancaster's links with its Roman past – the remains of a bath house which also served soldiers as an inn.

Close by is **Lancaster Castle** (see panel on page 152), one of the best-preserved Norman fortresses in the country. Dating back to 1200 and with a massive gatehouse flanked by sturdy twin towers, the castle dominates the centre of the city. For centuries, the castle served as a prison, relinquishing that function as recently as 1996. At the back of the castle, the **Shire Hall** is still in use as a Crown Court and one of its more macabre attractions is the Drop Room, where

THE SUN CAFÉ

25 Sun Street, Lancaster, Lancashire LA1 1EW
Tel: 01524 845599 Fax: 01524 60843

The Sun Café, one of the most stylish and relaxed places in town, is housed in Sun Street Studios, one of the most handsome and distinguished buildings in town.

Behind the 200-year-old facade, the café is stylishly modern in both look and philosophy. The chefs embrace all culinary continents without prejudice or pretension in creating food that will suit any taste and waistline, and that philosophy is reflected in the range of wines, beers and spirits carefully selected to complement the food.

The music is laid-back and jazzy, sometimes live but never intrusive, and the array of original artwork on display is evidence of

the restaurant's commitment to supporting local artists. The Sun Cafe is open Mon to Sat 10am-3pm, and 5pm to 10pm serving coffee, cakes, lunches,early evening and an excellent a la carte menu. The restaurant also offers a Sunday evening set menu from 5pm. The restaurant is available to be wholly or partly booked for private functions. Sun Street runs between Market Street and Church Street in the heart of the city.

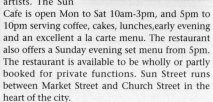

LANCASTER CASTLE

c/o P O Box 26, County Hall, Preston PR1 8RE
Tel: 01524 64998 Fax: 01524 847914
website: www.lancashire.gov.uk/resources/ps/
castle/index.htm

Lancaster Castle is owned by Her Majesty the Queen in right of her Duchy of Lancaster. For most of its history the castle has been the centre of law and order for the county, and this magnificent building is still in use as a prison and a crown court.

The castle has dominated the town for almost 1000 years, ever since it was first established in 1093. But the hill on which it stands has a history which goes back a thousand years further, almost to the birth of Christ. The Romans built the first of at least three military forts on the site in AD79.

Little is known about Lancaster until 1093 when the Norman Baron, Roger of Poitou, built a small motte and bailey castle which was replaced 50 years later by a large stone Keep which still stands today as the oldest part of the Castle.

Throughout its long history it has witnessed many trials, including that of the Lancashire Witches of 1612, which resulted in the execution of ten people.

Although still a working building, guided tours of the castle include where the witches were condemned to die; the beautiful Gillow furniture in the Grand Jury Room; the dungeons and 'Drop Room' from where the condemned went to their deaths; the Crown Court from where thousands were transported to Australia; 'Hanging Corner' the site of public hangings and the magnificent Shire Hall with its display of heraldic shields.

Criminals and convicts, monarchs and majesty, dungeons and death, treason and transportation, witches and martyrs, all have their place in the history of this most fascinating building.

prisoners were prepared for the gallows.

A short walk from the castle is the largely pedestrianised city centre, full of shops, the market, and much besides. The **City Museum** in the Market Place occupies the Old Town Hall, built between 1781-3 by Major Jarrett and Thomas Harrison. As well as the city's art collection and an area of changing exhibitions, there are displays and collections of material illustrating aspects of the city's industrial and social history. Also here is the **Museum of the King's Own Royal Regiment**, a regiment which was based in Lancaster from 1880 onwards.

The Gatehouse Café & Restaurant

White Cross, South Road, Lancaster, Lancashire LA1 4XQ
Tel: 01524 849111 Fax: 01524 67728

The Gatehouse Café & Restaurant is a major attraction in White Cross, an impressive 'urban village' of small and medium-sized businesses developed on the site of an old mill on the banks of the Lancaster Canal. Many of the original buildings have been incorporated, and in a spacious, stylishly converted basement Nick Bailey runs the Gatehouse. The restaurant has many attractive features, including a comfortable bar for pre-dinner drinks with leather sofas, exposed stone walls, tiled floors and eyecatching artwork, some of it with a classical Greek look.

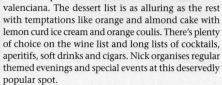

Greece and the Mediterranean also inspire much of the lunch and dinner menus with dishes such as moules marinière, meatballs

with a Provençal sauce, grilled halloumi, chicken kebabs or paella valenciana. The dessert list is as alluring as the rest with temptations like orange and almond cake with lemon curd ice cream and orange coulis. There's plenty of choice on the wine list and long lists of cocktails, aperitifs, soft drinks and cigars. Nick organises regular themed evenings and special events at this deservedly popular spot.

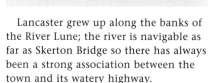

Lancaster grew up along the banks of the River Lune; the river is navigable as far as Skerton Bridge so there has always been a strong association between the town and its watery highway. Documents from 1297 make reference to the town's small-scale maritime trade, but it was not until the late 1600s and early 1700s that Lancaster's character as a port fully emerged. The splendid buildings of the 18th century Golden Age were born out of the port wealth, and the layout and appearance of the town was much altered by this building bonanza. Lancaster's importance as a port steadily declined throughout the 19th century so that many buildings originally intended for maritime purposes were taken over for other uses.

Lancaster enjoyed its era of greatest prosperity during the 18th century when its quays were busy servicing a thriving

Lancaster Maritime Museum

Custom House, St George's Quay, Lancaster LA1 1RB
Tel: 01524 64637 Fax: 01524 841692

The **Lancaster Maritime Museum** was opened in 1985 and occupies the former Custom House of 1764 by Richard Gillow and an adjacent warehouse.

Using sound, smells, reconstructions and audio visuals it tells the story of the port of Lancaster, the Lancaster Canal, fishing and the ecology of Morecambe Bay. A number of exhibitions can be seen and there is an education programme for children. Facilities include a shop, café, car parking and disabled access.

trade with the West Indies in rum, sugar, cotton – and slaves. The city's rich maritime history is celebrated at St George's Quay which, with its great stone warehouses and superb Custom House designed by Richard Gillow of furniture fame, is now the award-winning **Maritime Museum** (see panel on page 153). Visitors today are given a vivid insight into the life of the mariners and quayside workers with opportunities for knot-tying and the practising of other maritime skills. Every year, over the four days of the Easter weekend, St George's Quay is home to the Lancaster Maritime Festival with a programme that involves boisterous 'smugglers', sea songs, and shanties.

Fire destroyed most of Tudor and Jacobean Lancaster, but one notable survivor is the **Judge's Lodging** in Church Street, a charming Jacobean house built in the 1620s and now a

museum: two museums in fact. There's the **Museum of Childhood** which includes the Barry Elder Doll collection, and the **Gillow and Town House Museum** containing many examples of the fine workmanship produced by the famous Lancaster cabinet-makers, Gillows.

Close by is the **Cottage Museum** in a house, built in 1739, that was divided into two dwellings in the 19th century. Furnished in the style of an artisan's house of the early to mid-19th century, the museum is open from Easter to the end of September. Just around a corner or two, in Sun Street, is the **Music Room**, an exquisite early Georgian building originally designed as a pavilion in the long vanished garden of Oliver Marton. It is notable for some superb decorative plasterwork. **Lancaster University** has two important galleries. The Peter Scott Gallery houses an art collection that

---

Elizabeth Cottam

Far Barn, Gressingham, Nr Lancaster,
Lancashire LA2 8LW
Tel: 015242 21658

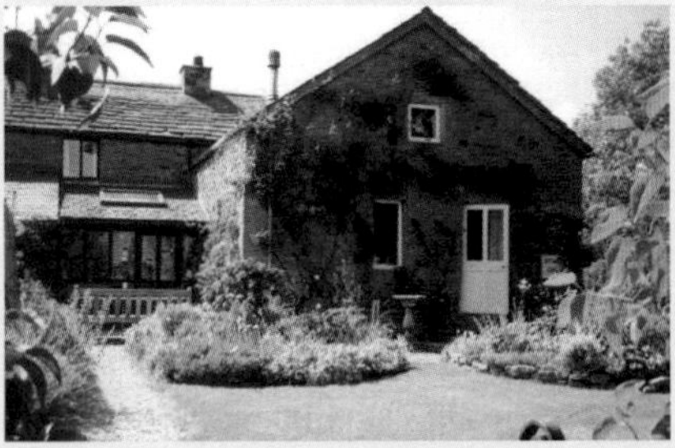

An idyllic, tranquil location in the beautiful Lune Valley is a perfect place to learn a new skill, and at **Elizabeth Cottam** that skill is fleece embroidery. Elizabeth uses materials from her beautiful organic garden for her wonderful wall hangings, which 'depict the myths which

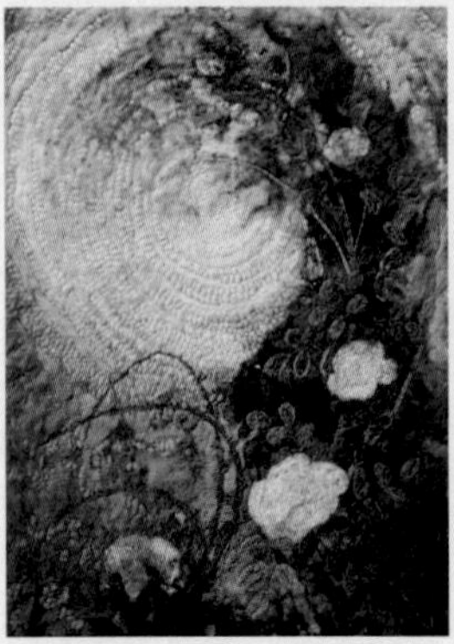

nature weaves around our lives'. Sheep's wool is dyed with bark, roots, and flowers and embroidered or hooked on to a hessian backing. Colours are blended in the process of carding to create the effect of a painting in wool, and the results are truly stunning, as shown by delicate masterpieces such as her Wild Rose, Tortoiseshell Butterfly or The Passage of Summer, which have been beautifully photographed by John McClements.

Visitors should telephone in advance for an appointment to visit her studio to view or to purchase, perhaps combined with a cup of tea in the garden. Elizabeth undertakes commissions and also runs workshops. Participants in the one-day workshops will practise the techniques for the craft of fleece embroidery while making a small hanging, and also learn something about the use of natural dyes. The workshop is suitable for all ages and abilities.

RIVER LUNE MILLENNIUM PARK

Lancaster
website: www.lancaster.gov.uk/millennium

The **River Lune Millennium Park** stretches some 15 kilometres along the banks of the Lune from Bull Beck near Caton to Salt Ayre in Lancaster. The Park offers leisure and everyday transport opportunities with linked footpaths and cycleways, artworks to discover and stations for information. At its heart is the Millennium Bridge providing a river crossing for pedestrians and cyclists.

A vast array of wildlife and birds can be seen in the park from gulls, ducks and waders at Salt Ayre where the river is tidal, to fishing birds such as cormorants and kingfishers further upstream. The Environment Agency is trying to encourage fish to spawn here to reverse the decline of fish populations Dragonflies can be seen skimming the water and in the evening, bats are on the wing hunting for insects.

Artworks in various forms can be seen along the route such as Colin Reid's River Rocks - rocks sculpted from glass and nestling by the riverside, and Marjan Wouda's Heron's Head, created from wrought iron and perched above a cycleway. A set of 16 stations, at points of interest along the river , gives detailed descriptions of what can be seen from each.

includes works by Miró, Picasso and Max Ernst and British artists Barbara Hepworth, Sir Terry Frost and Andy Goldsworthy. A stunning collection of Royal Lancaster Pottery is on display in the John Chambers Ceramics Room. The Ruskin Library, opened in 1998, contains an outstanding collection of the papers and drawings of John Ruskin.

To the east of the city rises its most prominent landmark, visible for miles around, the extravagant, temple-like Ashton Memorial – "the grandest monument in England" according to Nikolaus Pevsner. Erected in 1907 as a memorial to his wife by the local MP and millionaire linoleum manufacturer Lord Ashton, it stands on the highest point in Lancaster, set within a beautifully landscaped park and enjoying sweeping views of the Cumbrian hills and across Morecambe Bay. The building now houses exhibitions and multi-screen

presentations about the life and times of Lord Ashton and the Edwardian period.

Williamson Park was Lord Ashton's own personal project as a means of providing work for local people during the cotton famine crisis in the textile industry during the American Civil War in the 1860s. Constructed on the site of old quarries, which gives the park its undulating contours, the park was opened in 1896. As well as the magnificent Ashton Memorial there is also a delightful Butterfly House in the now restored Edwardian Palm House and a Conservation Garden and Wildlife Pool. Safely housed in the Mini-Beast centre are lizards, spiders, snakes and many other creepie-crawlies.

Another place the whole family can enjoy is **Lancaster Leisure Park** on Wyresdale Road. Set in 42 acres of landscaped parkland, the site includes a mini marina, a Wild West adventure

THE CASTLE HOTEL

Main Street, Hornby, Lancashire LA2 8JT
Tel: 01524 221204 Fax: 01524 222258
e-mail: information@diningroomhornby.co.uk
website: www.diningroomhornby.co.uk

Nestling in the beautiful and picturesque village of
Hornby, **The Castle Hotel** is one of Lancashire's best
known and best loved weekend retreats. Although a
small hotel, they are able to offer exciting
accommodation. A standard double room en suite is
available from as little as £50.00 inclusive of a stunning
3 course breakfast. They also offer executive doubles
from £70.00 and a duplex suite with its separate lounge
area for those extra special occasions from £90.00.

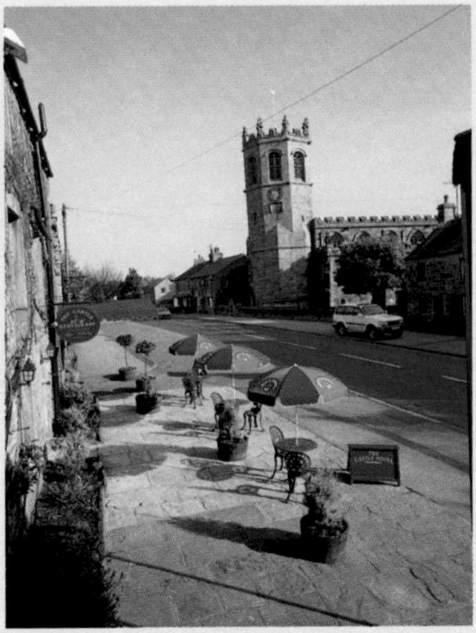

What makes the Castle unique is its ability to cater
for all your requirements - from a leisurely drink in
the comfortable bar, to a gala event in the Castle Ball
Room with full conference and banqueting facilities.

The Castle Hotel has been transformed into one of
the county's most elegant and upmarket hotels and

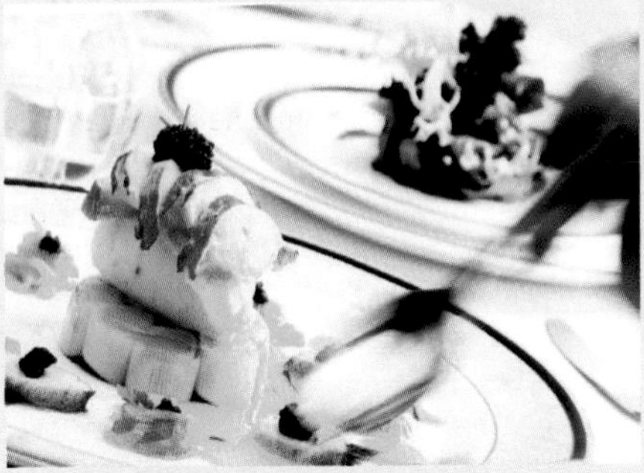

eating destinations. With its inclusion in the
Good Food Guide for 2004, Paul Reed, the chef-
patron, carefully guards the reputation of his
two restaurants at The Castle.

The Castle Barns is an informal alfresco
brasserie-style restaurant which is open
lunchtime and evening all year round. Serving
a delicious menu of light snacks and tantalising
dishes, The Castle Barns really has brought
metropolitan-style brasserie cuisine to the
country.

As one of the country's most well-respected
chefs, Paul Reed was the first chef in the North
of England to win a coveted Michelin star. Paul
explains, "over the last twelve months I have
assembled a great team to compliment the existing staff
at the Castle. I have appointed Lee Stainthorpe as my Head
Chef (formerly Heathcotes), Edward Charles as my General
Assistant (formerly The Dorchester) and J. C. Massonet as
my Restaurant Manager (formerly Heathcotes and The
Studio)". In the next twelve months the team intends to
establish **Paul Reed's Dining Room.** It's a superbly
designed fine-dining restaurant which is developing a first-
class reputation for itself with the county's culinary elite.
Reservations in this restaurant are essential and it's wise
to book well ahead.

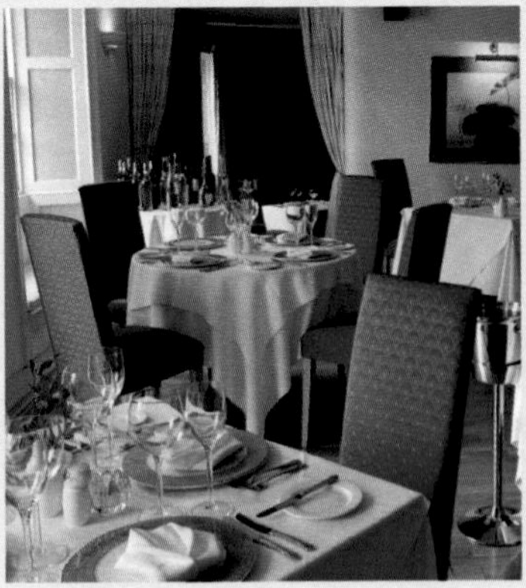

PAUL REED'S DINING ROOM

Main Street, Hornby, Lancashire LA2 8JT
Tel: 01524 221204 Fax: 01524 222258
e-mail: information@diningroomhornby.co.uk
website: www.diningroomhornby.co.uk

playground, a miniature railway, a rare breeds unit, a children's farmyard, pony rides, a gift shop, a tea garden, and a pottery shop.

The Lune Valley Ramble is a 16-mile signed and waymarked walk that follows the River Lune between Lancaster and Kirkby Lonsdale through some of northern England's finest lowland countryside.

Running along the banks of the River Lune from Salt Ayre in Lancaster to Bull Beck near Caton is the **River Lune Millennium Park** (see panel on page 155). The Park offers leisure and everyday transport opportunities, footpaths and cycleways, artworks to discover and a series of viewpoints. At its heart is the Millennium Bridge for pedestrians and cyclists, which traces an ancient crossing point of the river at St George's Quay. The route takes in Skerton Weir, where salmon and sea trout can be seen travelling through the fish pass; the monumental aqueduct bridge that takes the Lancaster Canal over the Lune; Denny Beck, near Halton Station, where on summer evenings bats can be seen on the wing; and Gray's Seat, where the poet Thomas Gray enjoyed the view and Turner painted it.

AROUND LANCASTER

HALTON
3 miles NE of Lancaster off the A683

The high mound, **Castle Hill**, which rises above this ancient village on the River Lune was firstly the site of a Roman camp and later a Saxon castle. The village's parish **Church of St Wilfrid** was founded in the 7th century and although nothing survives of that original foundation there are some stone crosses, both inside the building and out, that

date from the 9th century. One of them, unusually, bears both pagan and Christian symbols. Roman remains, in the form of a votive altar (where offerings were made before a military operation began), were found on the site in the late 18th century. Around the same time, a labourer tilling his allotment on Halton Moor unearthed more than 1,000 coins from the reign of King Canute (1017-35) and a gold necklace. This treasure trove is now in the British Museum.

NETHER KELLET
4 miles N of Lancaster off the B6254

This farming village has a traditional village green, which as well as being the central focus of the community also features several old wells and pumps. This is appropriate since the Old Norse word *chellet*, now Kellet, means 'spring'. Local brewers of home ale still use the spring water because of its purity and absence of chemicals. Quarrying has taken place here for many centuries and lime burning has been an important local industry. Its remains, in the form of lime kilns, can still be seen around the village and the local pub is named the Lime Burners Arms.

The village also has its own cave, Dunold Mill, through which flows a large stream that dives underground to appear 2 miles further north at Carnforth. During the mid 1800s the cave was occupied by a hermit who lived there until his death at the age of 100. His descendants still live in the village.

CARNFORTH
5 miles N of Lancaster on the A6

The town lies around what was once a major crossroads on the A6 but it is, perhaps, its fame as a busy railway junction town (the station was used as

the setting for the 1940s film classic *Brief Encounter*) by which most people know Carnforth. Though the station has declined in importance – it is now an unstaffed halt – the old engine sheds and sidings are occupied by **Steamtown**, one of the largest steam railway centres in the north of England. Visitors are likely to see such giants of the Age of Steam as the *Flying Scotsman* or an A4 Gresley Pacific being stabled here, together with a permanent collection of over 30 British and Continental steam locomotives.

YEALAND

8 miles N of Lancaster off the A6

To the south of the village lies **Leighton Hall**, a fine early 19th century house open to the public. During the Middle Ages the land on which it stands, together with much of the surrounding area, was owned by the d'Avranches family. Over the centuries, the house and the land passed through many hands before becoming the property of the Gillows family of Lancaster. Now in the hands of the Reynolds family, a branch of the Gillows, the fine furniture seen in the hall reflects the trade that made the family fortune.

As with many estates in Lancashire, Leighton Hall was a Catholic house and one owner, Sir George Middleton, was fined heavily by Cromwell after the Civil War for his loyalty to Charles I and to his religion. Later, another owner of the hall, Albert Hodgson, suffered for his loyalty to Catholicism and the Stuart claim on the throne of England. Taking part in the Jacobite rebellion of 1715, Hodgson was captured at Preston and the Government troops inflicted such damage on the hall that little remained of the Tudor structure.

The hall, today, dates from 1800 when it was built out of pale, local sandstone to the Gothic designs of Harrison, a Chester architect. One of the finest houses in the county, the views from the extensive grounds are magnificent and take in the nearby Leighton Moss Bird Reserve.

SILVERDALE

8 miles N of Lancaster off the A6

The village lies at the northwesternmost corner of the county and has the Lakeland hills as a backdrop as well as superb views over Morecambe Bay. The latter half of the 19th century saw Silverdale develop as a quiet seaside resort where those so inclined could take medicinal baths of fresh sea water in one of the many small villas situated along the coast. One frequent visitor was Elizabeth Gaskell, who is said to have written some of her books while holidaying here. However, Silverdale's history goes back well beyond the days of a genteel Victorian resort. Its name comes from a Viking family that settled here and which signifies that this was Sigward's or Soevers' valley. Fishing, naturally, was the key provider of local income but in the 18th century a copper smelting works was built here. All, however, that remains of the foundry is the chimney near **Jenny Brown's Point**, said to be named after an old woman who lived here in the 1700s.

Essentially, now a small residential village, Silverdale is well worth visiting for the network of footpaths from here that pass through the limestone woodlands that are such a joy for the botanist, being rich in wild flowers in spring – primroses, violets, orchids, bird's eye primroses, rockroses, and eglantines abound.

Leighton Moss near Silverdale is a nationally known RSPB bird sanctuary. The reed beds are the most important part of the reserve because they have become a northern stronghold of the

GREEN CLOSE STUDIOS

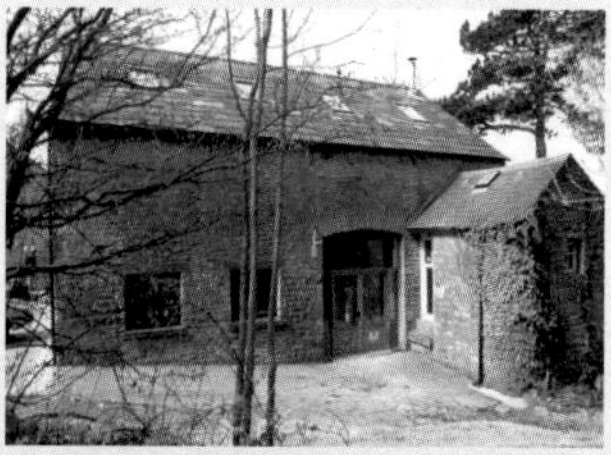

Green Close Barn, Melling, Nr Carnforth,
Lancashire LA6 2RB
Tel/Fax: 015242 21233 e-mail: info@greenclosestudios.co.uk
website: www.greenclosestudios.co.uk

In the heart of the Lune Valley, between the Yorkshire Dales
and the Lake District, **Green Close Studios** provides studio and
workshop facilities for professional artists. It also offers a range
of creative workshops and events. Established in 1998, it is
committed to bringing contemporary art practice to a rural audience, developing a programme of
cultural and cross-cultural initiatives for schools, local groups and the wider global arena.

Once a derelict barn, it has an open-plan layout on three floors, with disabled facilities on the
ground floor. Besides open studio exhibitions, the artists exhibit nationally and internationally, and
their work features in many private, public and corporate collections. Artists Sue and Pete Flowers are
the main stay of this exciting and developing business, and the sculptor Ailsa

Josland is another whose work can be seen
at the studio. The environment of the Lune
Valley always plays a prominent part in the
work of the studio, not only in the artwork
but also in events such as tree dressing,
which aims not only to celebrate trees but
also to motivate people to look after trees
in their own environment. As this is a
working studios please telephone in
advance to arrange suitable visiting times.

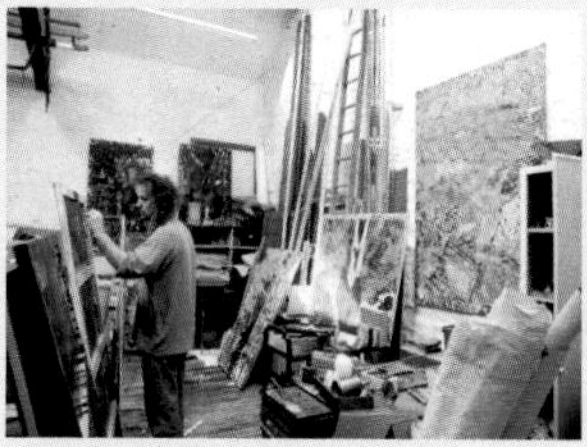

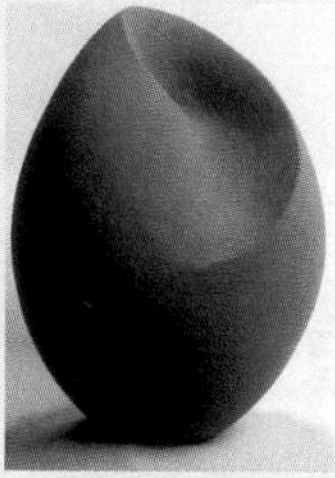

rare bearded tit and are also the major
British breeding centre for the bittern.

THE LUNE VALLEY

CATON

3 miles NE of Lancaster on the A683

Caton climbs up the hillside from the
leafy glades of the Crook o'Lune, subject
of one of Turner's paintings, to heather
moorlands commanding a panoramic
view of Morecambe Bay. A popular
commuter town nowadays, in the 19th
century Caton was a busy place with no
fewer than eight cotton and woodturning bobbin mills. Just to the south of
the village, tucked away among the hills
on the northern edges of the Forest of
Bowland, is **Littledale**, one of
Lancashire's most hidden gems. Chiefly
wooded, a walk through the dale

CORNERSTONES

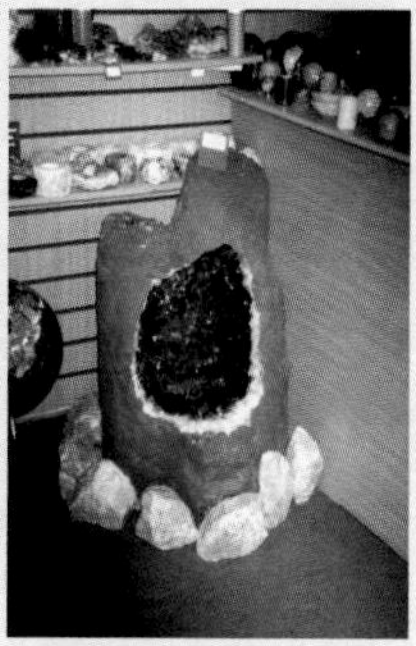

2 Main Street, Ingleton, North Yorkshire LA6 3EB
Tel: 015242 42135
e-mail: enquiries@cornerstones-ingleton.co.uk

Cornerstones is a delightful little shop whose floor-to-ceiling shelves are
crammed with crystals, minerals, fossils, jewellery, carvings and unusual gifts.
Owner John Owen is a retired police officer with a lifelong interest in minerals
and fossils, and he has built up a very good reputation and an extensive
customer base that is still expanding. He employs the services of a silversmith
and jeweller to make high-quality jewellery to order. Browsers and buyers are
very welcome at Cornerstones, which is open daily from April to October and
five days a week at other times.

COUNTRY HARVEST

On the A65 at Ingleton,
North Yorkshire LA6 3PE
Tel: 015242 42223 Fax: 015242 42226
e-mail: info@country-harvest.co.uk
website: www.country-harvest.co.uk

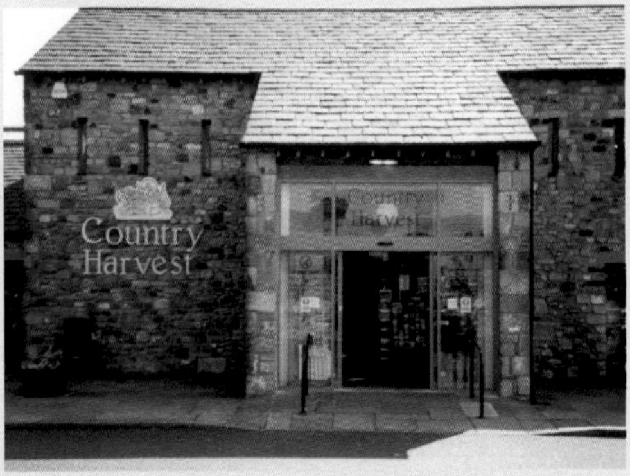

In a purpose-built barn on a 2-acre site west of Ingleton, **Country Harvest** is a partnership between two local farmers who decided to diversify their businesses in 1993. Local produce features prominently in the vast selection on mouthwatering display in the Food Hall, where the famous cheese department, with over 120 varieties, has been a winner of UK Cheese Retailer of the Year. The popular Coffee Shop, with huge windows overlooking the surrounding countryside, is renowned for its choice of quality teas and coffees, served in the traditional way with cakes and pastries, sandwiches, hot and cold snacks, light lunches and afternoon teas.

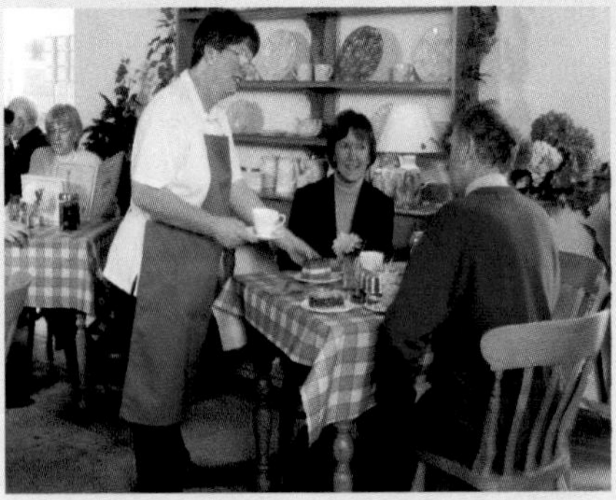

Food is by no means all that Country Harvest has to offer: there's also a wide selection of gifts, crafts and cards, as well as books concerned with the countryside, wildlife, food and cooking. The Clothes Department, while specialising in quality weatherproof jackets and fleeces, also stocks a large variety of other clothing along with handbags and holdalls in natural leather and other fabrics. Country Harvest is open daily and has ample free parking. Children can romp in safety in a playground while their parents fill their baskets with goodies.

alongside Artle Beck to Littledale Hall is well worthwhile and provides a view of Lancashire that is not normally seen.

CLAUGHTON
6 miles NE of Lancaster on the A683

The Old Toll House Garage on the road into this village (which is pronounced Clafton), is famous for a rather curious reason. In the 1920s the garage owner painted the first white lines on the road at the nearby corner because of the many accidents that had occurred there. After much debate their value was recognised by the government of the day and from then onwards the use of white lines became accepted as a means of road

marking, eventually spreading worldwide.

HORNBY
9 miles NE of Lancaster on the A683

Immortalised in paint by JMW Turner, the ruins of **Hornby Castle** (private) were incorporated into a picturesque mock medieval Hall in the 19th century. Perched atop a hill, the castle dominates the attractive village of Hornby. Sadly, it isn't open to the public but it's visible for miles around and there's a particularly pleasing view of it from the bridge over the River Wemming at the southern edge of the village.

The situation of this attractive village,

by a bluff overlooking the valley of the River Lune, not only gives Hornby panoramic views of the surrounding countryside but also makes this a strategic position that has been utilised over the centuries. Just to the north of the village is the attractive stone-built **Loyn Bridge**, which takes the road over the River Lune and on to Gressington. Constructed in 1684, it replaced a ford. Beside the bridge is **Castle Stede**, the best example of a Norman motte and bailey castle in Lancashire.

The graceful **Church of St Margaret of Antioch** dates from around 1300 when it was built as a chapel of ease to the parish church at Melling. Its unusual and impressive octagonal tower was ordered by Sir Edward Stanley, Lord Mounteagle, who made a vow before the Battle of Flodden Field in 1513 that if he returned victorious he would construct the tower in honour of his patron saint, St Margaret.

TUNSTALL

11 miles NE of Lancaster on the A683

The village is famous for its fine 15th century **Church of St John the Baptist**, that was known to the Brontë sisters and which is referred to in *Jane Eyre* as "Brocklebridge church". When the sisters were attending the Clergy Daughters' School at Cowan Bridge they walked the six mile round trip to the church each morning. After attending service, they had their midday meal in the room above the church porch.

COWAN BRIDGE

13 miles NE of Lancaster on the A65

In 1823, the Rev. William Carus Wilson, vicar of neighbouring Tunstall, opened his Clergy Daughters' School at Cowan Bridge. Among his early pupils were 4 daughters of the Rev Patrick Brontë of Howarth – Maria, Elizabeth, Charlotte

and Emily. Charlotte immortalised the school and its austere regime in *Jane Eyre* where it appears as Lowood. It can still be seen, though it is now part of a row of terraced cottages just north of the bridge on the A65. The school moved to Casterton in 1833.

LECK

13 miles NE of Lancaster off the A65

Over the A65 from Cowan Bridge lies the small village of Leck. To the northeast of this village lies **Green Hill**, surrounded by moorland and the highest point, at 2,060 feet, in the county. At just over three feet higher than the top of the neighbouring fell, Gragarth, it was only a recent, more accurate survey, that distinguished Green Hill as the higher. This is the most northerly part of Lancashire and from the summit there are superb views of both Cumbria and North Yorkshire, as well, of course, as Lancashire.

WHITTINGTON

12 miles NE of Lancaster on the B6254

This delightful village, in the green and sheltered valley of the River Lune, is well worth a visit. It was Wordsworth, in his *Guide to the Lakes*, who recommended that Kendal be approached via the Vale of Lune and it remains a popular place today.

WEST OF LANCASTER

MORECAMBE

3 miles NW of Lancaster on the A589

Featuring prominently on the Lancashire coastline, Morecambe has long been one of the most successful and popular seaside resorts in the North, and it can truly be said to enjoy one of the finest views from its promenade of any resort

MAGENTA NEW AGE GIFTS

12 Pedder Street, Morecambe, Lancashire LA4 5DZ
Tel: 01524 831013

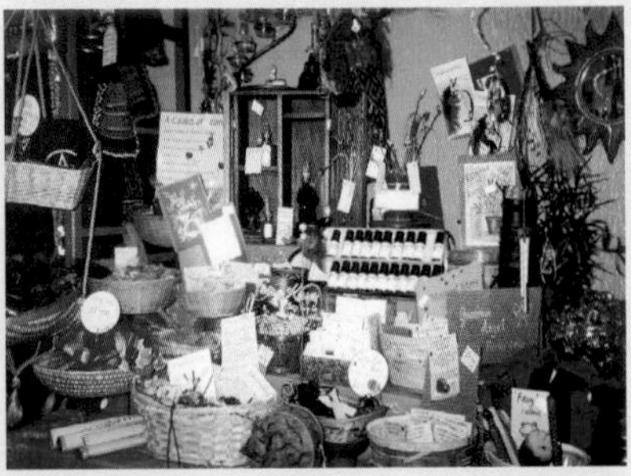

The popular coastal resort of Morecambe has many attractions for the visitor, including all the expected amenities of a seaside town, Some of these attractions are a little more unexpected, and therefore all the more delightful, and if there's a hint of mystery and

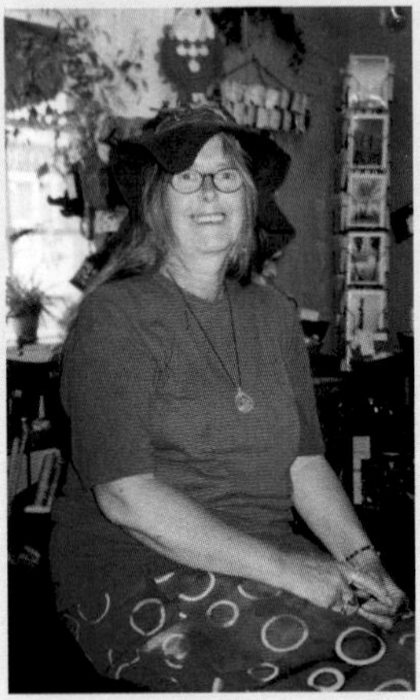

witchcraft in the air, so much the better. 'New Age Gifts, Trinkets and Eccentricities' reads the sign outside a 200-year-old, three-storey building in striking shades of blue close to the centre of town. And behind that eyecatching façade **Magenta New Age Gifts** is a treasure trove of unusual gifts that fill every inch of space and almost hide the bright blue walls.

Owner Elaine Schroder spent many years in the teaching profession before embarking on this venture; she lives above the shop, where visitors can spend happy hours browsing before deciding on the perfect present for themselves, family or friends. It is truly amazing how much is crammed into quite a small space The choice is prodigious, from New Age clothes, silk scarves, witches hats to tarot cards, charms and talismans, incense, oils, candles and cards. Hand crafted mobiles and dangles fill the ceiling giving an atmosphere of calm spitituality. A mail order catalogue available on request.

in England – a magnificent sweep of coastline and bay, looking across to the Lakeland mountains.

Morecambe Bay, a vast wide, flat tidal plain situated between Lancashire and Cumbria, is the home of many forms of marine life as well as being a very popular and important habitat for birds. The Rivers Lune, Kent, Keer, Leven, and Crayke create the gulleys, mud, and sandbanks that make this not only one of the most important ornithological sites in Europe but also a great source of mussels and shrimps.

The largest estuary in Britain, Morecambe Bay is noted for its rich marine and bird life, for its vast expanse of sands and mudflats – and for their treacherous nature. Over the years, many have lost their lives in the Bay's ever-

shifting quicksands while attempting to make the apparently straightforward crossing from Morecambe to Grange-over-Sands on the Cumbrian coast. In medieval times, this perilous track formed part of the main west coast route from Scotland to England and at one time the monks of the Furness peninsula acted as guides to those wishing to make their way to Cumbria without taking the long overland route. Today, you can join one of the **Cross Bay Walks** led by the Queen's Guide to the Sands.

Modern Morecambe is a relatively recent town that grew up as a direct result of the expansion of the railways to the north Lancashire coast. There were originally three villages, Bare, Poulton and Torrisholme that were quiet fishing communities. In 1848 all this changed as

the railways brought visitors from the textile towns of Lancashire and, especially, Yorkshire to what was jokingly called Bradford-by-the-Sea. Hotels and boarding houses were built as well as the usual seaside amenities such as parks and promenades and soon the villages were absorbed into one thriving resort.

Of the many buildings dating from Morecambe's heyday as a holiday destination, one in particular, the **Midland Hotel** stands out. Situated on the seafront, on the central promenade, the hotel, which was built in the early 1930s to designs by Oliver Hill, is concave towards the sea and convex facing inland. The elegant, sweeping balconies of the luxurious rooms remain a superb feature of the hotel and, while filming *Brief Encounter* at nearby Carnforth both Celia Johnson and Trevor Howard made their home here along with others working on the film.

Perhaps the town's most popular attraction is the **Eric Morecambe Statue** near the Stone Jetty. Few can resist the opportunity of posing in suitably one-legged fashion beside sculptor Graham Ibbeson's life-size statue. Lyrics from Eric's best-known song, *Bring Me Sunshine*, are carved into the granite steps leading up to the statue which is surrounded by flower beds and flashing lights that bring this 'stage' to life even after dark. In 1990 Morecambe was given substantial government funding for programmes of coastal protection and derelict land clearance. The theme chosen was the bird life of Morecanbe Bay, and the concept of the **Tern Project** was

born. A team of engineers, landscape architects, planners, artists, sculptors and RSPB education officers set out to celebrate the bird life of the Bay, introducing various features into the new coastal defences and the Promenade. Among the eyecatching results are steel cormorants and gannets on pieces of quarried rock on Central Drive, and flocks of metal birds on the perimeter fencing. At the heart of the project is the rebuilding and extending of the Stone Jetty, all that remains of the 1853 harbour. The designers created a series of circular pavement features that include a huge stainless steel compass set in granite, a maze and a word search containing the names of over 70 birds.

HEYSHAM
5 miles W of Lancaster on the A683

Southwards along the coast, Morecambe merges imperceptibly into Heysham, an ancient settlement with a quaint old main street that winds down to the shore. The town is notable for the tiny **St Patrick's Chapel** which is reckoned to be the oldest religious building in Lancashire. According to tradition, St Patrick himself built the now ruined

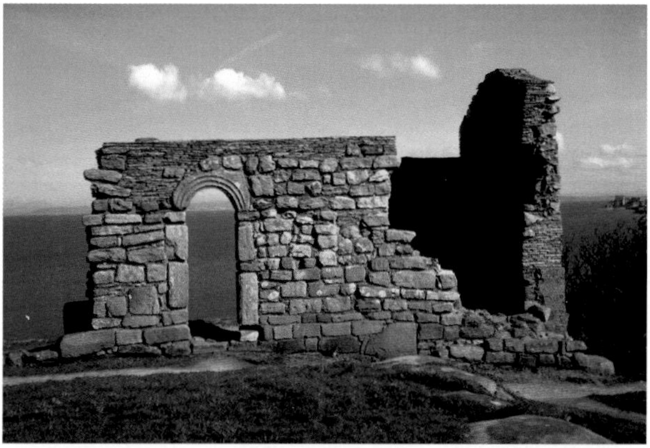

St Patrick's Chapel

chapel as a thanks offering to God after surviving a shipwreck on the rocks below. Historians aren't too sure about the veracity of that legend, but there's no doubting the interest of the chapel graveyard. Hewn out of the rock are six body-shaped coffins with an incised space above them in the shape of a cross. These 8th or 9th century coffins were originally covered by a similarly shaped slab of stone and would have been created as the final resting place for Saxon notables.

The little **Church of St Peter** on the headland below the chapel is equally interesting. It dates back to Saxon and Norman times, with an Anglo-Saxon cross on which the Madonna and other figures have been crudely carved by 9th century masons and there is a rare Viking hog-back gravestone. It is one of the oldest churches in western Europe to have been in continuous use.

SUNDERLAND
6 miles SW of Lancaster off the A683

This is, unbelievably, an old port and seaside resort which flourished until larger-berthed ships, silting channels, and the growth in the 19th century of rail-served Morecambe caused it to decline. A little wharf, quiet cottages, some with faded and evocative elegance, a sandy shore where sea thrift flourishes among the pebbles, are all that remains. The River Lune estuary is now a Site of Special Scientific Interest because of its wildlife value – visitors are likely to see such birds as redshank feeding on the rich supplies of worms, shellfish, and shrimps on the salt marshes, while a variety of wildfowl such as shell duck, widgeon, and mallard, are to be seen in autumn.

A particularly sad story acts as a reminder of Sunderland's time as a port.

THE SHIP HOTEL & OLD ROOF TREE INN

The Ship: Main Street, Overton, Lancashire
Tel: 01524 858231
The Old Roof Tree Inn: Low Road, Middleton, Lancashire LA3 3JT
Tel: 01524 852434

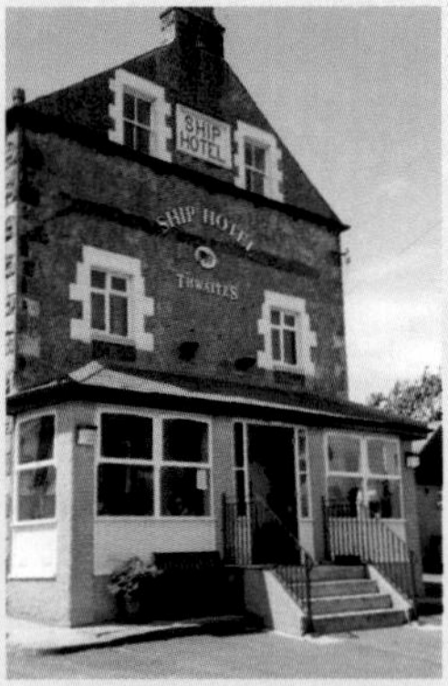

Geoffrey and Cynthia Webber are rightly proud of the reputation they have built over nearly ten years at **The Ship Hotel**, a fine old building recently renovated using many of the original timbers, furnishings and fittings. The Victorian Bar is an atmospheric spot for relaxing over a glass of real ale and a snack or a meal – potted shrimps from Morecambe Bay and home-baked ham are two of the favourites. A games room is separate from the bar, and upstairs is a popular wine bar. The Ship has two letting rooms for overnight guests.

In the nearby village of Middleton, the Webbers also own the **Old**

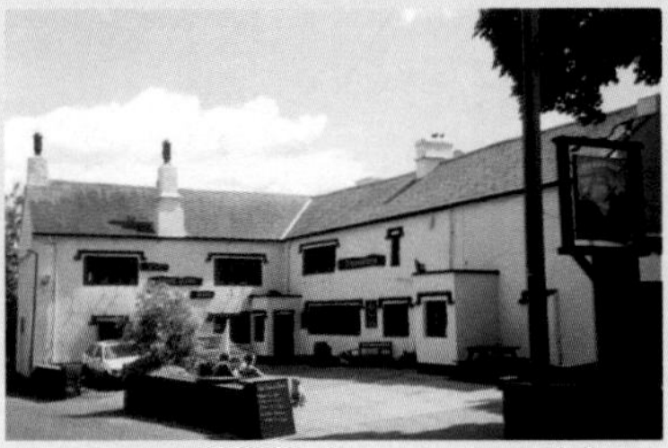

Roof Tree Inn, a Grade II listed building with its origins in the 13th century. The inn has great period appeal, with bare stone walls, black beams, copper and brass ornaments, prints, watercolours and plenty of cosy nooks and crannies. A choice of real ales is always on tap, and a menu of home-cooked dishes runs from traditional delights such as potted shrimps or Cumberland sausage to more modern choices like grilled tuna or lime & coriander salmon goujons. The inn has a large car park at the front and a pleasant garden at the back.

Sambo was a sea captain's servant at the time of the slave trade into Lancaster. Sambo fell ill of a fever just before the captain was setting off to the West Indies and was left in the care of an innkeeper. Sambo, believing himself abandoned, willed himself to die. Because he was not a baptised Christian, Sambo was not allowed to be buried in consecrated ground. In later years, his death and grave, marked by a simple cross and stone, became a potent local symbol of the anti-slavery cause.

His grave can be still seen, in a field at the west side of Sunderland Point. It can be reached by walking along The Lane from the village foreshore, past Upsteps Cottage, where Sambo died, and turning left at the shore then over a stile on the left which gives access to the simple gravestone. Fresh flowers are usually to be seen here, anonymously placed on the grave.

GLASSON

4 miles SW of Lancaster on the B5290

A few miles south of Heysham, the river Lune pours into Morecambe Bay. On its south bank lies **Glasson Dock**, once an important commercial port for larger boats unable to negotiate the tricky river as far upstream as Lancaster. The dock was built in 1791 and the tiny lighthouse erected at the same time is still in place.

The dock could accommodate 25 sea-going ships and traded extensively in slaves, rum, tobacco, sugar, and cotton. Glasson Dock today is a busy, colourful marina, serving both sea-going craft and boats arriving at the western terminus of the Lancaster Canal. Constructed in 1797, the Lancaster Canal is one of the earliest engineering marvels of the Industrial Age. 'The Lanky', as it is known, is a favourite with canal travellers since there's not a single lock in the whole of its 41 mile length from Preston to Tewitfield, thanks to the ingenuity of the canal's designer, John Rennie. He accomplished his engineering tour de force by linking the level stretches with six elegant aqueducts, the most impressive of them the five arched **Lune Aqueduct** near Lancaster, which has attracted visitors ever since it was first opened in 1797.

The canal was supplemented by the arrival of a railway line in 1883. This railway, long dismantled, is now the footpath and cycle-way to Lancaster's St George's Quay.

From Glasson there is a footpath along the coast to Plover Scar, where a lighthouse guards the River Lune estuary, and further along lie the ruins of **Cockersand Abbey**. The abbey was founded in 1190 by the Premonstratensian Order on the site of a

---

LAKEWOOD COTTAGES

c/o Cragg Hall Farm, Galgate, Nr Lancaster, Lancashire LA2 0HN
Tel: 01524 751053

Peace and relaxation are guaranteed at **Lakewood Cottages**, where Alec and Christine Sayer provide superb self-catering accommodation in the lovely Lancashire countryside. Set in the grounds of a country house on a small working farm, stone barns have been converted into three cottages finished to the highest standard and equipped with everything needed for a comfortable, go-as-you-please stay. Stone barn sleeps six, Mill Cottage sleeps four, and Granary Cottage is a cosy retreat for two. Guests are welcome to fish on an adjacent private lake, and the surrounding countryside offers a wealth of enjoyable walks. No smoking, no pets. Please telephone for brochure and price list.

hospital that had been the home of a hermit, Hugh Garth, before becoming a colony for lepers and the infirm. The 13th century Chapter House of the abbey remains since it was a burial chapel for the Dalton family of nearby Thurnham, descendants of Sir Thomas More.

GALGATE
4 miles S of Lancaster on the A6

The village of Galgate was originally located on the banks of the River Conder, which, for about half a mile, forms part of the Lancaster Canal. The village still contains some of its original mills, though they have now been put to other uses. One of them, a silk mill, was reputed to be the oldest working mill in the country, dating back to 1760, closed down in the 1960s. Galgate has a craft centre, a marina for around 100 boats and there's a well maintained pathway that leads from the village through locks to Glasson Dock.

DOLPHINHOLME
6 miles S of Lancaster off the A6

This small village of around 600 souls sits in the foothills of the Pennines at the edge of the Forest of Bowland. Dolphinholme was one of the first villages with a main street lit by gas. This was around 1806 and remains of the old gas holder can still be seen. A single street lamp has survived, now fuelled by bottled gas.

COCKERHAM
6 miles S of Lancaster on the A588

This sleepy little village lies on the shore of Morecambe Bay between the estuaries of the Lune and the Wyre. Cockerham once boasted a windmill but it was in such an exposed position that a gale in 1802 sent the sails spinning and the friction set fire to the mill. **Cockerham**

Hall (private) is a fine and rare example of a medieval timber-framed building that dates from the late 15th century. It is now a farmhouse.

QUERNMORE
3 miles E of Lancaster off the A683

Lying at the head of the Conder Valley, this peaceful farming village had a pottery industry as well as slate quarrying in the 17th century. The word quern refers to a particularly ancient form of hand-mill that was hewn from the rocks found on the nearby moorside and, indeed, corn milling continued here until World War II.

To the east of the village lies **Clougha Pike**, on the western edges of the Forest of Bowland, an Area of Outstanding Natural Beauty and one of the few places in the area that is accessible to walkers.

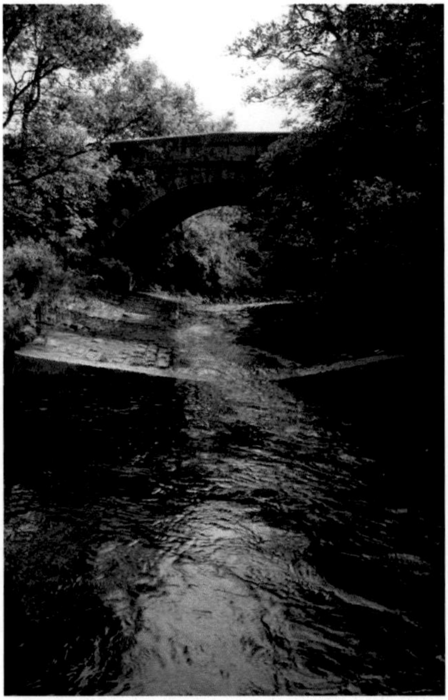

River Wyre, Trough of Bowland

Although it is not the highest peak in the forest – it rises to just over 1,300 feet – the walk up Clougha Pike is very pleasant and offers splendid views from the summit, not only of the Lakeland Fells but also of Morecambe Bay and, on a clear day, Blackpool Tower.

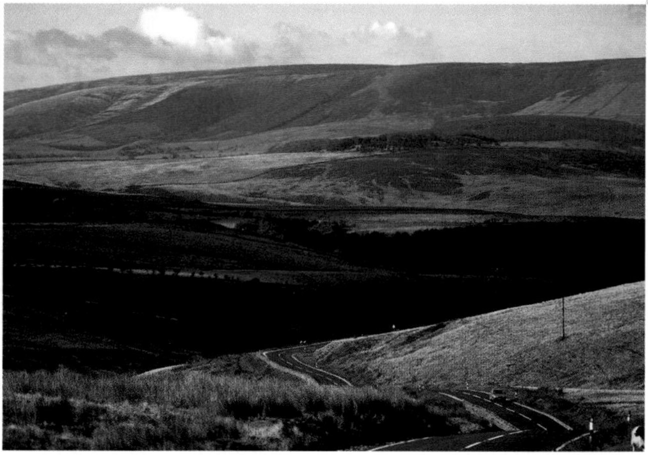
Newton Fells, Forest of Bowland

LEE

7 miles SE of Lancaster off the A6

To the northwest of this typical Bowland village soars the highest summit in the forest, **Ward's Stone**. Dotted with outcrops of gritstone boulders, the top of the fell is marked by two triangulation pillars: one of which is just over three feet higher than the other, though on first inspection, they look the same height. The panoramic views from this point are magnificent and, to the north and east, the Three Peaks of Yorkshire can be seen while the Lakeland fells roll away to the northwest.

FOREST OF BOWLAND

Designated an Area of Outstanding Natural Beauty in February 1964, this large scenic area is a veritable paradise for walkers and country lovers and is dotted with picturesque villages. The 11th largest of such designated areas, the Forest of Bowland is something of a misnomer, the term 'forest' is derived from the Latin 'foris' which was formerly used to denote a royal hunting ground, an unenclosed tract of land, rather than

a distinct wooded area. Before 1066, the broad acres of Bowland were the personal property of Earl Tostig of Northumbria, a brother of King Harold. Banished from his earldom, Tostig, with the help of the King of Norway, attempted to regain his lands and both he and the Norwegian king were killed at Stamford Bridge, just weeks before the fateful Battle of Hastings.

Following the Norman Conquest, Bowland became part of the Honour of Clitheroe and the vast estates that belonged to the de Lacy family. In time, by marriage, they came into the hands of the Earls of Lancaster and in 1399, when the then Duke of Lancaster ascended the throne as Henry IV, Bowland finally became one of nearly a hundred royal hunting forests.

The remains of a Roman road can be clearly seen traversing the land and many of the village's names in this area date back to the Saxon period. Perhaps the most celebrated of the many routes across Bowland is the minor road from Lancaster to Clitheroe which crosses

Continued on page 170

WALK 5

Slaidburn and Newton

Start	Slaidburn
Distance	5 miles (8km)
Approximate time	2½ hours
Parking	Slaidburn
Refreshments	Pub and café at Slaidburn, pub at Newton
Ordnance Survey maps	Landranger 103 (Blackburn & Burnley), Outdoor Leisure 41 (Forest of Bowland & Ribblesdale)

Although a relatively short and undemanding route, there are superb views over the Bowland fells and Hodder valley, two attractive and interesting villages and pleasant moorland, woodland and riverside walking. The final stretch is a delightful and relaxing ramble beside the River Hodder.

A street of attractive stone cottages leads up from the old bridge over the River Hodder to the village centre and the Hark to Bounty Inn. Slaidburn used to be the administrative centre of the Forest of Bowland and the forest courts met in what is now the inn, where the courtroom is still preserved. The mainly 15th century church is on the edge of the village, seen near the end of the walk.

The walk begins at the car park by the bridge over the River Hodder. Turn right to walk up through the village, keep ahead past the Hark to Bounty and just after passing Slaidburn Health Centre, bear right through a fence gap **A** onto a path which heads downhill through trees to Croasdale Brook. The path continues beside the brook to a ladder stile. Climb it, keep ahead to emerge from the trees and head up away from the brook to climb another stile. Keep ahead along the right edge of a field and, just before reaching a ladder stile in the field corner, turn sharp left and head diagonally uphill to climb a stile onto a lane **B** .

Cross over and take the moorland track ahead to Pain Hill Farm. As it winds across the moorland, there are grand and imposing views to the right of the Bowland fells. Go through a gate into the farmyard, turn right in front of the house, go through another gate and turn left at the corner of a barn to continue along a track beside a wall on the left. After climbing a stone stile to the left of a gate, follow the track as it bears slightly left across the field corner to join a wall and keep beside it towards the next farm. Climb a stone stile to the left of a gate, head across a field to climb a ladder stile in the corner, then bear right and head across the next field, passing to the left of the farm buildings.

Climb two stiles in quick succession and walk across the next field, making for a stone stile. After climbing this, keep along the right edge of a field. On approaching a farm, bear left away from the field edge, keep to the left of the farm, climb a stile and cross a plank footbridge. Keep ahead to climb another stile onto a lane **C** . Turn left and follow the narrow

lane downhill into Newton, passing a Quaker burial ground and former meeting house, both dating from the 18th century. Persecution of the Quakers at the time caused them to seek out small and relatively isolated places like Newton.

At a T-junction, turn left through the village and, at a fork, take the right-hand road, signposted to Waddington and Clitheroe. Turn right at a T-junction, follow the road down to the bridge over the River Hodder, passing the Parkers Arms, and at a public footpath sign in front of the bridge **D**, turn left through a gate. Walk along the right edge of a field, go through another gate, descend some steps and continue along a rocky and uneven path beside the Hodder. Cross a footbridge over a tributary brook and keep ahead along the right edge of a field.

Look out for where you turn right over another footbridge and climb a stone stile. Turn left along the left edge of a meadow and, at the far tapering end, climb a stile and continue above the river along the bottom inside edge of

Great Dunnow Wood. After going through a kissing gate, keep ahead across a meadow to a track, turn left and follow it below steep, wooded slopes to a 'Riverside Path' footpath post. Ahead is a fine view of Slaidburn Church.

Walk past the footpath post to go through a gate and immediately turn right over a stile **E**, also signed 'Riverside Path'. A path – a permissive route – leads to a stile. Climb it, keep ahead through trees to climb another one and turn left to follow a path beside the Hodder, over stiles and through a kissing gate, back to the start.

Abbeydale Moor and the **Trough of Bowland** before descending into the lovely Hodder Valley around Dunsop Bridge. This is a popular route in the summer months, with most lay-bys and parking places filled as people pause to take in the breathtaking moorland views.

SLAIDBURN
15 miles SE of Lancaster on the B6478

This pretty village of stone cottages and cobbled pavements lies in the heart of the Forest of Bowland. The village's focal point is the 13th century public house **Hark to Bounty**. The inn was originally named The Dog but one day in 1875 the local Hunt gathered here. A visiting Squire, listening to the hounds giving voice outside, clearly distinguished the tones of his own favourite hound rising above the others. His exclamation of delight, "Hark to Bounty!", was so whole-hearted that the landlord changed the name of his pub on the spot. The inn also contains an old courtroom, with its original oak furnishings, where from around 1250 the Chief Court of Bowland, or Halmote, was held. The only courtroom between York and Lancaster, it was used by visiting justices from the 14th century onwards, is said to have also been used by Oliver Cromwell when he was in the area, and continued in use right up until 1937.

From the village, a network of beautiful, little used lanes radiate westwards up into the fell country with some of the best walking that Lancashire has to offer. One walk in particular that offers solitude as well as excellent views of the Bowland landscape, leads to the lonely valley of the River Whitendale, northwest of the village. To the northeast of Slaidburn lies Stocks Reservoir, another popular walker's destination. Beneath its waters lie the remains of 20-odd dwellings that made up the hamlet of Stocks-in-Bolland. They were submerged in 1925 but in very dry summers the remains of the old Chapel bridge can be seen where it crosses the original Hodder river, along with the foundations of houses.

BOLTON BY BOWLAND
21 miles SE of Lancaster off the A59

Lying alongside a 'bow', or bend, in the River Ribble this tranquil village with its two ancient green, stone cross and old stocks, lies on the southern edge of the forest area. Part of the Bolton Hall estate, the village has been protected from insensitive development – the most recent dwelling to be built is already more than a hundred years old.

The 15th century village Church of St

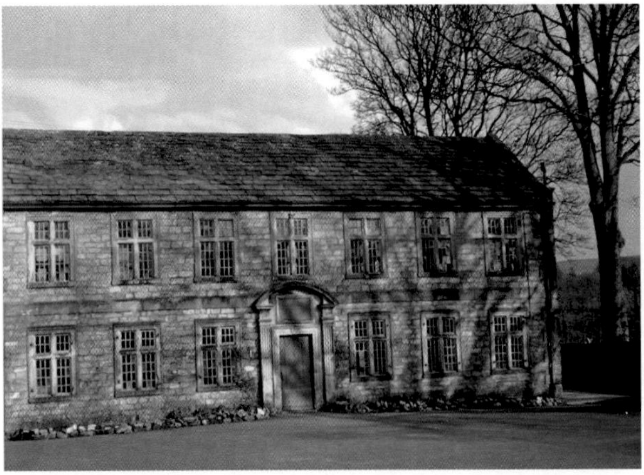
Slaidburn Grammar School

Springhead Farm Holiday Cottages

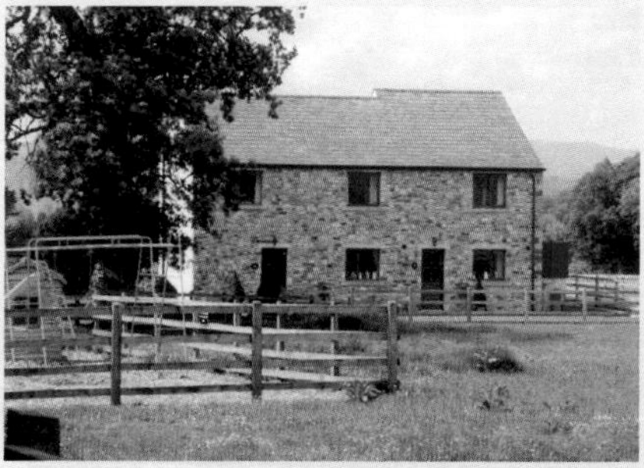

Bolton by Bowland, Nr Clitheroe,
Lancashire BB7 4LU
Tel: 01200 447245

In a serene setting in the beautiful Ribble Valley, **Springhead Farm Holiday Cottages** are ideally placed as a base for touring a particularly attractive part of the county. Susan and Richard Lund's cottages provide very comfortable self-catering accommodation in three properties sleeping 4 (Woodpecker), 6 (Kingfisher) or 8 (Mallard). All are tastefully decorated and full of character, with all the amenities needed for a relaxing, go-as-you-please stay. Equipment includes tv, video, fridge, dishwasher, full-size cooker, microwave and washing machine, and all linen and towels are provided.

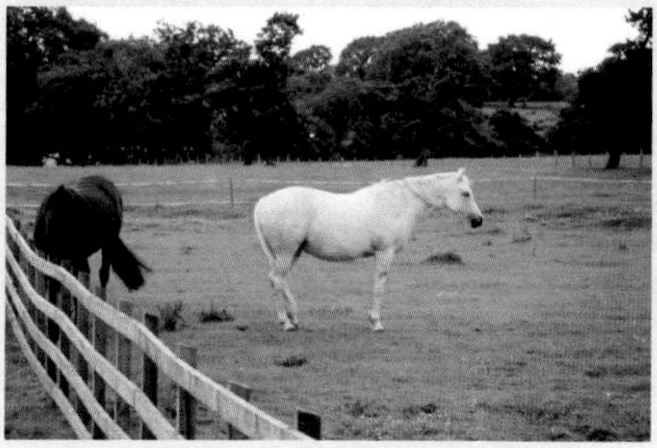

Each has central heating and two of the three also have open fires. One of Mallard's bedrooms is on the ground floor, which is fully accessible to wheelchair users. Children are very welcome, and cots and high chairs can be made available on request. This is excellent walking country, with the Forest of Bowland on the doorstep, but the farm itself also has plenty of interest, with cattle, calves and horses to see, a pleasant garden and a play area to keep the children occupied. A barbecue comes into its own on summer evenings. The village shop is a ten-minute walk away.

Peter & St Paul is home to the famous **Pudsey Tomb** with its engraved figure of Sir Ralph Pudsey in full armour alongside figures of his three wives and their 25 children. In the folds of each lady's gown is inscribed with a Roman numeral indicating how many children she bore – respectively six, two and 17.

NEWTON

15 miles SE of Lancaster on the B6478

Little more than a hamlet, Newton lies on the main route between Clitheroe and Lancaster and so, in their time, both John Paslew, the last abbot of Whalley, and the Pendle witches passed through on their way to trial in Lancaster. Here

Holden Clough Nursery

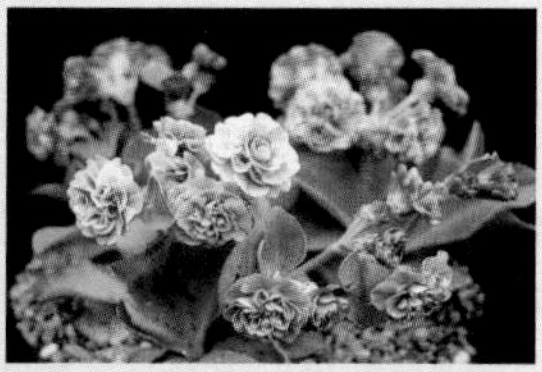

Holden, Bolton-by-Bowland, Nr Clitheroe, Lancashire BB7 4PF
Tel/Fax: 01200 447615   website: www.holdencloughnursery.co.uk
e-mail: enquiries@holdencloughnursery.co.uk

In the picturesque Ribble Valley, **Holden Clough Nursery** is a serious working nursery with a fine stock of hardy garden plants. Established in 1927, it is owned and run by Peter Foley, a plantsman all his working life and a well-known lecturer and broadcaster. Besides an impressive range of Alpine plants, the nursery stocks many herbaceous perennials, choice shrubs and climbers, dwarf conifers, heathers and hardy ferns, as well as ornamental grasses. The nursery is open from 9 to 5 Monday to Saturday, also Sunday afternoons on the spring Bank Holiday weekends. A worldwide mail order service is available.

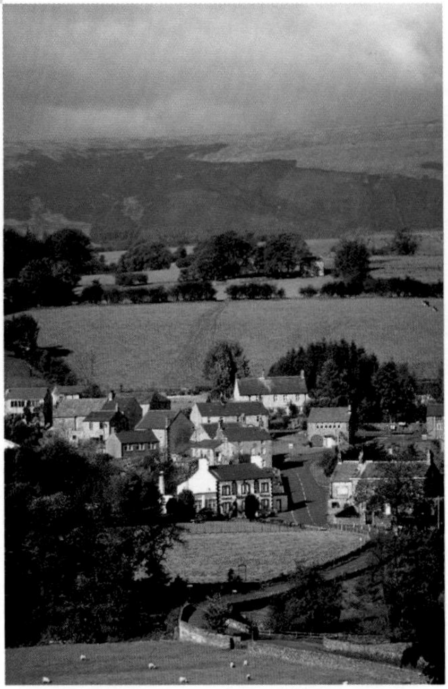

Newton Village

DUNSOP BRIDGE
14 miles SE of Lancaster off the B6478

Often known as the *'Gateway to the Trough of Bowland'* and located in a designated Area of Natural Beauty, Dunsop Bridge is, despite its remote location, the centre of the British Isles. The actual centre point, worked out by the Ordnance Survey, lies near Whitendale Hanging Stones and, to confirm the claim, the explorer Sir Ranolph Fiennes unveiled a commemorative plaque here. British Telecommunications bestowed a unique honour on the village by installing their 100,000th phone box here.

St Hubert's Roman Catholic Church on Lancaster Road has an unusual provenance. It was built by the Towneley family when their racehorse Kettledrum won the 1861 Derby. The family spent a further £1,000 on the huge white angel that stands in the graveyard and commemorates Richard Henry Towneley.

also is a **Quaker Meeting House** that was founded in 1767; the associated Quaker school, where the 19th century reformer John Bright was a pupil, has long since gone. Regarded with great suspicion by the Church of England, and by other nonconformists, because of their unorthodox views and their informality, the Quakers sought to settle in out of the way villages. Newton is typical of the places where they built their meeting houses and successfully lived according to their beliefs.

WHITEWELL
15 miles SE of Lancaster off the B6478

Little more than a hamlet in the heart of

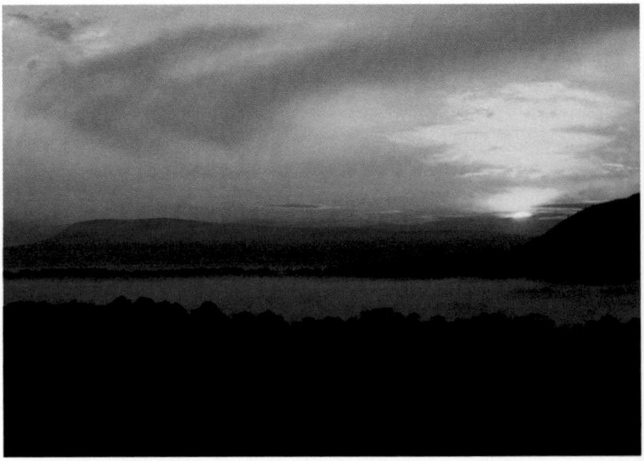

Sunset over Chipping

the Forest of Bowland, Whitewell consists of a small church, built in the early 19th century on the site of a medieval chapel, and an inn, built on the site of the old manor house.

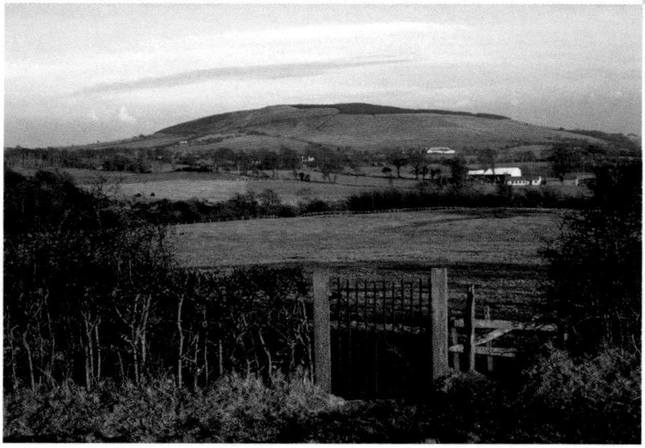

Beacon Fell Country Park

Just to the southeast lies **Browsholme Hall**, a Tudor mansion dating from 1507 that has the rare distinction of being occupied by the same family ever since. From the 16th century onwards, the owners, the Parker family, were also bowbearers, or warders, of the Forest of Bowland – the king's agent and upholders of the law in the forest. Though much of the original Tudor house can still be seen, there have been many additions over the centuries but it remains a homely building perhaps due to the continuous occupation by the same family and as a result of its remote location. The house is not open to the public.

CHIPPING
15 miles SE of Lancaster off the B6243

This picturesque village overlooking the River Loud is now a conservation area and it is also home to a post office, built in 1668, which claims to be Britain's oldest shop. Very much at the heart of the local agricultural communities, the annual village show is one of the best in Lancashire and its very name comes from the old English word for a market place - *chepyn*. In medieval times there were no fewer than five watermills along the banks of Chipping Beck and, later, one of the mills, Tweedies Mill, made ships' portholes which were used on the clipper ships bringing tea back from the east.

A little way west of Chipping is **Beacon Fell Country Park**, an area of rough moorland and woodland covering 185 acres. The land supports a wide variety of wildlife, and the Visitor Centre provides a wealth of information about the Fell and the Forest of Bowland Area of Outstanding Natural Beauty. Adjacent to the centre is the start of a sculpture trail with sculptures carved by local artist Thompson Dagnall from materials found in the locality.

LOCATOR MAP

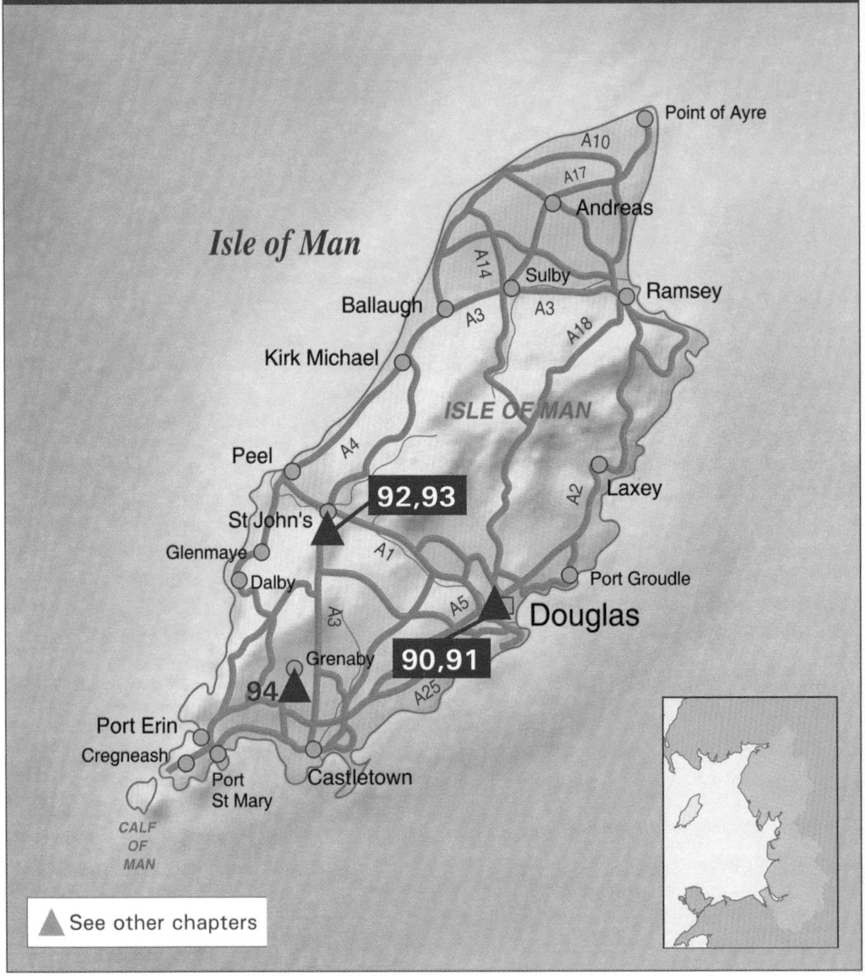

Isle of Man

Point of Ayre

A10

A17

Andreas

A14

Sulby

Ramsey

Ballaugh

A3

A3

A18

Kirk Michael

ISLE OF MAN

Peel

A4

St John's

92,93

Laxey

A2

Glenmaye

Dalby

A1

Port Groudle

A3

A5

Douglas

Grenaby

90,91

94

A25

Port Erin

Cregneash

Port
St Mary

Castletown

CALF
OF
MAN

▲ See other chapters

ADVERTISERS AND PLACES OF INTEREST

4 ISLE OF MAN

Although only 33 miles long and 13 miles wide, the Isle of Man contains a rich diversity of scenery and heritage and, perhaps best of all, exudes a sense of peacefulness epitomised by the Manx Gaelic saying 'traa-dy-liooar' – 'time enough'.

The island has an unusual status as a Crown Protectorate, with the Queen as Lord of Mann represented in the island by the Lieutenant-Governor. Its Parliament, the Tynwald, dates back more than a thousand years – the oldest continuously operating parliament in the world.

This island is perhaps best known for its annual TT (Tourist Trophy)

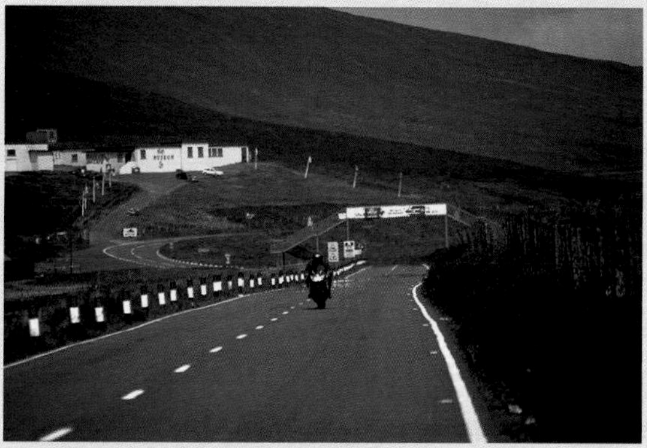

Competitor on TT Course

motorcycle races, its tailless cats, Manx kippers, and as a tax haven for the wealthy. However, there is much more to this beautiful island which, set in the heart of the Irish Sea, is truly a world apart, with its own laws, stamps, currency - even language, though of course everyone speaks English. With around 100 miles of coastline and several resorts, each with its own individual style and character, the Isle of Man has plenty to interest the visitor. The island is home to a wide range of species of birds, including chough, hen harrier, peregrine, long-eared and short-eared owls, puffins and the Manx shearwater. Natural attractions abound, and the Manx Wildlife Trust has 20 reserves throughout the island. Seventeen mountain and coastal glens are preserved and maintained in their natural state, havens of peace characterised by waterfalls, rock pools and lush vegetation.

This magical place became an island around 10,000 years ago when the melt water of the Ice Age raised the sea level. Soon afterwards, the first settlers arrived, working and developing the island into the landscape seen today. The distinctive influences of the various cultures who have lived here still remain, leaving a land with a unique and colourful heritage.

Among the first arrivals were the Vikings and evidence of their era, from the early chieftains to the last Norse King, abounds throughout the Isle of

Man. Against the skyline on the seaward side of road between Ballaugh and Bride are some ancient hilltop Viking burial mounds and, at the ancient castle in Peel, an archaeological dig revealed many hidden Viking treasures which are now on display at the Manx Museum in Douglas.

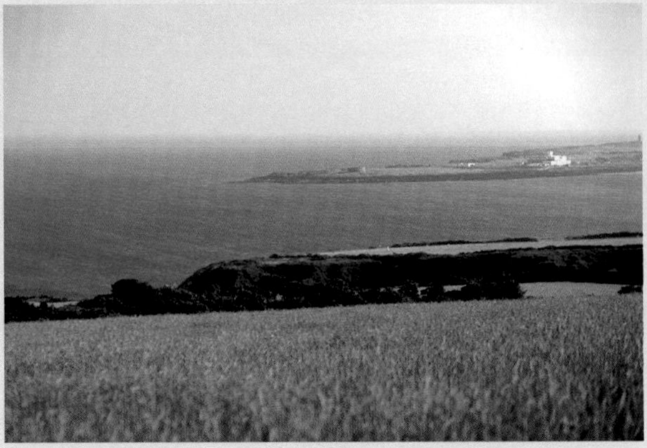

View from Santon

Despite their reputation for plunder, rape, and pillage, the Vikings also made some positive contributions to life on the island, not least of which was the establishment of the Manx governmental system, known as Tynwald. The Manx name for Tynwald Hill is 'Cronk Keeill Eoin', the hill of St John's Church. Although there is no evidence to confirm the story that it contains earth from all of the 17 parish churches here, it is not unlikely that token portions of soil were added to the mound in accordance with Norse tradition.

The Tynwald ceremony continues today with an annual meeting of the island's governors on Midsummer's Day at the ancient parliament field at St John's, where Manx citizens can also petition parliament.

The Isle of Man's most famous export is probably the Manx cat, notable for having no tail. There are several stories of how the cat lost its tail but one, in particular, is delightful. At the time that Noah was building the Ark there were two Manx cats, complete with tails. Noah sent for all the animals to come to the Ark, two by two, but the Manx cats replied that there was plenty of time and continued to play outside. Finally, when the cats did decide to board the Ark, Noah was just slamming the door and the cats lost their tails. A variation on this tale is that one of the cats reached the Ark safely, the other had its tail chopped off by the closing doors. The tailless cat went on to become the Manx cat and the one who managed to keep its tail became the ever grinning Cheshire cat. Manx cats actually originated among a population of cats whose common ancestry came from the same roots as the British Shorthair. A spontaneous mutation occurred, creating kittens born without the vertebrae that would normally form the tail. At Santon, on the south-east of the island, cat-lovers will purr with delight when visiting the Mann Cat Sanctuary, where many rescued cats and kittens, including some Manx, live happily in a pleasant rural setting.

The island's famous three-legged symbol seems to have been adopted in the 13th century as the armorial bearings of the native Kings of the Isle of Man, whose dominion also included the Hebrides. After 1266, when the native dynasty ended and control of the island passed briefly to the Crown of Scotland and then permanently to the Crown of England, the emblem was retained, and among the earliest surviving representations are those on the Manx Sword of State, thought to have been made in 1300. The Three Legs also appeared on Manx coinage from the 17th to the 19th century, and are still seen in everyday use in the form of the official Manx flag.

Why the Three Legs were adopted as the Royal Arms of the Manx Kingdom is unknown. Many heraldic emblems have no meaning and are simply chosen because they are distinctive. This may be the case with the Three Legs, though the emblem as such - something between a cross and a swastika - has a long history reaching far back into pagan times and was originally a symbol of the sun, the seat of power and light.

DOUGLAS

The island's capital (since 1869), Douglas is a lively resort with a sweeping sandy beach and a two-mile long promenade, the focus of the island's nightlife. There's excellent shopping around Strand Street, a fine park, Noble's Park, on the edge of town with facilities for tennis, bowls, putting, crazy golf and a children's play area. Other attractions include the magnificently restored Victorian Gaiety Theatre, the Manx Superbowl, a casino, the Summerland sport and leisure centre, which hosts live entertainment during the summer, The Villa Marina, an important venue for entertainment and cultural activities, a cinema complex and an Aquadrome. (Douglas once had a traditional Victorian pier, designed and built by the noted railway builder John Dixon in 1869, the year Douglas became the island's capital. A thousand feet in length, it was dismantled in 1896 and reconstructed at Rhos-on-Sea, near Colwyn Bay in North Wales.)

From dawn to dusk, visitors can take a leisurely ride along the wonderful promenade aboard the **Douglas Bay Horse Tramway**, a remarkable and beautiful reminder of a bygone era. It was the brainchild of a civil engineer, Thomas Lightfoot, who retired to the island and, seeing the need for a public transport system along this elegant promenade, designed in 1872 the system that is still in use today. That the

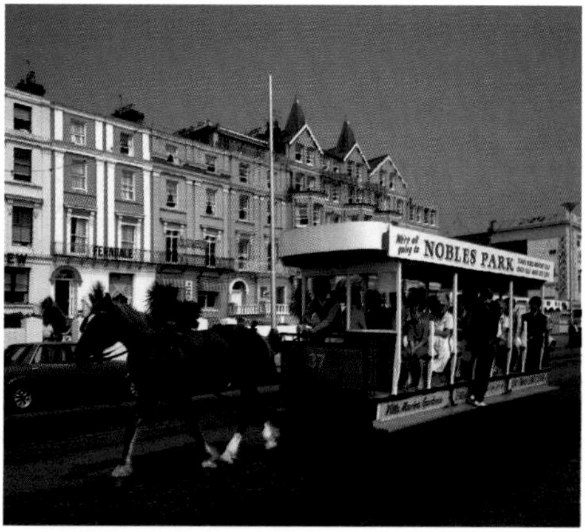

Douglas Bay Horse Tramway

MANX ELECTRIC RAILWAY

Douglas, Isle of Man
Tel: 01624 663366

An ideal way to discover what the island has to offer is by train. Supported by a good bus network, you can be somewhere different each day exploring the sights and the scenery. From Douglas, the **Manx Electric Railway** takes you along the east coast to Laxey. here you can climb to the top of the Great Laxey Wheel and go underground on the Mines Trail. Laxey is also the starting point for the Snaefell Mountain Railway which climbs the Island's highest peak. At the top you're rewarded with breathtaking views and refreshments in the Summit Hotel Café.

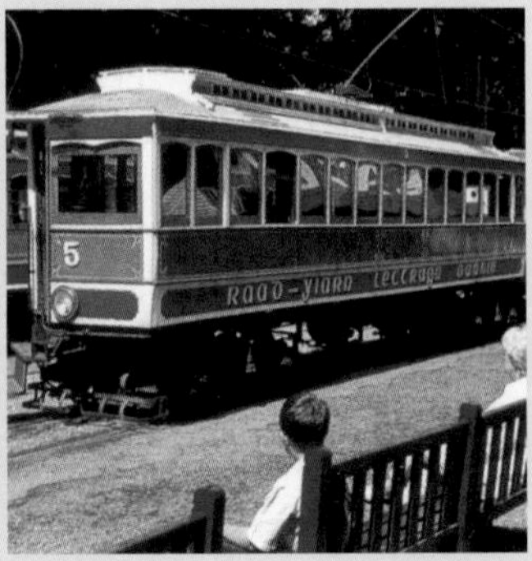

Further on from Laxey is the largest town in the north, Ramsey. In the town, there are plenty of shops to see, cafés to enjoy and pubs to visit. Nearby is Mooragh Park and boatinf alke. A short bus ride away is The Gibbs of the Grove. This Victorian period house was formerly the summer retreat of a Liverpool shipping merchant and his family. Inside the house you will find original furnishings, fittings and costumes. Outside in the spacious grounds and gardens are displays of vintage vehicles and agricultural equipment. The trains run daily between April and October and there are various themed events during the year.

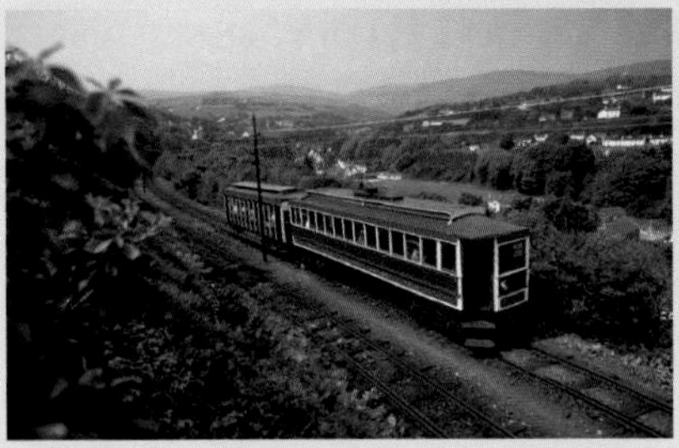

Douglas Tramway has survived into the 21st century is remarkable, especially since, in the early 1900s, attempts were made to electrify the line and extend the Manx electric railway along the promenade.

There is a story often told about the horses that pull the trams, which concerns a parrot that lived in a cage at a hotel close to one of the tram's stops. The bird learnt to mimic the sound of the tram's starting bell and used to practise this skill constantly. The tram horses would stop when they heard the bell and start off again immediately before the passengers could alight as the bird joined in the fun.

The Manx Electric Railway (see panel above), completed in 1899, is the longest narrow-gauge vintage line in the British Isles and operates the oldest working tramcars in the world. The 18-mile journey departs from the northern end of Douglas promenade, stops at Laxey, terminus of the Snaefell Mountain Railway, and then continues to Ramsey.

Another delightful means of travel is the narrow-gauge Victorian **Steam Railway** that runs between Douglas and Port Erin. Following the line of the cliff tops, the memorable journey also travels through bluebell woods and through steep-sided rocky cuttings. This section of line is all that remains of a railway that once served the whole of the island. Many miles of the old railway network have been developed as footpaths. From Quarterbridge in Douglas **The Heritage Trail** is a 10.5 mile former railway route that cuts across the island to Peel on the west coast. It's a scenic and undemanding trail that passes close to historic Tynwald Hill. Picnic sites and useful information boards are situated

along the way.

No trip to the island is complete without a visit to the **Manx Museum**, where the award-winning 'Story of Mann' audio-visual presentation uncovers 10,000 years of the island's history. The Manx Museum complex also contains the superb National Art Gallery, the National Library & Archives, as well as exhibits portraying many other aspects of life on the island, including the famous TT races. Also in

Douglas Harbour

Douglas is the Regimental Museum of the Manx Regiment.

One of the Isle of Man's most famous landmarks, the **Tower of Refuge**, looks out over Douglas Bay. Sir William Hilary, founder of the Royal National Lifeboat Institution, lived in a mansion overlooking the bay and, following a near disaster in 1830 when the Royal Mail Steam Packet *St George* was driven on to rocks in high seas, Hilary launched the Douglas lifeboat. Miraculously, all the crew of the *St George* were saved without the loss of a single lifeboatman despite the extremely treacherous conditions. It was following this incident

that Hilary decided that a form of refuge should be built for shipwrecked mariners to shelter in and so, with Hilary laying the foundation stone in 1832, the Tower of Refuge was built on Conister Rock out in the bay. Noble's Park leads to the Grandstand that is the control centre for the TT races, rightly billed as the greatest motorcycle show on earth in the road racing capital of the world. Road racing started on the island as a practice for a race to be run in France for the Gordon Bennett Cup, presented by James Gordon Bennett, owner of the *New York Herald*. An Act of Parliament outlawed racing on public highways in Britain, but at a special session of the Tynwald in 1904 a

---

THE DEVONIAN HOUSE

4 Sherwood Terrace, Broadway, Douglas, Isle of Man IM2 4EN
Tel: 01624 674676
website: www.thedevonian.co.uk

Behind a distinguished Victorian facade, **The Devonian** provides style and comfort in very civilised surroundings. Gillian and Kevin Salmon offer Bed & Breakfast accommodation in 14 well-appointed guest bedrooms, the majority of which have en suite facilities.

The Devonian, which has a fully licensed bar where light meals are served in the early evening, stands just off the promenade overlooking Glen Falcon Gardens. A fine cooked-to-order breakfast starts the day.

bill entitled The Highways (Light Locomotive) Act gave permission for limited racing on the roads of the island on a few days a year. Interest in racing, both cars and motorcycles, swiftly grew, and in 1907 the first TT race was run over a short course based on St John's. Twenty five machines started, ten finished, and the winner was CR (Charlie) Collier, who achieved an average speed of 38mph on his single-cylinder Matchless. In 1911 the mountain course was adopted and has remained more or less unchanged since.

Perched on a headland overlooking Douglas Bay is a *camera obscura* known as the **Great Union Camera**. The camera was originally situated on the old iron pier, but when this was demolished the camera was re-sited on Douglas Head. In the camera, the natural daylight is focused on to a white panel through a simple system of lenses and angled mirrors and so provides a living image of the scene outside. At first apparently still, as with a photograph, the 'picture' soon begins to move, to the fascination of viewers.

The Isle of Man was ruled for several centuries by the Stanley family, one of whom became Earl Derby. This notable gentleman organised the first Derby horserace, predating the Epsom Derby by many years. The main point of starting horse-racing on the island was to encourage the breeding of good horses. Fifty horses and donkeys who have retired or fallen on hard times are kept at the **Home of Rest for Old Horses**, set in 92 acres of open countryside just outside Douglas, on the A5 Castletown road.

NORTH OF DOUGLAS

Onchan, with a population of over 8,000, lies immediately north of Douglas and is the location of the Lieutenant-Governor's residence. An entry in the Onchan parish register records the marriage in 1781 of William Bligh RN to Miss Elizabeth (Betty) Betham, the daughter of the island's customs officer. In 1787 Captain Bligh took command of HMS *Bounty*, later the scene of the famous mutiny. The island has another connection with the Bounty. Peter Heywood, son of a deemster, was born on the island in 1773 and was 14 at the time of the mutiny. Though not on Bligh's ship at the time, he was put on trial in Tahiti and condemned to death. His sister Nessie travelled halfway across the world to beg for his life to be spared; her pleadings were successful, and Peter Heywood resumed his career in the Navy and rose to the rank of captain.

PORT GROUDLE
3 miles N of Douglas on the A11

Close to Port Groudle lies **Groundle Glen**, a deep and in places rocky valley with a bubbling stream running through its length. Excellent specimens of beech grow in the upper sections of the glen whilst, lower down, pines and larches are abundant. There is also a small waterwheel in the lower half of the glen. Railway enthusiasts will be delighted to learn that on certain days in the summer the **Groudle Glen Railway** operates. Running on a track just 2 feet wide for three-quarters of a mile along the cliffs, the railway's lovingly restored carriages are pulled by *Sea Lion*, the original 1896 steam engine.

LAXEY
5 miles N of Douglas on the A2

Set in a deep, wooded valley, this village is one of interesting contrasts. Tracing the river up from its mouth at the small tidal harbour leads the walker into **Laxey Glen**, one of the island's 17 National Glens that are preserved and

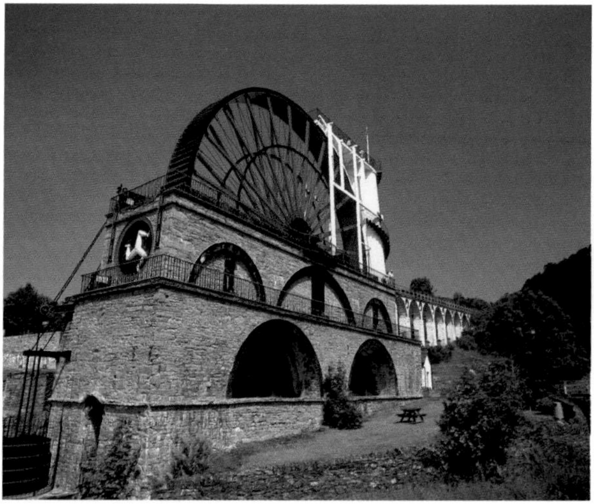

Great Laxey Wheel

just as it did when it first opened and it stands as a monument to Victorian engineering as well as the island's industrial heritage.

Situated above Laxey, in the beautiful Glen Roy, are the magnificent **Ballalheanagh Gardens**. The valley, of steep sides with winding paths and a crystal clear stream running through the bottom, is packed with rhododendrons, shrubs, bulbs and ferns, and is certainly a gardeners' paradise well worth seeking out.

maintained by the Forestry Department of the government

Further up the glen is one of the island's most famous sights, the **Great Laxey Wheel** that marks the site of a once thriving mining community. Known as the Lady Isabella Wheel, with a circumference of 228 feet, a diameter of 72 feet, and a top platform some 72 feet off the ground, it is the largest working waterwheel in the world.

It was Robert Casement, an engineer at the mines, who constructed this mechanical wonder and designed it to pump 250 gallons of water a minute from a depth of 200 fathoms. Officially opened in 1854, it was named the Lady Isabella after the wife of the then Lieutenant-Governor. After considerable repair and reconstruction work, the wheel now operates

From Laxey station, the **Snaefell Mountain Railway** carries visitors to the top of the island's only mountain. Built in 1895, the six original tram cars still climb the steep gradients to Snaefell's 2,036 foot summit and this is certainly the way to travel for those unwilling to walk. Those reaching the top are rewarded with outstanding views of the whole island and out over the sea to

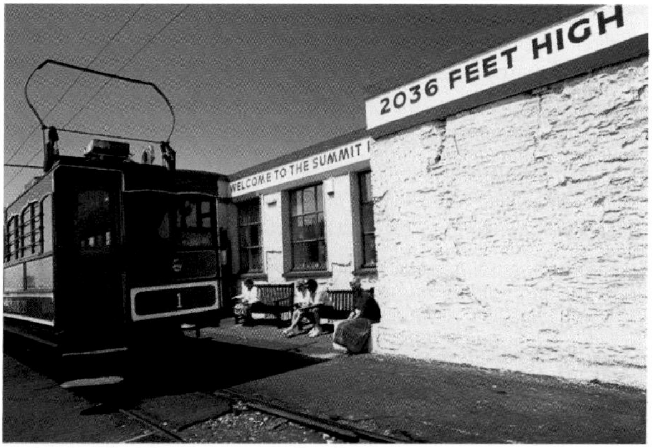

Snaefell Mountain Railway

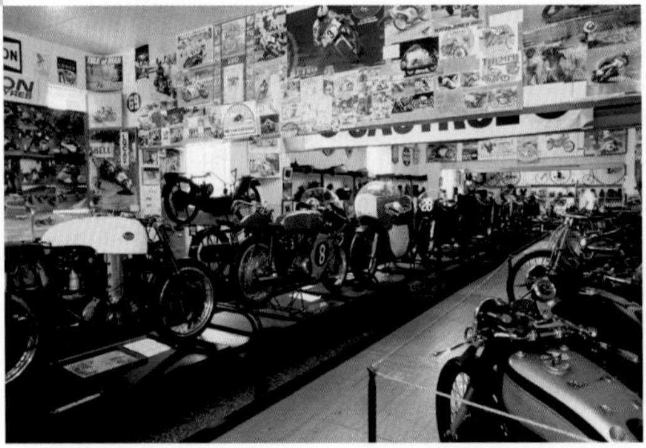

Murray's Motorcycle Museum

Ireland, Scotland, and England. There is also a café at the summit offering welcome refreshments. Snaefell is the location of **Murray's Motorcycle Museum**, where over 120 machines are on display, including Mike Hailwood's 1961 TT-winning Honda.

RAMSEY

12 miles N of Douglas on the A18

The second largest town in the island, Ramsey occupies a scenic location at the foot of North Barrule. This northernmost resort on the island has a busy working harbour, a long stretch of beach and a wide promenade. A popular amenity is **Mooragh Park**, a 40 acre expanse of gardens and recreational facilities with a 12 acre boating lake and lakeside café. During the summer months there's live musical entertainment in the park and around the third week of July each year the park is one of several venues hosting events during Yn Chruinnaght, an inter-Celtic festival of music, dance and literature.

Other major crowd-pullers are the Round-the-Island Yacht Race, held each summer and starting and finishing in Ramsey, and the Ramsey Motorcycle Sprint, part of the TT festival, when bikers show off their skills along Mooragh Promenade.

In the mid 1800s the town assumed the title of 'Royal Ramsey' following an unscheduled visit by Queen Victoria and Prince Albert in 1847. The royal yacht anchored in Ramsey Bay following a stormy crossing from Scotland so that the seasick Queen could recover. While Her Majesty recuperated on board, Prince Albert walked to the top of Lhergy Frissel and was much impressed by the view. A few years later the Albert Tower was erected to commemorate the Prince Consort's visit.

Just to the north of the town, lies the **Grove Rural Life Museum**, housed in a pleasantly proportioned Victorian house. Built as the summer retreat of Duncan Gibb, a wealthy Victorian shipping merchant from Liverpool, and his family, the rooms within the house have all been restored to their Victorian splendour and stepping into the museum is just like taking a step back in time. The outbuildings have not been neglected and they contain an interesting collection of vehicles and agricultural instruments that were seen on Manx farms in the late 19th century.

Ramsey is the northern terminus of the Manx Electric Railway, built in 1899. The **Manx Electric Railway Museum** tells the fascinating story of this world-famous Victorian transport system. From Ramsey the railway follows a scenic route southwards to Douglas, accompanied most of the way by the equally delightful coastal road, the A15/A2.

For serious walkers, there's the **Millennium Way**, which starts about a mile from Parliament Square in Ramsey. Established in 1979 to mark the

millennium year of the Tynwald parliament, the 28 mile long path passes through some magnificent countryside, picturesque towns and villages, before ending at the island's former capital, Castletown.

POINT OF AYRE
18 miles N of Douglas on the A16

This is the northernmost tip of the island and, not surprisingly, there is a lighthouse situated here. The area around the point is known as **The Ayres** and, at the Ayres Visitor Centre, a whole wealth of information can be found about this fascinating part of the island. Among the inland heath moorland, a variety of species of birds can be found nesting whilst, on the pebbled beaches, can be seen terns. The offshore sandbanks provide a plentiful supply of food for both the diving gannets and the basking grey seals.

ANDREAS
21 miles N of Douglas on the A17

Andreas was originally a Viking settlement and the village church contains intricately carved crosses dating back to the days of these early occupants. The church tower's mutilated spire goes back to the 1940s when part of it was removed in case it proved to be dangerous to aircraft from the nearby wartime airfields.

SULBY
14 miles N of Douglas on the A3

Situated in the heart of the island, the village lies on the famous TT course, a circular route on the island's roads that takes in Douglas, Ramsey, Kirk Michael, and St John's. There are several scenic and picturesque walks from the village which take in **Sulby Glen** and **Tholt-y-Will Glen**, both of which are renowned

beauty spots, and to the south, over moorland, to Sulby reservoir. Bird watchers particularly will enjoy the walks over the higher ground as it provides the opportunity to see hen harriers, kestrels, peregrines, and curlews.

BALLAUGH
13 miles N of Douglas on the A3

The village, which lies on the TT race course, is close to the island's most extensive area of marshland, the perfect habitat for a range of birds, including woodcock and grasshopper warbler, as well as being the largest roost for hen harriers in Western Europe.

Situated on the edge of the Ballaugh Curraghs, **Curraghs Wildlife Park** is home to a wide variety of wetland wildlife that come from all over the world. Curraghs is the Manx word for the wet, boggy, willow woodland that is typical of this part of the island and the site, which was opened in 1965, gives visitors the opportunity to see the animals in their natural environments. This world-renowned wildlife park has been divided into several different habitats, including The Pampas, The Swamp, The Marsh, and the Flooded Forest, and here endangered animals from around the world, such as Canadian otters, spider monkeys, rhea, and muntjac deer, live as they would in the wild.

The Curraghs Wildlife Park also has an enviable breeding record and, as many of the species are becoming rare in the wild, this is a very important aspect of the park's work. Not only have they successfully bred bald ibis, one of the most endangered birds in the world, but tapirs, lechwe antelope and many others also flourish in this environment. Not all the animals and birds are exotic – there are a great number of native species to be seen here too.

Visitors to the park are able to wander around the various habitats, following a well laid out path, and, aided by the illustrated brochure, the whole family will find this an interesting and informative trail. There is also a butterfly trail, an adventure play area for young children and, during the summer, a miniature railway runs around the park. The lakeside café is open during the day for refreshments and, during the main summer season when the park is open until 9pm, barbecues are held here.

KIRK MICHAEL

10 miles NW of Douglas on the A3

Close to the village lies **Glen Wyllin**, another of the island's 17 National Glens, and one that certainly deserves exploration. The varied woodland contains elm, ash, sycamore, alder, beech, lime, holm oak and chestnut and in spring the woodland floor is carpeted with bluebells, primroses, wood anemone and wild garlic. Kirk Michael also lies on a 16-mile footpath that follows the route of an old railway line from Peel to Ramsey. After following the coast, and part of the Raad ny Foillan, the footpath branches off through pastoral countryside before reaching the port of Ramsey on the other side of the island.

WEST OF DOUGLAS

PEEL

12 miles W of Douglas on the A1

Located on the western side of the island, Peel is renowned for its stunning sunsets and the town is generally regarded as best typifying the unique character and atmosphere of the Isle of Man. Traditionally the centre of the Manx fishing industry, including delicious

oak smoked kippers and fresh shellfish, Peel has managed to avoid any large scale developments. Its narrow winding streets exude history and draw the visitor unfailingly down to the busy harbour, sweeping sandy beach and magnificent castle of local red sandstone.

Peel Castle, one of Isle of Man's principal historic monuments, occupies the important site of St Patrick's Isle. The imposing curtain wall encircles many ruined buildings, including St Patrick's Church, the 11th century Round Tower and the 13th century Cathedral of St Germans – the cathedral of Sodor and Mann and the very first diocese established in the British Isles, pre-dating even Canterbury. The great curtain wall also encloses the later apartments of the Lords of Mann. In the 11th century the castle became the ruling seat of the Norse Kingdom of Man and the Isles, first united by Godred Crovan – the King Orry of Manx folklore. Today, the castle provides a dramatic backdrop for a variety of plays and musical events during the summer.

Recent archaeological excavations have discovered exciting new evidence relating to the long history of the site. One of the most dramatic finds was the

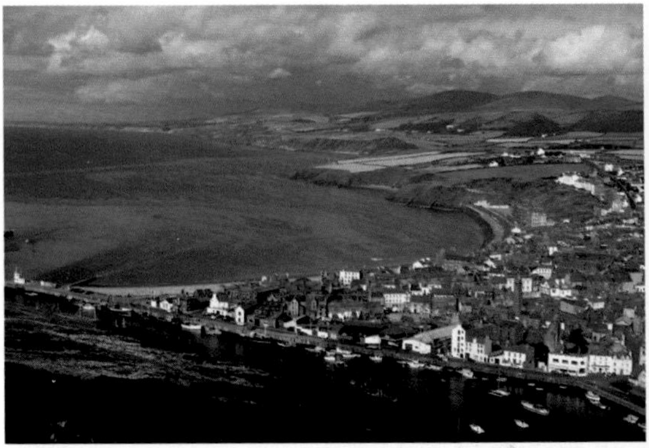

Peel Harbour

Norse grave of a lady of high social status buried in pagan splendour. The jewellery and effects buried with her can be seen on display, with other excavation finds, at the Manx Museum. The castle is also said to be haunted by the Black Dog, or Mauthe Dhoo. On dark windy nights, it can be heard howling in the castle's dungeons.

Connoisseurs of kippers speak highly of the tasty Manx kipper. At **Moore's Traditional Museum** you can watch a kipper curing process that remains unchanged since around 1770. Another major museum is **The House of Manannan**, a state of the art heritage attraction on the harbourside that was voted British Isles Museum of the Year in 1998. And for those researching their family history, **The Leece Museum** has

an archive of docluments and photographs of the town along with a varied display of artefacts connected with the life of a busy fishing port. Peel gave its name to the only production car ever made on the island. The three-wheel Peel, produced between 1962 and 1966, was one of the tiniest cars ever made - the first model was only 4½ feet long and was powered by a 49cc DKW engine. The claim that it could carry a driver and a shopping bag was disputed by some who thought that it was a question of one or the other!

ST JOHN'S

3 miles E of Peel on the A1

Roads from all over the island converge at the village of St John's because this is the site of the ancient **Tynwald Day**

The Courtyard, Tynwald Mills Craft Centre,
St John's, Isle of Man IM4 3AD
Tel/Fax: 01624 801913
e-mail: weaversandclay@manx.net

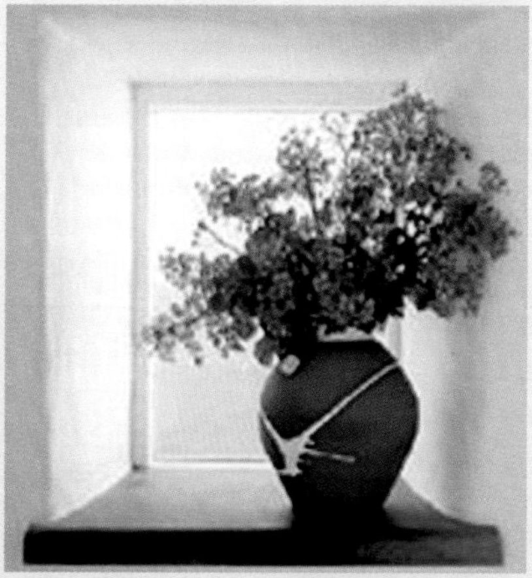

Cathy Matthews moved from Dublin to the Isle of Man to set up **Weavers & Clay** as a showcase for some of the finest Irish crafts and gourmet food. Her beautifully appointed shop in the Tynwald Mills Craft Centre exclusively stocks a wide range of pottery and crafts from Ireland, including Stephen Pearce Pottery, Stoneware Jackson Pottery, exquisite handmade leather bags by Chesneau, silverware by Paul Costelloe, wood-craft by Philip Kenny, handmade scented candles by Oberg, fine Irish linen and pure wool throws by Avoca Handweavers.

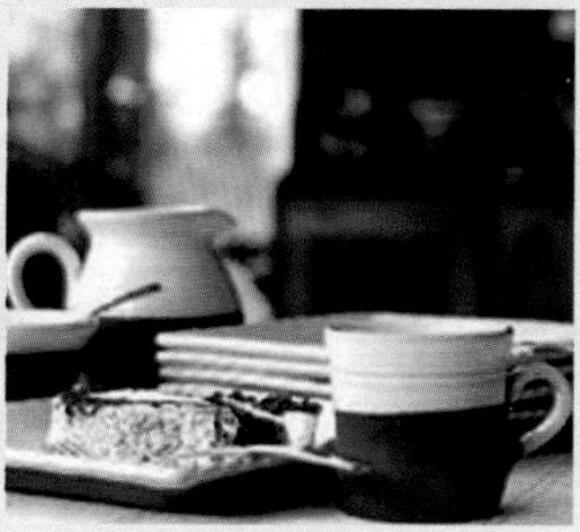

The shop also provides a gourmet taste of Ireland with such delights as handmade Skelligs Chocolates, teas and coffees from Clive McCabe, Odlums breads, sauces and biscuits from renowned Castle Leslie and a wonderful range of relishes and cookery books from the world-famous Ballymaloe Cookery School in Cork. Cathy and her friendly helpful staff are always happy to help visitors looking for the perfect gift at this really lovely shop, which is open from 10.30 to 5 Monday to Saturday and from 2 to 5 on Sunday.

PINEWOOD STUDIO

The Old Ballacraine Hotel, St John's, Isle of Man IM4 3NF
Tel: 01624 801829

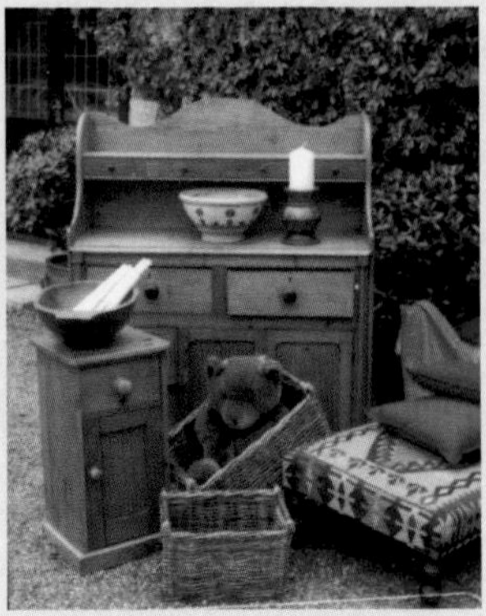

A hotel on one of the island's main routes is now the home of **Pinewood Studio**, which Beth Waterworth and Maree Murphy established in 1986. Behind the pretty flower-decked pink frontage, the display areas are filled with all kinds of decorative furnishings and beautiful and unusual gifts for all occasions. The studio exclusively stocks Bridgewater Pottery and Matthew Rice products, and the range on show also includes basketware, soft furnishings and table accessories; scented candles and lavender goods imbue the whole place with a wonderful aroma.

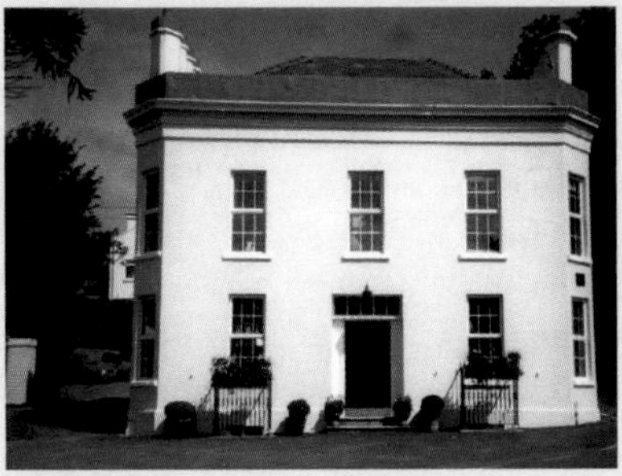

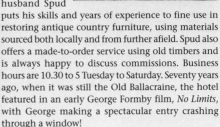

In the workshop Maree's husband Spud

puts his skills and years of experience to fine use in restoring antique country furniture, using materials sourced both locally and from further afield. Spud also offers a made-to-order service using old timbers and is always happy to discuss commissions. Business hours are 10.30 to 5 Tuesday to Saturday. Seventy years ago, when it was still the Old Ballacraine, the hotel featured in an early George Formby film, *No Limits*, with George making a spectacular entry crashing through a window!

Ceremony, held on July 5th, which is a public holiday throughout the island. This grand open-air event takes place on Tynwald Hill just north of the village. Here the Tynwald Court – a parliament that can trace its origins to the 9th century – assembles and the new laws of the land are proclaimed in both Manx and English. The serious business over, the rest of the day is devoted to various celebrations and activities culminating in a firework display.

Adjoining Tynwald Hill, the 25-acre **Tynwald Arboretum** was established in 1979 to mark the millennium of the island's parliament.

GLENMAYE

3 miles S of Peel on the A27

A spectacular bridged gorge and waterfall dominate this glen, which is one of the most picturesque on the island. Comprising over 11 acres, its

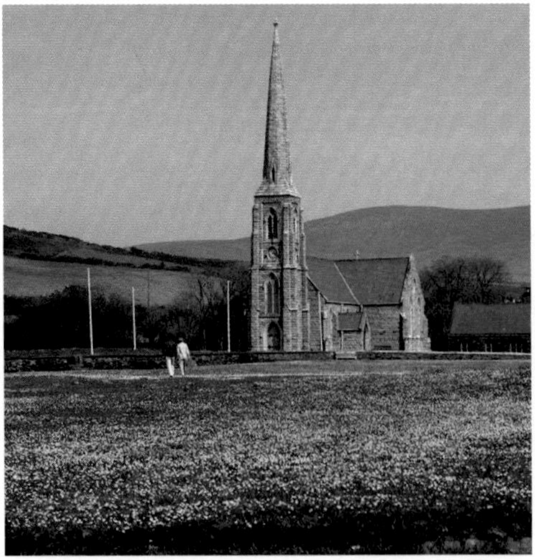

St John's Church, Tynwald Hill

beautiful sheltered woodland includes some relics of the ancient forests that once covered much of the Isle of Man. Another feature of this glen is the Mona Erin, one of the many waterwheels which once produced power for the Manx lead mines.

Dalby

4 miles S of Peel on the A27

Just southwest of Dalby village, **Niarbyl Bay** takes its name from the Manx Gaelic, Yn Arbyl, meaning 'the tail', so named because of the long reef that curves out from the shoreline. There are stunning views to the north and south, and the grandeur of the southwestern coast is seen at

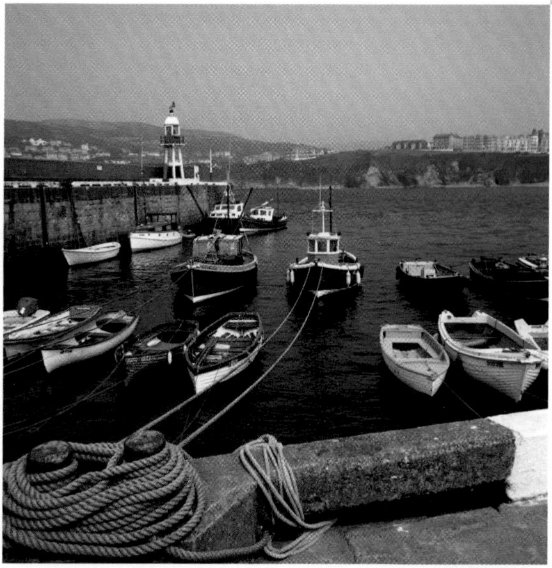

Port Erin Harbour

its best from this typically Manx setting. The beach here is an ideal place for picnics, relaxing and enjoying the tranquillity of the setting.

Port Erin

16 miles S of Peel on the A5

Situated between magnificent headlands, Port Erin's beach is certainly a safe haven. It is also a place of soft sands cleaned daily by the tide with rock pools to one side and a quay to the other. A long promenade above the sheltered sandy beach has a number of cafés and other amenities include bowls, tennis, putting, nearby Rowany golf course and some superb walks along coastal paths out to Bradda Head. Port Erin is also the terminus for the Steam Railway which runs from here to Douglas.

The town has its own Erin Arts Centre, which since 1975 has hosted the annual **Mananan International Festival of Music and the Arts**, now recognised as

one the island's most prestigious cultural events. The two week long festival takes place from mid to late June and the eclectic programme ranges through classical music, opera and ballet, jazz and theatre, to films, Indian music and art exhibitions as well as special events for children.

Calf of Man

18 miles S of Peel

This small island, situated just off the southwestern tip of the island, is now a bird sanctuary owned by the National Trust; it was given to the Trust in 1937 and almost immediately declared a bird sanctuary. The puffins should be grateful – one of the previous owners, the Dukes of Athol, requested that his tenants living on the Calf should catch the nesting puffins and pickle them! In 1777, a stone was found on the isle in the garden of Jane's Cottage, though in those days it was called The Mansion.

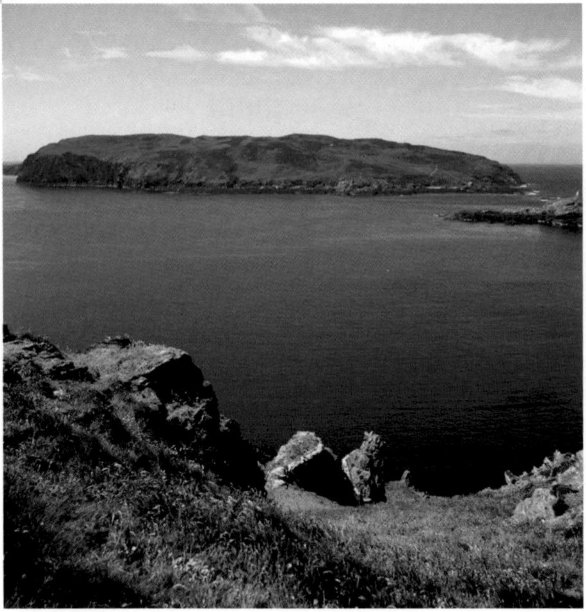

Calf of Man

off to invade Ireland. Centuries later, men from nearby Port St Mary were granted a gallantry medal by Napoleon, thought to be the only such medal he presented to British subjects, when they came to the rescue of the crew of the *St Charles* schooner from France which foundered in the sound.

One mile south of the Calf is the Chicken Rock and lighthouse; it was particularly associated with storm petrels, often known as Mother Carey's chickens.

CREGNEASH
19 miles S of Peel off the A31

Known as the Calf Crucifixion Cross, the stone is believed to date from the 8th century and it is one of the earliest Christian finds in Europe. The cross can be seen in the Manx Museum in Douglas.

In 2002, a new **Visitor Centre** was opened at the southernmost top of the island. The scenic 4 acre site also has a shop, café and car park and provides grand views of Spanish Head, the Calf of Man and the Irish Mountains of Mourne. This is one of the most important breeding areas for seabirds, and the British Bird Observatory keeps detailed records from March to November each year.

Calf Sound, the stretch of water between the island and the Isle of Man has seen many ships pass through and it was here that the largest armada of Viking longships ever assembled in the British Isles congregated before setting

Perched close to the southwestern tip of the island, this village is now a living museum - **Cregneash Village Folk MuseuM** - which offers a unique experience of Manx traditional life within a 19th century crofting community. Its isolated position led the village to become one of the last strongholds of the island's ancient skills and customs and all this is beautifully preserved today.

By combining small scale farming with other occupations, a small settlement of Manx men and women have successfully prospered here since the mid 1600s. In the carefully restored buildings, visitors can see the conditions in which they lived and managed to sustain life in this rugged landscape. The centrepiece of Cregneash is without doubt **Harry Kelly's Cottage**. Kelly, who died in 1934, was a renowned Cregneash crofter and a fluent speaker of the Manx language.

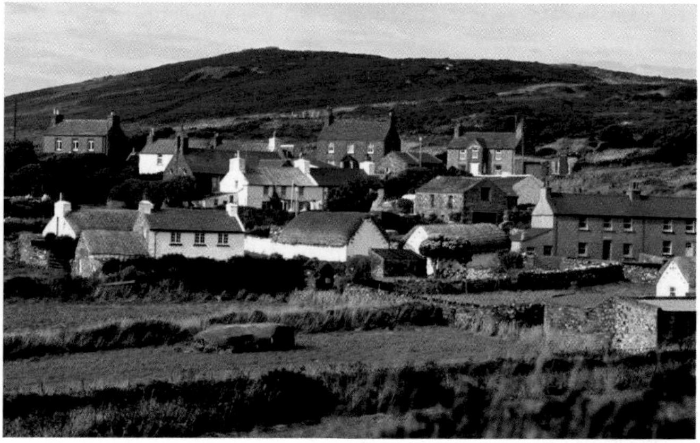

Cregneash Village Folk Museum

most sheltered part of the island.

One of the finest walks on the Isle of Man is the cliff-top route from Port St Mary to Port Erin along the **Raad ny Foillan** - the road of the gull - a long distance footpath that follows the coastline right around the island. From Port St Mary, the first part of the walk takes in **The Chasms**, gigantic vertical rifts that, in some places, descend the full 400 feet of the cliffs.

Opened to the public in 1938, his cottage, still filled with his furniture, is an excellent starting point to any tour of the village. There are various other buildings of interest, including Turner's Shed, a smithy, and the Karran Farm.

The village is also one of the few remaining places where visitors get a chance to view the unusual Manx Loaghtan four-horned sheep, a breed which, thanks to Manx National Heritage and other interest groups, now has a secure future.

CASTLETOWN
9 miles SW of Douglas on the A7

The original capital of the island, Castletown is full of character and charm, especially around the harbour area. Here, in August, the **World Tin Bath Championship** is held, one of the sporting world's more unusual contests,

PORT ST MARY
13 miles SW of Douglas off the A31

This delightful little working port has both an inner and outer harbour, two piers, and excellent anchorage for visiting yachts. The beach, along a scenic walkway from the harbour, is no more than two miles from the beach at Port Erin but it faces in almost the opposite direction and lies in the

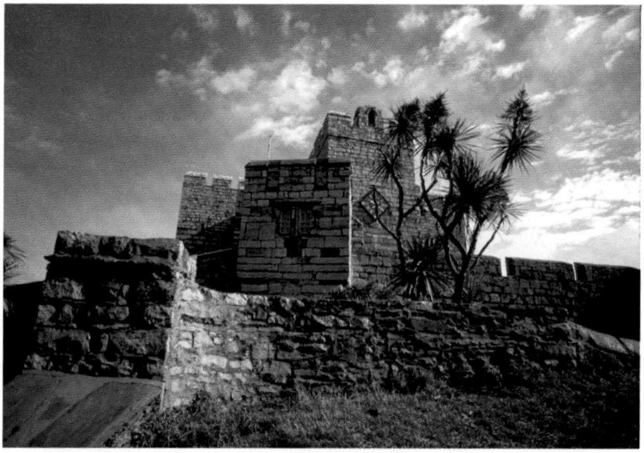

Castle Rushen

as well as snake racing and many other aquatic events.

The harbour lies beneath the imposing battlements of the finely preserved **Castle Rushen**, once home to the Kings and Lords of Mann. The present building was mostly constructed between 1340 and 1350 and has recently been restored to provide today's visitors with a vivid impression of what life was like in the fortress many years ago by presenting in authentic detail the sights, sounds, and smells of its heyday. Among the various points of interest is a unique one-fingered clock that was presented to the castle by Elizabeth I in 1597 and which still keeps perfect time.

The castle is also still used as a courthouse, for the swearing-in of new governors, and for registry office weddings. During the summer months there are regular spectacular displays re-enacting scenes from the castle's history, especially the events of 1651 when Royalists were forced to surrender Castle Rushen to Cromwell's parliamentary troops.

Like Peel Castle, Rushen too is said to be haunted, by a ghost known as the White Lady. Believed to be the ghost of Lady Jane Gray who travelled to the island from Scotland with her family, the spectre has been seen walking the battlements at night and occasionally passing straight through the castle's closed main gate during the day.

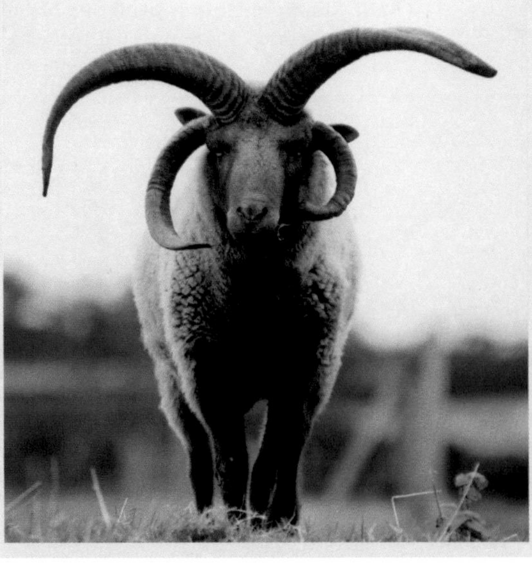

Also recently restored to its 19th century state of grace is the **Old House of the Keys**, the seat of the Manx parliament until it removed to Douglas in 1874. In the rather cosy former debating chamber visitors can vote on various issues which the parliament faced in the past, and some they may face in the future.

Castletown is also home to the island's **Nautical Museum**, where the displays centre around the 1791 armed yacht *Peggy* which sits in her contemporary boathouse. Part of the original building is constructed as a cabin room from the time of the Battle of Trafalgar and there are many other artefacts on display, all with a maritime theme.

A mile or so northeast of Castletown is Ronaldsway, the island's principal airport, where the Aviation Museum is worth a visit. Nearby, in the village of **Ballasalla**, is **Rushen Abbey** – the most substantial medieval religious site in the Isle of Man. This ancient Cistercian monastery now has an interpretative centre that explains the abbey's past importance and illustrates the daily life of the monks.

A couple of miles further along the A5 road towards Douglas, visitors should look out for the **Fairy Bridge**. For centuries, Manx people have taken no chances when it comes to the little people and it is still customary to wish the fairies who live under the bridge a respectful tip of the hat and a 'Good Morning' when crossing.

LOCATOR MAP

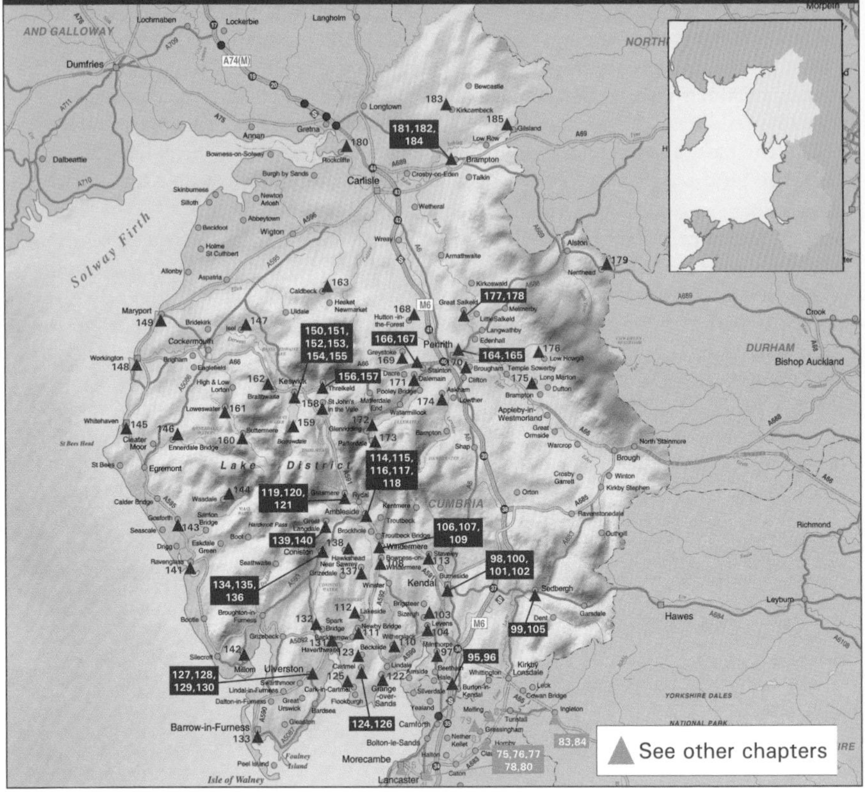

See other chapters

ADVERTISERS AND PLACES OF INTEREST

5 CUMBRIA AND THE LAKE DISTRICT

Visitors from all over the world are drawn in their millions to the Lake District, with its irresistible combination of enchanting lakes, picturesque villages and some of the most dramatic scenery in England. The highest mountain in the country, Scafell Pike (3,205ft), the largest and deepest lakes, Windermere and Wast Water respectively, are all found here, along with hundreds of other mountains, another 14 lakes (but apart from Bassenthwaite they are called 'meres' or 'waters'), challenging crags and lovely wooded valleys.

Despite the huge influx of visitors, most do not venture far from the main tourist 'honey-pots' so it's still easy to find the peaceful glades and windswept, isolated fells celebrated by the Lake Poets, Wordsworth, Coleridge and Southey. Between them, this lyrical trio transformed the pervading 18th century perception of the most northwesterly corner of England as an intimidating wilderness into an appreciation of its majestic scenery.

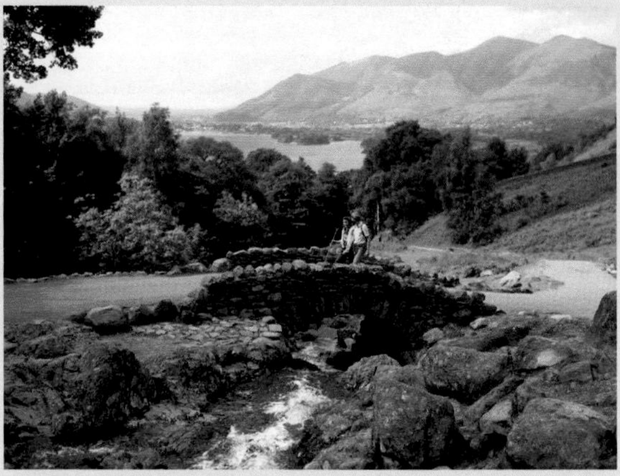

Ashness Bridge, nr Keswick

Almost exactly one third of the county's 2,636 square miles lies within the boundaries of the Lake District National Park, created in 1951 to protect the area from "inappropriate development and to provide access to the land for public enjoyment". Its 22,292 square kilometres include a wonderfully varied landscape, and the opportunities for enjoying the great outdoors are almost boundless. For many people travelling from the south into Cumbria, their first experience of the county is the area around Kendal and Kirkby Lonsdale. These ancient settlements both provide an excellent introduction to the history, people, and economy of Cumbria.

The southeastern corner of the extensive Lake District National Park is Cumbria's best known and most popular area, with the main resort towns of Windermere, Bowness-on-Windermere and Ambleside, and, of course, Lake Windermere itself. They are certainly busy with tourists during the summer months but their charm and attraction remain for all to see. Also, with the unpredictability of Lakeland weather, they provide a whole host of indoor amusements to appeal to all ages.

The whole area opened up to tourism as a result of the Victorians' growing

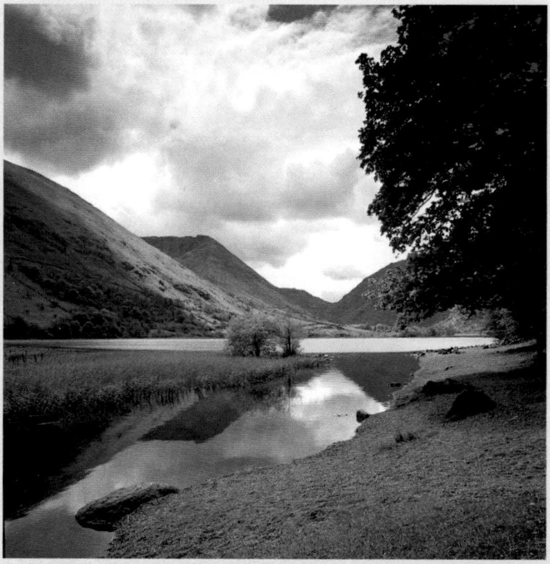

Brothers Water

interest in the natural landscape and their engineering ability in providing a railway service. So these villages, once little more than places where the fell farmers congregated to buy and sell their livestock and exchange gossip, grew into inland resorts with fine Victorian and Edwardian villas, houses, and municipal buildings.

Lying between the lakes and mountains of the Lake District and the sandy estuaries of Morecambe Bay, the Cartmel and Furness Peninsulas are an area of gentle moorland, craggy headlands, scattered woodlands, and vast expanses of sand. It was once a stronghold of the Cistercian monks, whose influence can still be seen in the buildings and fabric of the landscape. This is Cumbria's ecclesiastical centre and there were several monasteries here. The rapid growth of Barrow-in-Furness, which will be forever linked with the shipbuilding industry, changed the face of much of the area, but as the iron industry declined so did the town.

The arrival of the railways in the mid-19th century saw the development of genteel resorts such as Grange-over-Sands overlooking the treacherous sands of Morecambe Bay. Grange is still an elegant little town and has been spared the indignity of vast amusement parks and rows of slot machines, retaining its character as a quiet and pleasant holiday centre.

The North Cumbrian coast, from Workington in the south to the Solway Firth in the north, is one of the least known parts of this beautiful county but it certainly has a lot to offer. It is an area rich in heritage, with a network of quiet country lanes, small villages, old ports, and seaside resorts. The coast's largest town, Workington, on the site of a Roman fort, was once a large port, prospering on coal, iron and shipping. It later became famous for fine-quality steel, and though its importance has declined, it is still the country's largest producer of railway lines. Further up the coast is Maryport, again a port originally built by the Romans.

A short distance inland lies Cockermouth on the edge of the Lake District National Park, a pretty market town with some elegant Georgian buildings. However, most visitors will be more interested to see and hear about the town's most famous son, the poet William Wordsworth, who was born here in 1770.

The northernmost stretch of coastline, around the Solway Firth, is an area of tiny villages with fortified towers standing as mute witness to the border struggles of long ago. These villages were the haunt of smugglers, wildfowlers, and half-net fishermen. What is particularly special about this coastline is its rich birdlife. The north Cumbrian coast was also the setting for Sir Walter Scott's novel *Redgauntlet*, and the fortified farmhouse by the roadside beyond Port Carlisle is said to be the White Ladies of the novel.

The River Eden, one of the few large rivers in England that flows northwards, rises on the high limestone fells above Mallerstang Common, near the North Yorkshire border, and runs to the outskirts of Carlisle where it turns sharply east and flows into the Solway Firth. For much of its course, the river is accompanied by the famous Settle to Carlisle Railway, a spectacularly scenic route saved from extinction in the 1960s by the efforts of local enthusiasts.

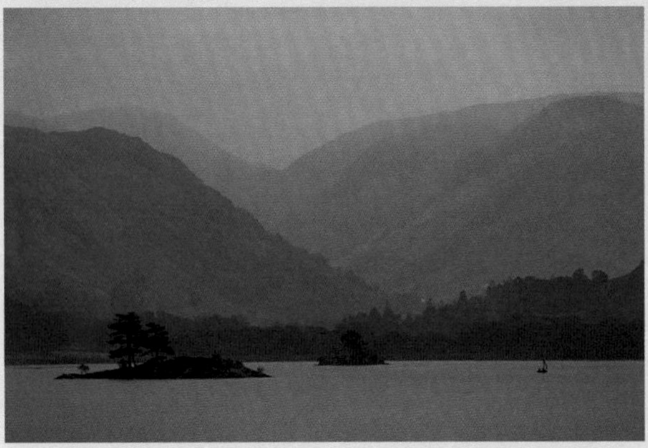

Ullswater Lake

For more than 350 years the area around Carlisle was known as the Debatable Lands, a lawless region where the feared Border Reivers sacked and plundered at will. Every winter, when their own food stocks were almost depleted, armed gangs from across the border would ride southwards to seize the cattle and sheep of their more prosperous neighbours. Stealing and murdering, they wreaked havoc in this area and almost every village would have had a fortified structure, usually a pele tower, where the inhabitants and their animals could hide safely.

This is, too, the country of Hadrian's Wall, the most important monument built in Britain by the Romans; many stretches of the wall are still visible, and Birdoswald and other centres give an excellent insight into Roman border life.

KIRKBY LONSDALE

One fine day in 1875 John Ruskin came to Kirkby Lonsdale and stood on the stone terrace overlooking the valley of the River Lune. It was, he declared, "one of the loveliest scenes in England, therefore in the world". He was equally enthusiastic about the busy little market town - "I do not know in all my country", he continued, "a place more naturally divine than Kirkby Lonsdale".

Ruskin had been inspired to visit the town after seeing Turner's painting of that view, and Turner himself had come in 1816 on the recommendation of William Wordsworth. All three of them made a point of going to see the **Devil's Bridge** over the Lune, a handsome, lofty structure of three fluted arches reputedly built by Satan himself in three days. According to legend an old woman, unable to cross the deep river with her cattle, had asked the Devil to build her a bridge. He agreed but demanded in return the soul of the first creature to cross but his evil plan was thwarted by Cumbrian cunning. The old woman threw a bun across the bridge which was retrieved by her dog and thus she cheated the Devil of a human soul.

Kirkby's Main Street is a picturesque jumble of houses spanning several centuries, with intriguing passages and alleyways skittering off in all directions, all of them worth exploring. It's still a pleasure to stroll along the narrow streets bearing names such as Jingling Lane, past the 16th century weavers' cottages in Fairbank, across the **Swine Market** with its 600-year-old cross where traders have displayed their wares every Thursday for more than 700 years, past ancient hostelries to the even more venerable **St Mary's Church** with its noble Norman doorway and massive pillars. In the churchyard, a late

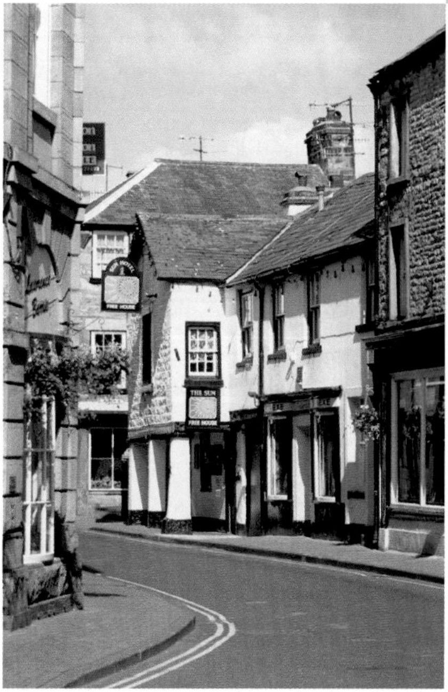

Kirkby Lonsdale Town Centre

Georgian gazebo looks across to the enchanting view of the Lune Valley painted by Turner.

The town has three times been national winner of the 'Britain in Bloom' competition and also attracts thousands of visitors for its **Victorian Fair**, held on the first full weekend in September, and again in December for the Yuletide procession through streets ablaze with coloured lights and decorated Christmas trees.

AROUND KIRKBY LONSDALE

HALE

7 miles W of Kirkby Lonsdale off the A6

This tiny village surrounded by woodland and close to the Lancashire border is home to the **Lakeland Wildlife Oasis** (see panel on page 199), where a

THE DUTTON ARMS

Station Lane, Burton-in-Kendal, Cumbria LA6 1HR
Tel: 01524 781225
e-mail: geoff.ditchfield@virgin.net
website: www.duttonarms.com

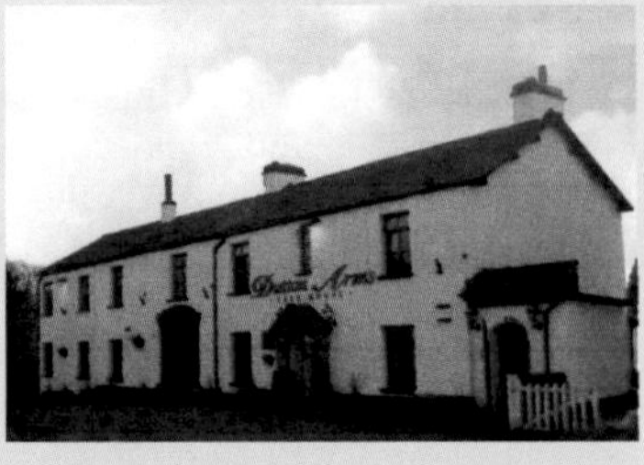

Situated in open countryside on the edge of the picturesque village of Burton-in-Kendal, the **Dutton Arms** is a lovely old country inn where Annie and Geoff Ditchfield enjoy welcoming old friends and new into a delightfully relaxed ambience. Formerly the Old Station House, the inn has a friendly bar serving a wide variety of ales and wines, a spacious conservatory, well-appointed accommodation in traditional style and an excellent 90-cover restaurant.

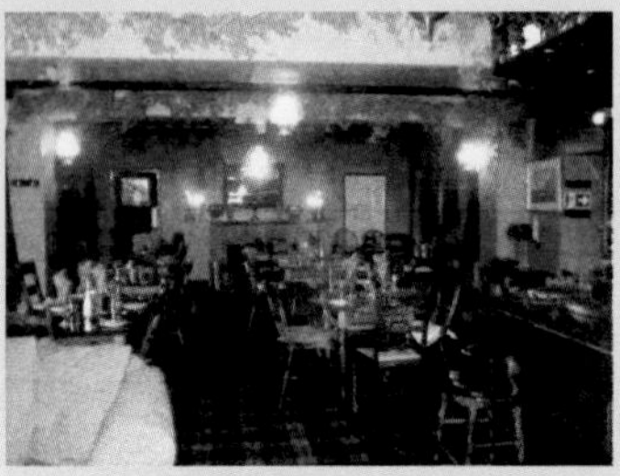

The extensive à la carte menu reflects the best of English country cooking and includes local specialities such as Morecambe Bay shrimps and Cumberland sausages. Steaks are always the best cuts, and the daily specials always include several fish and seafood dishes. Filled jacket potatoes and sandwiches are available until 6pm, and children can choose from their own special menu. The food, for which the inn has a growing reputation, is complemented by a very interesting wine list. The bedrooms, all with en suite facilities, include family rooms (children also have an adventure playground and an indoor play area) and a bridal suite with a four-poster bed.

WATER GARDEN RESTAURANT

A6 Road, Burton-in-Kendal,
Cumbria LA5 9RW
Tel: 01524 782888
e-mail: jasonyorke@btconnect.com
website: www.watergardenrestaurant.co.uk

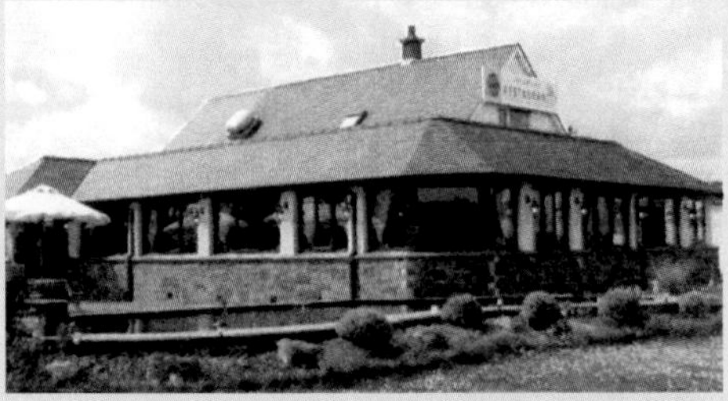

Jason and Karen Yorke took over **Water Garden Restaurant** in February 2002 and have worked hard to provide a stylish, comfortable setting for enjoying fine food accompanied by excellent wines. Jason seeks out the very best local produce for the extensive menu, which changes daily and is always supplemented by specials. Typical dishes run from freshly baked black pudding roulade or whitebait in a caper and dill butter to Cumberland sausage, steaks, guinea

fowl with pine nut and redcurrant jus and plaice with prawn and parsley butter. Meals stay delicious to the end with some splendid desserts. The Water Garden enjoys superb views over the surrounding countryside, and the beautiful garden has some magnificent water features.

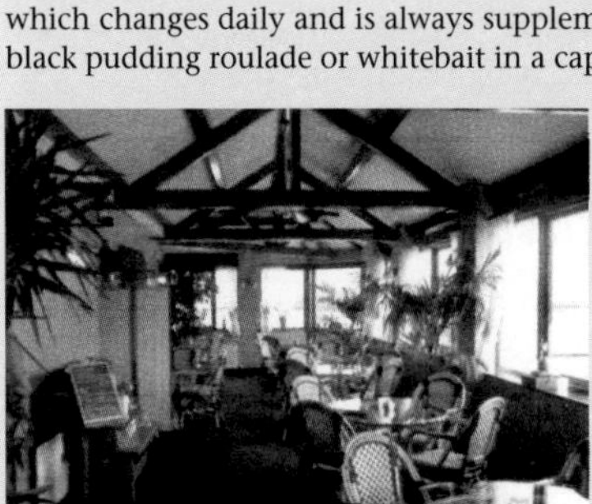

Jason & Karen and Geoff & Annie are frequent diners at each others' restaurants and have devised a great idea for visitors to enjoy both: on production of a receipt from the Water Garden at the Dutton Arms, or vice versa, customers are entitled to a complimentary bottle of house wine with lunch or dinner. Additionally, a receipt for a full meal at the Water Garden brings a 20% reduction off the room tariff at the Dutton Arms.

wide range of animals and birds can be seen and a hands-on exhibition tells the evolutionary story. Visitors can drape a snake around their neck, exchange inquisitive glances with a ruffled lemur or a meerkat squatting on its haunches, and admire creatures rarely seen in captivity such as flying foxes or poison arrow frogs. The tropical hall is the home of numerous free-flying birds, bats and butterflies, and other exhibits range from leaf-cutter ants to pygmy marmosets. The Oasis was established in 1991 by Dave and Jo Marsden, who were keepers at Chester Zoo before setting up this popular family attraction, which is open throughout the year.

ARNSIDE
10 miles W of Kirkby Lonsdale off the B5282

This quiet town on the Kent Estuary, with its short but elegant promenade, was once a busy port with its own shipbuilding and sea-salt refining industry. As the estuary silted up during the 19th century, a process accelerated by the construction of the striking 50-arch railway viaduct, so the port declined. Today, it is a favourite retirement destination and a peaceful holiday resort.

Around Arnside itself there is a wonderful choice of country walks, particularly over and around **Arnside Knott**. This limestone headland, now a nature reserve rich in old woods and wild flowers, is part of the Arnside and Silverdale Area of Outstanding Natural Beauty. Knott comes from the Saxon word meaning 'rounded hill', which, in this case, rises 521 feet above sea level and gives extensive views of the Lakeland fells, the Pennines, and the southern Cumbrian coast. There is a beautiful path around the headland and along the shoreline past Blackstone Point.

LAKELAND WILDLIFE OASIS

Hale, Milnthorpe, Cumbria LA7 7BW
Tel: 015395 63027
e-mail: mail@wildlifeoasis.co.uk
website: www.wildlifeoasis.co.uk

Opened in 1991, **Lakeland Wildlife Oasis** quickly established itself as one of the Lake District's premier visitor attractions. "Half Zoo, half Museum, and totally fascinating" the Oasis takes visitors on an amazing journey through the world of wildlife using a unique

combination of live animals and imaginative "hands-on" computer displays. Visitors can drape a snake around their neck, exchange inquisitive glances with a Ruffled Lemur or a beautifully poised Meerkat squatting on its haunches, and admire creatures rarely seen in captivity such as Flying Foxes and Poison Arrow Frogs. Or you can just relax in the tropical hall, colourful with free-flying birds, bats and butterflies. Many rare species have found a secure home here, amongst them the fossa, of which there are only 44 in captivity. Friendly staff are always on hand to answer questions and let you meet some of the inhabitants face to face! The Oasis was established by Dave and Jo Marsden, both of whom were animal keepers at Chester Zoo before setting up this popular family attraction. It is open every day of the year, (except for Christmas Day and Boxing Day), there is access throughout for the disabled, and other amenities include picnic areas, a snack bar and a gift shop. For parties of more than 30 people, it is advisable to book ahead and the Oasis will then provide a tour guide.

Inland, and found down a quiet lane, is **Arnside Tower**, one of the many pele towers that were built in the area in the 14th century. This particular tower dates from the 1370s and it may have been part of the chain of towers designed to form a ring of protection around Morecambe Bay.

BEETHAM

8 miles W of Kirkby Lonsdale on the A6

Approached through a pergola of rambling roses, the **Church of St Michael and All Angels** dates from Saxon times and, during restoration work in the 1830s, a hoard of around a hundred coins, minted in Norman times, was discovered inside the building at the base of a pillar. Although badly damaged during the Civil War, when its windows were smashed and effigies broken, a glass fragment of Henry IV in an ermine robe has survived the centuries. The village is also home to an unusual 19th century **Post Office** with a distinctive black and white studded door.

Just outside the village lies **Heron Corn Mill**, a restored and working watermill with fully operational grinding machinery. A fine example of a traditional corn mill which operated for trade in the Westmorland farming area, the mill ceased trading as recently as the 1950s. Visitors to the mill can see an exhibition about its history and view the milling process. Also here is the **Museum of Paper Making**, which was established in 1988 to commemorate 500 years of papermaking in England.

KENDAL

A survey a few years back by Strathclyde University revealed that the highest quality of life of any town in England was to be found in Kendal, the 'capital' of South Lakeland. That assessment came

as no surprise to the residents of this lively, bustling town which was once one of the most important woollen textile centres of northern England. The Kendal woollen industry was founded in 1331 by John Kemp, a Flemish weaver, and it flourished and sustained the town for almost 600 years until the development of competition from the huge West Riding of Yorkshire mills during the Industrial Revolution of the 19th century. The town's motto 'Wool is my Bread' reveals the extent to which the economy of Kendal depended on the wool from the flocks of Herdwick sheep that roamed the surrounding fells. The fame of the cloth was so great that Shakespeare refers to archers clad in Kendal Green cloth in his play *Henry IV*. These archers were the famous **Kendal Bowmen** whose lethal longbows were made from local yew trees culled from the nearby limestone crags. It was these men who clinched the English victories at Agincourt and Crécy and fought so decisively against the Scots at the Battle of Flodden Field in 1513.

Kendal has royal connections too. The Parr family lived at **Kendal Castle** until 1483 - their most famous descendant was Catherine Parr, the last of Henry VIII's six wives. Today, the castle's gaunt ruins stand high on a hill overlooking the town, with most of the castle wall and one of the towers still standing, and two underground vaults still complete. Castle Hill is a popular place for walking and picnicking and in summer the hillside is smothered with wild flowers. From the hilltop there are spectacular views and a panorama panel here assists in identifying the distant fells.

Anyone wandering around the town cannot help but notice the numerous alleyways, locally known as yards, that are such a distinctive feature of Kendal. An integral part of the old town, they are

Kendal Castle

Shopping Centre, **Blackhall Yard** and **Elephant Yard**, all in the heart of the town, and the **K Village Factory Shopping** complex on the outskirts, make it easy to shop until you drop. One local product well worth sampling is **Kendal Mint Cake**, a tasty, sugary confection which is cherished by climbers and walkers for its instant infusion of energy. Another once-popular local medication, **Kendal Black Drop**, is sadly no longer available. 'A more than commonly strong mixture of opium and alcohol', Kendal Black Drop was a favourite tipple of the poets Samuel Taylor Coleridge and Thomas de Quincey.

a reminder that the people of Kendal used to live under a constant threat of raids by the Scots. The yards were a line of defence against these attacks, an area that could be secured by sealing the one small entrance, with the families and livestock safe inside.

Shoppers are spoilt for choice in Kendal. In addition to all the familiar High Street names, the **Westmorland**

Kendal's excellent sporting facilities include the **Kendal Leisure Centre**, which offers a one-week tourist pass, Kendal Wall, which is one of the highest indoor climbing facilities in the country, Kendal ski slope, two local golf courses and a driving range. Drama, music and the visual arts are presented in a regularly changing programme of exhibitions, live music, theatre

ABBOT HALL ART GALLERY AND MUSEUM

Kendal, Cumbria LA9 5AL
Tel: 01539 722464
Fax: 01539 722494

Abbot Hall Art Gallery forms part of a complex within Abbot Hall park and includes work by John Ruskin and the celebrated portrait painter, George Romney, who was born nearby at Dalton-in-Furness in 1734. The permanent collection also includes a wide range of 18th, 19th and 20th century British paintings and watercolours, and the Gallery hosts regular touring exhibitions.

boho

Unique Apparel - Individual Attire

The Old Pottery, Howgill Lane, Sedbergh, Cumbria LA10 5DE
Tel: 015396 22108
e-mail: sunell@telco4u.net

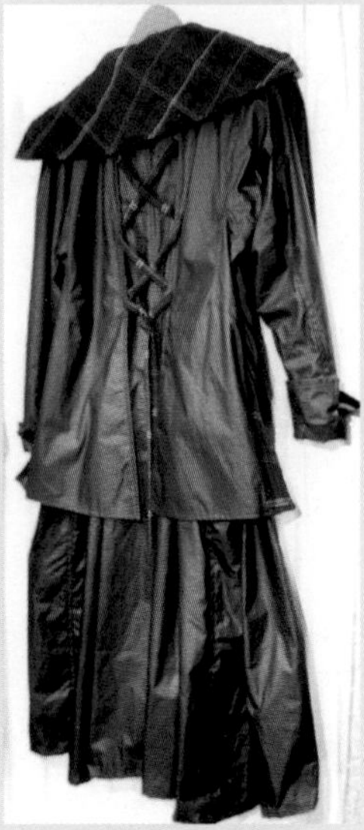

Tucked away up a narrow lane in Sedbergh, North Cumbria, you will find **boho**, a veritable Aladdin's Cave of designer clothes and accessories and all the more delicious because it is such an unexpected find....

You will be dazzled by colour, wafted by rich and exotic aromas and beguiled by wonderful music as you go about the rails and shelves, and you will discover delightful pieces of wearable art by designers such as Terry Macey, Angel Circle, Shepard Linen, Flax, Blueberry Hill, and many many others....

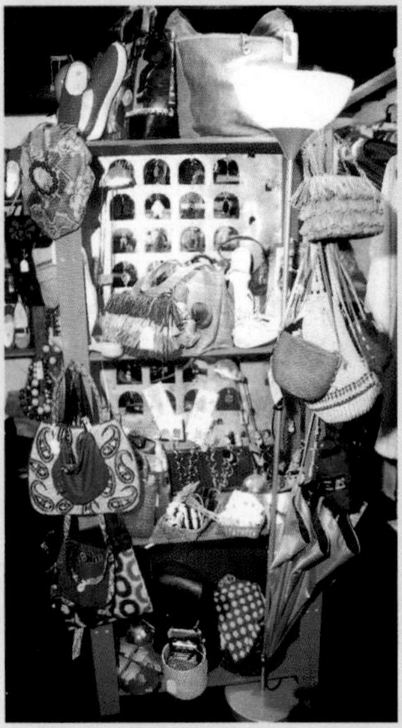

You will also find stunning jewellery in innovative designs, wearable yet wacky headgear, umbrellas in colours to chase away the rainy day blues, and shoes .... oh the shoes...! boho is also the home of the Amazing Rainforest Collection, wearable pieces of art, the tailoring so intricate it boggles the mind, and in shapes that will entrance... these coats are not just pretty though, they are also made to keep out the worst the elements can throw at you - quite a good thing in Cumbria!!

Many of the designers garments you will find here at boho are made by small local or UK craftspeople who have few or no 'shop window' of their own. Their designs are delightful, different and in some cases quite exclusive to boho. You will find hand painted silk dresses, coats, luscious wraps and stoles, hand woven and felt knitwear in colours that practically 'zing' off the rails, and there are heavy linen pieces which can be worn all year round - they are big fans of the layered look at boho!!

Chunky silver rings, wrist cuffs and wide silver watches are waiting to be discovered too - all made by local silversmiths. Woven and felted bags, felted silk and wool hats both stylish enough for the grandest occasion or to wear to walk in the mountains on a cold day - the colours will warm you, as will all the admiring glances you will receive!!

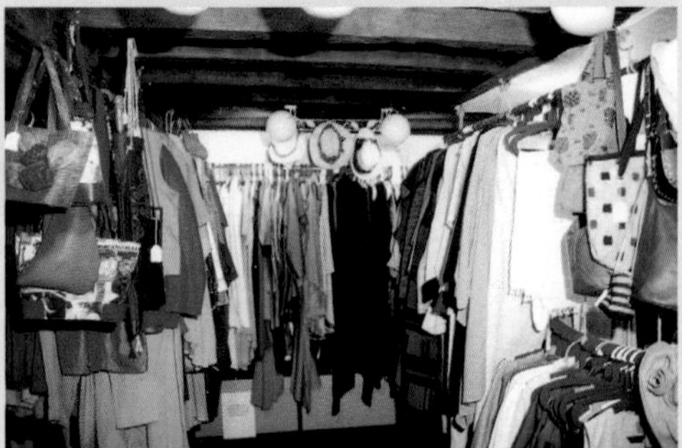

Evening wear in flowing or fitted styles, all unusual and very very stylish will also be found at boho along with the accessories you might crave to go with it .... richly embroidered stoles, bags and shawls, dashing and chic jewellery, dainty evening slippers in unexpected and alluring colours.

Whatever you may be looking for, if your taste is for the unconventional, the unusual or the 'far from everyday', be sure you will find it at boho.

productions and craft workshops at the **Brewery Arts Centre**. The Centre also houses Kendal's cinema which presents a mixture of mainstream, classic and art house films.

A number of interesting museums and galleries are also located in Kendal. The **Museum of Lakeland Life and Industry**, which is themed around traditional rural trades of the region, and **Abbot Hall Art Gallery** (see panel on page 201) form part of a complex within Abbot Hall park. The museum, in re-created farmhouse rooms, contains a wide variety of exhibits, including Arthur Ransome memorabilia, craft workshops, a Victorian street scene, artefacts from the Arts and Crafts movement, nautical displays and Captain Flint's Locker, a pirates activity area for children and families. The gallery, in an elegant Georgian villa, houses a collection of society portraits by the locally born George Romney and watercolour scenes by Ruskin and Turner, while the 20th century and contemporary scene is represented by Walter Sickert, Ben Nicholson, Lucien Freud and Bridget Riley. The **Museum of Natural History and Archaeology**, founded in 1796, is one of the oldest museums in the country. Based on the collection first exhibited by William Todhunter in the late 18th century, the Museum takes visitors on a journey from prehistoric times, a trip which includes an interactive exhibit which tells the story of Kendal Castle.

The famous fellwalker and writer, Alfred Wainwright, whose handwritten guides to the Lakeland hills will be found in the backpack of any serious walker, was honorary clerk here between 1945 and 1974. Many of his original drawings are on display. In the summer of 2004 a small exhibition will open chronicling

LAKELAND NATURAL VEGETARIAN GUESTHOUSE

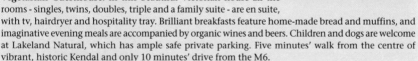

Low Slack, Queen's Road, Kendal, Cumbria LA9 4PH
Tel/Fax: 01539 733 011 e-mail: relax@lakelandnatural.co.uk
website: www.lakelandnatural.co.uk

A peaceful location, spacious surroundings, stunning views - all this and much more is guaranteed at the family-run **Lakeland Natural Vegetarian Guesthouse**. In this beautiful Victorian house all the rooms - singles, twins, doubles, triple and a family suite - are en suite, with tv, hairdryer and hospitality tray. Brilliant breakfasts feature home-made bread and muffins, and imaginative evening meals are accompanied by organic wines and beers. Children and dogs are welcome at Lakeland Natural, which has ample safe private parking. Five minutes' walk from the centre of vibrant, historic Kendal and only 10 minutes' drive from the M6.

WATERSIDE WHOLEFOODS VEGETARIAN CAFÉ & SHOP

Kent View, Waterside, Kendal, Cumbria LA9 4DZ
Tel: 01539 729 743 Fax: 01539 733 011
e-mail: relax@lakelandnatural.co.uk website: www.lakelandnatural.co.uk

A stunning riverside location close to the centre makes **Waterside Wholefoods Vegetarian Café & Shop** a unique venue in this bustling market town. The food, too, is unique - GM-free, scare-free, largely local, organic and all prepared on the premises. Morning coffee comes with a mouthwatering selection of scones, cakes and tray bakes; lunch offers exciting salads and daily changing hot and cold dishes; and afternoon tea is a relaxing treat not to be missed. Organic wines and beers accompany a meal, and all the food is available for takeaway.

the life of a local eccentric called Millican Dalton. Affectionately known as the **Cave Man of Borrowdale**, he lived for 50 years in a cave blasted from the slate of Castle Crag near Keswick and propounded his views on Quaker pacifism, vegetarianism and the outdoor life. He achieved notoriety between the two World Wars by offering women the chance to go on expeditions involving camping, river crafting and shooting rapids.

Adjacent to the elegant Georgian Abbot Hall and Museum is the 13th century **Parish Church** of Kendal, 'the Church of the Angels', one of the widest in England, with five aisles and a peal of 10 bells.

Perhaps the most unusual attraction in Kendal is the **Quaker Tapestry Exhibition** (see panel below) at the Friends Meeting House in the centre of the town. This unique exhibition of 77 panels of community embroidery explores Quaker history from the 17th century to the present day. These colourful, beautifully crafted tapestries are the work of some 4,000 people, aged between four and 90, from 15 countries. A Quaker costume display, embroidery demonstrations, workshops and courses, and a large screen colour video combine to provide a fascinating insight into the Quaker movement and its development.

AROUND KENDAL

LEVENS
5 miles S of Kendal off the A590

At the southern tip of Scout Scar, overlooking the Lyth Valley and the lower reaches of the River Kent, stands **Levens Hall** with its unique topiary gardens. The superb Elizabethan mansion (described as 'one of the wonders of Lakeland') developed from a 14th century pele tower and the gardens were first laid out in 1694. They were the work of Colonel James Grahme, a keen gardener, who purchased the hall in 1688 and employed a Frenchman, Guillaume Beaumont, to create the amazing topiary work (Beaumont also

---

THE QUAKER TAPESTRY

Friends Meeting House, Stramongate, Kendal, Cumbria LA9 4BH
Tel: 01539 722975
e-mail: leaflet@quaker-tapestry.co.uk
website: www.quaker-tapestry.co.uk

The Quaker Tapestry provides a fascinating insight into the Quaker movement and vividly illustrates the Quaker way of life. This unique exhibition of 77 panels of community embroidery delights visitors of all ages. It explores the Quaker journey from the 17th century to the present day as it uncovers over 300 years of social history, beautifully created by 4000 men, women and children from 15 countries between 1981 and 1996. The exhibition is enhanced by the use of personal headphones and a large screen colour video which graphically supplements the background information on the making of the tapestry.

Embroidery demonstrations are given by an experienced embroiderer and there is a small costume display for those interested in the dress codes of an earlier age. The well stocked gift shop offers a wide selection of souvenirs and gifts for purchase. There is easy access for wheelchairs and groups and school parties are welcome if booked in advance. Open Spring to late Autumn 10am - 5pm.

Levens Hall Gardens

and plasterwork, a dining room with walls covered in goatskin, and paintings by Rubens, Lely and Cuyp. A major location for the BBC-TV serial *Wives and Daughters*, the Hall's other attractions include a collection of working steam engines, a tea room, gift shop and plant centre.

Only a couple of miles north of Levens Hall, just off the A591, is another stately old residence, **Sizergh Castle**, the impressive home of the Strickland family since 1239 although the property is now administered by the National Trust. Originally a pele tower built to withstand border raiders, the house has been added to and altered over the intervening centuries to provide the family, as times became less violent, with a more comfortable home. Now boasting intricately carved chimney mantels, fine

redesigned the gardens at Hampton Court for James II). The topiary is by no means the only attraction in the grounds, which also include a Fountain Garden created in 1994 to mark the tercentenary of the gardens. The interior of the house is equally rewarding - a wealth of period furniture, fine panelling

LOW SIZERGH BARN

Low Sizergh Farm, Sizergh, Nr Kendal, Cumbria LA8 8AE
Tel: 015395 60426 Fax: 015395 61475
e-mail: apark@low-sizergh-barn.co.uk
website: www.low-sizergh-barn.co.uk

Farmshop, tea room, craft gallery and farm trail - all these can be found at the Park family's organic farm on the A591 four miles south of Kendal. **Low Sizergh Barn**, a delightful 18th century stone building, houses a farm shop selling a huge array of speciality foods, including fell-raised lamb, local cheese,

home baking, organic vegetables and free-range eggs. The latest addition to the range is beautiful Lancashire cheese made from the farm's organic milk. In the old shippons beneath the barn is a gallery with a large collection of prints and watercolours, ceramics, baskets and rugs.

Also in the barn is a tea shop serving cakes and quiches, pies and daily specials, all made on the premises; visitors arriving for afternoon tea at around 3.45 can watch the cows being milked from the large viewing windows that overlook the milking parlour. The farm, which is rented from the National Trust, has 120 Holstein Friesian dairy cows and 250 organic free-range hens. A farm trail recently developed by the owners enables visitors to enjoy the lovely countryside and the diversity of wildlife while learning how organic principles are put into practice around this beautiful farm.

CATH'S GARDEN PLANTS

The Heaves Nursery, Heaves Hotel, Levens,
Nr Kendal, Cumbria. Tel: 01539 561126
Office Tel/Fax: 01524 735567

In a tranquil location close to the M6 and A6,
Cath's Garden Plants is a delightful place to
visit for gardeners and non-gardeners alike.
Nursery staff are always on hand to give help
and advice concerning the thousands of plants
of all kinds that are for sale, and the lovely old
stone walls that surround the garden add extra
charm to the superb setting. The Nursery is open
Friday to Monday 10.30am to 5.00pm, March
to October.

oak panelling, and a collection of
portraits of the Stuart royal family, the
castle stands in well laid out gardens and
1,500 acres of grounds which provide
superb views over the Lakeland fells.

BRIGSTEER

3 miles SW of Kendal off A591

This tiny hamlet lies under the limestone
escarpment of Scout Scar. From this
pretty settlement, the road leads into the
National Trust property of **Brigsteer
Woods** where, as the climate is milder
here due to its sheltered position, there
are wild daffodils in the spring.

BURNESIDE

2 miles N of Kendal off the A591

There has been a settlement here since
the Stone Age and the remains of a stone
circle can be seen close by on **Potter Fell**.
By the 15th century, Burneside was a
settled agricultural area and a rich
variety of mills sprang up along the River
Sprint - fulling, corn, cotton, wool,
bobbin, and the original rag paper mill
at **Cowan Head.**

The River Sprint, which meets the
River Kent just south of the village, has
its own remarkably beautiful
Longsleddale Valley which curves past
Garnett Bridge deep into the high fell

country. A bridle path climbs from the
head of the valley into Kentmere,
another spectacularly beautiful walk.

SEDBERGH

In 1974 Sedbergh was brusquely removed
from the West Riding of Yorkshire and
became part of Cumbria. However, it still
lies within the Yorkshire Dales National
Park and the surrounding scenery
certainly belongs to the Dales with the
mighty **Howgill Hills** - great pear-shaped
drumlins shaped by glaciers - soaring to
more than 2,200 feet (670 metres).
Winder Hill, which provides a dramatic
backdrop to the little market town, is
half that height, but with its sleek grassy
flanks and domed top, seems much
loftier. Four valleys and four mountain
streams meet here and for centuries
Sedbergh (pronounced Sedber) has been
an important centre for cross-Pennine
travellers. During the golden age of stage
coach travel, the town became a staging
post on the route between Lancaster and
Newcastle-upon-Tyne. The complete
journey between Lancaster and
Newcastle took from 4 o'clock in the
morning to 7 o'clock at night: 15 hours
to cover a distance of about 120 miles,
an average speed of 8 miles per hour. At
the **King's Arms Hotel**, the four horses

would be swiftly changed before the equipage rattled off again across the moors to Teesdale, Durham and Newcastle.

In those days, the stage-coach would have been used frequently by the boys attending Sedbergh's famous **Public School**. Its founder was Roger Lupton, a Howgill boy who rose to become Provost of Eton: he established the school because he felt that one was desperately needed "in the north country amongst the people rude in knowledge". In later years, Wordsworth's son studied here and Coleridge's son, Hartley, became a master. The school's extensive grounds, through which visitors are welcome to wander, seem to place the old-world town within a park.

That impression is reinforced by following the path beside the River Rawthay to **Brigflatts**. Close to where George Fox stayed overnight with his friend Richard Robinson is the oldest **Quaker Meeting House** in the north of England. Built in 1675, and still with its original oak interior, this beautiful, simple building has changed little over the years.

This area is filled with Quaker history and **Firbank Knott**, on nearby Firbank Fell, can be said to be the birthplace of Quakerism for it was here, in 1652, that the visionary George Fox gave his great sermon to inspire a huge gathering from the whole of the north of England. This meeting was to lead to the development of the **Quaker Movement**. The simple boulder on the fell, from which Fox delivered his momentous words, is marked by a plaque and is now known as **Fox's Pulpit**.

Sedbergh seems a very friendly town. At **St Andrew's Church**, for example, Protestants and Roman Catholics take turns to use the building for their own

FARFIELD MILL

Garsdale Road, Sedbergh, Cumbria LA10 5LW
Tel: 015396 21958
e-mail: themanager@farfieldmill.org
website: www.farfieldmill.org

On the A684 a mile east of Sedbergh, **Farfield Mill** was built in 1837 beside the beautiful River Clough by a local woollen manufacturer. Washing, carding, spinning and weaving were among the processes undertaken, and at its height 30 looms were at work producing top-quality goods – one of the mills' best-known products were horse blankets, and Queen Victoria, King Edward Vii and King George V were among the customers. Now an important Arts and Heritage Centre, the mill re-opened in its present form in 2001, and two of the looms still produce traditional cloths.

Visitors can watch experienced and very talented local people creating unique pieces of work in their own studios, including artists/painters, photographer, weaver, felt-maker, knitter and workers in glass, ceramics, wood, silk and pewter. The mill also stages a changing programme of exhibitions

throughout the year. A wide variety of goods made at the mill or locally can be bought in the mill shop, and in the café a selection of cakes and hot and cold snacks is served, all made on the premises using fresh ingredients.

Farfield Mill is open daily up until 11 Jan 2004, from 10.30am-5pm. 12 Jan 2004 until 4 April 2004, Saturday and Sunday only. Admission £2, senior citizens and students £1.50, accompanied children free.

services, an arrangement believed to be rare in England.

To the east of the town, on a small wooded hill top, lies **Castlehaw**, the remains of an ancient motte-and-bailey castle. Built by the Normans in the 11th century, the castle guarded the valleys of the River Rawthey and the River Lune against the marauding Scots. Also just outside town, on the A683 Garsdale road, is **Farfield Mill** Heritage and Arts Centre, where spinners, weavers, potters, woodcarvers and other craftspeople use traditional skills to produce high-quality goods, all of it for sale in the shop.

AROUND SEDBERGH

DENT
4 miles SE of Sedbergh off the A684

This charming village, the only one in Dentdale - one of Cumbria's finest dales - has a delightful cobbled main street with tall cottages lining the road. Visitors to this tranquil place will find it hard to believe that, in the 18th century, Dent was of greater importance than nearby Sedbergh. The impressive **St Andrew's Church** is Norman in origin though it underwent an almost complete rebuilding in the early 15th century.

Inside can not only be seen the Jacobean three-decker pulpit that is still in use but also the local marble which paves the chancel.

Farming has, for many years, dominated the local economy but knitting, particularly in the village, has too played an important part. During the 17th and 18th centuries, the women and children, on whom this work fell, became known as the '**Terrible Knitters of Dent**' which, today, sounds uncomplimentary but the local use of the word terrible meant quite the opposite (like 'wicked' today!).

Dent's most famous son is undoubtedly the 'Father of Geology', **Adam Sedgwick**. Born the son of the local vicar in 1785, Sedgwick went on to become the Woodwardian Professor of Geology at Cambridge University and also a friend of Queen Victoria and Prince Albert. The fountain of pinkish Shap granite in the village centre is Dent's memorial to this great geologist. Dent stone, with no iron pyrites likely to cause sparks, was popular for millstones used in gunpowder works. The little valley of Dentdale winds from the village up past old farms and hamlets to **Lea Yeat** where a steep lane hairpins up to Dent Station, almost five miles from the village. This is a marvellous place to begin a ramble into Dentdale or over the Whernside. In the shadow of Whernside itself, **Whernside Manor** is a famous house with associations with the slave trade. Dent railway station is the highest in Britain, over 1,100 feet above sea level, and it lies on the famous Settle-Carlisle railway line.

Settle to Carlisle Railway, Nr Dent

GARSDALE
5 miles E of Sedbergh on the A684

Lying just north of Dentdale, Garsdale is both a dale and a

village and they are overlooked by the dramatic **Baugh Fell**. The River Clough follows down the dale from Garsdale Head, the watershed into Wensleydale, where a row of Midland Railway cottages lies alongside the former junction station on the Settle-Carlisle line. This is now a surprisingly busy little place during the summer months when, from time to time, preserved steam locomotives pause to take water from a moorland spring.

WINDERMERE

Birthwaite village no longer features on any map, thanks to the Kendal and Windermere Railway Company which built a branch line to it in 1847. With an eye on tourist traffic, and considering the name Birthwaite had little appeal, they named the station Windermere even though the lake is over a mile distant. In the early days carriages and, in later years, buses linked the station with the landing stages in the village of Bowness on the shores of the lake. As the village burgeoned into a prosperous Victorian resort, it became popularly, and then officially, known by the name of its station, while Windermere water was given the redundant prefix of Lake.

The Victorian heritage still predominates in the many large houses here, originally built as country retreats for Manchester businessmen - the railway made it possible for them to reach this idyllic countryside in just over two hours. Hotels, boarding houses, comfortable villas and shops sprang up around the station and spread rapidly down the hill towards the lake until Birthwaite and Bowness were linked together.

Windermere's railway is still operating, albeit now as a single track branch line. The **Lakes Line** is now the only surviving Railtrack line to run into the

Steam Launch, Lake Windermere

heart of the Lake District. Diesel railcars provide a busy shuttle service to and from the main line at Oxenholme. The route, through Kendal, Burneside and Staveley, is a delight and provides a very pleasant alternative to the often crowded A591.

Within a few yards of Windermere Station, just across the busy main road, is a footpath that leads through the woods to one of the finest viewpoints in Lakeland, **Orrest Head**. This spectacular vantage point provides a 360-degree panoramic view that takes in the ten-mile length of Windermere, the Cumbrian hills and even the fells of the Yorkshire Pennines. In Victorian times, visitors wandered through such ravishing scenery carrying, not cameras, but small, tinted mirrors mounted in elaborate frames. Arriving at a picturesque spot, they placed themselves

OLDFIELD HOUSE

Oldfield Road, Windermere, Cumbria LA23 2BY
Tel: 015394 88445
e-mail: sally.want@kencomp.net
website: www.oldfieldhouse.co.uk

Situated in a quiet area of Windermere, **Oldfield House** is a Victorian stone-built residence that now offers style, comfort and hospitality in the Lake District National Park. It is an ideal Bed & Breakfast base for

touring the Lake District, as many of the attractions within the Park can be reached by car, by guided tour and in some cases by boat. Oldfield's eight guest bedrooms are individually styled and all have tv, telephone and beverage tray. They comprise two premier rooms, one with a four-poster bed, doubles, singles, a twin and a family room, and all have either bath or shower en suite.

An outstanding breakfast menu makes a great start to the day, with a traditional English and scrambled egg with smoked salmon among the options. For a special event, resident Paul and Marion Want can provide a celebration pack with flowers, hand-made chocolates and champagne with cut-glass flutes to keep as a reminder of the occasion. Guests have the use of the leisure club (optional extra) at Windermere Marina, which has a swimming pool, steam room, sun bed and bar area. Oldfield House is a non-smoking establishment.

MATSON GROUND ESTATE

Estate Office, Matson Ground, Windermere,
Cumbria LA23 2NH
Tel: 015394 45756 Fax: 015394 47892
website: www.matsonground.co.uk
e-mail: info@matsonground.co.uk

The **Matson Ground Estate** Company manages a number of high-quality self-catering holiday homes near Windermere, Glenridding and Patterdale. Helm Farm, a short drive south of Windermere, has four units in an award-winning barn conversion. Sleeping from 2 to 5 guests, they are all very comfortably furnished, with well-equipped kitchens; they share a garden and a barbecue area. Footpaths lead from the doorstep into pleasant grazing land and connect with a wide network of paths, and the towns of Windermere and Bowness are a short drive away.

Similar quality and facilities are provided at Elm How, a fine old farmhouse with accommodation for up to 10 guests, and Cruck Barn, a spacious apartment for 2. These enjoy a scenic, out-of-the-way setting above Patterdale in the Grisedale Valley, while a little further north Eagle Cottage, which sleeps 4, sits up a steep, narrow drive slightly above Glenridding village. These three units are close to Ullswater, where rowing boats and canoes may be hired. All the Matson Ground Estate properties enjoy stunning scenery and provide ideal bases for walkers, tourists and lovers of the great outdoors.

with their back to the view, held the mirrors above them and so observed the view framed as in a painting. The image they saw recalled the romantic landscapes of Claude Lorraine: the mirrors accordingly were known as **Claude Glasses**.

AROUND WINDERMERE

Bowness-on-Windermere
1½ miles S of Windermere

It is from this attractive, but seasonally very busy town right on the edge of Windermere that most of the lake cruises operate. Lasting between 45 and 90 minutes, the cruises operate daily and provide connections to the Lakeside & Haverthwaite Steam Railway, the **Fell Foot Country Park** and the **Visitor Centre** at Brockhole - this centre (also easily reached by road) is idyllically situated in 30 acres of gardens and grounds and has two floors of interactive exhibitions. There are evening wine/champagne cruises during the summer months, and rowing boats and self drive

motor boats are also available for hire all year round.

Not only is **Windermere** the largest lake in Cumbria but it is, at 11 miles long, the largest in England. Across from Bowness, the lake is almost divided in two by **Belle Island**, which is believed to have been inhabited by the Romans. During the Civil War, it was owned by Colonel Phillipson (the Royalist supporter who disgraced himself by riding into Kendal Parish Church) and his family had to withstand an 80-day siege, successfully, while the Colonel was away on another campaign. In 1774, the island was bought by a Mr English, who constructed the round house which, at the time, caused such consternation that he sold the property and the island to Isabella Curwen, who planted the surrounding trees.

Fishermen, too, find great enjoyment practising their skills on this well-stocked lake. Once considered a great delicacy in the 17th and 18th centuries, the char, a deep-water trout, is still found here - though catching it is a special art.

Away from the marinas and car parks is the old village where **St Martin's Church** is of particular interest. It has a magnificent east window filled with 14th and 15th century glass, and an unusual 300-year-old carved wooden figure of St Martin depicted sharing his cloak with a beggar.

On the lake shore just to the north of the village is the **Windermere Steamboat Centre** (see panel on page 213). Housed here is a unique collection of Lake Windermere's nautical heritage. The exhibits, mainly

Bowness on Windermere

Victorian and Edwardian craft, include *Dolly*, the oldest mechanically powered boat in the world, and Beatrix Potter's rowing boat. The Swallows and Amazons exhibition features guided tours of *Esperance*, Arthur Ransome's inspiration for Captain Flint's Houseboat. The Museum grounds also includes a model boat pond, shop, tea room and picnic area.

Just down the road from the Steamboat Museum is the Old Laundry Visitor Centre, the home of **The World of Beatrix Potter**, one of the most popular visitor attractions in the country. Here visitors can enjoy fascinating re-creations of the Lakeland author's books, complete with the sounds, sights and even smells of the countryside. 2002 saw the centenary of the publication of the first *Tale of Peter Rabbit*, and to mark the occasion the Peter Rabbit Centenary springs to life every 15 minutes and features some

previously unpublished illustrations from the stories.

About a mile and a half south of Bowness, **Blackwell** is a treasure trove of the Arts and Crafts Movement. Completed in 1900, it is the largest and most important surviving masterpiece of the architect MH Baillie Scott (1865-1945). Inspired by Lakeland flora and fauna, he designed every last detail of this outstanding house, creating a symphony of art nouveau stained glass, oak panelling, intricate plasterwork and fanciful metalwork. From the gardens there are wonderful views of Windermere and the Coniston fells.

WINSTER
4 miles S of Windermere on the A5074

This charming hamlet has an old post office, originally built in the early 17th century as a cottage, that is much photographed. South from the village

FAIR RIGG

Ferry View, Bowness-on-Windermere, Cumbria LA23 3JB
Tel: 015394 43941
e-mail: rtodd51257@aol.com website: www.fairrigg.co.uk

Friendliness and personal service are watchwords at **Fair Rigg**, where Judith and Richard Todd offer Bed & Breakfast accommodation in their delightful Lakeland stone Victorian guest house. In a rural setting a short walk from Bowness and the shore of Windermere, the house has been fully refurbished by the owners to a commendably high standard, retaining many splendid original features and providing a most civilised and pleasant place for a holiday.

Fair Rigg has six spacious guest bedrooms, five doubles and a twin, all en suite and well equipped, with the emphasis on comfort and relaxation. Single occupancy is often available, and the tariff includes a full English breakfast which is served in an impressive dining-room. With lovely views over fields and trees to the lake and

the fells beyond, this charming place is an ideal spot to unwind and an excellent base for exploring South Lakeland and the Lyth Valley. The delights of lake and countryside are virtually on the doorstep, and the whole region is rich in scenic and historic interest, as well as providing a wide range of activities for all energy levels. Fair Rigg is a non-smoking establishment and is not suitable for children under 12.

runs the Winster Valley, which provided Wordsworth with one of his favourite walks. It was at **Low Ludderburn**, a couple of miles to the south, that Arthur Ransome settled in 1925 and here that he wrote his classic children's novel *Swallows and Amazons*.

While living here, Ransome discovered the peaceful churchyard at **Rusland** and decided that was where he wanted to be buried. And when he died in 1967 that is indeed where he was buried, joined later by his second wife Eugenia.

WITHERSLACK

9 miles S of Windermere off the A590

On the edge of the village is the **Latterbarrow Reserve** of the Cumbrian Wildlife Trust, a relatively small reserve that is home to some 200 species of flowering plants and ferns. Further from the village is **Witherslack Hall**, once the summer residence of the Earls of Derby and now a school.

WINDERMERE STEAMBOAT MUSEUM

Rayrigg Road, Windermere,
Cumbria LA23 1BN
Tel: 01539 445565

On the lake shore just to the north of the village is the **Windermere Steamboat Museum**, a unique collection of Victorian and Edwardian steam launches which includes the *SL Dolly*, the oldest mechanically powered boat in the world. *Dolly* celebrated her 150th birthday in 2000 and still has her original engine in working order despite its having lain on the bed of Ullswater for more than 60 years before being recovered.

Guided tours of the museum are available and also around the Esperance, the inspiration for Captain Flint's boat in Arthur Ransome's Swallows and Amazons. Some of the launches are still in working order and occasional cruises in one of these wonderful vintage craft are possible.

Private charters of an Edwardian steam launch for up to 12 passengers can also be arranged, with catering provided if required. The Museum grounds also includes a model boat pond, shop, tea room, picnic area, a self-catering flat for 2 persons, and free parking.

NEWBY BRIDGE

8 miles S of Windermere on the A592

The bridge here crosses the River Leven which runs from the southern tip of Windermere to Morecambe Bay. According to geologists, the mass of end moraines seen here show clearly that the village lay at the southernmost point of Windermere since they were deposited by the glacier while it paused having carved out the lake. Today, however, the village is some distance from the water's edge, which can be reached on foot, by car, or by taking the steam train on the Lakeside & Haverthwaite Railway. As the village

WITHERSLACK HALL EQUESTRIAN CENTRE

Witherslack Hall Farm, Witherslack, Grange-over-Sands,
Cumbria LA11 6SD
Tel: 015395 52244 Fax: 015395 52593
e-mail: info@whec.co.uk website: www.lakelandriding.co.uk

The stables at **Witherslack Hall Equestrian Centre** are arranged round a cobbled yard and schooling menage in magnificent Victorian farm buildings in the beautiful Winster Valley. Beginners, novices and experienced riders are all welcome, and Careth and Lynne offer private and group lessons, one-hour, two-hour, full day and pub rides, facilities for disabled riders and full livery facilities. Farmhouse Bed & Breakfast available on site.

George Barker & Sons - Timber Merchants

Backbarrow, Nr Ulverston, Cumbria LA12 8TA
Tel/Fax: 015395 31236
e-mail: sales@gbsltd.sagehost.co.uk
website: www.gbs-ltd.co.uk

Located by the River Leven surrounded by the splendour of the Lake District Hills, **George Barker & Sons** have been trading as a family firm since 1858. They have from the start been involved with timber in one way or another, and throughout their long and successful existence they have been committed to quality, integrity, value for money and personal service. The current product range, all hand-crafted to their own designs, includes garden and field gates, fencing and trellis, sheds and summer houses, bench seats, swing seats and tree seats, picnic benches, decking, Japanese-style bridges, planters, bird tables and bird boxes, dog kennels and rabbit hutches. These are among the most popular products, but the firm also produce one-off jobs and enjoy the challenge of new ideas and alternative designs.

All the European redwood timber used has been vacuum pressure treated for long life. Visitors can enjoy light snacks in the coffee shop, which the Barker family are planning to extend to incorporate a heritage centre and a viewing gallery over the current workshop area. George Barker & Sons are located on the A590 a mile south of Newby Bridge.

lies at the junction of two major south Cumbrian roads, it is also a popular tourist destination.

One mile north of the village, **Fell Foot Park** (National Trust) is a delightful 18-acre site of landscaped gardens and woodland laid out in late-Victorian times. Rowing boats can be hired at the piers from which there are regular ferries across to Lakeside, and pleasure cruises operate during the summer school holidays.

LAKESIDE
10 miles S of Windermere off the A590

Located at the southwestern tip of Windermere, Lakeside sits beneath gentle wooded hills. It's the northern terminus of the **Lakeside & Haverthwaite Railway** (see panel opposite), a four-mile route through the beautiful Leven valley which was once part of a line stretching to Ulverston and Barrow-in-Furness.

Throughout the season, hard-working steam locomotives chug along the track, their departure times set to coincide with boat arrivals from Bowness - a joint boat and train return ticket is available. The locomotives in use include 42073 and 42085, ex-LMR Fairburn 0-6-4 tank engines, and 5643, an ex-GWR 0-6-0 tank. Also present on display or under steam (when not occasionally required elsewhere) is FR20, built for the Furness Railway and Britain's oldest working standard gauge steam locomotive (see also under Haverthwaite).

Nearby lies Britain's only freshwater aquarium, the **Aquarium of the Lakes** with the largest collection of freshwater fish in the UK and also a number of playful otters and diving ducks. A unique attraction for visitors is to walk along a re-creation of Windermere's lake bed along an underwater tunnel.

The Lakeside & Haverthwaite Railway

Haverthwaite Station, nr Ulverston,
Cumbria LA12 8AL
Tel: 015395 31594

From the Victorian station at Haverthwaite, beautifully restored steam locomotives of the **Lakeside & Haverthwaite Railway** haul comfortable coaches through the Leven Valley. With connections at Lakeside by way of Windermere Lake Cruises, the train offers a unique perspective from which to enjoy the every-changing lake and river scenery of this picturesque part of the Lake District.

This former Furness Railway branch line runs for 3.5 miles, with a journey time of around 20 minutes, giving passengers a leisurely and relaxing trip. Whilst at Haverthwaite, visitors can sample a delicious home baked scone in the licensed Station Restaurant - an ideal way to start or end the journey.

A mile or so north of Lakeside, **Stott Park Bobbin Mill** (English Heritage) is a must for anyone interested in the area's industrial heritage. One of the best preserved in the country, it's a genuine working 19th century mill and stands in a lovely woodland setting at the southern end of the Lake. Visitors can join the inclusive 45-minute tour, watch wooden bobbins being made as they were 200 years ago and browse over the informative exhibition.

Troutbeck Bridge

1 mile NE of Windermere on the A591

Just north of this little village in the valley of Trout Beck lies the Royal Horticultural Society's four-acre garden at **Holehird**. In 1945, Edward Leigh Groves bequeathed the mansion and the estate 'for the better development of the health, education and social welfare services of the County of Westmoreland'. Some time later, the Lakeland Horticultural Society took over responsibility for the garden, which is still run by volunteers of that society, whose primary aim is to promote 'knowledge on the cultivation of plants, shrubs and trees, especially those suited to Lakeland conditions'. Highlights include the borders in the walled garden, the many specimen trees, the summer-autumn heathers and the National Collections of astilbes and hydrangeas.

Troutbeck

3 miles NE of Windermere off the A592

Designated a conservation area, Troutbeck has no recognisable centre, as the houses and cottages are grouped around a number of wells and springs which, until recently, were the only form of water supply. Dating from the 16th, 17th, and 18th centuries, the houses retain many of their original features, including mullion windows, heavy cylindrical chimneys, and, in some cases, exposed spinning galleries, and are of great interest to lovers of vernacular architecture. **Troutbeck Church**, too, is worthy of a visit as there is a fine east window, dating from 1873, that is the combined work of Edward Burne-Jones, Ford Maddox Brown, and William Morris.

However, perhaps the best known building at Troutbeck is **Townend** (National Trust), another enchanting example of Lake District vernacular architecture. Built in 1626, the stone and slate house contains some fine carved woodwork, books, furniture and

domestic implements collected by the Browne family, wealthy farmers who lived here for more than 300 years until 1944. Open from April to October, the house runs a regular 'living history' programme, so if you visit on a Thursday you can meet Mr George Browne - circa 1900. Another notable resident of Troutbeck was the 'Troutbeck Giant' - Thomas Hogarth, uncle of the painter William Hogarth.

KENTMERE

8 miles NE of Windermere off the A591

This hamlet, as its name implies, lies in part of the valley that was once a lake; drained to provide precious bottom pasture land. A large mill pond remains to provide a head of water on the River Kent for use at a paper mill. Inside

St Cuthbert's Church is a bronze memorial to Bernard Gilpin, who was born at Kentmere Hall in 1517 and went on to become Archdeacon of Durham Cathedral. Known as The Apostle of the North, Gilpin was also a leader of the Reformation and, in 1558, he travelled to London to face charges of heresy against the Roman Catholic Church. During the journey, Gilpin fell and broke his leg but, fortunately, while he was recovering Catholic Queen Mary died and was succeeded by Protestant Queen Elizabeth. The new queen restored Gilpin to favour and saved him from being burnt at the stake.

The beautiful valley of the River Kent is best explored on foot. A public footpath runs up its western side, past **Kentmere Hall**, a fortified pele tower

that is now a private farmhouse. Following the river southwards, the **Dales Way** runs down into Kendal and on into the Yorkshire Dales.

BROCKHOLE
3 miles NW of Windermere off the A591

The **Lake District Visitor Centre** at Brockhole provides enough activities for a full family day out. Lake cruises depart from the jetty here for 45-minute circular trips and groups of more than 20 can even organise their own private boat. The gardens and grounds were the work of Thomas H Mawson, a Lancastrian who trained in London and set up in business in Windermere in 1885. He soon became fashionable and landscaped the gardens of many wealthy industrialists. Within the beautifully landscaped grounds at Brockhole, visitors can join an organised walk accompanied by one of the gardening team, leave their children in the well-equipped adventure playground, enjoy a lakeside picnic or visit the rare breeds of sheep. A wide variety of events takes place during the season - among them a Medieval Living Weekend, a Taste of Cumbria Food Fair, a Christmas Craft Fair and much more. Brockhole itself is a fine Victorian mansion, originally built for a Manchester silk merchant.

AMBLESIDE
5 miles NW of Windermere on the A591

Standing less than a mile from the head of Lake Windermere, Ambleside is one of the busiest of the Lakeland towns, a popular centre for walkers and tourists, with glorious walks and drives radiating from the town in all directions. Ambleside offers a huge choice of pubs, restaurants, cafés, hotels and guest houses, as well as art galleries, a 2-screen cinema and a mix of traditional family-run shops supplemented by a modern

Bridge House

range of retailers in the new **Market Cross Centre**. Because of its many shops specialising in outdoor clothing, the town was recently described as 'the anorak capital of the world' and it would certainly be hard to find a wider selection anywhere of climbing, camping and walking gear.

Many of Ambleside's buildings are constructed in the distinctive grey green stone of the area which merges attractively with the green of the fields and fells all around. The centre of the town is now a conservation area and perhaps the most picturesque building here is **The Bridge House**, a tiny cottage perched on a packhorse bridge across Stock Ghyll. Today it's a National Trust shop and information centre, but during the 1850s it was the home of Mr and Mrs Rigg and their six children. The main room of this one-up, one-down residence

ADRIAN SANKEY - DESIGNER MAKERS

Rydal Road, Ambleside, Cumbria LA22 9AN
Tel: 015394 33039 Fax: 015394 31139
e-mail: adrian@glassmakers.co.uk
website: www.glassmakers.co.uk

In their Lake District studio, **Adrian Sankey - Designer Makers**
work with glass to create striking contemporary designs that
emphasise the remarkable properties of glass while
complementing and enhancing
living and working spaces. The
glassmaking skills of Adrian and
his team, passed down largely
unchanged through the
generations, are inspired in no small measure by the location, and the
splendour of the landscape, the dramatic fells and the rich colours, are
reflected in many of the pieces.

All the studioware is entirely hand-blown and hand-made, working
from their own furnace, and ensuring that each item is an individually
crafted, unique piece. The traditional way of working allows the
glassmakers to produce one-off designs to a specific brief or to
complement a particular setting. Besides the studio glass, which includes
bowls and plates, vases, jugs and decanters, drinking glasses, perfume
bottles, candlesticks, kitchenware and paperweights, Adrian Sankey
provides a bespoke service for lighting with a range that covers the whole
spectrum from period pieces and retro designs to modern minimalist creations, halogen pendant
shades and special commissions. The catalogue also includes beautiful tables and chairs, tables and
mirrors, all designed to make the most of light and space and to add character to any setting.

THE GLASSHOUSE RESTAURANT

Rydal Road, Ambleside, Cumbria
Tel: 015394 32137
website: www. theglasshouserestaurant.co.uk

The Glasshouse Restaurant is housed in a cleverley restored
former mill and retains many parts of the old machinery. A series
of mezzanine floors was constructed with the aid of an oak

framework and an
impressive glass
frontage floods the
restaurant with
light, making a
delightful ambience
for enjoying the best of Lakeland produce from a menu
that combines classic British cuisine with modern
European influences. Freshness, quality and simplicity are
keynotes wether it's a light lunch or an a la carte meal
you want. The restaurant can seat 100 and is an ideal
venue for special occasions where guests can mingle across
the four floors, or equally can provide cosy privacy for
small numbers. The cellar and bar offer an eclectic choice
of beers from Europe, a wide-ranging wine list and a
stupendous collection of vintage armagnacs.

Loughrigg Fell

watercolours - exquisite studies of fungi and mosses - and a fascinating collection of photographs by Herbert Bell, an Ambleside chemist who became an accomplished photographer.

The popular panoramic view of Ambleside, looking north from the path up **Loughrigg Fell**, reveals the town cradled within the apron of the massive Fairfield Horseshoe which rises to nearly 3,000 feet. Within the townscape itself, the most impressive feature is the rocket-like spire, 180 feet high, of **St Mary's Church**.

measures just 13 feet by six feet, so living chez Rigg was decidedly cosy. Close by, at **Adrian Sankey's Glass Works**, visitors can watch craftsmen transform molten material into glass in the age-old way and also purchase the elegant results.

A short walk from the mill brings the visitor to the **Armitt Museum** (see panel below) and Library dedicated to the area's history since Roman times and to its most famous literary luminaries, John Ruskin and Beatrix Potter. Among the highlights are Beatrix Potter's early

The church was completed in 1854 to a design by Sir George Gilbert Scott, the architect of London's St Pancras Station and the Albert Memorial. Inside the church is a chapel devoted to the memory of William Wordsworth and an interesting 1940s mural depicting the ancient ceremony of rush-bearing. The ceremony, dating back to the days when the floor of the church was covered by rushes, is still held on the first Saturday in July. Some 400 children process through the town bearing colourful

Continued on page 222

THE ARMITT MUSEUM

Rydal Road, Ambleside, Cumbria LA22 9PL
Tel: 01539 431212

A short walk from the mill brings you to **The Armitt**, an attractive new building which contains a museum and library dedicated to the area's history since Roman times and to its most famous literary luminaries, John Ruskin and Beatrix Potter. Visitors can "talk" to John Ruskin, watch a 19th century lantern slide show, and marvel at Beatrix Potter's pre-Mrs Tiggywinkle watercolours - exquisite scientific studies of fungi and mosses. Other exhibits include a lock of Ruskin's hair, a life mask of Harriet Martineau, the political writer and author of an early *Guide to the Lakes*, and a fascinating collection of photographs by Herbert Bell (1856-1946), an Ambleside chemist who became an accomplished photographer, concentrating on lakeland scenes. The Armitt hosts regular exhibitions, lectures and concerts, and also has its own shop selling items produced exclusively for sale only at the museum.

WALK 6

Low and High Sweden Bridges

Start	Ambleside
Distance	3½ miles (5.6km)
Approximate time	2 hours
Parking	Ambleside
Refreshments	Pubs and cafés at Ambleside
Ordnance Survey maps	Landranger 90 (Penrith, Keswick & Ambleside) and Outdoor Leisure 7 (The English Lakes – South Eastern area)

This short and easy route, ideal for a leisurely afternoon stroll, heads up out of Ambleside to Low Sweden Bridge and then climbs steadily above the valley of Scandale Beck before descending to the picturesque High Sweden Bridge. Initially, the return section passes through attractive woodland beside the beck, and on the final stretch there are impressive views over the surrounding fells and the head of Windermere.

Situated on a main road at the head of Windermere, Ambleside has developed into one of the Lake District's major tourist centres. Although a visitor might come away with the overriding impression of a 19th century town, the period when most of its hotels and guest houses were built, Ambleside is not just a creation of the Victorian tourist era; the Romans built their fort of Galava here, an important centre for their communications network in north-west England. At the far end of the town stands what is undoubtedly Ambleside's most photographed building: the tiny

17th century Bridge House, built above the bridge over Stock Ghyll and now a National Trust Information Centre.

Start by the cross, Market Hall and Queen's Hotel and walk along North Road. At a junction, turn left down Smithy Brow and take the first turning on the right, Nook Lane. Follow this narrow tarmac lane gently uphill, passing to the right of the buildings of Charlotte Mason College (part of the University of Lancaster) and, after passing between farm buildings, continue along a rough track.

WALK 6

Turn left over Low Sweden Bridge 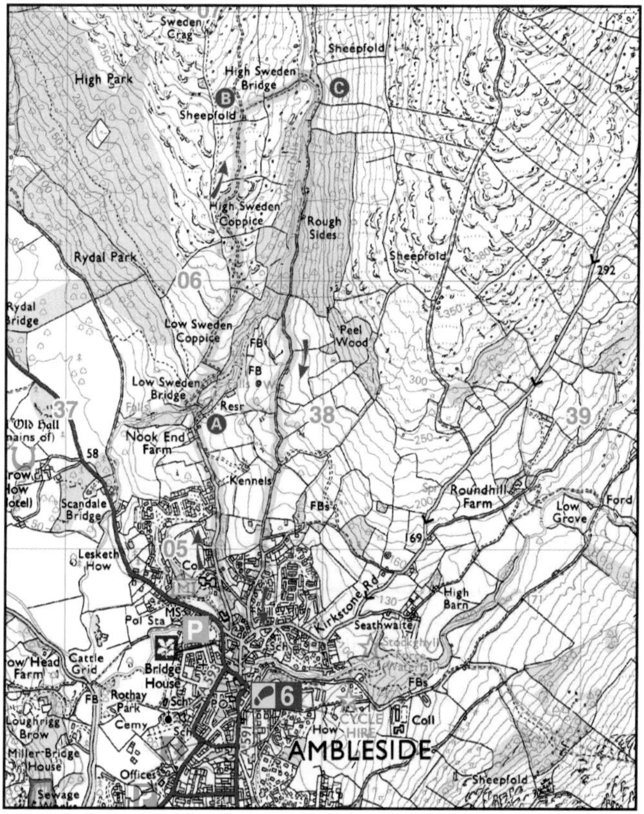 – to the right are some impressive wooded falls – and continue along the track, which bends sharply to the right. Head steadily and unrelentingly uphill above the wooded valley on the right, follow the track around left and right bends and continue uphill, by a wall on the left, passing through several wall gaps to the left of what are now redundant ladder-stiles. At a fork, take the right-hand track, pass through another wall gap to the left of a ladder-stile, continue ahead for another 50 yds (46m), passing a sheepfold on the right, and then turn right B along an obvious grassy path between bracken down to a ladder-stile.

Climb the stile and continue downhill, by a wall on the left, to cross High Sweden Bridge C, an old pack-horse bridge in a beautiful setting. Now follow an attractive wooded path beside the rocky waters of Scandale Beck to a gate. Go through, continue through the woodland of Rough Sides, go through another gate and walk along a walled track, soon emerging from the trees.

After a brief, gentle climb to leave the beck, you continue along an enclosed track gently downhill, enjoying the grand views to the right of Rydal Water and particularly impressive views ahead of Ambleside and the head of Windermere. Go through a gate, continue downhill along a tarmac lane into Ambleside, turn right at a T-junction and bear left along North Road to return to the start.

TOUCHSTONE INTERIORS

Skelwith Bridge, Ambleside,
Cumbria LA22 9NN
Tel: 015394 34711
website: www.touchstoneinteriors.com

Surrounded by woodland in the heart of The Lakes, an old bobbin mill has been the home of **Touchstone Interiors** for nearly forty years. But that is where the past ends.

Beautiful and peaceful, this riverside setting is the last place you would expect to find chic and contemporary. Step inside and the surprise discovery is good design, quality and originality. From kitchen to conservatory stylish displays reflect current trends in home furnishing. This is the place for inspiration.

Find furniture by Conran, Philippe Starck and Tom Schneider, lighting by Foscarini, coffee makers by Gaggia and elegant kitchen utensils designed for Nigella Lawson. Experience colour deftly used to co-ordinate or create impact in a wide variety of displays. Perhaps a maple coffee table sits by a chocolate leather sofa that is piled with Mongolian sheepskin cushions. Or a glass top dining table is set with simple white crockery, filigree handled cutlery and elegant flowers.

Touchstone Interiors is not a temple to contemporary design and minimalism. It is an infinitely more approachable mix of serious purchases and the fun and frivolous. You may choose from limestone, slate or glass tiles and work surfaces that will last a lifetime. Or perhaps you'll indulge in some sequined slippers, scented candles, or toys for the children. Whatever your purpose enjoy the moment.

Taste fat, juicy olives, smell sensuous bath oils, slip on a trendy watch, then drift into Chesters Café for a cappuccino and a huge piece of heavenly, home-made cake. It's all about spoiling yourself, in town you probably wouldn't have time!

New ranges are arriving continually, some of them exclusive, and displays are changed often. There is always something new to see. Touchstone Interiors is innovative and enterprising, a complete one-off designed to inspire. Take time out, relax in beautiful surroundings, leave brimming with ideas of new ways to furnish your home.

decorated rushes and singing the specially commissioned Ambleside Rushbearer's Hymn.

A few weeks later the famous **Ambleside Sports** take place, an event distinguished by the variety of local traditional sports it features. In addition to carriage-driving, ferret or pigeon racing, and tugs of war, the Sports include Cumberland and Westmorland wrestling (a little like Sumo wrestling but without the rolls of fat), muscle-wrenching fell racing, and hound trailing.

Another experience not to be missed while staying at Ambleside is a boat cruise on Lake Windermere to Bowness. There are daily departures from the pier at **Waterhead**, about a mile south of the town. At Bowness, there are connections to other lakeland attractions and, during the summer months, evening wine cruises. Rowing boats and self drive motor boats can also be hired. Just to the

west of the pier is **Borrans Park**, a pleasant lakeside park with plenty of picnic spots, and to the west of the park, the site of Galava Roman Fort. There is little to be seen of the fort but the setting is enchanting. Also well worth a visit is nearby **Stagshaw Garden** (NT), a spring woodland garden which contains a fine collection of shrubs, including some impressive rhododendrons, azaleas and camellias. Parking is very limited and vehicular access is hazardous, so it's best to park at Waterhead car park and walk.

Perhaps the most unusual visitor attraction in Ambleside is the **Homes of Football**, described by the Sunday Times as a national treasure. It began as a travelling exhibition of football photographs and memorabilia but now has a permanent home in Lake Road. Photographer Stuart Clarke recorded games and grounds at every kind of venue from the Premier League down to

OLD COURTHOUSE GALLERY

Market Place, Ambleside, Cumbria LA22 9BU
Tel: 015394 32022 Fax: 015394 33022
e-mail: sylvia@ocg-arts.com
website: www.ocg-arts.com

From small beginnings 10 years ago **Old Courthouse Gallery** has grown into one of the best independent contemporary art galleries in the North. The Courthouse, which covers three floors, is large, spacious and airy, and along with the newly refurbished ground floor gallery (the work of Chris Brammall), provides a unique backdrop for the display of some of the best-known - and exciting unknown - artists and makers. The family atmosphere of the gallery extends to the running of the business by the Brammall family; regular contributors have become friends, as have many of the

customers who buy the very special pieces to cherish.

Mike Scott, Maureen Minchin, Stewart Hearn, Sarah Cox, Olivia Brown, Melanie Adkins and Norman and Lesley Stuart Clarke are just a few of the selected artists, who now number over 200. In a shop opposite the gallery, also designed with verve and panache by Chris, over 70 jewellers are housed. The range of diamond jewellery includes 'D' flawless (perfect) and natural coloured diamonds set in platinum and 18 carat gold. Unusual silver, semi-precious stones, acrylic and enamelled pieces by some of the country's leading designers also feature in the collection.

amateur village teams. There are now 60,000 photographs on file and a massive selection on show, framed and for sale. Some of the memorabilia retail for £200 or more but a free picture postcard of your favourite soccer ground is included in the modest entrance fee.

From Ambleside town centre, a steep road climbs sharply up to the dramatic **Kirkstone Pass** and over to Ullswater. The pass is so called because of the rock at the top which looks like a church steeple. Rising to some 1,489 feet above sea level, the road is the highest in the Lake District and, though today's vehicles make light work of the climb, for centuries the Pass presented a formidable obstacle. The severest incline, known as **The Struggle**, necessitated passengers to step out of their coach and to make their way on foot, leaving the horses to make the steep haul with just the empty coach.

RYDAL

7 miles NW of Windermere on the A591

In 1813, following the deaths of their young children Catherine and Thomas, William and Mary Wordsworth were too grief stricken to stay on at the Old Rectory in Grasmere. They moved a couple of miles down the road to **Rydal Mount**, a handsome house overlooking tiny **Rydal Water**. By now, the poet was well-established and comparatively prosperous. A salaried position as Westmorland's Distributor of Stamps (a tax official), supplemented his earnings from poetry. Although Wordsworth only ever rented the house, it is now owned by his descendants and has been open to the public since 1970. The interior has seen little change, retaining a lived-in atmosphere. It contains first editions of the poet's work and many personal

Rydal Mount

possessions, among them the only surviving portrait of his beloved sister, Dorothy. William was a keen gardener and the four-acre garden remains very much as he designed it.

GRASMERE

9 miles NW of Windermere on the A591

In 1769 Thomas Gray described Grasmere as "a little unsuspected paradise". Thirty years later, Wordsworth himself called it "the loveliest spot that man hath ever found". Certainly, Grasmere enjoys one of the finest settings in all Lakeland, its small lake nestling in a natural scenic amphitheatre beside the compact, rough-stone village.

For lovers of Wordsworth's poetry, Grasmere is the pre-eminent place of pilgrimage. They come to visit **Dove Cottage** where Wordsworth lived in dire poverty from 1799 to 1808, obliged to line the walls with newspaper for warmth. The great poet shared this very basic accommodation with his wife Mary, his sister Dorothy, his sister-in-law Alice and, as almost permanent guests, Coleridge and De Quincey. (Sir Walter Scott also stayed, although he often sneaked off to the Swan Hotel for a dram since the Wordsworths were virtually teetotallers.) Located on the outskirts of the village, Dove Cottage has been

Wordsworths Relics, Dove Cottage

preserved intact: next door is an award-winning museum dedicated to Wordsworth's life and works. Dove Cottage, Rydal Mount, another of the poet's homes near Grasmere, and his birthplace, Wordsworth House at Cockermouth, are all owned by the **Wordsworth Trust**, which offers a discount ticket covering entrance to all three properties.

In 1808, the poet moved to **The Rectory** (private) opposite St Oswald's Church. In his long poem, *The Excursion*, he describes the house and its lovely garden beside the River Rothay. The church, too, is remembered in the same poem:

> *Not raised in nice proportions was the pile,*
> *But large and massy, for duration built,*
> *With pillars crowded and the roof upheld*
> *By naked rafters intricately crossed,*
> *Like leafless underboughs in some thick wood.*

WORDSWORTH HOTEL

Grasmere, Cumbria LA22 9SW
Tel: 015394 35592
e-mail: enquiry@wordsworth-grasmere.co.uk
website: www.grasmere-hotels.co.uk

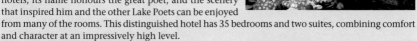

In the heart of Lakeland, in one of its loveliest villages, the **Wordsworth Hotel** stands in landscaped grounds next to the churchyard where William Wordsworth is buried. One of the best and most welcoming of all the Lake District hotels, its name honours the great poet, and the scenery that inspired him and the other Lake Poets can be enjoyed from many of the rooms. This distinguished hotel has 35 bedrooms and two suites, combining comfort and character at an impressively high level.

All have en suite bathrooms (whirlpool baths in the suites), tv, radio, direct-dial telephone and

computer point, and three of the rooms provide the added romance of four-poster beds. The antique-furnished lounges, the conservatory and the cocktail bar are ideal places to relax, and in the Prelude Restaurant our talented chef and his young brigade make excellent use of fresh local produce on their menus. The hotel also has its own pub, the Dove & Olive Branch, where a fine range of beers and snacks is served. Other amenities of the Wordsworth include an indoor pool, sauna and mini-gym; it holds a licence for civil marriages, and the Coleridge Suite is a memorable setting for a private celebration.

CRAGLANDS OF GRASMERE

Stock Lane, Grasmere, Cumbria LA22 9SJ
Tel: 015394 35283 Fax: 015394 35368
e-mail: christine@craglands.com
website: www.craglands.com

The name of **Craglands** is associated with the finest quality lambswool and cashmere knitwear, and visitors to the shop are welcome to browse through the exciting range of goods that are always on display. This family business specialise in their own exclusive designs and colours of tweeds, which can be purchased in a tailored skirt or by the metre. There is no difference in price for ready made or made-to measure skirts. The tweeds are dyed in subtle shades to co-ordinate with an extensive range of cashmere and lambswool knitwear in various original designs.

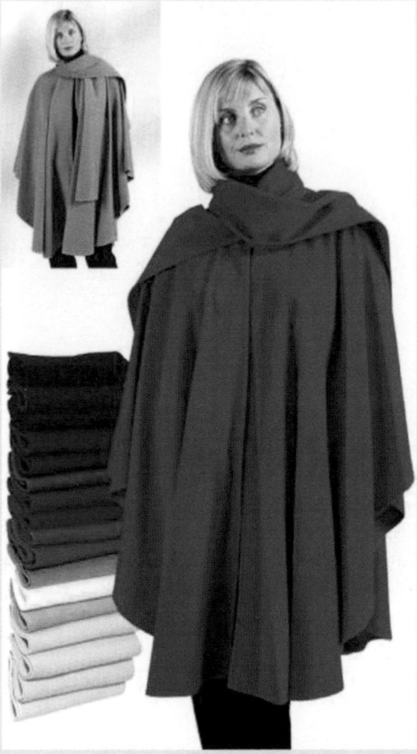

Christine Shaw, textile designer turned retailer, and her knowledgeable staff are always happy to help. They also offer a knit-to-order service at no extra charge, allowing customers to match specific style, colour and size requirements. Beautiful costume jewellery made to match the knitwear and silk scarves finish off an outfit. Gentlemen have not been forgotten, the shop stocks an interesting selection of classic knitwear, ties in silk and wool and luxurious scarves.

Apart from their own designs, Craglands carry ranges from many other leading British manufacturers. Firm favourites are John Smedley sweaters for both ladies and gentlemen in finest Sea Island cotton and merino wool, Pringle of Scotland cashmere and lambswool sweaters and Barbour jackets and country wear. Over the years this family business have built up a worldwide clientele who if they can't visit in person shop by mail order or on the web site. Garments can be mailed anywhere in the world.

BECK STEPS GIFT SHOP

College Street, Grasmere, Cumbria LA22 9SZ
Tel: 015394 35820
e-mail: sandrablackb@aol.com

When the opportunity arose for Iain and Sandra Blackburn to buy a business in Grasmere, they gave up their jobs in Manchester and opened **Beck Steps Gift Shop** in a traditional slate-fronted building on the green. They have never regretted the move, neither have the many visitors to the shop, which is stocked with a wide selection of gifts for all occasions, from unusual clocks and candles to Lakeland souvenirs and local crafts, aromatics and essential oils (blended on site), local slate products and toys. At one end is a section selling Lakeland ice cream and confectionery.

In 1850, the Poet Laureate was buried beneath yew trees he himself had planted in **St Oswald's** churchyard. He was joined here by his sister Dorothy, in 1885, and his wife Mary, in 1889. In Grasmere town cemetery is the grave of **William Archibald Spooner**, sometime Warden of New College, Oxford. He gave his name to Spoonerisms, in which the initial letters of two words are transposed, with amusing results. Here are a few of his gems, some genuine, others perhaps apocryphal:

Kinquering Kongs their titles take.

You have hissed all my mystery lessons.

You have deliberately tasted two worms and you can leave Oxford by the town drain.

Yes indeed: the Lord is a shoving leopard.

He spent many holidays in Grasmere with his wife at her house, How Foot.

Like Ambleside, Grasmere is famous for its **Sports**, first recorded in 1852, which still take place in late August. The most celebrated event in the Lake District, they attract some 10,000 visitors and feature many pursuits unique to Cumbria such as Cumberland and Westmorland wrestling as well as the more understandable, though arduous, fell running.

Collectors of curiosities who happen to be travelling north on the A591 from Grasmere should look out for the vintage black and yellow AA telephone box on the right hand side of the road. Still functioning, **Box 487** has been accorded Grade II listed building status by the Department of the Environment.

GRANGE-OVER-SANDS

Grange, as it's known locally, is an attractive little town set in a natural sun-trap on the north shore of Morecambe Bay. Much of its Victorian charm can be credited to the **Furness Railway Company**, which developed the town after building the Lancaster to

Morecombe Bay from Grange-over-Sands

HAZELMERE CAFÉ & BAKERY

1 & 2 Yewbarrow Terrace, Grange-over-Sands,
Cumbria LA11 6ED
Tel: 015395 32972 Fax: 015395 34101
e-mail: hazelmeregrange@yahoo.co.uk

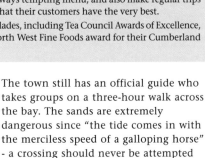

Set in a natural suntrap on the north shore of Morecambe Bay, Grange-over-Sands is an attractive little town with a quiet, pleasant and very civilised atmosphere that is epitomised by the **Hazelmere Café & Bakery**. Set in a Victorian parade of shops fronted by ornate glass and cast iron, it is owned and run by Dorothy and Ian Stubley, who have worked really hard to achieve the delightful ambience and to maintain the high level of quality that is the hallmark of their café.

All the baking is done in the bakery on the premises for customers to enjoy served by charming staff either inside, at an outside table overlooking a beautiful park or to take away. A measure of the owners' enthusiasm and dedication is that they seek out the very best local produce for their always tempting menu, and also make regular trips overseas in search of teas and coffees to make sure that their customers have the very best.

Their efforts have been rewarded with many accolades, including Tea Council Awards of Excellence, North West Café and Foodshop of the Year and a North West Fine Foods award for their Cumberland rum nicky cake.

Whitehaven line in 1857. The railway provided a safe alternative to this hazardous journey. At Grange the company built an elegant mile-long promenade (now traffic free) and set out the colourful ornamental gardens. Prosperous merchants built grand country homes here and it wasn't long before local residents began referring to their town as the 'Torquay of the North'.

The route to Grange, across the sands of **Morecambe Bay**, is a treacherous one, though it was used not only by the Romans but also by the monks of Furness Abbey and, later, even by stage coaches looking to shorten their journey time. Avoiding the quicksands of the bay, which have taken many lives over the centuries, is a difficult task. Back in the 16th century, the Duchy of Lancaster appointed an official guide to escort travellers over the shifting sands and also provided him with a house at Grange.

The town still has an official guide who takes groups on a three-hour walk across the bay. The sands are extremely dangerous since "the tide comes in with the merciless speed of a galloping horse" - a crossing should never be attempted without the help of a qualified guide.

Away from the hotels, shops, and cafés of the town there are some lovely walks and none is more pleasant than the path behind Grange which climbs through magnificent limestone woodlands rich in wild flowers. The path finally leads to the 727-foot **Hampsfell Summit** and **The Hospice**, a little stone tower from which there are unforgettable views over the bay and, in the opposite direction, the craggy peaks of the Lake District.

Grange is also the starting point of the **Cistercian Way**, an exceptionally interesting 33 mile long footpath through Furness to Barrow which takes in, naturally, many Cistercian sites.

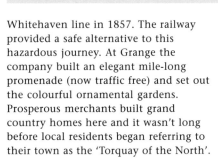

Wall Nook Cottage

Wall Nook, Beckside, Nr Cartmel, Cumbria LA11 7SP
Tel: 015395 36043 Fax: 015395 36119
e-mail: karen@hboi.com website: www.lakeland-cottage.com

Set in the lovely open countryside of the Cartmel Valley, **Wall Nook Cottage** is a perfect luxury Lakeland hideaway. Converted from Karen and Martyn's 200-year-old barn, it combines the best of traditional and modern features, with old oak beams and a polished oak floor, central heating and a fully equipped kitchen. The two bedrooms have beautiful private bathrooms, and the double-height sitting room boasts a complete entertainment centre and French windows looking out on to glorious views; teak garden furniture offers the delightful prospect of alfresco dining on hot summer evenings.

AROUND GRANGE-OVER-SANDS

Lindale

2 miles NE of Grange-over-Sands off the A590

This small village was the birthplace of a man who defied the scepticism of his contemporaries and built the first successful iron ship. 'Iron Mad' John Wilkinson also built the first cast iron barges and later created the castings for the famous Iron Bridge at Coalbrookdale. After his death in 1808 he was buried in an iron coffin (naturally) in an unmarked grave, and the lofty **Wilkinson Obelisk** to his memory that stands near the village crossroads is also cast in iron. The admirers who erected it however omitted to provide the iron column with a lightning conductor. A few years later it was struck to the ground by a lightning bolt. The obelisk lay neglected in shrubbery for some years but has now been restored and towers above the village once again. Just outside Lindale, at **Castle Head**, is the imposing house that Wilkinson built by the River Winster.

Cartmel

2 miles W of Grange-over-Sands off the B5278

One of the prettiest villages in the Peninsula, Cartmel is a delightful cluster of houses and cottages set around a square from which lead winding streets and arches into back yards. The village is dominated by the famous **Cartmel Priory**, founded in 1188 by Augustinian canons. Like all monastic institutions, the priory was disbanded in 1537 and several of its members were executed for participating in the Pilgrimage of Grace.

L'enclume

Cavendish Street, Cartmel, Cumbria LA11 6PZ
Tel: 015395 36362 Fax: 015395 38907
e-mail: info@lenclume.co.uk website: www.lenclume.co.uk

Chef-patron Simon Rogan has masterminded the stylish conversion of an old building in the attractive Cumbrian village of Cartmel into a gastronomic restaurant with rooms. Simon's sophisticated cooking is complemented by an impressive choice of wines, and aperitifs and coffee can be enjoyed in a delightful conservatory with a view of the famous Priory. Comfortable, elegant overnight accommodation is provided in seven individually designed bedrooms with fine fabrics and furnishings and spotless en suite bathrooms. The restaurant is closed on Mondays, the accommodation available every night.

LAKELAND MOTOR MUSEUM

Holker Hall and Gardens, Cark-in-Cartmel,
Grange-over-Sands, Cumbria LA11 7PL
Tel/Fax: 015395 58509
e-mail: info@lakelandmotormuseum.co.uk
website: www.lakelandmotormuseum.co.uk

A nostalgic reminder of transport bygones, the
Lakeland Motor Museum has more than 100
vehicles on show ranging from pioneer vehicles of
the early 1900s through to the exuberant models
of the swinging 40s and fabulous 50s. As well as
these classic cars, the Museum also houses a
fascinating collection of "magnificent motorbikes,
superb scooters, bygone bicycles and triumphant
tractors!" Also amongst the 10,000 exhibits,
probably the most extensive presentation of
automobilia on display in the UK, are "Authentic
automobilia, reminiscent rarities, micro cars and mechanical marvels". This unique and carefully
maintained collection is housed in a quaint former
Shire horse stable and its courtyard. Prominent
contributors to 20th century motoring are all
honoured - amongst them Walter Owen Bentley, Colin
Chapman, Henry Ford, Cecil Kimber, William Lyons,
Alec Issigonis and Frederick Henry Royce. The world
of agriculture is not neglected either, with Henry
Ferguson and the horticultural reformer Charles H.
Pugh both featured. Interpretive displays and
strategically positioned push-button narrative centres,
together with a well-researched exhibit listing, provide
added interest and enjoyment.

The recent recovery of Donald Campbell's *Bluebird*
from the depths of Coniston Water gives an added
interest to the Campbell Legend Bluebird Exhibition
which pays tribute to Sir Malcolm Campbell and his
son Donald who between them captured 21 world land

and water speed records for Britain. Highlights of
the exhibition include full size detailed replicas of
the 1935 *Bluebird* car and the famous jet
hydroplane, *Bluebird K7*. There's even a replica of
Donald Campbell's lucky mascot, teddy bear Mr
Whoppit, together with a continuous video
detailing the lives, careers, failures and
achievement of these two sporting celebrities.

Also on site is an exhibition celebrating
Britain's horticultural heritage, a comprehensive
display of vintage mechanical rotavators, trimmers,
cutters and rollers, plus a fine collection of
historical lawnmowers. The Potting Shed contains
a display of gardening hand tools and other
equipment of the past, as well as a re-creation of a
pre-war glasshouse. Other attractions include the
Coach House Café and a gift shop.

Cartmel Sticky Toffee Pudding Co Ltd

The Square, Cartmel, Cumbria LA11 6QB
Tel/Fax: 015395 36201
e-mail: stpudcartmel@fsbdial.co.uk
website: www.stickytoffeepudding.co.uk

The Johns family have been making sticky toffee pudding since 1984, first in their restaurant in Grange and then here in Cartmel Village Shop on the Square. **Cartmel Sticky Toffee Pudding Co Ltd** uses only the very best ingredients for this traditional Cumbrian pudding, which is made on the premises and sold in five sizes. The shop also sells its own sticky toffee pudding sauce – delicious with ice cream, barbecued bananas or baked apples – as well as a wide range of high-quality comestibles from other producers.

Today, substantial remains of the 12th century Gatehouse (National Trust) survive, but the rest of the Priory was cannibalised to build many of the village's cottages and houses. After the Dissolution, only the south aisle of the **Church of St Mary and St Michael** was still standing but, in 1620, George Preston of Holker began restoring the entire building and the richly carved black oak screens and stall canopies date from this restoration. St Mary & St Michael's has recently been described as *"the most beautiful church in the northwest"*.

Inside, in the southwest corner of the church, is a door known as **Cromwell's Door**. The holes in it are said to have been made by indignant parishioners firing at Parliamentarian soldiers who had stabled their horses in the nave. Cartmel is also famous for its attractive **Racecourse**, set beside the River Eea, on which meetings are held in May, July and August. Located close to the village, the course must be one of the most picturesque in the country and it is certainly one of the smallest. A holiday atmosphere descends on the village for race days and, though the competition is fierce, it is a wonderful and relaxing day out.

FLOOKBURGH

3 miles SW of Grange-over-Sands on the B5277

An ancient Charter Borough, Flookburgh is still the principal fishing village on Morecambe Bay. Roads from the square lead down to the shore where fishermen still land their catches of cockles, shrimps and (less often nowadays) flukes, the tasty small flat fish from which the village takes its name. In **Coach House**, Winder Lane, is an unusual attraction in the form of a miniature village - 120 buildings made of local Coniston slate are accurate down to the last detail.

CARK-IN-CARTMEL

3 miles SW of Grange-over-Sands on the B5278

Cumbria's premier stately house, **Holker Hall** is one of the homes of the Cavendish family, the Dukes of Devonshire. An intriguing blend of 16th century, Georgian and Victorian architecture, is a visitor-friendly place with no restraining ropes keeping visitors at a distance, a fire burning in the hearth and a lived-in, family atmosphere. There's an impressive cantilevered staircase, a library with some 3,500 leather bound books (plus a few dummy covers designed to hide electricity sockets), and an embroidered panel said to be the work of Mary, Queen of Scots.

Holker Hall

ULVERSTON

It was way back in 1280 that Edward I granted Ulverston its market charter; more than seven centuries later, colourful stalls still crowd the narrow streets and cobbled market square every Thursday. It's a picturesque scene but a walk up nearby **Hoad Hill** is rewarded with an even more striking view of the town. The great expanse of Morecambe Bay with a backdrop of the Pennines stretches to the south, the bulk of Ingleborough lies to the east, Coniston Old Man and the Langdale Pikes lie to the

Each year, Holker's 25 acres of award-winning gardens host the **Holker Garden Festival**, which has been hailed as the 'Chelsea of the North'. The gardens are the pride of Lord and Lady Cavendish, who developed the present layout from the original 'contrived natural landscape' of Lord George Cavendish 200 years ago. The Great Holker Lime and the stunning spring display of rhododendrons are among the delights not to be missed. Here, too, are a wonderful rose garden, an azalea walk and a restored Victorian rockery. Lord and Lady Cavendish put their pride into words: "If you gain from your visit a small fraction of the pleasure that we ourselves get from them, then the work of generations of gardeners will not have been in vain."

The Holker Hall estate contains a wide variety of other attractions - formal gardens, water features, a 125-acre deer park, picnic and children's play areas, a gift shop and café. Also within the grounds is the **Lakeland Motor Museum** (see page 230) which, as well as boasting a completely restored 1920s garage, has more than 100 vehicles on show among well over 20,000 well-presented exhibits.

Laurel and Hardy Museum

4c Upper Brook Street, Ulverston (town centre),
Cumbria LA12 7BH
Tel: 01229 582292

The world famous museum devoted to Laurel & Hardy is based in Ulverston, the town where Stan was born on 16th June 1890. Everything you want to know about them is here. The late Bill Cubin, the founder of the museum, devoted his life to these famous comedians and collected an amazing variety of memorabilia, believed to be the largest in the world, including letters, photographs, personal items and furniture. A large extension gives ample room to browse and a small cinema shows films and documentaries all day. Disabled persons have full access.

west and north. Crowning the hill is a 100ft-high **Replica of the Eddystone Lighthouse**, raised here in 1850 to commemorate one of Ulverston's most distinguished sons, Sir John Barrow. Explorer, diplomat and author, he served as a Lord of the Admiralty for more than forty years, his naval reforms contributing greatly to England's success in the Napoleonic Wars.

An even more famous son of Ulverston was Stanley Jefferson, born at number 3, Argyle Street on June 16th, 1890. Stanley is far better known to the world as Stan Laurel. His thirty-year career in more than 100 comedy films with Oliver Hardy is celebrated in the town's **Laurel and Hardy Museum** (see panel opposite) in King Street. The museum was founded in 1976 by the late Bill Cubin, who devoted his life to the famous duo and collected an extraordinary variety of memorabilia, believed to be the largest in the world. Everything is here, including letters, photographs, personal items, and even furniture belonging to the couple.

The oldest building in the town is the **Church of St Mary** which, in parts, dates from 1111. Though it was restored and rebuilt in the mid-19th century and

THE TINNERS' RABBIT

50 Market Street, Ulverston, Cumbria LA12 7LS
Tel: 01229 588808 Fax: 01229 596585
e-mail: chris@tinnersrabbit.freeserve.co.uk

The Tinners' Rabbit is a gallery and craft shop established in 1998 by professional artist Chris Benefield. The main gallery room hosts regular exhibitions from painters and photographers with both local and national reputations. In many cases limited edition prints are available during and after the shows. In the workshop, more than 4,000 frame mouldings are available and Chris and his staff put their skills to excellent use in meeting the growing demand for high-quality professional framing. Six studios have been made available to painters and crafts people, all of whom – painter, potter, printmaker, shoemaker, furniture maker – are pleased to talk about their work and to accept commissions.

The Tinners' Rabbit
Market Street, Ulverston
Martin Procter

THE BOOKSHOP AT THE TINNERS' RABBIT

48 Market Street, Ulverston, Cumbria LA12 7LS
Tel: 01229 588858 e-mail: bookshop@thetinnersrabbit.co.uk

Liz Drew's bookshop is a higgledy piggledy sort of place full of books on every subject. There's a cosy children's area, good range of local books and strong fiction section. The staff are knowledgeable and friendly and will research the most obscure of titles. **The Bookshop** has become a focal point for the local literary community and organises regular events as well as reading groups for adults and children.

TWO BY TWO

54 Market Street, Ulverston LA12 7LS.
Tel: 01229 480338

Two By Two, a dress shop, owned by the Tinners' Rabbit Team, has a reputation for original, distinctive clothing in natural fabrics and great colours. The shop caters for women who like easy to wear designer fashion.

the chancel was added in 1903, it has retained its splendid Norman door and some magnificent stained glass, including a window designed by the painter Sir Joshua Reynolds.

Ulverston also boasts England's shortest, widest and deepest **Canal**. Visitors can follow the towpath walk alongside which runs dead straight for just over a mile to Morecambe Bay. Built by the famous engineer John Rennie and opened in 1796, the canal ushered in a half-century of great prosperity for Ulverston as an inland port. At its peak, some 600 large ships a year berthed here but those good times came to an abrupt end in 1856 with the arrival of the railway. The railway company's directors bought the canal and promptly closed it.

The town's other attractions include **The Lakes Glass Centre**, which features the high-quality Heron Glass and Cumbria Crystal.

Also at the Centre is the **Gateway to Furness Exhibition**, providing a colourful snapshot of the history of the Furness Peninsula. There's more history at the **Ulverston Heritage Centre**, which also has a gift shop selling souvenirs and crafts made in Cumbria, while modern entertainment is provided at the Coronation Hall theatre complex and the traditional Roxy Cinema.

The open area to the north of the town, known as **The Gill**, is the starting point for the 70-mile Cumbria Way. The route of the Cumbria Way was originally devised by the Lake District area of the Ramblers Association in the mid-1970s and provides an exhilarating journey through a wonderful mix of natural splendour and fascinating heritage. The first section is the 15-mile walk to Coniston.

T H Barker & Son

Baines Paddock Nursery, Haverthwaite, Nr Ulverston, Cumbria LA12 8PF
Tel: 015395 58236
e-mail: rachel@ukclematis.co.uk website: www.ukclematis.co.uk

Halfway between Haverthwaite and Holker Hall is a nursery unique to the Lake District. **Baines Paddock Nursery** is an old-fashioned family business specialising primarily in clematis; they propagate many of their own plants, and the collection runs to 450 varieties which can be seen in various stages of development. This traditional working nursery, owned and run by Peter Watson and Winnie Thornley helped by daughter Rachel Sullivan, also has a fine selection of cottage garden perennials with enough unusual varieties to delight those hunting for something 'a bit different'. Open 1st Feb-31st Oct, 9.30am-5.30pm. Closed Tuesday mornings.

Summer Hill Holidays

Spark Bridge, Nr Ulverston, Cumbria LA12 7SS
Tel: 01229 861510 Fax: 01229 861090
e-mail: lodges@summerhill.co.uk

Summer Hill is an excellent base for exploring Lakeland and an ideal retreat for a relaxing holiday. Brian and Rosemary Campbell offer comfortable, characterful self-catering accommodation in four self-contained authentic log cabins, all with two bedrooms, shower room, living room and adjoining fully fitted kitchen area. Each Lodge is pine-clad, centrally heated, double-glazed and fully carpeted. The Verandah has its own seating, allowing guests to enjoy the incredible garden, which includes majestic trees, ponds, rhododendrons and azaleas and a broad fountained lawn.

AROUND ULVERSTON

HAVERTHWAITE
5 miles NE of Ulverston off the A590

Haverthwaite is the southern terminus of the Lakeside & Haverthwaite Railway, a branch of the Furness railway originally built to transport passengers and goods to the steamers on Lake Windermere. It was one of the first attempts at mass tourism in the Lake District. Passenger numbers peaked in the 1920s, but the general decline of rail travel in the 1960s led to the railway's closure in 1967. However, a group of dedicated rail enthusiasts rescued this scenic stretch, restored its engines and rolling stock to working order and now provide a full service of steam trains throughout the season.

SWARTHMOOR
1 mile S of Ulverston off the A590

Swarthmoor Hall was built in around 1586 by George Fell, a wealthy landowner. It was his son, Judge Thomas Fell, who married Margaret Askew, who, in turn, became a follower of George Fox after hearing him preach in 1652. At that time, many people were suspicious of Fox's beliefs but Margaret was able to persuade her husband to use his position to give Fox protection and shelter, and the hall became the first settled centre of the Quaker Movement. Missionaries were organised from here and the library was stocked with both Quaker and anti-Quaker literature. Judge Fell died in 1658 and, 11 years later, Margaret married George Fox. The hall is open during the summer and it gives a fascinating insight into the history of the early Quakers.

LINDAL-IN-FURNESS
3 miles SW of Ulverston on the A590

The **Colony Country Store** combines the aromatic character of an old-fashioned country general stores with the cost-cutting advantages of a Factory Shop. There's a huge range of textiles, glassware, ceramics and decorative accessories for the home, but the Colony is also Europe's leading manufacturer of scented candles, supplying millions of scented and dinner candles every year to prestigious stores around the world.

GREAT URSWICK
3 miles S of Ulverston off the A590

The ancient village **Church of St Mary and St Michael** is noted for its unusual and lively woodcarvings that were created by the Chipping Campden Guild of Carvers. As well as the figure of a pilgrim to the left of the chancel arch, there are some smaller carvings in the choir stall of winged children playing musical instruments. Also worthy of a second look is the 9th century wooden cross which bears a runic inscription.

Lying between Great Urswick and Bardsea and overlooking Morecambe Bay is **Birkrigg Common**, a lovely area of open land. Here, on the east side of the common, is the **Druid's Circle**, with two concentric circles made up of 31 stones up to three feet high.

BARDSEA
2 miles S of Ulverston off the A5087

The village stands on a lovely green knoll overlooking the sea and, as well as having a charming, unhurried air about it, there are some excellent walks from here along the coast either from its Country Park or through the woodland.

Just up the coast, to the north, lies **Conishead Priory**, once the site of a leper colony that was established by Augustinian canons in the 12th century. The monks from the priory used to act as guides across the dangerous Cartmel Sands to Lancashire. After the Dissolution, a superb private house was

built on the site and the guide service was continued by the Duchy of Lancaster. In 1821, Colonel Braddyll demolished the house and built in its place the ornate Gothic mansion that stands here today. He was also responsible for the atmospheric ruined folly on **Chapel Island** that is clearly visible in the estuary.

Latterly, the Priory has been a private house, a hydropathic hotel, a military hospital and a rest home for Durham miners; it is now owned by the Tibet Buddhist Manjushri Mahayana Buddhist Centre, who came here in 1977. During the summer months, visitors are welcome to the house, which is open for tours, and there is a delightful woodland trail to follow through the grounds. A new Buddhist temple was opened in 1998, based on a traditional design which symbolises the pure world (Mandala) of a Buddha.

BARROW-IN-FURNESS

Undoubtedly the best introduction to Barrow is to pay a visit to the **Dock Museum** (see panel opposite), an impressive glass and steel structure which hangs suspended above a Victorian Graving Dock. Audio-visual displays and a series of exhibits describe how Barrow grew from a tiny hamlet in the early 1800s to become the largest iron and steel centre in the world and also a major shipbuilding force in just 40 years. The museum has some spectacular models of ships of every kind, an Art Gallery hosting both permanent and travelling exhibitions, and a high tech interactive film show where characters from Barrow's history come to life to tell the town's story. It was James (later Sir James) Ramsden who established the first Barrow Iron Ship Company in 1870,

taking advantage of local steel production skills. In 1896, the firm was acquired by **Vickers**, a name forever linked with Barrow, and for a number of years was the largest armaments works in the world. Sir James was also the General Manager of the Furness Railway and the town's first mayor. At the Ramsden Square roundabout is a statue to Sir James, and at the next roundabout is a statue of HW Schneider, one of the men who developed the Furness iron mines and was involved in the Barrow Haematite Steel Company.

Barrow is the western starting point of the **Cistercian Way**, a 33-mile-walk to Grange-over-Sands through wonderfully unspoilt countryside.

AROUND BARROW-IN-FURNESS

GLEASTON

3 miles E of Barrow-in-Furness off the A5087

This village is typical of the small, peaceful villages and hamlets that can be found in this part of the peninsula. Here, standing close by the ruins of **Gleaston Castle**, can be found **Gleaston Water Mill**. The present buildings date from 1774, with the massive original wooden gearing still in place. The machinery is operational most days - an 18ft water-wheel and an 11ft wooden pit wheel serviced by an intriguing water course. Evening tours with supper are available by prior arrangement.

FOULNEY ISLAND

5 miles E of Barrow-in-Furness off the A5087

The island, like its smaller neighbour Roa Island, is joined to the mainland by a causeway. The site of the local lifeboat station, the island is small and sheltered from the Irish Sea by Walney Island.

THE DOCK MUSEUM

The Dock, North Road, Barrow-in-Furness,
Cumbria LA14 2PW
Tel: 01229 894444

The Dock Museum is a spectacular modern museum built over an orginal Victorian dock. Its displays trace the fascinating history of Barrow showing how it grew from a tiny nineteenth century hamlet to the biggest iron and steel centre in the world and a major shipbuilding force in just 40 years.

New for 2001 is a permanent exhibition entitled "Shipbuilders to the World" which opens in May to coincide with Barrow's submarine centenary. This impressive exhibition looks at the development of shipbuilding in the town and will include an exciting interactive display using images from the museum's nationally important collection of glass negatives.

The Dock Museum has a fully landscaped waterfront site, with paths linking to the Cumbria Coastal Way, an adventure playground and picnic area. A wide range of tempting snacks and hot meals are available in our Strollers Coffee Shop. The museum has no admission charge and car parking is also free.

PIEL ISLAND

5 miles SE of Barrow-in-Furness via foot ferry from Roa island. Though this tiny island was probably visited by both the Celts and the Romans, its first recorded name is Scandinavian - Fotheray - from the Old Norse meaning 'fodder island'.

Piel Castle

In 1127 the islands were given to the Savignac Monks by King Stephen and, after the order merged with the Cistercian monks in the middle of the 12th century, the monks of Furness Abbey began to use Piel Island as a warehouse and storage area.

Piel Castle, on the island, was a house fortified in the early part of the 14th century and at the time it was the largest of its kind in the northwest. Intended to be used as one of the abbey's warehouses and to offer protection from raiders, in later years the castle also proved to be a useful defence against the King's Customs men and a prosperous trade in smuggling began. The castle has, over many years, been allowed to fall into ruin and now presents a stark outline on the horizon.

Continued on page 241

WALK 7

Low Furness

Start	Furness Abbey
Distance	7½ miles (12.1km). Shorter version 4½ miles (7.2km)
Approximate time	3½ hours (2 hours for shorter version)
Parking	Amphitheatre car park on south side of Furness Abbey
Refreshments	Pub by Furness Abbey, pubs at Newton, pubs and café at Dalton-in-Furness
Ordnance Survey maps	Landranger 96 (Barrow-in-Furness & South Lakeland) and Explorer OL6 (The English Lakes – South Western area)

Furness literally means 'far ness', and this formerly inaccessible area comprises the fells of High Furness, part of the Lake District National Park, and the peninsula of Low Furness, a region of green, rolling hills and shallow valleys. This walk explores part of the latter region: starting at one of the foremost monastic sites in the country, passing through three hamlets, visiting the medieval capital of Furness (Dalton-in-Furness) and finishing off with a walk through the lovely wooded Vale of Nightshade. Furness was an important source of iron ore, hence the sudden rise of Barrow in the 19ᵗʰ century, but there is little evidence of this industrial heritage on this peaceful walk, except for some abandoned iron mines and views over Barrow shipyards and Walney Channel. There may be cattle on some pastures passed through. The shorter version omits two of the three hamlets.

The extensive and well-preserved red sandstone ruins of Furness Abbey occupy such a peaceful and beautiful setting in the well-wooded Vale of Nightshade that it is difficult to believe Barrow lies just over the next hill. Founded in 1127, the abbey rapidly grew into one of the wealthiest Cistercian monasteries in England and, in this far flung region well away from the main centres of power, the abbots of Furness exercised almost quasi-monarchic powers. Its wealth was based on sheep farming, quarrying and iron-mining on its extensive estates, though it was subject to Scottish sea-borne raids from time to time. the transepts and east end of the church are almost complete, as is the east range of the cloisters, the latter noted for the flamboyant, decorative Norman arches that lead into the 13th-century chapter-house. Furness suffered the same fate as all the other great abbeys and was dissolved on the orders of Henry VIII in 1537.

Start by turning right along the lane and after about 50 yds (45m) turn right along a path through trees, which soon becomes a tarmac path enclosed by iron fencing. Cross a railway line, go through a metal kissing-gate and bear right to walk along the right-hand edge of a field, soon joining and keeping by Mill Beck on the right, up to the attractive Bow Bridge. This is thought to date from the 15th century and was one of the links in the large number of routes that radiated from the abbey at the height of its power.

Go through a metal kissing-gate onto a road, turn left beneath an avenue of trees and turn right by a road junction Ⓐ through a metal kissing-gate, by a public footpath sign to Newton. Follow the direction of the signpost uphill across rough pasture to a waymarked post, where you pass through a wall gap and continue uphill, by a hedge on the left. Where the hedge peters out, keep

ahead to a metal kissing-gate  , and ahead are the houses of Newton.

For the shorter version of the walk, go through the gate, head gently downhill along the right-hand edge of a field, by a hedge on the right, and go through another metal kissing-gate onto a lane on the edge of Newton. Continue along the lane opposite, bearing first right and then left, follow it through the village and at a public footpath sign to Long Lane turn left onto a tarmac track, here rejoining the full walk.

For the full walk, do not go through the gate but turn right to keep along the top edge of the field, by a fence and hedge on the left, to a stile. From here there are views over Barrow and Walney Channel, and out in the channel Piel Castle, owned by the medieval abbots of Furness, can be seen. Climb the stile, continue along the top edge of the next field, made uneven by the remains of disused iron mines, and turn left over a ladder-stile, just before reaching the brow of the hill in front. Bear right and head diagonally across a field; note that there is no visible path here. Make for a metal kissing-gate, go through this and continue on to a lane and turn right downhill into the hamlet of Stank.

Just before reaching farm buildings, turn left **C** through a metal gate along a track to a footpath sign and turn right around the end of a barn. Climb a stile, bear slightly left and head across to a waymarked post to the left of

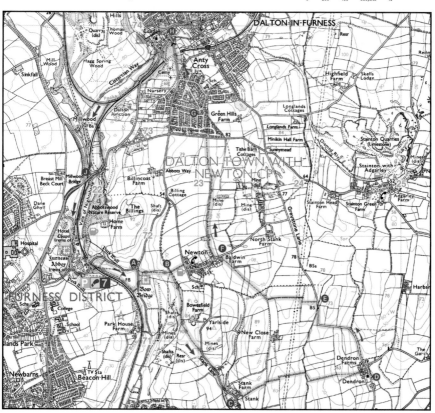

WALK 7

a barn. Continue past it to the field corner and turn left to walk along the right-hand edge of the field, by a hedge on the right. Climb a stile a few yards to the left of the field corner, keep along the left edge of the next field for a short distance and then climb a stile in the hedge on the left to continue uphill, now along the right edge of a field, by a hedge on the right. Over the brow, a fine view across Furness is revealed, with the outline of the Lakeland mountains to the left. Descend into a 'dip', climb a stile in the field corner, turn right along the bottom edge of the next field and turn left in the field corner to continue uphill along the right-hand edge of the field. In the top corner, climb a stile and keep ahead across the next field, heading downhill in the direction of Dendron church, to go through a metal gate in the bottom right-hand corner.

Walk through a farmyard, follow a track to right and left and continue down to a lane **D** just to the left of Dendron's 17th century church, one of the few to be built during the Civil War. Turn left along the lane for nearly ¾ mile (1.2km), following it around left and right bends, and at a public footpath sign turn left through a metal kissing-gate **E**. Veer right across the field. Go through another kissing-gate, turn right and at the end of the field turn left onto a farm track. Keep along the right-hand edge of a field, by a hedge on the right – it later becomes an enclosed track – to reach a metal gate. Go through, turn right over a waymarked stile a few yards ahead, bear left and head across a field to a squeezer stile; this may be difficult to spot but it is about 100 yds (91m) to the left of the right-hand field corner.

Go through the stile, continue in the same direction across two fields, going through more squeezer stiles, and bear right after the second one and make for a wide gap in the field corner. Climb a stile a few yards to the right of the gap and continue in the same direction across the next field, descending to go through a squeezer stile onto a lane (difficult to spot until you are close) **F** . Turn left into Newton and, just before reaching a pub, turn right, at a public footpath sign Long Lane, along a tarmac track, which soon continues as a hedge-lined, enclosed path. Where this path bends right, keep ahead

through a squeezer stile and continue across a succession of fields and through a series of squeezer stiles to emerge onto a road on the edge of Dalton-in-Furness. Cross over, take the tarmac path opposite between new houses, cross another road and continue along a narrow path. Bear left on joining another path and eventually turn left along a track to reach a road, by a public footpath sign North Stank **G** .

Turn right, at a T-junction turn right again and at the next T-junction turn left along a road to another T-junction. Here turn right along the main road and follow it steeply downhill to a junction **H**, where the route continues sharply to the left. Turn right if visiting the centre of Dalton-in-Furness, which was the 'capital' of Furness in the Middle Ages. Around the market square is Dalton Castle, a 14th century tower in which the abbots of Furness held their courts, some attractive cottages and an ornate Victorian cast-iron fountain in the middle. Nearby is the large, mainly 19th century church.

After turning left, take the first turning on the right, Goose Green, follow the lane as it curves left and, at a public footpath sign to Millwood, bear right along a tarmac drive. After a few yards, turn left to cross a footbridge over a stream, go through a kissing-gate and continue along a track through the pleasant, well-wooded valley.

The track narrows to a path and continues along the right inside edge of woodland. Go through a metal kissing-gate, continue to go through another and shortly turn left to pass under a railway bridge. Continue to the right, turn left to pass under another railway bridge, turn right, and the path later becomes a hedge- and tree-lined track that heads uphill to a road **J** . Cross over and, at a public footpath sign Furness Abbey, take the path opposite, which bends right and continues through woodland. Emerging from the trees, continue along an enclosed path through the Vale of Nightshade, then turn right to pass once more under a railway bridge and turn left to continue to a lane.

Walk along the lane, passing under an arch to the right of the Abbey Tavern and following it past the abbey ruins to return to the start.

WALNEY ISLAND

2 miles W of Barrow-in-Furness on the A590

This 10-mile-long island is joined to the Furness Peninsula by a bridge from Barrow docks and is home to two important nature reserves that are situated at either end of the island. **North Walney National Nature Reserve** covers some 350 acres within which are a great variety of habitats including sand dunes, heath, salt marsh, shingle, and scrub. As well as having several species of orchid and over 130 species of bird either living or visiting the reserve, there is also an area for the preservation of the Natterjack toad, Britain's rarest amphibian. Unique to the Reserve is the Walney Geranium, a plant that grows nowhere else in the world. North Walney also boasts a rich prehistoric past, with important archaeological sites from mesolithic, neolithic, Bronze, and Iron Age times.

Situated on the island's long foot, **South Walney Nature Reserve** is home to the largest nesting ground of herring gulls and lesser black-backed gulls in Europe. It is also the most southerly breeding ground of such species as the oystercatcher, tern, and ringed plover, and in all, over 250 bird species have been recorded. A stopover for many migratory birds, the reserve has considerable ecological interest with mudflats, sandy beaches, rough pasture, and fresh water. There are waymarked trails around the reserve, with a number of hides.

The island's southernmost tip, **Walney Point**, is dominated by a 70ft lighthouse which was built in 1790 and whose light was, originally, an oil lamp.

DALTON-IN-FURNESS

5 miles N of Barrow-in-Furness off the A590

Lying in a narrow valley on the part of Furness which extends deep into Morecambe Bay, it is difficult to imagine that this ancient place was once the leading town of Furness and an important centre for administration and justice. The 14th century pele tower, **Dalton Castle**, was built with walls six feet thick to provide a place of refuge for the monks of Furness Abbey against Scottish raiders and it still looks very formidable. It is now owned by the National Trust and houses a small museum with an interesting display of 16th and 17th century armour, along with exhibits about iron mining, the Civil War in Furness, and the life and work of George Romney, the 18th century portrait painter. He was best known in his day for his many portraits of Nelson's mistress, Lady Hamilton, with whom he formed a romantic attachment, in spite of having a wife in Kendal. He is buried in the graveyard of the red sandstone **Church of St Mary**, where his grave is marked with the inscription 'pictor celeberrimus'

Visitors to Dalton will find that it is time well spent looking around the many fascinating facades in and close to the market place, such as the unique, cast-iron shop front at No 51, **Market Street**. In the market place itself is an elegant **Victorian Drinking Fountain** with fluted columns supporting a dome of open iron work above the pedestal fountain. Nearby stands the market cross and the slabs of stone that were used for fish-drying in the 19th century.

From the mostly pedestrianised Tudor Square, visitors can board a bus to the award-winning **South Lakes Wild Animal Park**, which has been designated the Region's Official Top Attraction by the Cumbria Tourist Board. It's the only place in Britain where you can see rare Amur and Sumatran tigers (the world's biggest and smallest tigers). At feeding time (14.30 each day) they climb a 20

foot vertical tree to 'catch' their food. Ring-tailed lemurs wander freely through the park, visitors can walk with emus and hand feed the largest collection of kangaroos in Europe. The 17 acres of natural parkland are also home to some of the rarest animals on earth, among them the red panda, maned wolves and tamarin monkeys as well as some 150 other species from around the world, including rhinos, giraffes, tapirs, coatis and the ever-popular meerkats. Other attractions include a Safari Railway, adventure play area, many picnic spots, a gift shop and café.

Furness Abbey

To the south of the town lies **Furness Abbey** (English Heritage), a magnificent ruin of eroded red sandstone set in fine parkland, the focal point of south Cumbria's monastic heritage. Furness Abbey stands in the **Vale of Deadly Nightshade**, a shallow valley of sandstone cliffs and rich pastureland. The abbey itself was established in 1123 at Tulketh, near Preston, by King Stephen. Four years later it was moved to its present site and, after 20 years, became absorbed into the Cistercian Order. Despite its remoteness, the abbey flourished, with the monks establishing themselves as guides across the treacherous sands of Morecambe Bay.

GRIZEBECK
15 miles N of Barrow-in-Furness on the A595/A5092

This small village on the edge of the Lake District National Park nestles against the flanks of the **Furness Fells**. Although it stands at the junction of roads leading to the Furness Peninsula and the South Cumbria coast, the village and the area around is peaceful and unhurried, offering the visitor an inviting alternative to some of the busier and more crowded Lakeland towns.

BROUGHTON-IN-FURNESS
19 miles N of Barrow-in-Furness on the A595/A593

At the heart of this attractive, unspoilt little town is the **Market Square** with its tall Georgian houses, commemorative obelisk of 1810, village stocks, fish slabs and some venerable chestnut trees. The old Town Hall, occupying the whole of one side, dates back to 1766 and now houses the town's Tourist Information Centre and the Clocktower Gallery, which exhibits paintings, ceramics, mirrors and glassware. On August 1st each year, Broughton's Lord of the Manor comes to the Square to read out the market charter granted by Elizabeth I, while Councillors dispense pennies to any children in the crowd.

One of the town's famous short-term residents was Branwell Brontë, who was

employed here as a tutor at **Broughton House**, a splendid double-fronted, three-storey town house just off the Square. Branwell apparently found time to both enjoy the elegance of the town and to share in whatever revelries were in train. Wordsworth often visited Broughton as a child. Throughout his life he loved this peaceful corner of Lakeland and celebrated its charms in some 150 poems; his 20th century poetical successor, Norman Nicholson, was similarly enchanted.

Some of the Lake District's finest scenery - the Duddon Valley, Furness Fells, Great Gable and Scafell are all within easy reach, and about 3 miles west of the town is **Swinside Circle**, a fine prehistoric stone circle, some 60 feet in diameter, containing 52 close-set stones and two outlying 'portal' or gateway stones.

About three miles north of the town, the peaceful hamlet of **Broughton Mills** will attract followers of the Coleridge Trail. During the course of his famous 'circumcursion' of Lakeland in August 1802, the poet stopped to refresh himself at the **Blacksmith's Arms** where he "Dined on Oatcake and Cheese, with a pint of Ale, and two glasses of Rum and water sweetened with preserved Gooseberries". The inn, built in 1748, is still there and barely changed since Coleridge's visit.

CONISTON AND SOUTHWEST CUMBRIA

Three distinct areas lie within the southwest quarter of Cumbria. The enchanting scenery around Coniston Water and its environs is very much on the tourist trail, and also has strong literary connections. John Ruskin, the 19th century author, artist, and critic

made his home at Brantwood on the shore of Coniston and the lake is also the setting for many of the adventures recounted in *Swallows and Amazons* as told by Arthur Ransome. Wordsworth went to school in Hawkshead where the desk he defaced with his name can still be seen. But probably the most popular of Coniston's literary denizens is Beatrix Potter, who, after holidaying at Near Sawrey as a child, later bought a house at Hill Top as well as many acres of farms which she bequeathed to the National Trust. Further west is Cumbria's 'Empty Quarter', a vast terrain of magnificent mountains and desolate fells beloved of climbers and walkers. England's highest mountain, Scafell Pike, rises here; the country's deepest lake, Wast Water, sinks to a depth of some 200 feet and is surrounded by sheer cliffs soaring up to 2,000 feet, and the village of Wasdale Head claims to have the smallest church in England.

Bordering this untamed landscape is the narrow coastal strip, stretching from Whitehaven down to Millom, which has its own identity as well as a quiet charm. The coastline is dominated by small 18th and 19th century iron mining communities set between the romantic outline of the Lakeland fells and the grey-blue waters of the Irish Sea

CONISTON

Beatrix Potter, John Ruskin, Arthur Ransome, Sir Donald Campbell - all of them have strong connections with **Coniston Water**, the third largest and one of the most beautiful of the central Cumbrian lakes. Beatrix Potter lived at Sawrey near Lake Windermere but she owned the vast **Monk Coniston** estate at the head of Coniston Water. On her death, she bequeathed it to the National Trust, a body she had helped to establish

View of Coniston Lake from Nibthwaite

Arthur Ransome's *Swallows and Amazons* has delighted generations with its tales of children's adventures set in and around the Lake District. As a child he spent his summer holidays near Nibthwaite at the southern end of the lake and recalled that he was always "half-drowned in tears" when he had to leave. Later he bought a house overlooking Coniston Water and many locations in his books can be recognised today.

and to which she devoted much of her time and fortune.

Ruskin came to Coniston in 1872, moving into a house he had never seen. Brantwood, on the eastern side of the lake, is open to the public and enjoys superb views across the water to the great crumpled hill of the **Old Man of Coniston**, 800 metres high. From its summit there are even more extensive vistas over Scotland, the Isle of Man, and on a clear day as far as Snowdonia.

Sir Donald Campbell's associations with the lake were both glorious and tragic. In 1955 he broke the world water speed record here; twelve years later, when he was attempting to beat his own record, his boat, **Bluebird**, struck a log while travelling at 320mph. In March 2001 his widow was present as the tailfin of the boat was at last hauled up to the surface. For 34 years the 15 feet rear section had lain on a bed of silt, 140 feet

CONISTON LAUNCH

Coniston Water, Coniston, Cumbria LA22 0LF
Tel/Fax: 015394 36216
e-mail: info@conferry.co.uk
website: www.conistonlaunch.co.uk

Coniston Launch provides the perfect way to enjoy the glorious scenery and the historic sights of Coniston Water. All the local landmarks are visited by the traditional motor launches *Ruskin* and *Ransome*, and the options include regular North and South Lake sailings, Swallows & Amazons cruises, early morning cruises followed by breakfast, late evening cruises with wine, boat trips combined with guided walks, and Campbells on Coniston cruises that follow the history of Sir Malcolm's and Donald's speed record attempts on the lake.

down and right in the middle of the lake. Plans are still under way for the boat to be restored and placed on display at the Ruskin Museum, but it could take some time. Sir Donald's body was later recovered and was buried on September 12th 2001 in the village cemetery - an event that was comparatively little covered by the media, who were obviously concerned with the tragic events in New York and Washington the day before.

Nowadays, boats on Coniston Water are restricted to a 10 mph limit, which is an ideal speed if you're travelling in the wonderful old steamship, the **Gondola**. So called because of its high prow which enabled it to come in close to shore to pick up passengers, *Gondola* was commissioned by Sir James Ramsden, General Manager of the Furness Railway Company and first Mayor of Barrow, and was launched on Coniston Water in 1859. She retired in 1936, but found a new career as a houseboat in 1945. Abandoned after a storm in the 1960s, she was saved by a group of National Trust enthusiasts and restored and rebuilt by Vickers Shipbuilding. She was relaunched in 1980. Up to 86 passengers can now travel in opulent comfort on her regular trips around the lake. Coniston Launch also offers lake cruises in its two timber launches, and at the boating centre craft of every kind are available to rent.

Coniston village was once an important copper mining centre and it was from the Old Man of Coniston and some of the surrounding hills that copper was extracted. Mined from the days of the Romans, the industry's heyday in Coniston was in the 18th and 19th centuries but, with the discovery of more accessible deposits, the industry went into decline and the village

Ruskin Museum

The Institute, Yewdale Road, Coniston, Cumbria LA21 8DU
Tel: 015394 41164 Fax: 015394 41132
website: ruskinmuseum.com

John Ruskin, critic, social reformer, artist, amateur geologist and master of English prose, was Coniston's most distinguished 19th century resident, and the **Ruskin Museum** is a notable permanent memorial to the great man. With funds from the Heritage Lottery, the European Community and other benefactors, the Museum was redeveloped and extended in 1999 and is now widely cited as an example of how a small independent museum can help to regenerate a rural community through stimulating cultural tourism.

Many of Ruskin's letters, manuscripts, paintings, drawings and personal possessions are on display, and his concern for the local people and the local economy are shown in arrays of Langdale Linen and Ruskin Lace. Local farming, geology, mining and quarrying are also featured in this superb museum, along with the life and times of others notable figures with Coniston connections: Arthur Ransome of *Swallows and Amazons* fame, and Donald Campbell, who came to Coniston in the wake of his intrepid father Sir Malcolm and lost his life in 1967 while attempting a water speed record in his *Bluebird*.

BRANTWOOD

Coniston, Cumbria LA21 8AD
Tel: 015394 41396 Fax: 015394 41263
e-mail: enquiries@brantwood.org.uk
website: www.brantwood.org.uk

A popular 'port of call' on the Coniston Launch North Lake service is **Brantwood**, the home of John Ruskin from 1872 to 1900. The most beautifully situated house in the Lake District, it preserves the legacy of a man of great intellectual power whose influence spread to many notable thinkers and covered many subjects – art and art criticism, society and economics, the environment and man's effect on it. An entire day can be spent exploring at Brantwood, whose attractions include the house itself, filled with original furniture, artwork and decorations, the extensive estate and gardens, art exhibitions, a bookshop, a craft gallery and the Jumping Jenny restaurant.

returned to pre-boom peacefulness. At 2,631 feet, the Old Man of Coniston is a considerable climb but many make the effort and the summit can be bustling with fell walkers enjoying the glorious views.

Coniston's most famous inhabitant was John Ruskin, the 19th century author, artist, critic, social commentator and one of the first conservationists. He lies buried in Coniston churchyard and the **Ruskin Museum** (see panel on page 245) nearby contains many of his studies, pictures, letters, photographs and personal belongings, as well as his collection of geological specimens. Here, too, is his funeral pall made of Ruskin lace embroidered with wild flowers. The lace was so called because Ruskin had encouraged the revival of flax hand-spinning in the area. Lace pieces made to his own designs and based on the sumptuous ruffs worn by sitters in portraits by Titian, Tintoretto and Veronese were attached to plain linen to make decorative cushions, table covers and bedspreads - many of these are on display.

From the jetty at Coniston, a short ferry trip takes visitors to John Ruskin's home, **Brantwood** (see panel above),

which occupies a beautiful setting on the eastern shores of Coniston Water. It was his home from 1872 until his death in 1900. When he arrived for the first time he described the house, which he had bought for £1,500 without ever seeing it, as "a mere shed". He spent the next 20 years extending the house, by adding another 12 rooms, and laying out the gardens. The view from the Turret Room he had built was, Ruskin declared, "the best in all England". Sadly, Ruskin's later years were blighted by mental illness: "He was," said a biographer, "at times quite mad".

AROUND CONISTON

GRIZEDALE
3 miles SE of Coniston off the B5285

The village lies at the heart of the 9,000-acre **Grizedale Forest** which was acquired by the Forestry Commission in 1934 and is famous for its Theatre and Sculpture. The Commission's original intention of chiefly cultivating the forest for its timber met with much resistance and, over the years, many pathways have been opened and a variety of recreational activities have been

Grizedale Forest Tree Sculpture

encouraged. The Visitor Centre vividly illustrates the story of the forest as well as showing how the combination of wildlife, recreation, and commercial timbering can work together hand in hand. The forest, too, is famously the home of some 80 tree sculptures commissioned since 1977.

NEAR SAWREY
4 miles E of Coniston on the B5285

After holidaying here in 1896, the authoress fell in love with the place and, with the royalties from her first book, *The Tale of Peter Rabbit*, she purchased **Hill Top** in 1905. After her marriage in 1913 to a local solicitor, she actually lived in another house in the village and used the charming 17th century cottage as her study. Oddly, she wrote very little after the marriage, spending most of her time dealing with the management of the farms she had bought in the area.

SAWREY HOUSE

Near Sawrey, Ambleside, Cumbria LA22 0LF
Tel: 015394 36387 Fax: 015394 36010
e-mail: enquiries@sawreyhouse.com
website: www.sawreyhouse.com

In a part of the world rich in scenic delights, the Whiteside family's **Sawrey House** is an exceedingly comfortable and civilised base for touring the Lake District. The house was built around 1830 for a vicar who came from Cambridge to run nearby Hawkshead School. Some of the style of his Cambridge house is reflected at Sawrey in ecclesiastical touches like the stained glass window in the hall or the lych gate entrance. The bedrooms, each with its own character, are beautifully decorated, and many enjoy views of the lake. All have bath or shower en suite, tv, direct-dial telephone and beverage tray; some rooms boast king or queen size beds with canopies, and one room has a splendid four-poster.

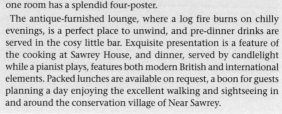

The antique-furnished lounge, where a log fire burns on chilly evenings, is a perfect place to unwind, and pre-dinner drinks are served in the cosy little bar. Exquisite presentation is a feature of the cooking at Sawrey House, and dinner, served by candlelight while a pianist plays, features both modern British and international elements. Packed lunches are available on request, a boon for guests planning a day enjoying the excellent walking and sightseeing in and around the conservation village of Near Sawrey.

Tarn Hows

HAWKSHEAD
3 miles E of Coniston on the B5285

There are more Beatrix Potter connections in the enchanting little village of Hawkshead. Her solicitor husband, William Heelis, worked from an office in the Main Street here and this has now been transformed into **The Beatrix Potter Gallery**. The gallery features an exhibition of her original drawings and illustrations alongside details of the author's life.

Following Beatrix Potter's death in 1943, the house and the land she had bought on the surrounding fells became the property of the National Trust and, in accordance with her will, Hill Top has remained exactly as she would have known it. One of the most popular Lakeland attractions, Hill Top is full of Beatrix Potter memorabilia, including some of her original drawings. The house is very small, so it is best avoided at peak holiday times. **Tarn Hows**, part of the 4,000-acre Monk Coniston estate bought and sold on to the National Trust, was created to resemble a Swiss lake and is very rich in flora and fauna - it has been designated a Site of Special Scientific Interest.

Hawkshead has specific Wordsworth connections, too. **Hawkshead Grammar School** was founded in 1585 by Edwin Sandys, Archbishop of York, and between 1779 and 1787 the young William Wordsworth was a star pupil. The earliest of his surviving poems was written to celebrate the school's 200th year. The school is open from Easter to September and visitors can inspect the classrooms during the summer holidays, see the desk where William carved his name and have a look around the headmaster's study. Ann Tyson's Cottage, where Wordsworth lodged while he attended the school, has also survived. It stands in Wordsworth Street and is now a guest house.

Situated at the head of **Esthwaite Water**, enjoying glorious views of Coniston Old Man and Helvellyn, Hawkshead is a delightful village of narrow cobbled lanes with a pedestrianised main square dominated by the Market House, or Shambles, and another square linked to it by little snickets and arched alleyways which invite exploration. The poet Norman Nicholson observed that, "The whole village could be fitted into the boundaries of a large agricultural show; yet it contains enough corners, angles, alleys and entries to keep the eye happy for hours".

The **Church of St Michael & All Angels**, with its massive 15th century tower, seems rather grand for the village but it too was built at a time when Hawkshead was a wealthy town. Inside, there are some remarkable wall paintings from the late 1600s and also look out for the "Buried in Woolen" affidavit near the vestry door. In 1666 the Government had decreed that corpses must not be buried in shrouds made from "flaxe, hempe, silke or hair, or other than what is made of sheeps wool onely". The idea was to help maintain the local woollen industry and this was one way of ensuring that even the dead got to help out. The church is the focal point of the annual Lake District Summer Music Festival and a popular venue for concerts and recitals. In the churchyard is a war memorial erected in 1919 and modelled on the ancient runic cross at Gosforth.

Some lovely walks lead from Hawkshead to **Roger Ground** and Esthwaite Water, possibly the least frequented of the Lakes, and also to the nearby hamlet of **Colthouse** where there's an early Quaker Meeting House built around 1690. Esthwaite Water was much loved by Wordsworth, as he shows in *The Prelude*:

> *My morning walks were early; oft before the hours of school*
> *I travelled round our little lake, five miles*
> *Of pleasant wandering. Happy time!*

GREAT LANGDALE
9 miles N of Coniston on the B5343

One of the most dramatic of the Lake District waterfalls is **Dungeon Ghyll**,

Great Langdale

MILLBECK FARM

Great Langdale, Nr Ambleside, Cumbria LA22 9JU
Tel: 015394 37364 Fax: 015394 37570
e-mail: millbeck@lineone.net

In a traditional Lakeland farm setting near the head of the Langdale Valley , Susan Taylforth welcomes guests with a choice of delightful accommodation. The Bed & Breakfast rooms in the main house, which dates from 1621, enjoy idyllic views of the valley, and days start in great style with Susan's superb home cooking – dinner is available with a little notice. Two recently renovated National trust properties on the other side of the B5343 provide a splendid base for a

self-catering holiday, with everything on hand for a carefree stay. Side House Farm sleeps six in great comfort, while Side House Cottage, part of the dairy of the old farmhouse, is an equally pleasant holiday home for three. The accommodation can be booked separately or for one big party.

The other part of the business is the rearing of Herdwick sheep and Angus cattle, both of which enjoy a stress-free life grazing wild and free on the Fells. The lamb - a traditional breed indigenous to the Lake District - and the beef can both be ordered direct from the farm for collection or delivery.

THE OLD DUNGEON GHYLL HOTEL

Great Langdale, Ambleside, Cumbria LA22 9JY
Tel/Fax: 015394 37272
website: www.odg.co.uk

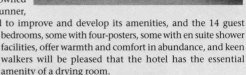

In a magnificent and spectacular setting at the head of the Great Langdale Valley, the **Old Dungeon Ghyll Hotel** has been dispensing hospitality to fellwalkers, climbers and tourists for more than 300 years.

Since 1984 this fine old inn has been owned and run by Neil Walmsley, a keen fell runner, and his wife Jane. They have continued to improve and develop its amenities, and the 14 guest

bedrooms, some with four-posters, some with en suite shower facilities, offer warmth and comfort in abundance, and keen walkers will be pleased that the hotel has the essential amenity of a drying room.

The first port of call for many visitors is the Hikers Bar, where a selection of real ales is on hand to quench outdoor thirsts. The owners both enjoy cooking, and the accent is very much on home-made food, from bar meals to evening meals served in the comfort of the dining room (open to non-residents by advance booking). The hotel takes its name from one of the most dramatic of the Lake District waterfalls, which tumbles 60 feet down the fellside.

which tumbles 60 feet down the fellside. The 'dungeon' is actually a natural cave. Nearby is the well-known Old Dungeon Ghyll Hotel, which makes an excellent starting point for walks in this spectacularly scenic area where the famous peaks of Crinkle Crags, Bowfell and the Langdale Pikes provide some serious challenges for hikers and ramblers.

Hardknott Fort

SEATHWAITE

5 miles W of Coniston via minor road off the A593

A mere five miles or so from Coniston as the crow flies, by road Seathwaite is nearly three times as far. It stands in one of the Lake District's most tranquil and least known valleys, **Dunnerdale**. Little has changed here since the days when William Wordsworth, who knew the area as Duddon Valley, captured its natural beauty in a sequence of sonnets. In his poem *The Excursion*, he wrote about the Rev Robert Walker, the curate of Seathwaite. Nicholas, or 'Wonderful Walker' as Wordsworth referred to him, served the church here for some 67 years though he also filled various other jobs such as farm labourer and nurse as well as spinning wool and making his own clothes. Fell walkers and hikers who prefer to escape the masses will delight not only in the solitude of this glorious valley but also in the wide variety of plant, animal, and birdlife that have made this haven their home.

HARDKNOTT PASS

5 miles W of Coniston off the A593

Surrounded by the fell of the same name, this pass is one of the most treacherous in the Lake District yet it was used by the Romans for the road between their forts at Ambleside (Galava) and Ravenglass (Glannaventa). Of the remains of Roman occupation, **Hardknott Fort** on a shoulder of the fell, overlooking the Esk Valley, is the most substantial and also provides some of the grandest views in the whole of the Lake District.

BOOT

8 miles W of Coniston off the A595

Lying at the eastern end of the **Ravenglass and Eskdale Railway**, this is a wonderful place to visit whether arriving by train or car. A gentle walk from the station at Eskdale brings you to this delightful

Eskdale Green

Continued on page 254

WALK 8

Boot

Start	Dalegarth Station, Boot
Distance	4¼ miles (6.8km)
Approximate time	2¼ hours
Parking	Station car park at Dalegarth, near Boot
Refreshments	Café at Dalegarth Station, pub and café at Boot, Woolpack Inn to east of point D
Ordnance Survey maps	Landranger 89 (West Cumbria) and Explorer OL6 (The English Lakes – South Western area)

The valley of the River Esk is among the loveliest and possibly least disturbed in the Lake District. Apart from La'al Ratty, the narrow-gauge railway whose steam trains carry visitors up and down the first 7 miles (11.3km), there has been no tourist development so its pleasures are all natural ones, not least its riverside and fellside walks. This walk starts with a gentle stroll uphill past a series of waterfalls before crossing open moorland, from where there are grand panoramas of some of the finest Lakeland mountains, including the Sca Fell group and Great Gable. After reaching a little tarn set among hills, the way descends steeply, with expansive views of stone farmhouses in a pattern of neatly walled fields along the Esk valley, and ends with a level walk beside the river. There is no rough terrain, and the height reached should be safe in all weather, but walking-shoes or boots are recommended, as is protective clothing against the wind chill above the valley.

From Dalegarth Station Ⓐ turn left along the road to Brook House and left again up the lane to Boot and Eskdale Mill. The first stop on the walk could be at Eskdale Mill just up the lane beside the bridge over Whillan Beck. It has been working since 1578 and still does when it has visitors, who – strangely for so interesting a place – are rather few. Almost as fascinating as its complex internal workings is the system that diverts water from higher up the beck, which is controlled by sluices and fed to a 12ft (3.7m) overshot wheel by a wooden leat. A path through the woods follows the course of this water system.

Through a gate just beyond the mill, turn left onto the fell to see what was once the terminus of the Ravenglass and Eskdale Railway, which was built originally to service Nab Gill iron ore mines near the top of the fell above Boot. Down the fellside there is what

looks like a great smudge of pink paint. This is spillage of haematite, or iron ore, along the line of the self-acting inclined railway that used to bring the ore down to the then 3ft (1m) gauge railway. A cable ran round a wheel at the top of the incline, and loaded wagons running down pulled a string of empty ones up to the top to be loaded. At the foot of the now much decayed and overgrown incline the layout of Boot Station with its passenger platform and ore-loading bays can still be made out. The shell of a stone building was the mine manager's office. A low circular stone-walled enclosure is the remains of the store for gunpowder, which was used until 1874, when it was replaced by Alfred Nobel's new dynamite. The mines closed down in 1882.

From this site of industrial archaeology go back over the bridge, turn left up a gated lane beside two holiday cottages and walk up

beside Whillan Beck. For some way the beck is a succession of falls 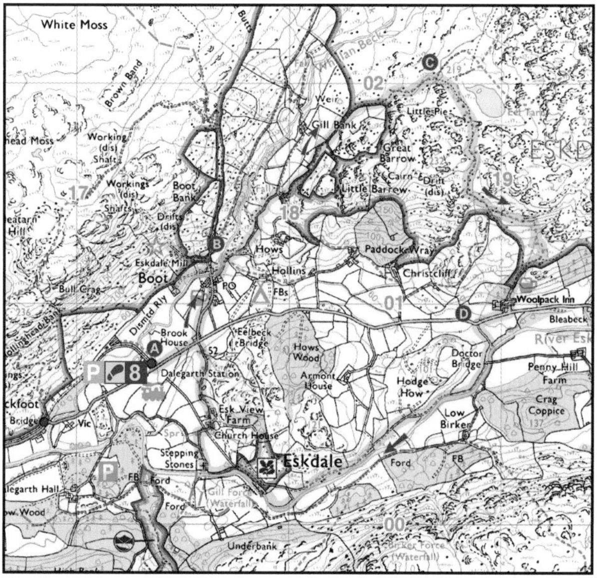 where, except when in full spate in winter, it is possible to walk about on great slabs of rock with the water rushing and tumbling around you. The point at which the falls can be easily reached is about 200 yds (183m) from the start of the lane opposite a gate on the right. The lane continues as a good farm road to Gill Bank, but halfway there a public footpath sign to Eel Tarn directs you through a gate and then another sign leads uphill to the left on a rough, stony path. This path continues with a slight curve all the way round the crags of Little Barrow, Great Barrow and Little Pie. On the way, one is treated to a clear view of the southern side of Sca Fell with Great Gable peeping over its shoulder on the left. Scafell Pike is hidden behind the fell. Near a high point on the path it is crossed by a small stream, and a course should be taken to the right about 50 yds (45m) beyond the stream and parallel to it. This is a fairly obvious grass way over a shallow shoulder, beyond which is Eel Tarn. This is a pretty piece of water decorated with water-lilies and lying in a peaty basin surrounded by bobbing cotton grass and boulders, the latter providing seats for a rest or picnic.

At the far end of the tarn a clearly marked peat and grass path starts to wind gently between rock outcrops down the hillside to the road on the valley bottom. For most of the way there are oblique views up and down the middle of Eskdale with the steep high rock faces of Birker, Harter and Ulpha fells forming the far horizon. Shoulder-high bracken softens the immediate scene and gives a feeling of protection against the ever-present, looming crags above. Eventually the path comes out onto the road beside the Woolpack

Inn. Here, turn right and almost immediately left along the lane to Penny Hill Farm but, instead of crossing the stone Doctor Bridge to the farm, keep on the path alongside the Esk all the way to St Catherine's Church on the riverbank. It is a relatively level and pleasant walk, always within sight or sound of the pebble-strewn river. Gill Force is in a little ravine with deep pools that attract hardy divers into the cold mountain water. St Catherine's Church is well over 600 years old but was largely rebuilt in 1881 at the enormous cost of £750, equivalent to the incumbent's stipend for ten years. Until 1901 the churchyard was the burial ground for both Eskdale and Wasdale. The rough track that runs from Wasdale Head up to Burnmoor Tarn and then down beside the iron ore mines, now a popular fell walk, was until early in this century maintained as a corpse road. Follow the walled lane that runs up from the church past Eskview Farm to the crossroads at Brook House and turn left along the road to return to the start.

village with its pub, post office, museum, waterfall and nearby St Catherine's Church in its lovely secluded riverside setting.

ESKDALE GREEN
10 miles W of Coniston off the A595

One of the few settlements in this beautiful and unspoiled valley, the village lies on the route of the Ravenglass and Eskdale Railway. Further up the valley lies a group of buildings that make up Eskdale Mill where cereals

Ravenglass

have been ground since 1578, when it is recorded that the brothers Henry and Robert Vicars were the tenants, paying an annual rent of eight shillings (40p). The original machinery for grinding oatmeal is in full working order and operated daily.

RAVENGLASS

Lying as it does at the estuary of three rivers - the Esk, the Mite, and the Irt - as well as enjoying a sheltered position, it is not surprising that Ravenglass was an important port from prehistoric times. The Romans built a naval base here around AD78, which served as a supply point for the military zone around Hadrian's Wall. They also constructed a fort, **Glannaventra**, on the cliffs above the town, which was home to around 1,000 soldiers. Little remains of Glannaventra except for the impressively preserved walls of the Bath House. Almost 12 feet high, these walls are believed to be the highest Roman remains in the country.

One of the town's major attractions is the 15 inch narrow gauge **Ravenglass and Eskdale Railway** which runs for seven miles up the lovely Mite and Esk

River valleys. Better known as "La'al Ratty", it was built in 1875 to transport ore and quarried stone from the Eskdale Valley and opened the following year for passenger traffic. Since then the railway has survived several threats of extinction. The most serious occurred at the end of the 1950s when the closure of the Eskdale granite quarries wiped out the railway's freight traffic at a stroke. However, at the auction for the railway in 1960 a band of enthusiasts outbid the scrap dealers and formed a company to keep the little railway running.

Today, the company operates 12 locomotives, both steam and diesel, and 300,000 people a year come from all over the world to ride on what has been described as 'the most beautiful train journey in England'. There are several stops along the journey and at both termini there is a café and a souvenir shop. At Ravenglass Station there is also a museum which brings to life the history of this remarkable line and the important part it has played in the life of Eskdale.

A mile or so east of Ravenglass stands **Muncaster Castle** (see panel opposite), which has been in the ownership of the Pennington family since 1208. In 1464

MUNCASTER CASTLE

Ravenglass, Cumbria CA18 1RQ
Tel: 01229 717614 Fax: 01229 717010

Muncaster Castle is an impressive castellated mansion which has been owned by the Pennington family since 1208. Back in 1464 the Penningtons gave shelter to King Henry VI after his defeat at the Battle of Hexham. On his departure Henry presented them with his enamelled glass drinking bowl saying that as long as it remained unbroken the Penningtons would live and thrive at Muncaster. It remains intact and the Penningtons are indeed still here - your audio tour guide is narrated by Patrick Gordon-Duff-Pennington, the present owner, who enlivens the tale with old legends and family anecdotes. The tour also introduces visitors to the many Muncaster treasures (including tapestry, silver, and porcelain collections), the stunning Great Hall, Salvin's octagonal library and the barrel ceiling in the drawing room.

Muncaster is also famous for its gardens and, in particular, the rhododendrons, azaleas, and camellias which are best viewed between March and June. The woodland gardens themselves cover some 77 acres and, as well as the beauty of the vegetation, there are some splendid views over the Lakeland fells. These extensive grounds also contain a fascinating Owl Centre which is home to more than 180 birds of 50 different species. Here, visitors can meet the birds daily at 14.30 (late March to early November) when a talk is given on the work of the centre and, weather permitting, the owls display their flying skills. Other attractions include a very well-equipped children's play area with an aerial runway, scramble net and fireman's pole; a nature trail and orienteering course, plant centre, gift shop and licensed café. The gardens and owl centre are open daily throughout the year; the castle is open each afternoon from the end of March to the end of October (closed Saturday).

the Penningtons gave shelter to King Henry VI after his defeat at the Battle of Hexham. On his departure Henry presented them with his enamelled glass drinking bowl, saying that as long as it remained unbroken the Penningtons would survive and thrive at Muncaster. Apart from the many treasures, the stunning Great Hall, Salvin's octagonal library and the barrel ceiling in the drawing room, Muncaster is also famous for its gardens. The collection of rhododendrons is one of the finest in Europe, gathered primarily from plant-hunting expeditions to Nepal in the 1920s, and there are also fine azaleas, hydrangeas and camellias as well as many unusual trees. For many visitors the chief attraction is the **World Owl Centre**, where many endangered owl species are bred. Snowy owls have become great favourites on the back of the Harry Potter craze, and many visitors have enquired about keeping them as pets. The staff at the Centre have to point out that the snowy owl is a mighty predator with a five feet wingspan. Mighty as he is, he is not the mightiest of the owls at the Centre: that honour goes to the Eurasian eagle owl, whose full splendour can be seen at the daily demonstrations. Muncaster's latest attraction is the Meadow Vole Maze (these little creatures are the staple diet of barn owls, and visitors can find out what it's like to be a vole on the run from a hungry owl).

Originally part of the Muncaster Castle Estate, **Muncaster Water Mill** can be traced back to 1455, though it is thought that this site may be Roman. The situation is certainly idyllic, with the mill race still turning the huge wooden water wheel and the Ravenglass and Eskdale Railway running alongside. In November 1996, Pam and Ernie Priestley

came to the mill and Ernie put his years of engineering experience to use as the miller. The mill is open every day from Easter to the end of October, working just as it has done for hundreds of years. Visitors can see the machinery in action, and also enjoy some delicious refreshments in the 17th century byre tea rooms. Naturally, the organic flour ground here is used in all the cakes, breads, and scones, and the flour is also on sale.

AROUND RAVENGLASS

BOOTLE
7 miles S of Ravenglass on the A595

This ancient village is particularly picturesque and quaint. The river Annas flows beside the main road and then dives under the village on its way to the sea. High up on **Bootle Fell**, to the southeast of the village, lies one of the best stone circles in Cumbria. Over the years, many of the 51 stones that make up the **Swinside Stone Circle** have fallen over. When it was originally constructed and all the stones were upright, it is likely, as they were also close together, that the circle was used as an enclosure.

SILECROFT
10 miles S of Ravenglass off the A595

Perhaps of all the villages in this coastal region of the National Park, Silecroft is the perfect example. Just a short walk from the heart of the village is the beach, which extends as far as the eye can see. On the horizon lies the distant outline of the Isle of Man. There is also a Site of Special Scientific Interest close by, a

UNDERWOOD COUNTRY GUEST HOUSE

The Hill, Millom, Cumbria LA18 5EZ
Tel: 01229 771116 Fax: 01229 719900
e-mail: enquiries@underwoodhouse.co.uk
website: www.underwoodhouse.co.uk

On the edge of woodland overlooking the picturesque Whicham Valley and the Duddon Estuary, **Underwood Country Guest House** offers a delightful combination of comfort, luxury and hospitality. Andrew and Wendy Miller personally run this charming house, a beautifully restored Victorian vicarage situated in eight acres of grounds, gardens and paddocks. The seven guest bedrooms - five double rooms and two twins - are all en suite, each with its own distinctive decor and character. All are equipped with tv, radio alarm, tea/coffee making facilities and hairdryers.

Two elegant lounges provide ample room for relaxation, and Underwood's amenities include a

tennis court and an indoor heated swimming pool with steam room. A multi-choice breakfast - as hearty or healthy as you like - makes a perfect prelude to a day exploring the surrounding area, while for the less adventurous or less energetic, a stroll round the grounds or a gentle game of croquet might fit the bill. Every evening Andrew and Wendy, both with international culinary experience, prepare a splendid four-course dinner using the best of local produce, complemented by a carefully selected wine list. Underwood is a non-smoking guest house and is unsuitable for children under 14.

tract of coastal scrubland which provides the perfect habitat for the rare Natterjack toad.

Millom
13 miles S of Ravenglass on the A5093

This small and peaceful town stands at the mouth of the River Duddon with the imposing **Black Combe Fell** providing a dramatic backdrop. Originally called Holborn Hill, the present day name was taken from nearby **Millom Castle** which is now a private, working farm. Like many neighbouring towns and villages in Furness, Millom was a small fishing village before it too grew with the development of the local iron industry. **Millom Folk Museum** tells the story of the town's growth and also has a permanent memorial to Norman Nicholson (1914-1987) who is generally regarded as the best writer on Lakeland life and customs since Wordsworth himself. Nicholson's book *Provincial Pleasures* records his affectionate memories of Millom, the town where he spent all his life. Other displays include a full-scale reproduction of a drift and cage from nearby Hodbarrow mine. South of Millom, at Haverigg, is the **RAF Millom Museum** situated in the former Officers Mess. Visitors to the site will find a fascinating collection of over 2,000 photographs of the wartime activities of the RAF in the area, various artefacts connected with the period and a number of items recovered from local crash sites. The museum also has a fine collection of aero engines including a Rolls Royce Merlin, a Westland Whirlwind helicopter, the cockpit section of a De Havilland Vampire jet trainer and an example of the HM14 or Flying Flea. The Duddon Estuary is an important site for wildlife, and the RSPB site at **Hodbarrow** is home not only to birds but to many kinds of flora and fauna. **Hodbarrow**

Beacon, which still stands, was built in 1879 as a lighthouse to assist vessels taking iron ore from the mines to destinations in Europe.

Drigg
2 miles N of Ravenglass on the B5343

The main attractions here are the sand dunes and the fine views across to the Lakeland mountains and fells. There is an important nature reserve, **Drigg Dunes**, on the salt marshes that border the River Irt but - take note, adders are common here. The reserve is home to Europe's largest colony of black-headed gulls.

Santon Bridge
3 miles NE of Ravenglass off the A595

The churchyard of **Irton Church**, reached from Santon Bridge via an unclassified road, offers the visitor not only superb views of the Lakeland fells to the west but also the opportunity to see a beautiful Anglican Cross, in excellent condition, that is certainly 1,000 years old. The Bridge Inn here plays host each November to the 'World's Biggest Liar' competition (see Gosforth on page 260).

Seascale
4 miles N of Ravenglass on the B5343

One of the most popular seaside villages in Cumbria, Seascale enhanced its resort status in 2000 by restoring the **Victorian Wooden Jetty** to mark Millennium Year. Stretching out into the Irish Sea, it is the focal point for fishing, beach casting, wind surfing and water-skiing, and also provides the starting point for many walks, including the Cumbrian Coastal Way which passes along the foreshore. Two Victorian buildings stand out: the **Water Tower**, medieval in style and with a conical roof, and the old **Engine Shed** which is now a multi-purpose Sports Hall.

A couple of miles north of the village is the site of the world's first commercial nuclear power station, the Magnox power station at Calder Hall.

GOSFORTH

5 miles N of Ravenglass on the A595

On the edge of this picturesque village, in the graveyard of **St Mary's Church**, stands the tallest ancient cross in England. Fifteen feet high, the **Viking Cross** towers above the huddled gravestones in the peaceful churchyard. Carved from red sandstone and clearly influenced by both Christian and pagan traditions, the cross depicts the crucifixion, the deeds of Norse gods and Yggdrasil, the World Ash Tree that Norsemen believed supported the universe. The interior of the church also contains some interesting features. There's a **Chinese Bell**, finely decorated with Oriental imagery, which was captured in 1841 at Anunkry, a fort on the River Canton, some delightful carved faces on the chancel arch and a collection of ancient stones the most notable of which dates from Saxon times and depicts the Lamb of God trampling on the serpents of pagan faith.

A major attraction in this appealing village is **Gosforth Pottery**, where Dick and Barbara Wright produce beautifully crafted work and also give pottery lessons.

To the east of Gosforth runs Wasdale, the wildest of the Lake District valleys but easily accessible by road. The road leads to **Wast Water**, which is just three miles long but is the deepest lake in England. The southern shores are dominated by huge screes some 2,000 feet high that plunge abruptly into the lake and they provide an awesome backdrop to this tranquil stretch of water. A lake less like Windermere would be hard to find as there are no

GOSFORTH HALL HOTEL

Gosforth Village, Cumbria CA20 1AZ
Tel: 019467 25322 Fax: 019467 25992
e-mail: enquiries@gosforthhallhotel.co.uk
website: www.gosforthhallhotel.co.uk

Located on the quiet western edge of the Lake District National Park, **Gosforth Hall Hotel** has a history going back almost 350 years. In keeping with its status as Grade 2* listed, the building retains many original features, including a magnificent sandstone hearth and wooden beams said to be taken from the hull of a sunken ship. Owners Rod and Barbara offer a warm welcome in a friendly, relaxed atmosphere, and the nine guest bedrooms, some en suite, all with tv and tea/coffee making facilities, provide comfort and character in abundance.

Top of the range is the suite, with a four-poster bed and a huge, magnificent bath. The owners take great pride in the food at the Hall, all of it home cooked using local produce as much as possible; they will always do their best to cater for special dietary needs. The hotel is close to the deepest lake in England, Wastwater, and the country's highest peak, Scafell, and it stands next to the little Church of St Mary with its famous 15ft Viking Cross. This is great walking and climbing country but equally appealing for touring or just relaxing and enjoying the lovely scenery.

Wast Water

from here there are many footpaths up to some of the best fells in Cumbria.

Wasdale Head, just to the north of the lake, is a small, close-knit community with a far-famed Inn that has provided a welcome refuge for walkers and climbers since the mid-1800s. who have been out discovering Wasdale and the lake. **Wasdale Church** is claimed to be the smallest in England - although this title is hotly disputed by Culbone in Somerset and Dale Abbey in Derbyshire. The church was built in the 14th century and it is hidden away amidst a tiny copse of evergreen trees. Local legend suggests that the roof beams came from a Viking ship and it is certainly true that until late Victorian times, the church had only an earth floor and few seats.

motorboats ploughing their way up and down the lake; this is very much the country of walkers and climbers and

YEWTREE HOLIDAYS IN WASDALE

Yewtree, Wasdale, Cumbria CA20 1EU
Tel/Fax: 019467 26285
e-mail: pauline@corleyp.freeserve.co.uk
website: www.yewtreeholidays.co.uk

Yewtree Holidays in Wasdale offers excellent self-catering holiday accommodation in a magnificent, peaceful setting on the north side of Wasdale. Bank Barn, built around 1820 and the only building remaining from the old Yewtree Farm, has been sympathetically converted to provide delightful accommodation for four, plus a cot for a baby; it comprises two bedrooms, a well-equipped shower room and an open-plan living area with a fully fitted modern kitchen. It has its own private parking and access to a garden with patio furniture. The Garden Flat is a cosy self-contained retreat for two, plus bunk beds for one or two children and a cot for a baby. This flat, too, is very comfortable and well equipped and has access through French windows to its garden with spectacular views. The properties have been given a 3-4 star self catering rating by The English Tourism Council .

Linen and duvets are included, and the use of a washing machine and tumble dryer is available on request. No smoking indoors. Gosforth, Nether Wasdale and Wasdale Head provide a choice of pubs, restaurants and shops, and the fuller amenities of Egremont and Whitehaven are within an easy drive. Yewtree is a family run hill farm with 100 acres of land and a flock of Herdwick sheep. There is direct access from Bank Barn and the Garden Flat to the fellside, with excellent opportunities for walkers, climbers, artists, photographers and lovers of wildlife and glorious scenery.

Sca Fell Pike

As well as the deepest lake and the smallest church, Wasdale also boasts the highest mountain, **Sca Fell Pike** (3,205ft) - and the world's biggest liars. This latter claim goes back to the mid-1800s when Will Ritson, "a reet good fibber", was the publican at the inn. Will enthralled his patrons with tall stories of how he had crossed foxes with eagles to produce flying foxes and had grown turnips so large he could hollow them out to make a comfortable residence. In the same spirit, the 'World's Biggest Liar' Competition takes place every November, usually at the Bridge Inn at Santon Bridge, when contestants from all over the country vie in telling the most prodigious porkies.

CALDER BRIDGE
7 miles N of Ravenglass on the A595

From this small, grey, 19th century settlement there is an attractive footpath to **Calder Abbey**. It was founded by monks of Savigny in 1134 but amalgamated with the Cistercians of Furness Abbey when it was ransacked by the Scots a few years later. After the Dissolution the monastery buildings lapsed slowly into the present-day romantic ruin. To the northeast of the village, the River Calder rises on Caw

Fell. **Monk's Bridge**, the oldest packhorse bridge in Cumbria, was built across it for the monks of Calder Abbey.

EGREMONT
12 miles N of Ravenglass on the A595

This pretty town is dominated by **Egremont Castle** with walls 20 feet high and an 80 foot tower. It stands high above the town, overlooking the lovely River Ehen to the south and the market place to the north. The castle was built between 1130 and 1140 by William de Meschines on the site of a former Danish fortification. The most complete part still standing is a Norman arch that once guarded the drawbridge entrance. Nearby is an unusual four-sided sundial and the stump of the old market cross dating from the early 13th century.

Egremont's prosperity was based on the good quality of its local red iron ore and jewellery made from it can be bought at the nearby **Florence Mine Heritage Centre**. Visitors to the mine, the last deep working iron ore mine in Europe, can join an underground tour (by prior arrangement) and discover why the miners became known as the Red Men of Cumbria. The museum here also tells story of the mine, which was worked by the ancient Britons, and there is a re-creation of the conditions that the miners endured at the turn of the 20th century.

In September every year the town celebrates its **Crab Fair**. Held each year on the third Saturday in September, the Fair dates back more than seven centuries - to 1267 in fact, when Henry III granted a Royal Charter for a three-day fair to be held on "the even, the day and the morrow after the Nativity of St. Mary the Virgin". The celebrations

World Gurning Championship

include the Parade of the Apple Cart when a wagon loaded with apples is driven along Main Street with men on the back throwing fruit into the crowds. Originally, the throng was pelted with crab apples - hence the name Crab Fair - but these are considered too tart for modern taste so nowadays more palatable varieties are used. The festivities also feature a greasy pole competition (with a pole 30 feet high), a pipe-smoking contest, wrestling and hound-trailing. The highlight, however, is the **World Gurning Championship** in which contestants place their heads through a braffin, or horse collar, and vie to produce the most grotesque expression. If you're toothless, you start with a great advantage!

Lowes Court Gallery, in a listed 18th century building, holds fine art exhibitions throughout the year. The premises also house the Tourist Information Centre.

WHITEHAVEN

The first impression is of a handsome Georgian town but Whitehaven was already well established in the 12th century as a harbour for use by the monks of nearby St Bees Priory. After the reformation, the land was acquired and developed by the Lowther family in order to expand the coal industry. By the mid-1700s, Whitehaven had become the third largest port in Britain, its trade based on coal and other cargo business, including importing tobacco from Virginia, exporting coal to Ireland, and transporting emigrants to the New World.

When the large iron-steamships arrived however, the harbour's shallow draught halted expansion and the port declined in favour of Liverpool and Southampton. For that reason much of the attractive harbour area - now full of pleasure craft and fishing smacks - and older parts of the town remain largely unchanged.

The harbour and its environs have been declared a Conservation Area and located here is **The Beacon** (see panel on page 262), where, through a series of

Whitehaven Harbour

THE BEACON

West Strand, Whitehaven, Cumbria, CA28 6LY
Tel: 01946 592302 Fax: 01946 598150
e-mail: thebeacon@copelandbc.gov.uk
website: www.copelandbc.gov.uk

Situated on Whitehaven's attractive harbourside, The Beacon is home to the town's museum collection. It traces the social, industrial and maritime heritage of the area, using local characters, audio-visual displays and fascinating museum pieces. The Met Office Weather Gallery, where you can monitor, forecast and broadcast the weather, offers panoramic views of the town and coast. Also, don't miss the Harbour Gallery, which offers free entry to the changing exhibitions; our gift shop and café. Guided heritage walks are available through town and over the headland to Haig Colliery Mining Museum. Disabled access and facilities.

innovative displays, the history of the town and its harbour are brought to life. The displays reflect the many aspects of this harbour borough with a collection that includes paintings, locally made pottery, ship models, navigational instruments, miners' lamps, and surveying equipment. The Beilby 'Slavery' Goblet, part of the museum's collection, is one of the masterpieces of English glass-making and is probably the finest example of its kind in existence.

Also here are the **Harbour Gallery**, with an ongoing arts programme, and the **Met Office Gallery**, where visitors can monitor, forecast and broadcast the weather. They can also learn about the "American Connection" and John Paul Jones' attack on the town in 1778, or settle down in the cinema to watch vintage footage of Whitehaven in times past. John Paul Jones had been an apprentice seaman at Whitehaven before going to the New World, where he became well known in the War of Independence. In 1777 he became Captain of the privateer *The Ranger* and led a raid on Whitehaven with the intention of firing the ships in the harbour. Thwarted by light winds, the party raided the fort and spiked the guns, then managed to damage only

three ships before retreating under fire.

There's more history at **The Rum Story**, which tells the story of the town's connections with the Caribbean. The display is housed in the original 1785 shop, courtyards, cellars and bonded warehouses of the Jefferson family, the oldest surviving UK family of rum traders. Visitors can learn about the various processes involved in the making of rum, travel through realistic re-creations of far-off villages and experience the sights, sounds and smells of life on board the slave ships.

In Solway Road, Kells, the **Haig Colliery Mining Museum** features the world's only Bever Dorling Winding Engines, various displays about the mining industry and exhibits on mining disasters. Haig Colliery was the last deep coal mine worked in the West Cumberland coalfield. Sunk between 1914 and 1918, it closed in 1986 and was later sold for restoration. As well as the elegant Georgian buildings that give the town its air of distinction, there are two fine parish churches that are worth a visit. Dating from 1753, **St James' Church** has Italian ceiling designs and a beautiful Memorial Chapel (dedicated to those who lost their lives in the two World Wars and also the local people who were killed in

mining accidents) while the younger **St Begh's Church**, which was built in the 1860s by EW Pugin, is striking with its sandstone walls. In the graveyard of the parish church of **St Nicholas** is buried Mildred Gale, the grandmother of George Washington. In 1699, this widow and mother of three married George Gale, a merchant who traded from Whitehaven to Maryland and Virginia. Her sons were born in Virginia but went to school in Appleby. When their mother died they returned to Virginia; one of them, Augustin, became the father of George Washington, first President of the United States of America.

Whitehaven is interesting in other ways. The grid pattern of streets dating back to the 17th century gives substance to its claim to be the first planned town in Britain. Many of the fine Georgian buildings in the centre have been restored and **Lowther Street** is a particularly impressive thoroughfare. Also of note is the **Harbour Pier** built by the canal engineer John Rennie, and considered to be one of the finest in Britain. There is a fascinating walk and a Nature Trail around **Tom Hurd Rock**, above the town.

AROUND WHITEHAVEN

St Bees
3 miles S of Whitehaven on the B5343

St Bees Head, a red sandstone bluff, forms one of the most dramatic natural features along the entire coast of northwest England. Some four miles long and 300 feet high, these towering, precipitous cliffs are formed of St Bees sandstone, the red rock which is so characteristic of Cumbria. Far out to sea, on the horizon, can

be seen the grey shadow of the Isle of Man and, on a clear day, the shimmering outline of the Irish coast. From here the 190-mile **Coast to Coast Walk** starts on its long journey across the Pennines to Robin Hood's Bay in North Yorkshire.

Long before the first lighthouse was built in 1822, there was a beacon on the headland to warn and guide passing ships away from the rocks. The present 99ft high lighthouse dates from 1866-7, built after an earlier one was destroyed by fire. St Bees Head is now an important Nature Reserve and the cliffs are crowded with guillemots, razorbills, kittiwakes, gulls, gannets, and skuas. Bird watchers are well-provided for with observation and information points all along the headland. There is a superb walk of about eight miles along the coastal footpath around the headland from St Bees to Whitehaven. The route passes Saltam Bay and Saltam Pit, which dates from 1729 and was the world's first undersea mineshaft. The original lamp house for the pit has been restored and is now used by HM Coastguard.

St Bees itself is a delightful place to explore, with its main street winding up the hillside between old farms and cottages. The Priory at St Bees grew in size and importance until it was

View from St Bees

destroyed by the Danes in the 10th century: the Benedictines later re-established the priory in 1129. **The Priory Church of St Mary and St Bega** is all that is now left and although it has been substantially altered there is still a magnificent Norman arch and a pre-Conquest, carved Beowulf Stone on a lintel between the church and the vicarage, showing St Michael killing a dragon. The most stunning feature of all is much more modern, a sumptuous Art Nouveau metal work screen. In the south aisle is a small museum.

Close by the church are the charming Abbey Cottages and **St Bees School** with its handsome clock-tower. The school was founded in 1583 by Edmund Grindal, Archbishop of Canterbury under Elizabeth I, and the son of a local farmer.

The original red sandstone quadrangle bears his coat-of-arms and the bridge he gave to the village is still in use. Among the school's most famous alumni is the actor and comedian Rowan Atkinson, creator of the ineffable Mr Bean.

CLEATOR MOOR
3 miles SE of Whitehaven on the B5295

Cleator developed rapidly in the 19th century because of the insatiable demand during the Industrial Revolution for coal and iron ore. As the Cumbrian poet Norman Nicholson wrote:

From one shaft at Cleator Moor
They mined for coal and iron ore.
This harvest below ground could show
Black and red currants on one tree.

Cleator is surrounded by delightful

FAR MOOR END

Ennerdale Bridge, Cumbria CA23 3AS
Tel: 01946 861046
website: www.ennerdalelakedistrict.co.uk
e-mail: claremessenger@aol.com

Far Moor End is a traditional Lakeland house set in delightful gardens and grounds at the end of a long private drive on the outskirts of Ennerdale Bridge. The magnificent secluded position, with the backdrop of Grike Fell, Crag Fell and the High Stile range, provides a very tranquil environment for a stay, and the house and adjoining newly converted barn offer superb non-smoking en suite

accommodation for up to six guests. All the rooms have central heating, tv and access to cooking facilities, and the residents' sitting/dining room is supplied with a tv/dvd/video/music system and a good selection of books, maps and information about the locality.

A splendid breakfast with locally sourced produce starts the day, after which guests might take a stroll through the private woodland, watch the visiting red squirrels and the many species of wildlife in and around the three ponds. The house also has a long frontage along the River Ehen, which is designated a Site of Special Scientific Interest. There are many beautiful walks starting from the doorstep and catering for all energy levels: a relaxed four-hour walk round Ennerdale Water, perhaps, or a more energetic seven-hour walk taking in Steeple and Haycock (packed lunches can be provided), and for walkers returning exhausted and thirsty a lift to the local pub (1 mile away) can be arranged.

countryside and little evidence of the town's industrial past is visible. But there is a thriving business nearby - the **Kangol Factory Shop** in Cleator village which stocks a huge range of hats, scarves, bags, caps and golf wear.

ENNERDALE BRIDGE

7 miles E of Whitehaven off the A5086

The bridge here crosses the River Ehen, which, a couple of miles upstream runs out from **Ennerdale Water**, one of the most secluded and inaccessible of all the Cumbrian lakes. The walks around this tranquil lake and through the quiet woodlands amply repay the slight effort of leaving the car at a distance. The Coast to Coast Walk runs the whole length of Ennerdale and this section is generally considered to be by far the most beautiful.

COCKERMOUTH

A market town since 1226, Cockermouth has been fortunate in keeping unspoilt its broad main street, lined with trees and handsome Georgian houses, and dominated by a statue to the Earl of Mayo. The Earl was Cockermouth's MP for ten years from 1858 before being appointed Viceroy of India. His brilliant career was brutally cut short when he was stabbed to death by a convict at a prison settlement he was inspecting on the Andaman Islands.

But Cockermouth boasts two far more famous sons. Did they ever meet, one wonders, those two young lads growing up in Cockermouth in the 1770s, both of them destined to become celebrated for very different reasons? The elder boy was Fletcher Christian, who would later lead the mutiny on the *Bounty*; the younger lad was William Wordsworth, born here in 1770 at Lowther House on Main Street, an imposing Georgian house now maintained by the National Trust. Now known as **Wordsworth House**, it was built in 1745 for the Sheriff of Cumberland and then purchased by the Earl of Lowther; he let it to his land agent, John Wordsworth, William's father. All five Wordsworth children were born here, William on 7th April 1770. Many of the building's original features survive, among them the staircase, fireplace, and fine plaster ceilings. A few of the poet's personal effects are still here and the delightful walled garden by the River Cocker has been returned to its Georgian splendour. The garden is referred to in *The Prelude*.

Built in 1134 by the Earl of Dunbar, **Cockermouth Castle** saw plenty of action against Scottish raiders (Robert the Bruce himself gave it a mauling in 1315), and again during the Wars of the Roses; in the course of the Civil War it was occupied by both sides in turn. Mary, Queen of Scots, took refuge at the castle in 1568 after her defeat at the Battle of Langside. Her fortunes were so low that she was grateful

Wordsworth House

IRTON HOUSE FARM

Isel, Nr Cockermouth, Cumbria CA13 9ST
Tel: 017687 76380
e-mail: almond@farmersweekly.net
website: www.almondirtonhousefarm.com

Guests return year after year to enjoy the warm welcome, the
peace and beauty of the setting, the superb accommodation and
the freedom of a self-catering holiday at **Irton House Farm**. On
their working sheep farm, Joan and Reg Almond offer a choice
of non-smoking self-catering apartments with luxury accommodation for two, four or six guests, all
beautifully designed and furnished, fully equipped and centrally heated. Laundry facilities are available
on site, and a games area includes pool, snooker and table tennis. All the apartments have wheelchair
access and other design features for the disabled.

for the gift of 16 ells (about 20 yards) of
rich crimson velvet from a wealthy
merchant. Part of the castle is still lived
in by the Egremont family; the
remainder is usually only open to the
public during the Cockermouth Festival
in July.

Opposite the Castle entrance,
Castlegate House is a fine Georgian
house, built in 1739, which hosts a
changing programme of monthly
exhibitions of the work of Northern and
Scottish artists - paintings, sculptures,
ceramics and glass. To the rear of the
house is a charming walled garden
which is open from time to time
during the summer.

Just around the corner from Castlegate
House is the **Toy & Model Museum**
which exhibits mainly British toys from
around 1900 to the present. There are
many visitor operated displays including
0 and 00 gauge vintage tinplate trains,
Scalextric cars, Lego models and even a
1950s helicopter to fly. There are prams
and dolls houses, and a working railway
in a garden shed.

Almost next door, **Jennings Brewery**
offers visitors a 90-minute tour which
ends with the option of sampling some of
their ales - Cumberland Ale, Cocker Hoop
or the intriguingly named Sneck Lifter.
The last independent brewing company
in Cumbria, Jennings have been brewing

traditional beers since the 1820s and
today there are more than 100 Jennings
pubs across the north of England.

A short walk from the Brewery brings
you to the **Kirkgate Centre**, which is
housed in a converted Victorian primary
school. Run by volunteers, the Centre
offers a wide range of events and activities
including live music, amateur and
professional drama, films, dance,
workshops, exhibitions of art and
local history.

The **Printing House Museum** occupies
a building dating back to the 16th
century and follows the progress of
printing from its invention by Johann
Gutenberg in 1430 to the end of the
letterpress era in the 1960's, when
computers took over. On display is a wide
range of historical presses and printing
equipment, the earliest being a Cogger
Press dated 1820. Visitors are offered the
opportunity to gain hands-on experience
by using some of the presses to produce
cards or keepsakes.

Located just south of the town, the
Lakeland Sheep & Wool Centre provides
an introduction to life in the Cumbrian
countryside with the help of a spectacular
visual show, 19 different breeds of live
sheep and a wide variety of exhibits. The
Centre also hosts indoor sheepdog trials
and sheep-shearing displays for which
there is a small charge.

AROUND COCKERMOUTH

BRIGHAM

2 miles W of Cockermouth off the A66

St Bridget's Church, which was probably founded as part of a nunnery, contains many interesting features, including pre-Norman carved stones, a rare 'fish window' and a window dedicated to the Rev John Wordsworth, son of William and vicar of Brigham for 40 years. One of the tombs in the graveyard is that of Charles Christian, the father of Fletcher Christian, the *Bounty* mutineer. Fletcher himself was baptised in the church on the day of his birth, as it was thought unlikely that he would survive.

BRIDEKIRK

2 miles N of Cockermouth off the A595

The village **Church** contains one of the finest pieces of Norman sculpture in the country, a carved font with a runic inscription and a mass of detailed embellishments. It dates from the 12th century and the runic inscription states that:

> *Richard he me wrought*
> *And to this beauty eagerly me brought.*

Richard himself is shown on one side with a chisel and mallet. Not only is this a superb example of early English craftsmanship but it is exceedingly rare to find a signed work. Ancient tombstones stand round the walls of this cruciform church and inside it has unusual reredos of fleur-de-lys patterned tiles.

HIGH & LOW LORTON

5 miles SE of Cockermouth on the B5289

There is a yew tree, pride of Lorton Vale... wrote Wordsworth in his poem *Yew Trees*, and astonishingly it's still there behind the village hall of High Lorton. It was in the shade of its branches that the Quaker George Fox preached to a large gathering under the watchful eye of Cromwell's soldiers. In its sister village, Low Lorton, set beside the River Cocker, is **Lorton Hall** (private) which is reputed to be home to the ghost of a woman who carries a lighted candle. Less spectral guests in the past have included King Malcolm III of Scotland, who stayed here with his queen while visiting the southern boundaries of his Kingdom of Strathclyde of which this area was a part.

EAGLESFIELD

2 miles SW of Cockermouth off the A5086

The most famous son of this small village is **John Dalton**, who was born here in 1766. The son of Quaker parents, Dalton was teaching at the village school by the time he was 12. Despite having had no formal education himself, he became one of the most brilliant scientists, naturalists, and mathematicians of his age and was the originator of the theory that all matter is composed of small indestructible particles called atoms. He was also the first to recognise the existence of colour blindness. He suffered from it himself and in medical circles it is known as Daltonism. A memorial to this remarkable man now marks the house where he lived in Eaglesfield.

WORKINGTON

The largest town on the Cumbrian coast, Workington stands at the mouth of the River Derwent and on the site of the Roman fort of **Gabrosentum**. Its prosperity was founded on the three great Cumbrian industries - coal, iron and shipping. In later years, Workington became famous for its fine quality steel, especially after Henry Bessemer developed his revolutionary steel making process here in 1850. The seat of the Curwen family for over 600 years,

HELENA THOMPSON MUSEUM

Park End Road, Workington, Cumbria CA14 4DE.
Tel: 01900 326255Fax: 01900 326256

Visit the **Helena Thompson Museum** and discover Workington's fascinating social and industrial heritage. The Museum is housed in a fine, listed mid Georgian building. It was bequethed to the people of Workington in 1940 by local philanthropist Miss Helena Thompson. Displays in the museum include; pottery, silver, glass and furniture, dating from Georgian, Regency and Victorian times; women's and childrens dresses from the 18th to the early 20th century, together with accessories and jewellery; the social and industrial history of Workington, the coal mining, ship building, iron and steel industry for which Workington became world renowned. Admission is free.

Workington Hall has an interesting history. Originally built around a 14th century pele tower, the hall was developed over the years with extensive alterations being made in the 18th century by the then lord of the manor, John Christian Curwen. Now a stabilised ruin, it has several commemorative plaques which give a taste of the hall's history. The most famous visitor was Mary, Queen of Scots who sought refuge here when she fled from Scotland in 1558. She stayed for a few days during which time she wrote the famous letter to her cousin Elizabeth I bemoaning her fate, "for I am in a pitiable condition....having nothing in the world but the clothes in which I escaped", and asking the Queen "to have compassion on my great misfortunes". The letter is now in the British Museum.

Workington's **Church of St John the Evangelist** is a very grand affair built at enormous expense in 1823 to give thanks for the defeat of Napoleon at Waterloo. It is a copy of St Paul's, Covent Garden, and its walls were built with stones from the local Schoose and Hunday quarries. The interior was splendidly restored by Sir Ninian Comper in 1931. St Michael's is the ancient parish church, restored after a fire in 1994.

The **Helena Thompson Museum** (see panel above) the story of Workington's coal mining, ship-building, and iron and steel industries for which the town became internationally renowned. The Georgian Room gives an insight into the variety of decorative styles which were popular between 1714 and 1830, with displays of beautiful cut-glass tableware, porcelain from China, and period pieces of furniture. Bequeathed to the town by the local philanthropist Miss Helena Thompson, MBE, JP, the museum was opened in 1949 and contains some of her own family heirlooms. One particularly interesting exhibit is the Clifton Dish, a locally produced 18th century piece of slipware pottery, while further displays demonstrate the links between this local industry and the famous Staffordshire pottery families. Fashion fiends will be interested in the display of women's and children's dresses from the 1700s to the early 1900s, together with accessories and jewellery. Workington is at the start of the C2C cycle route that runs to Sunderland and Newcastle. A short distance south of town is **Harrington Reservoir Nature Reserve**, a haven for wildlife with a rich variety of wild flowers, insects, butterflies, birds and animals.

AROUND WORKINGTON

MARYPORT
6 miles NE of Workington on the A596

Dramatically located on the Solway Firth, Maryport is a charming Cumbrian coastal town rich in interest and maritime history. The old part is full of narrow streets and neoclassical, Georgian architecture which contrast with sudden, surprising views of the sea. Some of the first visitors to Maryport were the Romans, who built a clifftop fort here, **Alauna**, which is now part of the Hadrian's Wall World Heritage Site. The award-winning **Senhouse Roman Museum** tells the story of life in this outpost of the empire. Housed in the striking Naval Reserve Battery, built in the 1880s, the museum holds the largest collection of Roman altars from a single site in Britain. Modern Maryport dates from the 18th century when Humphrey Senhouse, a local landowner, developed the harbour at what was then called Ellenport to export coal from his mines, and named the new port after his wife, Mary. Over the next century it became a busy port as well as a ship-building centre; boats had to be launched broadside because of the narrowness of the harbour channel. The town declined, along with the mining industry, from the 1930s onwards. It nevertheless attracted the artist LS Lowry, who was a frequent visitor and loved painting the harbour. Today, Maryport is enjoying a well-earned revival, with newly restored Georgian quaysides, clifftop paths, sandy beaches and a harbour with fishing boats.

The town's extensive maritime history is preserved in the vast array of objects, pictures and models on display at the **Maritime Museum** (see panel opposite) overlooking the harbour. Housed in another of Maryport's more interesting and historic buildings, the former Queen's Head public house, the museum tells of the rise and fall of the harbour and docks. Other exhibits include a brass

MARYPORT MARITIME MUSEUM

1 Senhouse Street, Maryport,
Cumbria CA13 6AB
Tel: 01900 813738 Fax: 01900 819496

Did you know that Maryport has connections with the ill fated 'Titanic', or Fletcher Christian, of Mutiny on the Bounty fame? Visit **Maryport Maritime Museum** and discover the fascinating and proud maritime heritage of this delightful town. The building, formerly the Queens Head Public House, is built on one of the earliest plots of land developed by Humphrey Senhouse 11 when the town was built.

The Museum houses a wealth of objects, pictures, models and paintings that illustrate Maryport's proud maritime tradition; from a whale's tooth to a blunderbuss; from sailmakers' tools to telescopes;from a mutineer, Fletcher Christian, to a great shipowner, Thomas Henry Ismay of the great White Star Line, owners of the ill fated Titanic.

telescope from the *Cutty Sark* and the town's connections with the ill-fated liner, the *Titanic*, and with Fletcher Christian, instigator of the mutiny on the *Bounty*. The *Titanic* was part of the fleet of the White Star Line, which was founded by a Maryport man, Thomas Henry Ismay. Fletcher Christian was also more or less a local man, being born at nearby Cockermouth in 1764.

Close by is the **Lake District Coast Aquarium**, where a series of spectacular living habitat re-creations introduce visitors to the profusion of marine life found in the Solway Firth - thornback rays (which can be touched), some small sharks, spider crabs and the comically ugly tompot blenny among them.

ASPATRIA
14 miles NE of Workington on the A596

Lying above the shallow Ellen Valley, Aspatria's main interest for most visitors lies in the elaborate **Memorial Fountain** to 'Watery Wilfred', Sir Wilfred Lawson MP (1829-1906), a lifelong crusader for the Temperance Movement and International Peace. According to one writer, "No man in his day made more people laugh at Temperance meetings". Also worth a visit is the much restored **Norman Church** that is entered through a fine avenue of yew trees. Inside are several ancient relics including a 12th century font with intricate carvings, a Viking hogback tombstone, and a grave cover with a pagan swastika engraving.

ALLONBY
11 miles N of Workington on the B5300

This traditional Solway village is backed by the Lake District fells and looks out across the Solway Firth to the Scottish hills. Popular with wind-surfers, the village has an attractive shingle and sand beach which received a Seaside Award in

1998. The Allerdale Way and the Cumbrian Cycle Way both pass close by, and the village is also on the **Smuggler's Route** trail. Smuggling seems to have been a profitable occupation around here - a Government enquiry into contraband trade reported in 1730 that "the Solway people were the first working-class folk to drink tea regularly in Britain".

In the early 1800s, Allonby was a popular sea-bathing resort and the former seawater baths, built in 1835 and now Grade II listed buildings, still stand in the old **Market Square**. In those days, the upper floor was in popular use as a ballroom for the local nobility. Allonby still keeps much of its Georgian and early Victorian charm with cobbled lanes, alleyways, and some interesting old houses. It was also an important centre for herring fishing and some of the old kippering houses can still be seen.

HOLME ST CUTHBERT
14 miles N of Workington off the B5300

This inland hamlet is also known as Rowks because, in the Middle Ages, there was a chapel here dedicated to St Roche. Northeast of the hamlet, and enveloped among low hills, is a lovely 30-acre lake known as **Tarns Dub**, which is a haven for birdlife. A couple of miles to the southwest, the headland of **Dubmill Point** is popular with sea anglers. When the tide is high and driven by a fresh westerly wind, the sea covers the road with lashing waves.

BECKFOOT
16 miles N of Workington on the B5300

At certain times and tides, the remains of a prehistoric forest can be seen on the sand beds here and, to the south of the village, is the site of a 2nd century Roman fort known as **Bibra**. According to an

inscribed stone found here, it was once occupied by an Auxiliary Cohort of 500 Pannonians (Spaniards) and surrounded by a large civilian settlement. The small stream flowing into the sea was used in World War I as a fresh water supply by German U-boats.

SILLOTH
18 miles N of Workington on the B5300

This charming old port and Victorian seaside resort is well worth exploring and its two-mile-long promenade provides wonderful views of the Solway Firth and the coast of Scotland. With the coming of the railways in the 1850s, Silloth developed as a port and railhead for Carlisle. The Railway Company helped to develop the town and had grey granite shipped over in its own vessels from Ireland to build the handsome church which is such a prominent landmark. The region's bracing air and low rainfall helped to make Silloth a popular seaside resort. Visitors today will appreciate the invigorating but mild climate, the leisurely atmosphere, and the glorious sunsets over the sea that inspired Turner to record them for posterity. The town remains a delightful place to stroll, to admire the sunken rose garden and the pinewoods and two miles of promenades. Silloth's 18-hole golf course was the 'home course' where Miss Cecil Leitch (1891-1978), the most celebrated woman golfer of her day, used to play. Another keen woman golfer was the great contralto, Kathleen Ferrier, who stayed in the town for part of her tragically short life. One of the most popular attractions is the **Solway Coast Discovery Centre**, where Auld Michael the Monk and Oyk the Oystercatcher guide visitors through 10,000 years of Solway Coast history.

WIGTON

For centuries, Wigton has been the centre of the business and social life of the Solway coast and plain, its prosperity being based on the weaving of cotton and linen. It has enjoyed the benefits of a Royal Charter since 1262 and the market is still held on Tuesdays. Horse sales are held every April (riding horses and ponies) and October (Clydesdales, heavy horses and ponies). Today, most of the old town is a Conservation Area and, particularly along the **Main Street**, the upper storeys of the houses have survived in an almost unaltered state. On street corners, metal guards to prevent heavy horse-drawn wagons damaging the walls can also still be seen.

One mile south of Wigton are the scant remains of the Roman fort of **Olenacum**; most of its stones were removed to rebuild Wigton in the 18th and 19th centuries.

AROUND WIGTON

SKINBURNESS
11 miles W of Wigton off the B5302

A lively market town, in the Middle Ages, Skinburness was used by Edward I in 1299 as a base for his navy when attacking the Scots. A few years later a terrible storm destroyed the town and what survived became a small fishing hamlet. From nearby **Grune Point**, the start of the **Allerdale Ramble**, there are some tremendous views over the Solway Firth and the beautiful, desolate expanse of marshland and sandbank. Grune Point, which was once the site of a Roman fort, now forms part of a designated Site of Special Scientific Interest notable for the variety of its birdlife and marsh plants.

ABBEYTOWN
5 miles W of Wigton on the B5302

As its name suggests, Abbeytown grew up around the 12th century **Abbey of Holm Cultram** on the River Waver and many of the town's buildings are constructed of stone taken from the abbey when it fell into ruins. The red sandstone **Church of St Mary** is still the parish church and was restored in 1883, a strange yet impressive building with the original nave shorn of its tower, transepts and chancel. The east and west walls are heavily buttressed and a porch with a new roof protects the original Norman arch of the west door. Within the church buildings is a room, opened by Princess Margaret in 1973, which contains the gravestones of Robert the Bruce's father and that of Mathias and Juliana De Keldsik, relations of Abbot Robert. Nearby, there are some lovely walks along the River Waver, which is especially rich in wildlife.

NEWTON ARLOSH
5 miles NW of Wigton on the B5307

Situated on the **Solway marshes**, the village was first established by the monks of Holm Cultram Abbey in 1307 after the old port at Skinburness had been destroyed by the sea. The village church is one of the most delightful examples of a Cumbrian fortified **Church**. In the Middle Ages, there was no castle nearby to protect the local population from the border raids and so a pele tower was added to the church. As an additional defensive measure, the builders created what is believed to be narrowest church doorway in the country, barely two feet seven inches across and a little over five feet high. The 12-inch arrow-slot east window is also the smallest in England.

View near Keswick

After the Reformation, the church became derelict but was finally restored in the 19th century. Inside, there is a particularly fine eagle lectern carved out of bog oak.

KESWICK AND THE NORTHERN LAKES

For many visitors this part of the county is classic Lakeland, the scenery dominated by the rounded, heather-clad slopes of the Skiddaw range to the north of Keswick, and the wild, craggy mountains of Borrowdale, to the south. Yet, despite this area's popularity, there are still many hidden places to discover and many opportunities to leave the beaten track.

The major town, Keswick, on the shores of Derwent Water, is a pleasant Lakeland town that has much to offer the visitor. The lake too, is interesting as, not only is it in a near perfect setting, but it is unusual in having some islands - in this case four. It was the view over the lake, from Friar's Crag, that formed one of John Ruskin's early childhood memories. The area is also rich in history, from prehistoric times through Roman occupation to the period of industrial growth.

Castlerigg Stone Circle

KESWICK

For generations, visitors to Keswick have been impressed by the town's stunningly beautiful setting, surrounded by the great fells of Saddleback, Helvellyn and Grizedale Pike. Tourism, now the town's major industry, actually began in the mid-1700s and was given a huge boost by the Lakeland Poets in the early 1800s. The arrival of the railway in 1865 firmly established Keswick as the undisputed 'capital' of the Lake District with most of the area's notable attractions within easy reach.

The grandeur of the lakeland scenery is of course the greatest draw but, among the man-made features, one not to be missed is the well-preserved **Castlerigg**

The Lakeland Fells are home to Herdwick sheep, one of the country's hardiest breeds. Their coarse fleece cannot be dyed, but Herdwick sheep of various ages yield wool in a variety of subtle shades of grey and black which produces an unusual and very durable tweed-like weave.

THE NECESSARY ANGEL

Packhorse Court, Keswick, Cumbria CA12 5JB
Tel: 017687 71379 Fax: 0870 0558225
e-mail: info@artangel.co.uk
website: www.artangel.co.uk

A friendly and relaxing ambience welcomes you to **The Necessary Angel**. The open plan gallery is set in a 17th century courtyard that originally stabled the Packhorses as they crossed the Lakeland Fells. Established in 1990, the gallery now showcases the

work of over 50 of the greatest British Contemporary Jewellery Designers, whose pieces range from the trendy accessible to platinum and diamond show stoppers!

The owner, Deborah Cowin, offers a personalised commission service specialising in unique diamond, 18ct and platinum engagement and wedding rings. In addition to contemporary jewellery there is a rolling exhibition of spectacular work by artists from Cumbria including Simon Bull one of the worlds best selling artists.

KESWICK POST OFFICE BUILDING

19 Station Street, Keswick,
Cumbria CA12 5HH
Tel: 017687 72440 Fax: 017687 75126

In 1890, in the Market Town of Keswick-upon-Derwentwater, on the site of Sir John Banke's Workhouse was built an imposing lakeland stone building which housed the Post Office, Telegraph Office and Sorting Office. Today a modern Post Office with Bureau de Change and all new services still exists to serve the local population and the thousands of visitors who flock to this picturesque Lakeland town. So up to date are the facilities, you will find the Lake District Trading Company (supplying an extensive range of Lake District maps, books, gifts and souvenirs), and U-Compute, a computer centre providing all computer facilities including cyber café with internet access, snacks and drinks available seven days a week.

Further up the town in Station Street exists an original farmhouse building, for many years a bookshop known as Chaplins. This building has retained it's character and now boasts an Aladdin's Cave of decorative accessories, teddy bears, witches, gifts for all occasions, candles, napkins, silverware and lovely things too numerous to mention. A visit to this shop is a must. Discover a wealth of treasures in and around the old farmhouse kitchen range. At Christmas time it transforms into a magical wonderland. Primrose Patch at Chaplins will delight you.

Stone Circle. About a mile to the east of the town, the 38 standing stones, some of them eight feet high, form a circle 100 feet in diameter. They are believed to have been put in place some 4,000 years ago and occupy a hauntingly beautiful position. Beautiful, but forbidding, as evoked by Keats in his poem *Hyperion*:

A dismal cirque of Druid stones, upon a forlorn moor,
When the chill rain begins at shut of eve.
In dull November, and their chancel vault,
The Heaven itself, is blinded throughout night.

Keswick old town developed along the banks of the broad River Greta, with a wide main street leading up to the attractive **Moot Hall**. A little further south, in **St John's Street**, the church of that name was built in the very same year as the Moot Hall and its elegant spire provides a point of reference from all around the town. In the churchyard is the grave of Sir Hugh Walpole, whose once hugely popular series of novels, *The Herries Chronicle* (1930-3), is set in this part of the Lake District.

In the riverside Fitz Park is the town's **Museum & Art Gallery** which is well worth a visit not just to see original manuscripts by Wordsworth and other lakeland poets but also for the astonishing 'Rock, Bell and Steel Band' created by Joseph Richardson of Skiddaw in the 19th century. It's a kind of xylophone made of sixty stones (some a yard long), sixty steel bars and forty bells. Four 'musicians' are required to play this extraordinary instrument.

Surrounded by a loop of the River Greta to the northwest of the town is a museum which must be pencilled in on any visit to Keswick. This is the **Cumberland Pencil Museum**, which boasts the six feet long 'Largest Pencil in the World'. The 'lead' used in pencils (not lead at all but

GRANGE COUNTRY HOUSE

Manor Brow, Keswick, Cumbria CA12 4BA
Tel: 017687 72500
e-mail: info@grangekeswick.com
website: www.grangekeswick.com

Owners Duncan and Jane Miller call on 25 years experience to offer Bed & Breakfast accommodation at **Grange Country House**. Their immaculate early-Victorian greystone Lakeland house is set in an acre of gardens a

ten-minute walk from Keswick town centre, and the ten bedrooms combine comfort and elegance at a very high level (AA and ETC 5 Diamonds). All have en suite facilities, central heating, television, telephone, radio, hairdryer, beverage tray and mineral water.

A full English breakfast gets the day off to a good start, and roomy, comfortable lounges are perfect places to relax, meet other guests and plan the day's activities. For walkers and cyclists a drying room and secure cycle storage are available, and the owners are happy to give advice on walks close to the Grange - these cater for all energy levels, from gentle nature trails to climbing some of the highest peaks in England. Golf, fishing, sailing and horse riding can also be arranged, and local attractions include National Trust properties, gardens, galleries, museums, shops and the famous Theatre by the Lake. Grange Country House is a non-smoking establishment.

actually an allotrope of carbon) was accidentally discovered by a Borrowdale shepherd in the 16th century and Keswick eventually became the world centre for the manufacture of lead pencils. The pencil mill here, established in 1832, is still operating here although the wadd, or lead, is now imported.

Other attractions in the town centre include the **Cars of the Stars Museum**, home to such gems as Laurel and Hardy's Model T Ford, James Bond's Aston Martin, Chitty Chitty Bang Bang, Batman's Batmobile, Lady Penelope's pink Rolls-Royce FAB 1, the Mad Max car and Mr Bean's Mini. There are film set displays and vehicles from series such as *The Saint, Knightrider, Bergerac* and *Postman Pat*, and Del Boy's 3-wheel Reliant from *Only Fools and Horses* is

KESWICK PERFUMERY

Derwent Street, Keswick, Cumbria CA12 5BZ
Tel: 017687 75555

One of Keswick's most attractive shops and one of its most historic, **Keswick Perfumery** occupies 400 year old premises with greenery adorning the pretty frontage. Inside is arrayed a wide range of famous brand and locally produced perfumes and toiletries for ladies and gentlemen. Owner Karin Gibson also stocks linen sprays, old and new scent bottles and a selection of gifts for all occasions, including lavender products, Isle of Bute jewellery and charming little characters from the Beatrice Potter stories. Keswick Perfumery offers a complimentary gift wrapping service to all its customers.

KESWICK PARK HOTEL

33 Station Road, Keswick, Cumbria CA12 4NA
Tel: 017687 72072 Fax: 017687 74816
e-mail: info@keswickparkhotel.com
website: www.keswickparkhotel.com

The **Keswick Park Hotel** is an elegant Lakeland stone house dating from about 1880, easy to find in an exceptional position on the corner of Victoria Street and Station Road. The town centre is a two-minute walk away, making the hotel a splendid base for exploring the delights of Keswick, among them the famous Pencil Museum and quiet walks along the nearby riverbank. Donald Rogers and his staff offer, quality, comfort and genuine hospitality in this lovely Lakeland setting, and the hotel combines traditional values with all the up-to-date amenities expected by today's guests.

The accommodation comprises three room styles – standard, superior and premier – from a choice of single, twin, double and family rooms. All rooms have en suite facilities, remote-control tv, radio/alarm clock, toiletries, hairdryer and refreshments; an iron and board are available on request. Breakfast, taken in the main dining room and the conservatory, consists of a self-service buffet and a choice of dishes from the menu served to the table. In the evening, fine home cooking using the best of fresh local produce is complemented by well-chosen wines. Keswick Park is a non-smoking hotel.

there, too. **The Teapottery** makes and sells a bizarre range of practical teapots in the shape of anything from an upright piano to an Aga stove.

A short walk from the town centre, along Lake Road, leads visitors to the popular **Theatre by the Lake**, which hosts a year-round programme of plays, concerts, exhibitions, readings and talks. Close by is the pier from which there are regular departures for cruises around Derwentwater and ferries across the lake to Nichol End where you can hire just about every kind of water craft, including your own private cruise boat. One trip is to the National Trust's **Derwent Island House**, an Italianate house of the 1840s on a wooded island.

Another short walk will bring the visitor to **Friar's Crag**. This famous view of Derwent Water and its islands, now National Trust property, formed one of John Ruskin's early childhood memories,

inspiring in him "intense joy, mingled with awe". Inscribed on his memorial here are these words: "The first thing which I remember as an event in life was being taken by my nurse to the brow of Friar's Crag on Derwentwater." The Crag is dedicated to the memory of Canon Rawnsley, the local vicar, who was one of the founder members of the National Trust, which he helped to set up in 1895. Keswick is host to several annual festivals, covering films, Cumbrian literature, jazz and beer. And on the first Sunday in December a colourful 'Christmassy' Fayre is held in the Market Place.

AROUND KESWICK

THRELKELD
3 miles E of Keswick off the A66

From Keswick there's a delightful walk along the track bed of the old railway

MJ CABINET MAKERS

Unit 15, Blancathra Business Centre, Threlkeld, Nr Keswick, Cumbria CA12 4TR
Tel: 017687 74285 mobile: 07769 942918
e-mail: matt@mjcabinetmakers.co.uk
website: www.mjcabinetmakers.co.uk

MJ Cabinet Makers creates furniture for the customer who puts quality first. The designer and maker, Matthew Jardine, prides himself in the skill of combining traditional techniques with contemporary design. Every piece of furniture is made from local hardwoods such as Oak, Ash, Elm and Sycamore, and comes with a 'history scroll', giving the origins of the wood used, the date made and the maker. Every piece carries the hand-carved MJ logo and is stamped with a number if it part of a range, making each piece unique.

The craftsmen believe that the conservation of native forests is important and try to use wood felled out of necessity, as well as supporting a local supplier with a replanting programme. MJ Cabinet Makers has a selection of standard pieces as well as welcoming individual commissions from customers looking for something that bit different. Matthew is also known for sculpting 'dug-out' chairs from hollow trees, all of them unique pieces of art as well as being both comfortable and extremely tactile. Personal visits are welcome, and they are always happy to discuss customers' ideas and inspirations.

THRELKELD MINING MUSEUM

Threlkeld Quarry, Keswick, Cumbria CA12 4TT
Tel: 017687 79747 / 01228 561883
e-mail: coppermaid@aol.com website: www.golakes.co.uk

Entranced by the spectacular scenery of the Lake District,
visitors are often unaware that in the past this was also a
significant mining area. This industrial heritage is brought
vividly to life at the **Threlkeld Quarry & Mining Museum**
where visitors can browse through the collection of mining

artefacts, wander through the locomotive shed and machine shop, or join the 40-minute tour through
a recreated mine.

At Threlkeld Quarry, men were employed from the 1870s until 1982 quarrying granite for railway
ballast and road making, as well as producing granite setts and masonry stone. Several of the original
buildings remain, including the locomotive shed which now houses various industrial diesel
locomotives which can be seen out on the track from time to time. A new acquisition to the museum
is the steam locomotive Sir Thomas Callender which should be in use from June 2001. On display in
the Museum is probably the finest collection of small mining and quarrying artefacts in the North -
everything from wedges, chisels and drills to candles, clogs and kibbles (large iron buckets used for

conveying the ore and spoil to the surface). There's also an
excellent mineral collection and in the Geology Room a
fascinating table top relief map of the Lake District, enhanced
by rock specimens.

The Museum Shop stocks the largest selection of mining,
geology and mineralogy books in the north of England,
(including a second-hand section), beautiful minerals from
around the world, along with gemstone jewellery and a complete
range of mine exploration and caving gear.

line to the charming village of Threlkeld,
set in a plain at the foot of mighty
Blencathra. The village is the ideal
starting point for a number of mountain
walks, including an ascent of Blencathra,
one of the most exciting of all the Lake
District mountains. Threlkeld is famous

for its annual sheepdog trials though its
economy was built up on the several
mines in the area and the granite quarry
to the south. At **Threlkeld Quarry &
Mining Museum** (see panel above)
visitors can browse through the
collection of vintage excavators, old

FORNSIDE FARM

St John's in the Vale, Keswick, Cumbria CA12 4TS
Tel: 017687 79173 Fax: 017687 79174
e-mail: cottages@fornside.co.uk
website: www.fornside.co.uk

At **Fornside Farm**, traditional stone barns have been converted into
four cottages providing comfortable self-catering accommodation
among the Lakeland Fells. All are furnished and equipped to a very
high standard, with central heating, open-plan living/dining rooms
with fitted kitchen areas and either two or three bedrooms. Guests
are welcome to help feed owners Pam and Robert Hall's sheep and
goats and to see the farm at work. A farm trail explores the beautiful
setting with its woods, streams, wildlife and spectacular views.

quarry machinery and other mining artefacts, wander through the locomotive shed and machine shop, or join the 40-minute tour through a re-created mine. The museum has interpretive displays of Lakeland geology and quarrying and is used as a teaching facility by several university geology departments.

MATTERDALE END
8 miles E of Keswick on the A5091

This tiny hamlet lies at one end of Matterdale, a valley that an essential stop on any Wordsworth trail: it was here, on April 15th 1802, that he and his sister saw that immortal

> Host of golden daffodils,
> Beside the lake,
> beneath the trees,
> Fluttering and dancing in the breeze.

THIRLMERE
4 miles S of Keswick off the A591

This attractive, tree-lined lake, one of the few in the Lakes that can be driven around as well as walked around, was created in the 1890s by the Manchester Corporation. More than 100 miles of pipes and tunnels still supply the city with water from Thirlmere.

The creation of the huge **Thirlmere Reservoir**, five miles long, flooded the two hamlets of **Armboth** and **Wythburn** and all that remains of these places today is Wythburn chapel towards the southern end. Overlooking the narrow lake is **Helvellyn**, Wordsworth's favourite mountain and one that is also very popular with walkers and climbers today. At 3,116 feet, it is one of the four Lakeland fells over 3,000 feet high and the walk to the summit should not

be undertaken lightly - but those reaching the summit will be rewarded with some spectacular views. The eastern aspect of the mountain is markedly different from the western as it was here that the Ice Age glaciers were sheltered from the mild, west winds.

BORROWDALE
Runs South from Keswick via the B5289

"The Mountains of Borrowdale are perhaps as fine as anything we have seen" wrote John Keats in 1818. Six miles long, this brooding, mysterious valley, steep and narrow with towering crags and deep woods, is generally regarded as the most beautiful in the Lake District. Just to the south of Derwent Water are the **Lodore Falls**, where the Watendlath Beck drops some 120 feet before reaching the lake. Further along the dale, in woodland owned by the National Trust, lies the extraordinary **Bowder Stone** which provides an irresistible photo-opportunity for most visitors. A massive 50ft square and weighing almost 2,000 tons, it stands

Borrowdale

THE BORROWDALE HOTEL

Borrowdale, Keswick-on-Derwentwater, Cumbria CA12 5UY
Tel: 017687 77224 Fax: 017687 77338
e-mail: theborrowdalehotel@yahoo.com
website: www.theborrowdalehotel.co.uk

The Borrowdale Hotel is a handsome Lakeland stone building
in the heart of the magnificent Lake District National Park, at
the southern end of Derwentwater. Resident owners Peter and
Jane-Louise Fidrmuc have built up a fine reputation for traditional
standards of service and hospitality, and they and their staff work
hard to see that guests have a very pleasant and relaxing stay.
The 33 stylish, individually designed bedrooms all have en suite
facilities, tv, radio, direct-dial telephone, hairdryer and beverage
tray; some rooms are family size, and superior four-poster rooms
make special occasions
even more special.

The bar lounge overlooking the conservatory is a favourite
place for relaxing, for meeting friends and for enjoying the bar
lunches for which The Borrowdale is renowned. Evening meals
offer an excellent choice of English and Continental dishes using
the pick of fresh local produce and complemented by an extensive
wine cellar. Residents can enjoy, free of charge, weekday golf at
the Keswick Golf Club (6225 yards par 71) and the varied facilities
of a nearby leisure club. Many other sporting and leisure activities
can be arranged.

BUTTERMERE AYRSHIRES ICECREAM AND BUTTERMERE LANDSCAPES & CRAFTS

Syke Farm, Buttermere,
Nr Cockermouth, Cumbria CA13 9XA
Tel: 017687 70277

Photography by Louise Kyle

'See and taste a real piece of Lakeland'

Set on a working farm, and run by husband and wife team Les and Louise
Kyle. They are ideally situated in the picturesque village of Buttermere,   *The Buttermere Ayrshires*
one of Lakeland's most beautiful valleys.

Buttermere Ayrshire's

Their luxury homemade icecream is made on the farm using milk and cream courtesy of their resident
herd of Ayrshire cows who have grazed Buttermere's pastures for over 45 years. Choose from an ever-
changing selection of mouth-watering flavours served exclusively in their quaint ice-cream parlour.

Buttermere Landscapes & Crafts

A cornucopia of locally produced craftwork, woodturning, pottery, ceramics, smellies, walking sticks
and much more including photography by Louise, who specialises in landscapes of the beautiful
Buttermere Valley and the wildlife and characters within it, many of these scenes are also available as
greetings cards and postcards, also exclusive to their shop. They are proud to sell a quality range of
Herdwick woollen products- their unique breed of sheep that roam freely throughout the valley, choose
from thick pile fireside rugs, caps, ties, jackets, jumpers, yarns etc.

precariously on one corner apparently defying gravity. Just south of Rosthwaite the road turns westwards to the village of **Seatoller** where there's a National Park Information Centre and a minor road turns off to **Seathwaite**, which enjoys the unenviable reputation of being the wettest place in England with an average of 131 inches a year. From Seatoller, the B5289 slices through the spectacular **Honister Pass**, overlooked by dramatic 1,000 foot high Honister Crag. At the top of the pass, the 18th century **Honister Slate Mine** has been re-opened and is once again producing the beautiful green slate that adorns so many Lakeland houses and is famous throughout the world. Buckingham Palace, The Ritz, New Scotland Yard and RAF Cranwell are among the prestigious buildings donned with this stone. Helmets and lights are provided for a guided tour through great caverns of the mine to show how a mixture of modern and traditional methods is still extracting the slate which was formed here some 400 million years ago.

Buttermere

BUTTERMERE

8 miles SW of Keswick on the B5289

Half the size of its neighbour, Crummock Water, Buttermere is a beautiful lake set in a dramatic landscape. To many connoisseurs of the Lake District landscape, this is the most splendid of them all. The walk around Buttermere gives superb views of the eastern towers of **Fleetwith Pike** and the great fell wall made up of High Crag, High Stile, and Red Pike.

Standing above the village is the small, picturesque **Church of St James**, where the special features of interest include an antique organ and a memorial to fellwalker Alfred Wainwright.

LOWESWATER

10 miles W of Keswick off the B5289

Reached by narrow winding lanes, Loweswater is one of the smaller lakes, framed in an enchanting fellside and forest setting. Because it is so shallow, never more than 60 feet deep, Loweswater provides an ideal habitat for

LOWESWATER HOLIDAY COTTAGES

Scale Hill, Loweswater, Nr Cockermouth,
Cumbria CA13 9UX
Tel/Fax: 0190085 232
e-mail: mike@loweswaterholidaycottages.co.uk
website: www.loweswaterholidaycottages.co.uk

Some 200 years ago, William Wordsworth stayed at the Scale
Hill Inn near Loweswater and recommended it as "a roomy
inn with very good accommodation." A coaching inn dating
back to 1620, Scale Hill continued to dispense hospitality
to travellers through this spectacular corner of the Lake District until 1990 when owners, the Thompson
family, decided to change its role from a hotel to self-catering accommodation.

They now live in the central part of the house while the wings have been converted into 2 luxurious
holiday cottages, each providing every possible convenience and comfort. Just across the cobbled
yard from the main building, the former Coach House, built in the colourful local stone, has been
imaginatively transformed into 4 beautifully furnished and decorated cottages. Two of them are on
the ground floor with easy access for the disabled and all of them are well equipped with modern
kitchens and colour TV. They sleep between 2 to 6 people and are available all year round. Scale Hill is

ideally situated for exploring the peaceful
western side of the Lake District. Walkers
and anglers will be in their element here,
so too will those who prefer just to "laze".
Also available nearby are facilities for
squash, tennis, sailing, paragliding and
mountain biking, and there's also a trekking
centre some 6 miles away and various golf
courses of which the nearest is at Silloth,
just 8 miles distant.

wildfowl, which also benefit from the
fact that this is perhaps the least visited
lake in the whole of Cumbria. To the east
of the lake lies the small village of the
same name, while to the north stretches
one of the quietest and least known parts
of the National Park, a landscape of low
fells through which there are few roads
or even paths.

CRUMMOCK WATER

9 miles SW of Keswick on the B5289

Fed by both Buttermere and Loweswater,
this is by far the largest of the three
lakes. In this less frequented part of
western Cumbria, where there are few
roads, the attractions of Crummock
Water can usually be enjoyed in solitude.
Best seen from the top of Rannerdale
Knotts, to the east, the lake has a

footpath running around it though, in
places, the going gets a little strenuous.

BRAITHWAITE

3 miles W of Keswick on the B5292

This small village lies at the foot of the
Whinlatter Pass, another of Cumbria's
dramatic routes. The summit of this steep
road, the B5292, is some 1,043 feet above
sea level and, on the westerly descent,
there are magnificent views over
Bassenthwaite Lake. The road runs
through the **Whinlatter Forest Park** (see
panel opposite), one of the Forestry
Commission's oldest woodlands, which
has a Visitor Centre, trails and walks for
all ages and abilities, an orienteering
course, adventure playground,
viewpoints, gift shop and a tearoom with
a terrace overlooking the woodlands and

valley. Many of the record numbers who visited the centre in 2002 came to see live footage of the Lake District ospreys beamed to a viewing facility or to see the birds through high-powered telescopes at the Dodd Wood viewing point. **The Lake District Osprey Project** is a partnership of the Forestry Commission, the Lake District National Park Authority and the RSPB whose aim is to protect the nesting ospreys and to encourage others to settle and breed in other suitable locations.

BASSENTHWAITE LAKE
4 miles NW of Keswick on the A66

Here's one for the Pub Quiz: Which is the only lake in the Lake District? Answer: Bassenthwaite, because all the others are either Waters or Meres. Only 70 feet deep and with borders rich in vegetation, Bassenthwaite provides an ideal habitat for birds - more than 70 species have been recorded around the lake.

Successful breeding is encouraged by the fact that no power boats are allowed on the lake and some areas are off limits to boats of any kind. Also, most of the shoreline is privately owned, with public access restricted mostly to the eastern shore where the Allerdale Ramble follows the lakeside for a couple of miles or so.

At the northern end of the lake, at Coalbeck Farm, **Trotters World of Animals** is home to many hundreds of animals - rare breeds, traditional farm favourites, endangered species, birds of prey and reptiles. In addition to the ring-tailed lemurs, wallabies, racoons and gibbons, 2002 saw the arrival of rough-coated lemurs, lechwe antelope, red, fallow and sika deer and guanaco. Visitors to the 25-acre site can bottle-feed baby animals, cuddle bunnies, meet Monty the python, take a tractor trailer ride, watch the birds of prey demonstrations, find a quiet picnic

WHINLATTER FOREST PARK

Braithwaite, Keswick, Cumbria CA12 5TW
Tel: 017687 78469 Fax: 017687 78049
e-mail: Rangers@whinlatter.demon.co.uk

The only Mountain Forest in England, **Whinlatter Forest Park** is also one of the Forestry Commission's oldest woodlands, providing a whole range of outdoor activities. The best place to start is at the Visitor Centre which has a wealth of information about the work of the Lakes Forest District and staff who will be happy to help you plan your day in the forest.

Visitors can also book a forest classroom or a forest discovery walk with the Rangers. There's a shop and tea room here, with a terrace overlooking the woodlands and valley, an adventure playground close by and the Centre is also the starting point for several trails suitable for the whole family. The trails are clearly waymarked to provide easily followed routes taking in some spectacular views across the fells and forests of North Lakeland. Cyclists will find many miles of forest roads with some routes offering off-road and technical sections for the enthusiastic mountain biker. And if you have never tried orienteering, Whinlatter's permanent orienteering course is the perfect place to start.

For children, there are Rabbit Run and Fox Trot orienteering trails, both starting from the Visitor Centre, while for those who prefer easier terrain or are less mobile, Europe's first permanent trail orienteering course combines the navigational skills of traditional orienteering with an easy-going route along forest roads and paths.

spot or sample the fare on offer in Trotters Tea Room. And for the smaller children there's an indoor soft play climbing centre.

Rising grandly above Bassenthwaite's eastern shore is **Skiddaw** which, ever since the Lake District was opened up to tourists by the arrival of the railway in the 19th century, has been one of the most popular peaks to climb. Although it rises to some 3,054 feet, the climb is both safe and manageable, if a little unattractive lower down, and typically takes around two hours. From the summit, on a clear day, there are spectacular views to Scotland in the north, the Isle of Man in the west, the Pennines to the east, and to the south the greater part of the Lake District.

Also on the eastern shore is the secluded, originally Norman, **Church of St Bridget & St Bega** which Tennyson had in mind when, in his poem *Morte d'Arthur*, he describes Sir Bedivere carrying the dead King Arthur:

"to a chapel in the fields,
A broken chancel with a broken cross,
That stood on a dark strait of barren land".

This then would make Bassenthwaite Lake the resting place of Excalibur but, as yet, no one has reported seeing a lady's arm, "clothed in white samite, mystic, wonderful", rising from the waters and holding aloft the legendary sword.

Set back from the lakeside, **Mirehouse** is a 17th century building which has been home to the Spedding family since 1688. Literary visitors to the house included Tennyson, Thomas Carlyle, and Edward Fitzgerald, the poet and translator of *The Rubaiyat of Omar Khayyam*. As well as some manuscripts by these family friends, the house also has a fine collection of furniture and visitors can wander around the wildflower

meadow, the walled garden and the lakeside walk.

ULDALE

11 miles N of Keswick off the A591

To the northeast of Bassenthwaite Lake stretches the area known locally as the 'Land Back of Skidda', a crescent of fells and valleys constituting the most northerly part of the Lake District National Park. This peaceful region is well off the tourist track and offers visitors a delightful landscape of gently undulating bare-backed fells and valleys sheltering unspoilt villages such as Uldale. The village boasts a friendly traditional pub, The Snooty Fox, and a Victorian school which now houses the **Northern Fells Gallery** where a wide range of work by Cumbrian artists - watercolours, jewellery, copperwork, ceramics, knitwear and woodcarvings - can be seen, all available to buy. This tranquil village has one small claim to fame: it was the daughter of an Uldale farmer who eloped with and married the legendary huntsman John Peel (see Caldbeck).

CALDBECK

13 miles N of Keswick on the B5299

Caldbeck is perhaps the best-known village in the northern Lakes because of its associations with **John Peel**, the famous huntsman who died in 1854 after falling from his horse. His ornate tombstone in the churchyard is decorated with depictions of hunting horns and his favourite hound. Also buried here are John Peel's wife Mary and their four children. John Peel was Master of Hounds for over 50 years and was immortalised by his friend John Woodcutt Graves, who worked in a Caldbeck mill making the grey woollen cloth mentioned in the song, "D'ye ken John Peel with his coat so grey?" The tune itself is based on an old

Cumbrian folk song adapted by William Metcalfe, a chorister and organist at Carlisle Cathedral.

A few paces from Peel's tomb lies 'The Fair Maid of Buttermere', mentioned earlier, whose grave bears her married name, Mary Harrison. With its picturesque church, village green, cricket pitch, pond and blacksmith's forge, Caldbeck has all the ingredients of a picture postcard village. Some 200 years ago Caldbeck was an industrial village, with corn mills, woollen mills, and a paper mill all powered by the fast-flowing 'cold stream' - the Caldbeck. **Priest's Mill**, built in 1702 by the Rector of Caldbeck, next to his church, was a stone grinding corn mill, powered by a waterwheel which has now been restored to working order. It is open to the public and has an accompanying Mining Museum and a collection of old rural implements.

About a quarter of a mile outside the village is the limestone gorge known as **The Howk**, a popular beauty spot where the Caldbeck rushes past the restored ruins of one of the old bobbin mills.

HESKET NEWMARKET

13 miles N of Keswick off the B5305

Set around a well-kept village green, this pleasing little village used to have its own market, as the name suggests, and much earlier there was probably also a racecourse here since that is what Hesket meant in Old Scandinavian. It could well be the reason why the village's main street is so wide. Although the market is no longer held, Hesket hosts two important agricultural events each year: an Agricultural Show and Sheepdog Trials. There's also a vintage motor cycle rally in May. In a converted barn at the back of the Old Crown pub, **Hesket Newmarket Brewery** was set up in 1988,

THE WOOL CLIP

Priest's Mill, Caldbeck, Nr Wigton, Cumbria CA7 8DR
Tel: 016974 78707
website: www.woolclip.com

For ALL Things Woollen

The Wool Clip is a local co-operative of 15 women producing high-quality items making extensive use of wool from Herdwick and other locally bred sheep. All the women have skills in farming or crafts and include spinners, weavers, knitters, dyers, felt-makers and rug-makers. Their output covers an impressive range, and each item is unique; the products are mostly hand-crafted but a few are machine or factory made to their own exclusive designs; the co-operative will also undertake commissions from customers. The stock includes wools and yarns, sheepskins, rugs, scarves and throws, hats, slippers, jumpers, socks, wall hangings, bags and cushions.

The members of the Wool Clip are very happy to teach others their skills, running regular workshops and visiting schools and local groups. The project is supported by the Carnegie UK Trust and the Leader Plus Programme and visitors are welcome between 11 and 4 Tuesday to Sunday and Bank Holiday Mondays. The setting is a beautiful converted early-18th century water mill in the centre of Caldbeck, a pretty village in the lovely Northern Fells of the Lake District; it lies just below the church where the renowned huntsman John Peel is buried. Priest's Mill also houses a number of other speciality shops and a delightful riverside restaurant.

Ullswater Lake

England and Scotland and built a fort nearby, although nothing visible of it remains today. Most of the town's oldest buildings have also disappeared, victims of the incessant Border conflicts down the centuries. Penrith today is a busy place, its location close to the M6 and within easy reach not only of the Lakes but also of the Border Country and the Yorkshire Dales making it a hub of this northwestern corner of England.

Only a few miles from the town, **Ullswater**, eight miles long and the second longest lake in Cumbria, is also one of its most beautiful. The area around Penrith has some interesting old buildings, notably Shap Abbey and Brougham Castle, as well as two outstanding stately homes, Hutton-in-the-Forest where the Inglewood family have lived since 1605, and Dalemain, a fine mixture of medieval, Tudor and Georgian architecture. Sadly, Greystoke Castle, which according to Edgar Rice Burroughs was the ancestral home of Tarzan, is not open to the public.

and beer sales, which were at first limited to the pub, soon spread across Cumbria. Many awards have come the way of Hesket Newmarket beers, which include Skiddaw Special Bitter, the nearly black Great Cockup Porter and the pale but potent Catbells Pale Ale.

IN AND AROUND PENRITH

Penrith is the most historic of Lakeland towns and was almost certainly settled long before the Romans arrived. They quickly appreciated its strategic position on the main west coast artery linking

PENRITH

In Saxon times Penrith was the capital of the Kingdom of Cumbria but after the

Normans arrived the town seems to have been rather neglected - it was sacked several times by the Scots before **Penrith Castle** was finally built in the 1390s. Richard, Duke of Gloucester (later Richard III) strengthened the castle's defences when he was Lord Warden of the Western Marches and was responsible for keeping the peace along the border with Scotland. By the time of the Civil War, however, the castle was in a state of ruin. The Cromwellian General Lambert demolished much of what was left and the townspeople helped themselves to the fallen stones to build their own houses. Nevertheless, the ruins remain impressive, standing high above a steep-sided moat.

A short walk from the castle leads to the centre of this lively town with its charming mixture of narrow streets and wide-open spaces.

Penrith has a splendid Georgian church in a very attractive churchyard, surrounded by a number of interesting buildings. The oldest part of **St Andrew's Church** dates from Norman times but the most recent part, the nave, was rebuilt between 1719 and 1772, possibly to a design by Nicholas Hawksmoor. Pevsner described it as "the stateliest church of its time in the county". Of particular interest is the three-sided gallery and the two chandeliers which were a gift from the Duke of Portland in 1745 - a reward for the town's loyalty during the Jacobite Rising. A tablet on the wall records the deaths of 2,260 citizens of Penrith in the plague of 1597.

The church's most interesting feature however, is to be found in the churchyard, in the curious group of gravestones known as **Giant's Grave** - two ancient cross-shafts, each 11 feet high, and four 10th century hogback tombstones which have arched tops and

WHITEMORE & THWAYTES

Foxton House, Lowther Street, Penrith, Cumbria CA11 7UW
Tel: 01768 863895 Fax: 01768 862459
e-mail: enquiries@whitemorenadthwaytes.co.uk
website: www.whitemoreandthwaytes.co.uk

'Interior by Design' is the business of **Whitemore & Thwaytes**, which occupies attractive premises in a converted stable block. Maureen Whitemore has been in the field of soft furnishings for more than 30 years, and her knowledge and expertise are second to none. Her business partner Deborah Thwaytes, who studied fine art and graphics, comes up with styling ideas which Maureen turns into reality with her great

technical know-how, and between them they offer an unrivalled service in interior design and home furnishing.

One of the rooms is filled with samples of fabrics and wallpapers, lighting, upholstery, sofas and chairs, rugs and carpets, poles and tracks, and they offer a making-up service and design assistance. The partners also run a year-round series of courses lasting either one or two days and catering for everyone from absolute beginners to workroom professionals. Among the courses are Soft Furnishings for the Beginner, Swags & Tails, Decorative Curtain Styles and Advanced Cushions and Bolsters. They also run occasional workshops with guest experts, and offer workroom training to any level. For those unable to attend courses, videos, manuals and books are available, including Maureen's acclaimed *Home Furnishing Workbook*.

RHEGED DISCOVERY CENTRE

Redhills, Stainton, Penrith,
Cumbria CA11 0DX
Tel: 01539 441164

Penrith's latest and most spectacular visitor attraction, **Rheged Discovery Centre**, opened in Easter 2000 and dedicates itself to "a celebration of 2000 years of Cumbria's history, mystery and magic - as never seen before". Open all year round,

the Centre is housed in the largest earth-covered building in Britain, and is carefully designed to blend harmoniously with the surrounding fells. Although it is built on 7 levels, from the outside Rheged looks like just another Lakeland hill. Inside, babbling brooks and massive limestone crags replicate the Cumbrian landscape but the centrepiece is a 6-storey high, giant cinema screen, 60ft wide and 48ft high, on which is shown a specially commissioned film, *The Lost Kingdom*, which relates the story of the ancient Kingdom of Cumbria which once extended from Strathclyde in Scotland to Cheshire. Only a couple of minutes drive from Exit 40 of the M6, Rheged also offers visitors a retail shopping street, a useful information centre, special exhibitions, and restaurants and coffee shops which specialise in local delicacies and also provide panoramic mountain views.

ALAN STONES' GALLERY

Rheged Discovery Centre, Penrith,
Cumbria CA11 0DQ
Tel: 01768 860061 or 01768 88688
website: www.alanstones.co.uk

Paintings, drawings and original prints by Alan Stones are on display and on sale at **Alan Stones' Gallery** within the award-winning Rheged Discovery Centre.

Many awards have also come the way of Alan, who was born in Manchester in 1947 and studied Fine Art at St Martin's School of Art in London. Since 1982 he has lived and worked in Blencarn near Penrith, and the landscape of the Eden Valley, along with the trees and

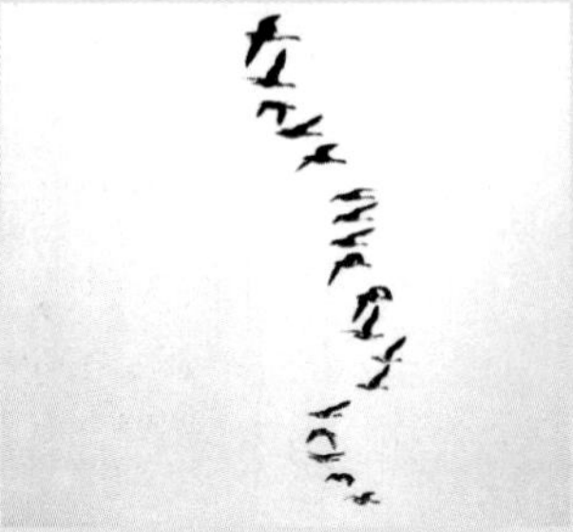

the birds and the people who live and work there, has provided the themes for much of his work. He makes oil paintings, charcoal drawings and original prints (lithographs and carborundum etchings).

In 1995 Alan worked for three months in the Falkland Islands on a commission to 'give the Islanders a view of themselves from the outside'. The result was 20 charcoal portraits and 30 larger oils and drawings, and the influence of that visit can be seen in many subsequent works.

Admission is free to the Gallery, which is open daily.

sharply sloping sides. According to a local legend the stones mark the burial place of a 5th century King of Cumbria, Owen Caesarius. Also buried somewhere in the churchyard is Wordsworth's mother, but her grave is not marked.

Overlooking the churchyard is a splendid Tudor house, bearing the date 1563, which is now a restaurant but was, at one time, Dame Birkett's School. The school's most illustrious pupils were William Wordsworth, his sister Dorothy, and his future wife, Mary Hutchinson. William is also commemorated by a plaque on the wall of the Robin Hood Inn stating that he was a guest there in 1794 and again in 1795.

Penrith's latest and most spectacular visitor attraction, **Rheged Discovery Centre** (see panel opposite), opened in Easter 2000 and dedicates itself to "a celebration of 2,000 years of Cumbria's history, mystery and magic - as never seen before". Named after Cumbria's Celtic Kingdom, this extraordinary grass-covered building is also home to Britain's only exhibition dedicated to mountains and mountain adventure. It also has a giant cinema screen, speciality shops, pottery demonstrations, an artists' exhibition, restaurants and a children's play area.

The town is dominated by **Beacon Hill Pike**, which stands amidst wooded slopes high above Penrith. The tower was built in 1719 and marks the place where, from 1296, beacons were lit to warn the townsfolk of an impending attack. The beacon was last lit during the Napoleonic wars in 1804 and was seen by the author Sir Walter Scott who was visiting Cumberland at the time. Seeing it prompted Scott to hasten home to rejoin his local volunteer regiment. It is well worth the climb from the Beacon Edge, along the footpath to the summit, to enjoy a magnificent view of the Lakeland fells. It was on top of this hill, in 1767, that Thomas Nicholson, a murderer, was hanged. The gibbet was left on the summit and so was Nicholson's ghost, seen in the form of a skeleton hanging from the noose. The red sandstone from which many of Penrith's Victorian houses were built was quarried along the escarpments of Beacon Edge, and one of the old quarries, at **Cowraik**, is now a local nature reserve and is a Site of Special Scientific Interest for the geological interest of the quarry faces.

AROUND PENRITH

Hutton-in-the-Forest
6 miles N of Penrith on the B5305

The home of the Inglewood family since 1605, Hutton-in-the-Forest was

---

Upfront Gallery & Coffee Shop

Nr Hutton-in-the-Forest, Penrith, Cumbria CA11 9TG
Tel: 017684 84538 Fax: 017684 84187
e-mail: john.f.parkinson@btinternet.com
website: www.upfront.co.uk

Upfront Gallery is the fulfilment of a lifetime ambition of owners John and Elaine Parkinson, who run it with their daughter Holly and son Ben. Much expanded since it opened in 1997, the Gallery hosts around 14 exhibitions each year, including one-man artist's shows, textiles shows and sculpture. The Coffee Shop serves an all-day selection of home-made vegetarian food, and in the Gift Shop a wide range of ceramics, jewellery, cards and crafts is for sale. Plans for the Gallery include a performance space and sculpture garden.

originally a medieval stronghold and the **Pele Tower** still exists. The house has been added to and altered by successive generations, with the result that an unusual number of architectural and decorative styles can be seen. Among the notable features are the 17th century Gallery, the Hall dominated by a Cupid staircase, and a room decorated in the Arts and Crafts style. The splendid grounds include a beautiful walled garden built in the 1730s, topiary terraces that were originally laid out in the 17th century, and fine specimen trees and a 17th century dovecote that form part of the Woodland Walk.

GREYSTOKE

5 miles W of Penrith on the B5288

According to Edgar Rice Burroughs, **Greystoke Castle** was the ancestral home of Tarzan, Lord of the Apes, a fiction which was perpetuated in the 1984 film *Greystoke*. Tarzan's aristocratic credentials would have come as something of a surprise to the dignified Barons of Greystoke whose effigies are preserved in **St Andrew's Church**. As imposing and spacious as a cathedral, St Andrew's boasts a wonderful east window with much 13th century glass and, in the Lady Chapel, a figure of the Madonna and Child carved by a German prisoner-of-war. About 100 yards from the church stands the **Plague Stone** where, during medieval times, coins were left in vinegar in exchange for food for the plague victims. An ancient **Sanctuary Stone**, now concealed behind a grille, marks the point beyond which fugitives could claim sanctuary.

Greystoke village itself is a gem, its attractive houses grouped around a trimly maintained village green. Nearby

BECKSTONES ART GALLERY

Beckstones, Greystoke Ghyll, Nr Penrith,
Cumbria CA11 0UQ
Tel: 01768 483601
website: www.beckstonesartgallery.co.uk

Beckstones Art Gallery, quietly tucked away down a Lakeland country lane, is a picturesque sandstone building nestling at the heart of the tiny village of Greystoke Ghyll, an idyllic location for a gallery dedicated to the highest standards of contemporary art. Seemingly well off the beaten track, the gallery is actually only two miles from the A66 and roughly five miles from Penrith, Ullswater and Junction 40 of the M6. In the 25 years since it opened, its resolute policy of pursuing excellence has given it a national reputation for exhibiting paintings of the highest quality. It is a family run business with a relaxed atmosphere, and visitors are made genuinely welcome by friendly, knowledgable staff.

The artists who exhibit at Beckstones are chosen as the best in their own particular categories and come from every part of the United Kingdom. Subject matter covers an impressive range, and oils, water-colours and other media are all featured. Around 40 artists exhibit on a regular basis, and between 300 and 500 pieces, all originals, are available at any one time.

are the stables where Gordon Richards (now Sir Gordon) trained his two Grand National winners, Lucius and Hello Dandy.

BROUGHAM
1 mile SE of Penrith off the A66

About a mile southeast of Penrith, the substantial and imposing remains of **Brougham Castle** (English Heritage) stand on the foundations of a Roman fort. The castle was inherited in the 1640s by the redoubtable and immensely rich Lady Anne Clifford, whose patrimony as Countess of Pembroke, Dorset and Montgomery also included another six northern castles. She spent a fortune restoring them all in medieval style and when told that Cromwell had threatened to destroy them replied "As often as he destroys them I will rebuild them while he leaves me a shilling in my pocket". Brougham was her favourite castle and she died here in 1676 at the age of 86. From the castle there's a delightful riverside walk to **Eamont Bridge** and the circular **Mayburgh Earthwork**, which dates from prehistoric times. Close to the village, on the banks of the River Eamont, is **Giant's Cave**, the supposed lair of a man-eating giant called Isir. This local tale is linked with the legend of Tarquin, a giant knight who imprisoned 64 men in his cave and was eventually killed by Sir Lancelot. Some people also claim that Uther Pendragon, King Arthur's father, lived here and that he too ate human flesh. A nearby prehistoric earthwork has been known as **King Arthur's Round Table** for many centuries. Lady Anne also rebuilt the chapel that stands on a hill above the castle, next to Brougham Hall. The old parish church of Brougham is the remotely located **St Ninian's**, also known as Ninekirks, which contains some family box pews that are screened so that they look almost like cages.

HORNBY HALL

Brougham, Nr Penrith, Cumbria CA10 2AR
Tel: 01768 891114
e-mail: enquire@hornbyhall.co.uk
website: www.hornbyhall.co.uk

Situated on a working farm in tranquil countryside three miles southeast of Penrith, **Hornby Hall** was built of local red sandstone in about 1550. Owner Ros Sanders offers country house accommodation of a very high standard in five main bedrooms with en suite or private facilities, and two single rooms with a shared shower room up the spiral stone staircase in the tower; all the bedrooms face south overlooking the garden. Guests have their own sitting room with a log fire.

The Grade II listed building has many interesting features and is full of handsome antique furniture.

In the 16th century Hall, now used as a dining room, with its original sandstone floor and a magnificent open fireplace, a traditional 3-course meal, using meat from the farm and fruit and vegetables from the garden, is available with advance booking. The dining room can be booked for private dinner parties, and room bookings can be taken for the whole house for fishing or shooting parties or for those wishing to entertain their own guests in a private house atmosphere. Dry Fly fishing is available on a two-mile stretch of the River Eamont for which day tickets can be obtained.

STAINTON

2 miles W of Penrith off the A66 or A592

At Stainton, off the A592, **The Alpaca Centre** was set up in 1997 and has become a focal point for the development and expanding knowledge of the alpaca. The Centre is a working farm, breeding, rearing and selling alpacas and welcomes visits at any time of the year.

DALEMAIN

3 miles SW of Penrith off the A592

Dalemain House (see panel below) is one of the area's most popular attractions - an impressive house with a medieval and Tudor core fronted by an imposing Georgian façade. The house has been home to the same family since 1679 and over the years they have accumulated fine collections of china, furniture and family portraits. The grand drawing rooms boast some very fine oak panelling and in the Chinese Room is some beautifully preserved 18th century Chinese wallpaper and a rococo chimneypiece by Nathaniel Hedges in Chinese Chippendale style;

visitors also have access to the Nursery (furnished with toys from all ages) and Housekeeper's Room. The Norman pele tower houses the regimental collection of the Westmorland and Cumberland Yeomanry, a troop of mounted infantry which the family usually led, while the 16th century Great Barn contains an interesting assortment of agricultural bygones. The extensive grounds include a medieval herb garden, a Tudor-walled knot garden with a fine early Roman fountain, a wild garden alongside Dacre Beck, a deer park, and woodland and riverside walks.

DACRE

4 miles SW of Penrith off the A66

There is much of historic interest in this village. The **Church** occupies a site of a former monastery which was mentioned by the Venerable Bede in his accounts of Cumberland in the 8th century. A later reference shows that in 926 the Peace of Dacre was signed between Athelstan of England and Constantine of Scotland. Fragments of masonry are reputed to

---

DALEMAIN HISTORIC HOUSE & GARDENS

Penrith, Cumbria CA11 0HB
Tel: 017684 86450 Fax: 017684 86223
e-mail: admin@dalemain.com

Dalemain has been a much loved family home since 1679 and is set against the grandeur and picturesque splendour of the Lakeland Fells and Parkland. Behind the impressive façade you will discover the surprise of Dalemain- its sheer variety. In the Georgian part of the house, the grand public rooms include the breathtaking Chinese Room with its original 18th century Chinese hand-painted wallpaper. Much of the house dates from Tudor times and here you will find a glorious confusion of winding passages, quaint stairways and unexpected rooms including the Fretwork Room with its magnificent 16th century plaster ceilings and oak panelling.

The gardens at Dalemain are a pure delight with a series of differing themes including a rose garden, a Tudor knot garden and a wild garden. A glorious woodland walk takes you high above Dacre Beck while other footpaths lead you by the walls of 14th century Dacre Castle or to Pooley Bridge.Besides the house and gardens, you can pause for refreshments in the Mediaeval Hall, with its range of home-made lunches and afternoon teas. A gift shop offers a selection of souvenirs and the Plant Centre sells a choice of English plants including old fashioned roses. The Agricultural and Countryside Collections can be found in the 16th century Great Barn. Open Sunday to Thursday March to October 10.30-5pm, (House and Gardens open 11am-4pm).

have come from the monastery and the four weather-beaten carvings of bears in the churchyard are probably of Anglo-Viking origin. The bears are shown, respectively, sleeping, being attacked by a cat, shaking off the cat and eating the cat. A 14th century pele tower, **Dacre Castle** (in private hands) is a typical example of the fortified house or small castle that was common in northern England during the Middle Ages. This was the seat of the Dacre family, Catholic Earls of Cumberland, and its turrets and battle-ments have walls, which are eight feet thick.

Pooley Bridge
5 miles SW of Penrith on the B5320

In Wordsworth's opinion Ullswater provides "the happiest combination of beauty and grandeur, which any of the Lakes affords", an opinion with which most visitors concur. The poet also noted the curious fact that the lake creates a sextuple echo, a natural phenomenon that the Duke of Portland exploited in the mid-1700s by keeping a boat on the lake equipped "with brass guns, for the purpose of exciting echoes".

The charming village of Pooley Bridge stands at the northern tip of Ullswater, and there are regular cruise departures from here during the season, stopping at

Glenridding and Howton. Rowing and powered boats are available for hire, and since Ullswater is in effect a public highway, private boats can also be launched. A speed limit of 10mph applies over the whole of the 8-mile-long serpentine lake. The oldest building in Pooley Bridge is part of **Holly House**, which dates back to 1691, while the Bridge of the village's name dates from 1763 when the elegant structure over the River Eamont was built at a cost of £400.

Watermillock
7 miles SW of Penrith on the A592

This small village, perfectly situated on the shores of Ullswater, is hidden amongst the woodland which occupies much of the lake's western shores. About 4 miles southwest of the village, there is a series of waterfalls which tumble down through a wooded gorge and then into Ullswater. The name of the largest fall is **Aira Force** (70 feet high) and the second largest is **High Force**. They can easily be reached on foot through the woodlands of **Gowbarrow Estate**, which is owned by the National Trust.

Glenridding
14 miles SW of Penrith on the A592

A popular base for walkers about to tackle the daunting challenge of **Helvellyn**,

Ullswater 'Steamers'

Glenridding Pier House, Glenridding,
Cumbria CA11 0US
Tel: 017684 82229 Fax: 017684 82669
e-mail: enquiries@ullswater-steamers.co.uk
website: www.ullswater-steamers.co.uk

Ullswater 'Steamers' have plied England's most spectacular lake for almost 150 years. 'Lady of the Lake' and 'Raven', both Victorian steamers, were joined by 'Lady Dorothy' in November 2001, when the introduction of winter sailing provided a year-round service for the first time. Passengers have various options, including 1-hour and 2-hour cruises, cruises + walks, cruises + lunch and cruises + visits to historic houses and other local attractions.

Glenridding is the largest and busiest of Ullswater's lakeside villages. Lake cruises depart from here, rowing boats are available for hire and there's plenty of room for waterside picnics.

PATTERDALE

15 miles SW of Penrith on the A592

It is this village's magnificent setting that makes it such a popular tourist destination. Close to the head of Ullswater and with a series of fells framing the views, the scenery is indeed splendid. On the north side of the village is **St Patrick's Well**, which was thought to have healing properties, and the medieval chapel dedicated to the saint was rebuilt in the 1850s.

CLIFTON

3 miles S of Penrith on the A6

One of the last battles to be fought on English soil took place at nearby **Clifton Moor** in December 1745. Bonnie Prince Charlie was in retreat and his exhausted troops were easily routed by the English forces. Eleven soldiers were killed and are buried in Clifton churchyard, but some of the wounded Highlanders were hanged from the Rebels' Tree on the outskirts of the village. The tree is a sorry sight nowadays with its gaunt, dead branches, but it is still a place of pilgrimage for the Scots.

To the southeast of the village is **Wetheriggs Country Pottery**, which was founded in 1855. Visitors can try their hand at the often messy business of throwing a pot, paint a pot, paint on glass and make a candle, and also take a conducted tour of the steam-powered pottery, the only one of its kind in the UK. The pottery was scheduled as an Industrial Monument in 1973, and its steam engine was restored by none other than Fred Dibnah, the famous steeplejack.

DEEPDALE HALL

Patterdale, Nr Penrith, Cumbria CA11 0NR
Tel: 017684 82369 Fax: 017684 82608
e-mail: brown@deepdalehall.freeserve.co.uk
website: www.deepdalehall.co.uk

A scenic driveway leads from the A592 south of Patterdale to **Deepdale Hall**, where successive generations of the Brown family have been welcoming guests for almost 50 years. The house, at the centre of a working hill farm, was built around 1670 and is an ideal base for a touring or walking holiday. A splendid wooden spiral staircase leads from the ground floor up to the comfortable, characterful guest bedrooms – a double room with private bathroom and a family room with en suite shower.

A hearty Cumbrian breakfast cooked on the Aga starts the day, and guests can take their ease in a lounge with log fire, tv, magnificent views and a selection of books on the surrounding area. An alternative to the farmhouse B&B is the adjoining cottage, offering self-catering accommodation for four; it consists of two bedrooms, a bathroom with bath and shower, a lounge/dining room with a Lakeland slate fireplace and a fully fitted kitchen. Outside is a garden with patio and picnic table. An adjoining barn conversion, offering self catering is due to be completed in 2004.

THE TOY WORKS

Holly House, Askham, Penrith, Cumbria CA10 2PG
Tel: 01931 712077
e-mail: info@thetoyworks.co.uk
website: www.thetoyworks.co.uk

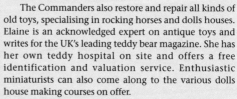

Situated in the centre of the picturesque Lake District village
of Askham within a listed 17th century stone barn, **The Toy
Works** is a unique toymaker's workshop. Paul and Elaine
Commander have been designing and making traditional
wooden toys since 1985, specialising in farms, castles and
commission models of clients' homes. Below the workshop, housed in the former stable and byre is
their amazing traditional toy shop selling all kinds of old-fashioned, hard to find quality toys, catering
for both first and second childhoods. Be sure to bring a 20p coin so you can see the Toy Works Express
chug around the display.

The Commanders also restore and repair all kinds of
old toys, specialising in rocking horses and dolls houses.
Elaine is an acknowledged expert on antique toys and
writes for the UK's leading teddy bear magazine. She has
her own teddy hospital on site and offers a free
identification and valuation service. Enthusiastic
miniaturists can also come along to the various dolls
house making courses on offer.

The toy shop is open Wednesdays to Saturdays 10am
till 5pm, Sundays 11am till 4pm. Closed Mondays and
Tuesdays (except Bank Holiday Mondays).

ASKHAM

3 miles S of Penrith off the A6

Askham is a pleasant village set around
two greens. In the centre of the village is
one of its most interesting shops, the **Toy
Works** (see panel above), which combines
a traditional toy shop with a toymaker's
workshop. **Askham Fell**, which rises to
the west, is dotted with prehistoric
monuments including one known as the
Copt (or Cop) Stone, which is said to
mark the burial site of a Celtic chieftain.

LOWTHER

4 miles S of Penrith off the A6

Lowther Castle is now only a shell, most
of it having been demolished in 1957,
but it was clearly once a grand place;
after one visit Queen Victoria is reputed
to have said that she would not return to
the castle as it was too grand for her. The

ancestral owners of the castle were the
illustrious Earls of Lonsdale, a family of
statesmen and sportsmen. The most
famous is perhaps the 5th Earl (1857-
1944), known as the Yellow Earl because
of the colour of the livery used on his
private carriage. He was the first
President of the Automobile Association
and permitted his family colours to be
used by that organisation. The Earl was
also a patron of amateur boxing and the
Lonsdale Belt emerged from his interest.

Lowther village itself was built in the
1680s by Sir John Lowther, who moved
his tenants here to improve the view
from the new house he was building. He
also built **St Michael's Church** where
several generations of the Lowthers are
buried in a series of magnificent tombs
beginning with a medieval style alabaster
monument to Sir Richard who died
in 1608.

BAMPTON

8 miles S of Penrith off the A6

For several hundred years this small village was well known for its **Grammar School**, two of whose pupils rose swiftly in the church hierarchy. One was Hugh Curwen, who as a Protestant became Chaplain to Henry VIII, as a Catholic under Queen Mary was elevated to the Archbishopric of Dublin, and then prudently re-embraced Protestantism when Elizabeth succeeded to the throne. Another Bampton boy was less pliable: Edmund Gibson was baptised in the church here in 1669 and later became a fiery Bishop of London who repeatedly denounced the degenerate morals of the age - with little apparent effect.

A couple of miles south of Bampton, **Haweswater** is the most easterly of the lakes. It is actually a reservoir, created in the late 1930s to supply the growing needs of industrial Manchester. Beneath the water lies the village of **Mardale** and several dairy farms for which Haweswater Valley was once famous. By 1940, the lake had reached its present extent of four miles and Manchester Corporation set about planting its shores with conifers and today the area is managed as a nature reserve. Walkers have a good chance of seeing woodpeckers and sparrowhawks, buzzards and peregrine falcons, and with luck may even catch sight of golden eagles gliding on the thermals rising above Riggindale. An observation is manned throughout the breeding season if the eagles are nesting.

Above Haweswater runs the **High Street**, actually a Roman road, which is now one of the most popular fell walks in the Lake District. It overlooks the remote and lovely Blea Tarn and the lonely valley of Martindale, a cul-de-sac valley to the south of Ullswater, where England's last remaining herd of wild red deer can often be seen.

SHAP

10 miles S of Penrith on the A6

This small village on the once congested A6 enjoys some grand views of the hills. In coaching days Shap was an important staging post for the coaches before they tackled the daunting climb up **Shap Fell** to its summit some 850 feet above sea level. Much earlier, in medieval times, the village was even more significant because of nearby **Shap Abbey**, constructed in the local Shap granite which has been used in many well-known buildings, St Pancras Station and the Albert Memorial in London among them.

The Abbey stands about a mile to the west of the village, just inside the National Park, and it's well worth seeking it out to see the imposing remains of the only abbey founded in Westmorland; the only one in the Lake District mountains; the last abbey to be consecrated in England (around 1199) and the last to be dissolved, in 1540.

From the Abbey there's a pleasant walk of well under a mile to **Keld**, a tiny village of just 17 houses. So quiet today, in medieval times Keld was a busy little place servicing the monks of Shap Abbey nearby. It was the monks of Shap Abbey who built the village's oldest building, the early-16th century **Keld Chapel** (National Trust).

ORTON

15 miles S of Penrith on the B6260

By far the best approach to Orton is along the B6290 from Appleby to Tebay. This scenic route climbs up onto the moors, passing **Thunder Stone**, some mighty limestone bluffs and the pavements of **Great Asby Scar**, the setting for BBC-TV's *The Tenant of Wildfell Hall*.

A pretty village now, for centuries Orton was a market town of some

consequence with a charter granted in the 13th century by Edward I and a licence to hold fairs accorded by the puritan Oliver Cromwell. There are reminders of Orton's former importance in the noble church tower, completed in 1504; in the attractive proportions of **Petty Hall**, an Elizabethan house at the lower end of the village (a private residence, incidentally); and in the grandeur of **Orton Hall**, built in 1662 and now converted into holiday apartments.

The Eden Valley

Orton's most famous visitor was Bonnie Prince Charlie, on his way northwards after the crushing defeat of his troops at Derby.

The village stands below **Orton Scar**, on which a beacon was lit to warn people to seek safety from advancing Scottish raiders. The village church, in common with many in the Eden Valley, has a massive 16th century tower that was built for defensive purposes and, presumably, was one place where the villagers sought shelter. Its features include an ancient oak parish chest and a stained glass window by Beatrice Whistler, wife of the American artist James McNeill Whistler.

THE EDEN VALLEY AND EAST CUMBRIA

Carved through boulder clay and red sandstone and sandwiched between the Lakeland fells and the northern Pennines, the Eden Valley is green and fertile - in every sense another Eden. This, too, is farming country and many of the ancient towns and villages have a market place. Appleby-in-Westmorland,

the old county town of Westmorland, had an important market and also an annual horse fair which continues today and has gained a large following.

An attractive man-made feature of the valley is the collection of specially commissioned stone sculptures known as Eden Benchmarks dotted along its length. Each created by a different sculptor, they have been located beside public paths and, since they also function as seats, provide the perfect setting in which to enjoy the valley's unspoilt scenery.

KIRKBY STEPHEN

Surrounded by spectacular scenery, the old market town of Kirkby Stephen lies at the head of the beautiful Eden Valley. Although essentially part of the Valley, Kirkby Stephen has a strong Yorkshire Dales feel about it. Indeed, the church, with its long, elegant nave, has been called the Cathedral of the Dales.

Dating from Saxon times, rebuilt in 1220 and with a 16th century tower, **St Stephen's Church** is one of the finest in the eastern fells, dominating the northern end of the town from its

Viaduct near Kirkby Stephen

elevated position. Until the last century the **Trupp Stone** in the churchyard received money from local people every Easter Monday in payment of church tithes and, at eight o'clock, the curfew is still sounded by the **Taggy Bell**, once regarded by local children as a demon. Inside the church are a number of pre-Conquest stones, some of which show Norse influence. The most remarkable is the 10th century **Loki Stone**, one of only two such carvings in Europe to have survived. Loki was a Norse God and presumably Viking settlers brought their belief in Loki to Kirkby Stephen.

Between the church and the market square stand the cloisters, which served for a long time as a butter market. The **Market Square** is surrounded by an ancient collar of cobblestones which marked out an area used for bull-baiting

- a 'sport' that ceased here in 1820 after a disaster when a bull broke loose. There are many delightful walks from the town, to **Croglam Earthworks** for example, a prehistoric fort, or to nearby Stenkrith Park where the second of the **Eden Benchmarks** can be found. Created by Laura White in Ancaster limestone and titled *Passage*, the sculpture is deceptively simple, suggesting perhaps the course of a river bed. There are also some pleasant strolls along the riverside to a fine waterfall where the River Eden cascades into Coop Karnel Hole. Look out for the unusual shapes of the weathered limestone rock. For more strenuous exercise, walkers could tackle a stretch of the **Coast to Coast** long distance footpath, which passes through the town.

AROUND KIRKBY STEPHEN

OUTHGILL
5 miles S of Kirkby Stephen on the B6259

This remote village has close links with the Clifford family of Skipton Castle, North Yorkshire. The village **Church of St Mary**, first built in 1311, was repaired by Lady Anne Clifford who, from 1643 when she finally obtained possession of the Clifford estates, devoted her life to restoring her many properties and lived in each of them for varying periods of time. Her estates included six castles - Skipton and Barden in Yorkshire; Appleby, Brough, Brougham and Pendragon in Westmorland. Lady Anne's zeal for restoration didn't stop at castles: she also repaired the Roman road between Wensleydale and the Eden Valley, a route she often travelled (along with a huge retinue) between her castles and her birthplace at Skipton. The route is now known as Lady Anne's Way but in

times past it was aptly called the **High Way** since it was a regular place of employment for highwaymen such as Dick Turpin and William 'Swift' Nevison.

The landscape around Outhgill is remote and beautiful. To the south is **Wild Boar Fell**, a brooding, flat-topped peak where the last wild boar in England was reputedly killed, while tucked down in the valley are the romantic ruins of Lammerside and Pendragon Castles.

Pendragon Castle, about a mile north of the village, is shrouded in legend but there are claims that it was the fortress of Uther Pendragon, father of King Arthur. If so, nothing remains of that 6th century wooden castle. The present structure dates from the 1100s and was built by Hugh de Morville, one of the four knights who murdered Thomas à Becket, to guard the narrow pass of **Mallerstang**. Twice it was burned by the Scots and twice restored, on the latter occasion by the formidable Lady Anne Clifford in 1660. Another mile or so downstream, **Lammerside Castle** dates from the 12th century but only the remains of the keep survive. They can be found along a bridle path between Pendragon and Wharton Hall.

RAVENSTONEDALE
5 miles SW of Kirkby Stephen on the A685

Known locally as Rissendale, this pretty village of stone-built cottages clustered along the banks of **Scandal Beck** lies on the edge of the Howgill Fells. The parish **Church of St Oswald** is especially interesting: built in 1738, it is one of the few Georgian churches in Cumbria. The window at the east end commemorates the last woman in England to be put to death for her Protestant faith. Elizabeth Gaunt was sentenced in 1685 by the notorious Judge Jeffreys to be burnt at the stake for sheltering a fugitive rebel. She met her end at Tyburn in London.

CROSBY GARRETT
4 miles W of Kirkby Stephen off the A685

Local legend has it that the Devil, seeing all the stones lying ready to build **Crosby Garrett Church**, carried them in his leather apron to the top of a nearby hill. He reasoned that, as people grew old, they would be unable to climb the hill and attend church and thus would come to him rather than go to Heaven. Such tales apart, the church itself is said to be of Anglo-Saxon origin though the visible fabric is 12th century. Inside there are some superb carvings, particularly near the font. The church is also famous for its hagioscope, cut through the wall to allow people in the north aisle to see the altar. Near the church gates is a tithe barn, built in the 18th century to store farm produce given to the church as a religious tax. To the west of the village runs the **Settle-Carlisle Railway** whose splendid viaduct dominates Crosby Garrett.

WINTON
3 miles N of Kirkby Stephen off the A685

The oldest building in this quiet and picturesque hamlet is **Winton Hall**, built of stone and dated 1665, but looking older with its stone buttresses and mullion windows with iron bars. Those taking a walk on **Winton Fell** are likely to see red grouse lifting off from the large tracts of heather on the fellside. Indeed, the wildlife is much more prolific around this area where the limestone provides more plentiful food than on the fells around the lakes.

APPLEBY-IN-WESTMORLAND

The old county town of Westmorland, Appleby is one of the most delightful small towns in England. It was originally built by the Norman, Ranulph de

River Eden, Appleby-in-Westmorland

some dating back to the 17th century. At its foot stands the 16th century **Moot Hall** (still used for council meetings and also housing the Tourist Information Centre); at its head rises the great Norman Keep of **Appleby Castle** which is protected by one of the most impressive curtain walls in northern England. Attractions here include the dramatic view from the top of the five-storey keep and the attractive grounds which are home to a wide variety of animals and include a **Rare Breeds Survival Centre**.

During the mid-1600s, Appleby Castle was the home of Lady Anne Clifford, the remarkable woman who has already been mentioned several times and to whom Appleby has good cause to be grateful. The last of the Clifford line, the diminutive Lady Anne (she was just four feet 10 inches tall) inherited vast wealth and estates, among them no fewer than six northern castles. She lavished her fortune on rebuilding or restoring them all. Churches and chapels in the area also benefited from her munificence and at Appleby, in 1651, she also founded the almshouses known as the Hospital of St Anne, for '12 sisters and a Mother'. Set around a cobbled square, the picturesque cottages and minuscule chapel still serve their original function, maintained by the trust endowed by Lady Anne.

Meschines, who set it within a broad loop of the River Eden which protects it on three sides. The fourth side is guarded by **Castle Hill**. The town's uniquely attractive main street, **Boroughgate**, has been described as the finest in England. A broad, tree-lined avenue, it slopes down the hillside to the river, its sides lined with a pleasing variety of buildings,

Lady Anne died in 1676 in her 87th year and was buried with her mother, Margaret Countess of Cumberland, in **St Lawrence's Church**. The church is well worth visiting to see their magnificent tombs and also the historic organ, purchased from Carlisle Cathedral in 1684, which is said to be oldest still in use in Britain.

Just a few years after Lady Anne's death, James II granted the town the right to hold a Fair during the week leading to the second Wednesday in June. More than three hundred years later, the **Gypsy Horse Fair** is still thriving with hundreds of gypsies flooding into the little town (population 1,800) with their caravans and horse-drawn carts. The trade, principally in horses, and the trotting races provide a picturesque and colourful spectacle.

AROUND APPLEBY-IN-WESTMORLAND

BROUGH
8 miles SE of Appleby-in-Westmorland on the A66/ A685

This small town, standing at the point where the **Stainmore Pass** opens into the Vale of Eden, is, in fact, two settlements: **Church Brough** and **Market Brough**. Church Brough is a group of neat houses and cottages clustered around a little market square in which a maypole stands on the site of the former market cross. **Brough Castle**, built within the ramparts of the Roman camp of Verterae, was constructed to protect the Roman road over Stainmore Pass. The building of this Norman castle was begun by William Rufus in 1095 but it was largely destroyed in 1174 by William the Lion of Scotland. Another fortification restored by the remarkable

Lady Anne Clifford, the castle, with its tall keep 60 feet high is well worth visiting, if only for the superb panorama of the surrounding fells seen from the battlements.

The distinctive low hills that lie to the west of Brough are drumlins - heaps of material deposited by Ice Age glaciers. In this area many drumlins are marked by broad, grassy ridges, remains of ancient lynchets or ploughing strips.

NORTH STAINMORE
10 miles SE of Appleby-in-Westmorland on the A66

The village lies on the Stainmore Pass which carries the old Roman road, now the A66, through a remote area of the North Pennines which David Bellamy described as "England's last wilderness". Near Stainmore summit are the foundations of **Maiden Castle**, a Roman fort built to guard the pass against marauders. A few yards over the Cumbrian border, into County Durham, is the stump of the ancient **Rey Cross** which was erected before AD 946 and which, until 1092, marked the boundary between England and Scotland. It is thought to be the site of the battle at which the last Viking King of York and North England, Eric Bloodaxe, was killed following his expulsion from the city.

WARCOP
5 miles SE of Appleby-in-Westmorland on the B6259

The largest village in this part of the Eden Valley, Warcop grew up as a crossing point of the river. The bridge, the oldest to cross the river, dates from the 16th century and the red sandstone buildings surrounding the village green, with its central maypole, make this a charming place to visit.

The **Church of St Columba** is built outside the village on the site of a

Roman camp. An interesting building in its own right, it is particularly famous for the rush-bearing ceremony, which takes place in late June each year.

GREAT ORMSIDE

2 miles SE of Appleby-in-Westmorland off the B6260

This was once an important fort guarded by a pele tower, and the ancient **Church of St James**, which dates from the 11th century, occupies a site on the steep-sided defence mound. Relics of pre-Christian burials have been found in the mound, as well as a Viking sword (now in the Tullie Museum in Carlisle). A silver gilt and enamel bowl from the 7th century has also been found and is regarded as one of the most important pieces of Anglo-Saxon metalware to survive. A particularly beautiful piece, richly decorated with vine scrolls, birds, and animals, it is now on permanent display in the Yorkshire Museum in York.

From the village a path leads across fields to the village of **Little Ormside**, with its large cedar tree said to have been brought back from Lebanon as a sapling by General Whitehead. On the voyage home he grew it in his hat and shared with it his daily ration of one pint of water.

BRAMPTON

2 miles N of Appleby-in-Westmorland off the A66

This village, along with the surrounding area, was said to be haunted by the ghost of Elizabeth Sleddall, the wife of a 17th century owner of nearby Crackenthorpe Hall. Elizabeth died believing that she had been cheated out of her share of the estate, so to shame the false inheritors her spirit was seen being driven around the countryside in a coach drawn by four black horses.

Her ghost became so troublesome that the local people exhumed her body and reburied the remains under a larger boulder. Her ghost, while no longer troubling the local people, is said still to visit the hall.

DUFTON

3 miles N of Appleby-in-Westmorland off the A66

Behind this delightful hamlet lies **Dufton Gill**, a beautiful, secluded wooded valley through which runs a footpath.

Also from Dufton there is a track carrying the Pennine Way up to High Cup Nick, a great horseshoe precipice at the edge of the northern Pennine escarpment that was formed by a glacial lake during the Ice Age.

LOW HOWGILL

Low Howgill, Milburn, Nr Penrith, Cumbria CA10 1TL
Tel: 017683 61595 Fax: 017683 61598
e-mail: holidays@low-howgill.co.uk
website: www.lowhowgill.f9.co.uk

John and Jane Taylor have farmed **Low Howgill** since 1975 and have recently converted an old barn to provide three en suite bedrooms for Bed & Breakfast accommodation. The mixed farm has an area of ancient woodland running alongside Milburn Beck and a small lake where fishing is available. Half a mile away, High Slakes is a former farmhouse offering very spacious and comfortable self-catering accommodation in three bedrooms; fishing is available here, too, and both properties are havens for nature-lovers and bird-watchers. Low Howgill has accommodation and grazing for horses.

TEMPLE SOWERBY

7 miles NW of Appleby-in-Westmorland on the A66

Temple Sowerby prides itself on the title 'Queen of Westmorland villages', an accolade justified by its lovely setting in the Eden valley. (Here's a bonus: the average rainfall here is half that recorded in the Lake District National Park to the west.) To the north, the massive bulk of **Cross Fell**, the highest point in the Pennines, swells skywards to provide a spectacular backdrop. The village itself, picturesquely grouped around a sloping green and an 18th century red sandstone church, takes its name from the medieval Knights Templar who owned the manor of Sowerby until their Order was suppressed in 1308.

From Temple Sowerby there are delightful walks through the Eden Valley or, if you prefer a gentle stroll, it's only a mile to the National Trust gardens at **Acorn Bank** where **Crowdundle Beck** splashes beneath an elegant 18th century bridge. The 16th century manor house is now a Sue Ryder Home and not open to the public, but visitors are welcome to explore the attractive gardens planted with a collection of some 250 medicinal and culinary herbs. A circular woodland walk runs along the beck to a watermill that was first mentioned on the site as far back as the 14th century. At different times it has been a saw mill, a corn mill and a source of power for the local gypsum mines; now restored, it is open for visits.

EDENHALL

3 miles NE of Penrith off the A686

An old tradition asserts that in the 8th century the monks of Jarrow, fleeing from Viking invaders with the body of St Cuthbert, stopped here briefly. As a result the village church is dedicated to the saint. Part of the **Church of St Cuthbert** appears to be pre-Norman but most of the structure dates from the 1100s. Close to the church is the **Plague Cross** which stands where there was once a basin filled with vinegar. This acted as a disinfectant into which plague victims put their money to pay for food from the people of Penrith. The plague of the 16th century killed a quarter of the village's inhabitants.

Edenhall is particularly famous for the story of the 'Luck of Eden Hall', a priceless glass cup which, according to legend, was stolen from some fairies dancing round the garden wall by a butler in the service of the Musgrave family back in the 15th century. Despite the fairies' entreaties, the butler refused to return the 6-inch high glass to them. As he departed with the precious goblet, the fairies laid a curse upon it: "If ever this cup shall break or fall, Farewell the luck of Eden Hall". On inspection, the glass was identified as a 13th century chalice of enamelled and gilded glass that is thought to have come from Syria and may well have been brought back by a Crusader. It was a treasured heirloom of the Musgraves for many generations and is now in the Victoria & Albert Museum in London. The goblet is still intact but Eden Hall has long since disappeared.

LANGWATHBY

4 miles NE of Penrith on the A686

Langwathby has a huge village green, which still hosts maypole dancing on the third Saturday in May. The green is medieval in origin and would once have been surrounded by wood and mud houses, perhaps to protect cattle but also for defence against border raids. After the Civil War and the growth in prosperity in the late 17th century, these wattle and daub cottages were replaced by stone buildings. West of the village, at

Langwathby Hall Farm, **Eden Ostrich World** offers visitors the chance to see these splendid birds in a farm setting in the heart of the Eden Valley. The farm is also home to rare breed sheep, cattle and pigs, donkeys, deer, wallabies, alpacas and many other creatures from around the world.

Little Salkeld

6 miles NE of Penrith off the A686

A lane from the village leads to **Long Meg** and her Daughters, a most impressive prehistoric site and second only to Stonehenge in size. Local legend claims that Long Meg was a witch who, with her daughters, was turned to stone for profaning the Sabbath, as they danced wildly on the moor. There are more than 60 stones in the Circle

(actually an oval), which is approximately 300 feet across. The tallest, Long Meg, is a 15 feet column of Penrith sandstone, the corners of which face the four points of the compass. Cup and ring symbols and spirals are carved on this stone which is over 3,500 years old. The circle is now known to belong to the Bronze Age but no one is certain of its purpose. It may have been used for rituals connected with the changing seasons since the midwinter sun sets in alignment with the centre of the circle and Long Meg herself. The brooding majesty of the site was perfectly evoked by Wordsworth:

A weight of awe, not easy to be borne,
Fell suddenly upon my spirit - cast
From the dread bosom of the unknown past,
When first I saw that family forlorn.

In 1725 an attempt was made by Colonel Samuel Lacy of Salkeld Hall to use the stones for mileposts. However, as work began, a great storm blew up and the workmen fled in terror believing that the Druids were angry at the desecration of their temple. It was the same Colonel Lacy who gave his name to the **Lacy Caves**, a mile or so downstream from Little Salkeld. The Colonel had the five chambers carved out of the soft red sandstone, possibly as a copy of St Constantine's Caves further down the river at Wetheral. At that time it was fashionable to have romantic ruins and grottoes on large estates and Colonel Lacy is said to have employed a man to live in his caves acting the part of a hermit.

Great Salkeld
6 miles NE of Penrith on the B6412

The River Eden formed the boundary between the two old counties of Westmorland and Cumberland so while Little Salkeld was in Westmorland its larger namesake stood in Cumberland. The village is a picturesque collection of 18th century cottages and farmhouses built in red sandstone which are typical of this area. Great Salkeld is best known for the impressive **Church** with its massive, battlemented pele tower built in the 14th century and complete with a dungeon. The Norman doorway in the porch is less than a yard wide and its arch has three rows of deeply cut zig-zags with five heads, one with a crown.

Kirkoswald
8 miles NE of Penrith on the B6413

The village derives its name from the **Church of St Oswald**: Oswald was the King of Northumbria who, according to legend, toured the pagan north with St Aidan in the 7th century. The church is unusual in having a detached bell tower

Wetheral Cottages

Great Salkeld, Cumbria CA11 9NA
Tel: 01768 898779 Fax: 01768 898943
e-mail: wetheralcottages@btopenworld.com
website: www.wetheralcottages.co.uk

A group of charming sandstone cottages, each well-equipped cottage is furnished with care to reflect its own character, set within extensive gardens, situated on the edge of an attractive Cumbrian village, near the River Eden and surrounded by rolling farmland. The village of Great Salkeld, with a Pub serving excellent food, offers tranquillity, yet there is easy access to the lakes and mountains of the Lake District, the Scottish Borders, also the many interesting villages of the Eden Valley and Northern Pennines. Local activities include: Walking, Cycling,

Golf, Swimming, Sailing, Fishing or visiting the many attractions and historic sites of the Eden Valley and Cumbria. Garth Cottage is nestled into a grassy bank with a quiet outdoor sitting area, shaded by wild cherry trees and sleeps a family of 8, has four bedrooms and a large living area with wood burning stove. Highcroft and Langriggs accommodation is all on one level, both sleep 4. Highcroft looks across the Eden to the North Pennine fells, while Langriggs features the original stone walls in the living area and is suitable for the less sprightly. The snug cottage Mickledale sleeps 3 and retains its original ceiling timbers in the lounge. Windale has an open plan lounge and kitchen area upstairs and will accommodate 3 or a family of 4. Sorry we are unable to accommodate pets.

standing on top of a grassy hill some 200 yards from the main building (this is in a valley, so the bells could not be heard by the villagers).

This once thriving market town still retains its small cobbled market place and some very fine Georgian buildings. There's also a striking ruined 12th century **Castle**, formerly the home of the Featherstonehaugh family.

One of Kirkoswald's most splendid buildings is the **College**, its name recalling the days when St Oswald's was a collegiate church. The two-storey house with its sloping-ended roof was originally built as a pele tower and converted into the college for priests in the 1520s. The manor house opposite has a particularly attractive entrance front in sandstone, which was added in 1696.

Just to the northwest of Kirkoswald are the **Nunnery Walks** which start at a Georgian house built in 1715 on the site of a Benedictine Nunnery founded during the reign of William Rufus. Narrow footpaths have been cut into the sandstone cliffs along the deep gorge of **Croglin Beck** and they pass through beautiful woodland to reveal exciting waterfalls. The walks are open to the public during the summer months.

ARMATHWAITE
10 miles N of Penrith off the A6

Set on the western bank of the River Eden, the village has a particularly fine sandstone bridge from which there is a lovely view of **Armathwaite Castle** (private), the home of the Skelton family, one of whose forebears was Poet Laureate to Henry VIII. Close by, visitors to the **Eden Valley Woollen Mill** can see traditional looms rattling away and browse through a huge range of knitwear produced from the finest wools and mohair. Also worth seeking out in

Coombs Wood to the south is another of the Eden Benchmarks. Entitled *Vista* and created by Graeme Mitchison, this remarkable sculpture seems to make the Lazenby Sandstone flow into liquid shapes.

MELMERBY
9 miles NE of Penrith on the A686

Melmerby nestles at the foot of **Hartside Pass**, its spacious village green dissected by three becks. Even today, every householder in Melmerby has grazing rights on the green. Horses are grazed more commonly now, but in the past it would have been more usual to see flocks of geese - indeed, there was once a cottage industry here making pillows and mattresses from goose feathers. Overlooking the 13-acre village green is **Melmerby Hall**, a defensive tower that was extended in the 17th and 18th centuries. The village church, with its tower, is a Victorian building, but the first known rector of the church on the site came here in 1332.

A curious meteorological feature here is what is known as the **Helm Winds**, localised gusts which sweep through the valley with the force of a gale while the surrounding countryside is perfectly calm.

From Melmerby the main road climbs out of the Eden Valley to the east and the landscape changes suddenly. The road passes Fiend's Fell, close to the highest point in the Pennine Chain, the summit of Cross Fell. Early Christians erected a cross on the highest point of the fell to protect travellers from the demons who haunted the moors. Today, a cairn marks the spot where the cross once stood.

ALSTON
18 miles NE of Penrith on the A689/A686

The town of Alston has a cobbled main street and, from the picturesque **Market**

Cross, narrow lanes radiating out with courtyards enclosing old houses. Many of the older buildings still have the outside staircase leading to the first floor - a relic from the days when animals were kept below while the family's living accommodation was upstairs. This ancient part of Alston is known as **The Butts**, a title acquired by the need of the townspeople to be proficient in archery during the times of the border raids.

An unusual feature of Alston was the number of watermills in and around the town and the mill race was once the central artery of the old town. The tall spire of **St Augustine's Church** is a well known local landmark and its churchyard contains a number of interesting epitaphs, as well as affording wonderful views of the South Tyne Valley.

Alston supports an astonishing diversity of shops and pubs. and is home to a wide variety of craftspeople, ranging from blacksmiths to candlemakers, wood turners to potters. **Gossipgate Gallery**, housed in a converted congregational church built 200 years ago and with its original gas lights still intact, is the premier centre in the North Pennines

for contemporary art and craft. A programme of exhibitions runs non-stop from February to December, and in the gallery shop a huge range of artefacts is for sale, including original watercolours and prints, jewellery, glass, ceramics, sculpture and striking turned wooden bowls made from native woods.

Another popular attraction in Alston is the **South Tynedale Railway**. This narrow gauge (2ft) steam railway runs regular services during the summer months and at the northern terminus of the 2½-mile long track travellers can join a stretch of the Pennine Way that runs alongside the River South Tyne. In between the station and the A686, is the **HUB Exhibition** of historic vehicles, a wealth of local images and the stories that bring them alive.

Alston Moor, to the south of the town, was once the centre of an extremely important lead mining region, one of the richest in Britain. Lead and silver were probably mined on the moor by the Romans, but the industry reached its peak in the early 19th century when vast quantities of iron, silver, copper, and zinc were extracted by the London Lead

NORTH PENNINES HERITAGE TRUST

Nenthead House, Nenthead, Alston, Cumbria CA9 3PD
Tel: 01434 382037

Welcome to **Nent Valley**. Visit the 200-acre centre at Nenthead, in the North Pennines, an Area of Outstanding Natural Beauty. It offers a unique insight into the lives of the miners who transformed these fells. Visitors have the chance to experience the underground world through guided trips in Carr's Mine, last commercially worked for lead in 1920. There is the huge "Power of Water" interactive area, where visitors can open sluice gates to operate water wheels and drive machinery. **Brewery Shaft** is an impressive 328 feet deep, with a viewing platform for visitors to gaze down into the depths and be amazed at the courage of anyone daring to descend.

Around the centre are various restored buildings, which contain exhibitions and interactive displays about the geology of the area, the local wildlife and social history of the area. The 200 acre site includes woodland walks, mountain streams and a waterfall, whilst the surrounding area is ideal for walkers of all ages and gives access to the spectacular scenery of the North Pennines. There is a café you can rest your legs and take refreshments, and a well-stocked shop to purchase postcards, books and gifts.

Company. A Quaker company, it was a pioneer of industrial welfare and also built the model village of Nenthead to house the miners. Here, not only were the workers and their families provided with a home, but education was compulsory and there were some public baths. **Nenthead Mines Heritage Centre** (see panel on page 307) is a 200-acre site high in the hills that tells the story of the lead and zinc mining industry. One of the main visitor attractions is 'The Power of Water', an impressive interactive area that looks at the technology used, including three working water wheels that drive model machinery. Another is the Brewery Shaft with its 328 feet drop and amazing virtual stone feature.

Carlisle Castle

CARLISLE

Carlisle is the largest settlement in Cumbria, with a population of around 130,000, and is also its county town. The city stands at the junction of three rivers, the Eden, the Caldew and the Petteril, and was already fortified in Celtic times when it was named Caer Lue, the 'hill fort'. It became a major Roman centre: it was the military base for the Petriana regiment, Luguvallum, guarding the western end of Hadrian's Wall, and also an important civilian settlement with fountains, mosaics, statues and centrally-heated homes.

Today, the squat outline of **Carlisle Castle** (English Heritage) dominates the skyline of this fascinating city. The original Norman Castle was built of wood but, during the Scottish occupation in the 12th century, King David I laid out a new castle with stones taken from Hadrian's Wall. The 12th century keep can still be seen enclosed by massive inner and outer walls. Entry is through a great 14th century gatehouse, complete with portcullis, and with a maze of vaulted passages, chambers, staircases, towers, and dismal dungeons. Children, especially, enjoy the legendary 'licking stones' from which parched Jacobite prisoners tried to find enough moisture to stay alive. Archaeologists working outside the castle walls unearthed the remains of three Roman forts, and many of the finds are on display in a special exhibition at the castle. Carlisle Castle is everything a real castle should be and is still the headquarters of the King's Own Royal Border Regiment, whose **Regimental Museum** is located within the castle walls.

Carlisle Cathedral has many interesting features, including an exquisite east window that is considered to be one of the finest in Europe. Below the beautifully painted wooden ceiling of the choir, with its gold star shimmering against deep blue, are the carved, canopied choir-stalls with their medieval misericords. These wonderful carved beasts and birds include two dragons

joined by the ears, a fox killing a goose, pelicans feeding their young, and a mermaid with a looking glass. In St Wilfrid's Chapel is the superb 16th century Flemish Brougham Triptych which was originally in Cologne Cathedral.

It was here that Edward I solemnly used bell, book, and candle to excommunicate Robert the Bruce, and here, too, the bells were rung to welcome Bonnie Prince Charlie in 1745.

Although an appointment is usually necessary, a visit to the nearby **Prior's Tower** is a must. On the first floor of this 15th century pele tower is a wonderful panelled ceiling incorporating the popinjay crest and arms of the Prior Senhouse. The 16th century Prior's gatehouse leads to a narrow lane called Paternoster which is named after the monks reciting their offices.

Like many great medieval cities, Carlisle was surrounded by walls. Guided walks and tours are available and the best view is to be found in a little street called **West Walls** at the bottom of Sally Port Steps, near the Tithe Barn. The walls date from around the 11th century and they remained virtually intact until the 1800s.

Close by is **St Cuthbert's Church**, the official city church of Carlisle and where the Lord Mayor's pew can be found. Although the present building dates from 1778, there has been a church on this site since the 7th century and the dedication is obvious, since St Cuthbert was Bishop of Carlisle in AD680. It is a charming Georgian building with several interesting features

including a moveable pulpit on rails.

The award-winning **Tullie House Museum & Art Gallery**, in the centre of the city close to the Cathedral, is certainly another place not to be missed. Through skilful and interpretive techniques the fascinating, and often dark, history of the Debatable Lands, as this border region was called, is told. The museum's centrepiece is its story of the Border Reivers who occupied the lands from the 14th to the 17th century. The horrific stories of the Reivers have been passed down through the generations in the Border Ballads, and many of the Reivers family names are still known - the museum even offers a genealogy service, so that visitors find out if their ancestry goes back to these people. The city of Carlisle dates back far beyond those desperate days and Tullie House also has an extensive collection of Roman remains from both the city and the Cumbrian section of Hadrian's Wall. The Art Gallery features contemporary

Carlisle Town Centre

arts and crafts, and the spectacular underground Millennium Gallery has a stunning collection of local minerals, archaeological finds of wood and leather, artist-made glass and interactive exhibits. Old Tullie House showcases paintings and drawings by renowned Pre-Raphaelite artists, as well as other artworks and a selection of fine English porcelain.

A short walk from the Museum leads to the **Linton Visitor Centre** in Shaddongate which provides an insight into the city's industrial heritage.

The **Guildhall Museum**, housed in an unspoiled medieval building constructed by Richard of Redeness in 1407, provides an ideal setting for illustrating the history of both the Guilds and the City.

Not far from the museum is the **Citadel**, which is often mistaken for the castle. In fact, this intimidating fortress with its well-preserved circular tower was built in 1543 on the orders of Henry VIII to strengthen the city's defences. Much of it was demolished in the early 1800s to improve access to the city centre but what remains is mightily impressive.

Across the road from the Citadel is the railway station. The first railway to Carlisle opened in July 1836 and Citadel Station, which opened in 1850, was built to serve seven different railway companies whose coats of arms are still displayed on the facade. So elegant was its interior - and much of it remains - that Carlisle was known as the 'top hat' station. Today it is still an important centre of communications; InterCity trains from Glasgow and London now link with lines to Dumfries, Tyneside, West Cumbria, and Yorkshire, and it is, of course, the northern terminus of the famous **Settle-Carlisle Railway** line.

One of the last great mainline railways to be built in Britain - it was completed in 1876 - the Settle to Carlisle line takes in some of the most dramatic scenery that the north of England has to offer. Scenic it may be but the terrain caused the Victorian engineers many problems and it is thanks to their ingenuity and skill that the line was ever finished. During the course of its 72 miles, the line crosses 20 viaducts and passes through 12 tunnels, each of which was constructed by an army of navvies who had little in the way of resources besides their strength and some dynamite to remove the rock.

Located on the northwestern edge of the city, **Kingmoor Nature Reserve** occupies an area of moorland given to the city in 1352 by Edward III. Citizens enjoyed the right to graze sheep on the moors and to cut peat for fuel. Later, Carlisle's first racecourse was established here with annual Guild races being held up until 1850. Then in 1913, Kingmoor became one of the first bird sanctuaries in England and today provides a peaceful retreat away from the bustle of the city. A half-mile circular path wanders through the woodland with gentle gradients of 1 in 20 making it fully accessible to wheelchairs and pushchairs, and with seats every 100 yards or so providing plenty of resting places. Another path links the reserve to **Kingmoor Sidings**, which since the old railway sheds closed has been colonised by a wide variety of wildlife.

AROUND CARLISLE

WREAY
5 miles S of Carlisle off the A6

This little village is known for its extraordinary **Church of St Mary**, designed by a local woman, Sarah Losh, in memory of her sister and her parents. It was built in 1835 and incorporates

CASTLETOWN FARM SHOP

Floriston Rigg, Rockcliffe, Carlisle, Cumbria CA6 4HG
Tel: 01228 674400 Fax: 01228 672251
website: www.castletownfarmshop.co.uk

Castletown Farm Shop stands within a 5000-acre working mixed farm either side of the A74 between Carlisle and Gretna. The shop sells a wide range of home produced meat and vegetables, a large selection of cheeses and it has an excellent delicatessen. The shop stocks a selection of organic produce but the emphasis is on locally produced or English foods. The Castletown Kitchen produces a large selection of home cooked frozen meals in varying sizes along with many different cakes and bakes. There is also The Coffee Shop serving baguettes, baked potatoes, soup and cakes from the kitchen as well as a daily special, all made without artificial preservatives or additives. Open 7 days a week Mon-Sat 9.30am-5.00pm, Sunday 10.00am-4.00pm.

many Italian Romanesque features. The church is full of beautiful touches, including the carvings, mostly by Sarah herself, on the font.

BURGH BY SANDS

5 miles W of Carlisle off the B5307

On 7th July 1307, the body of King Edward I was laid out in the village church: he was already a dying man when he left Carlisle to march against his old enemy, Robert the Bruce. A monument to Edward was erected on the marshes and a later monument still marks the spot. At the time of the king's death, the **Church of St Michael** was already well over a century old and is possibly the earliest surviving example of a fortified church. Dating from 1181 and constructed entirely of stones from a fort on the Roman wall, the church was designed for protection against Border raids, which is why its tower has walls seven feet thick.

BOWNESS-ON-SOLWAY

14 miles W of Carlisle off the B5307

Hadrian's Wall continues along the Solway coast to Bowness and many of the sandstone cottages around here contain stones from the Wall. Some of these stones can easily be identified, such as the small inscribed altar let into a

barn near the King's Arms. The Roman fort of **Maia** once covered a 7-acre site, but today there is only a plaque explaining where it used to be. Bowness is sometimes said to be the end of the Wall but in fact it just turned a corner here and continued south along the coast for another 40 miles.

Two miles south of the village lies **Glasson Moss National Nature Reserve**, a lowland raised mire extending to 93 hectares. Many species of sphagnum moss are to be found here, and the birdlife includes red grouse, curlew, sparrowhawk and snipe.

LONGTOWN

9 miles N of Carlisle on the A7

Situated on the north side of Hadrian's Wall, only a couple of miles from the Scottish border, this is the last town in England. Its position on the River Esk so close to the border has influenced its history from earliest times. The Romans occupied this land and they were followed by other conquerors. The legendary King Arthur attempted to organise the Northern Britons against the pagan hordes who tried to settle and control this territory. In AD573 the mighty battle of Ardderyd was fought here and, according to legend, 80,000 men were slain.

On the outskirts of Longtown is **Arthuret Church**. The earliest records of the church date from 1150 and it was originally served by the monks of Jedburgh. But it is thought that the earliest church here may have been founded by St Kentigern in the 6th century; recent research has led some to believe that King Arthur was actually interred here after his last battle, Camboglanna, was fought a few miles east of Longtown at Gilsland. The present church, dedicated to **St Michael and All Angels**, was built in 1609, financed by a general collection throughout the realm which James I ordered after a report that the people of Arthuret Church were without faith or religion. The people that he referred to, of course, were the infamous Reivers, ungoverned by either English or Scottish laws. Archie Armstrong, favourite Court Jester to James I and later to Charles I, is buried in the churchyard.

BEWCASTLE

14 miles NE of Carlisle off the B6318

Roman legionaries assigned to the fort at what is now Bewcastle must certainly have felt that they had drawn the short straw. The fort stood all on its own, about nine miles north of Hadrian's Wall, guarding a crossing over the Kirk Beck. The site covered around six acres and most of it is now occupied by the ruins of a **Norman Castle**. Most of the south wall is still standing but little else remains and the castle is best admired for its setting rather than its architecture.

A much more impressive survival dominates the village churchyard. Here stands the **Bewcastle Cross**, erected around AD670 and one of the oldest and finest stone crosses in Europe. Standing over 13 feet in height, its intricate Celtic carvings have survived the centuries of

weathering and much of the runic inscription can still be made out in the yellow sandstone. One of the carvings, a semicircle with 13 radiating lines, three of which have crossbars, is believed to be a sophisticated sundial which not only indicated the 12 hours of the Roman clock but also the three 'tides' of the Saxon day - morning, noon and eventide.

WETHERAL

4 miles E of Carlisle off the A69

Wetheral stands above the River Eden, over which runs an impressive railway viaduct, carrying the **Tyne Valley Line**, which was built by Francis Giles in 1830. Wetheral **Parish Church** lies below the village beside the river and contains a poignant sculpture by Joseph Nollekens of the dying Lady Mary Howard clasping her dead baby. Nearby, occupying a lovely riverside setting, is one of the **Eden Benchmarks**, a sculptured bench in St Bee's sandstone by Tim Shutter, entitled *Flight of Fancy*.

St Constantine was the local patron and the church is dedicated to the Holy Trinity, St Constantine and St Mary. Constantine is said to have lived in caves in what are now National Trust woodlands alongside the river, a location known as **Constantine's Caves**. Constantine died as a martyr in AD 657 and a life-sized statue of him can be seen in the grounds of **Corby Castle** to the south of the village. The castle, with its impressive 13th century keep and terraced gardens overlooking the Eden, is usually open during the summer months.

During the reign of William Rufus, one of his barons, Ranulph Meschin, founded a priory for Benedictine monks at Wetheral above a red-rock gorge of the River Eden. All that remains now is the imposing three-storey gatehouse.

CROSBY-ON-EDEN

4 miles NE of Carlisle off the A689

The tiny hamlet of **High Crosby** stands on the hillside overlooking the River Eden; the small village of **Low Crosby** sits beside the river, clustered around a Victorian sandstone church. Inside the church there's a modern square pulpit, intricately carved with pomegranates, wheat and vines. Apparently, it was carved from one half of a tree felled nearby; the other half was used to create a second pulpit, which was installed in the newly-built Liverpool Cathedral.

A couple of miles east of Crosby, The **Solway Aviation Museum** is one of only a few museums located on a 'live' airfield, in this case Carlisle Airport. Opened in 1997, the museum is home to several British jet aircraft of the 1950s and 1960s, among them the mighty Vulcan and the Canberra. Other exhibits include a wartime air raid shelter where a video presentation explains the story behind the museum, displays of the Blue Streak rocket programme, testing for which took place only a few miles from here, and a very impressive engine room which houses one of Frank Whittle's first development jet engines.

BRAMPTON

Nestling in the heart of the lovely Irthing Valley, Brampton is a delightful little town where the Wednesday market has been held since 1252, authorised by a charter granted by Henry III. Overlooking the Market Place is the town's most striking building, the octagonal **Moot Hall** topped by a handsome clock tower.

Just around the corner, in **High Cross Street**, is the house (now a shop) which once witnessed one of the high points in Bonnie Prince Charles' rebellion of 1745. It was here that the Prince stayed during

WINGED HEART STAINED GLASS

7 The Old Brewery, Brampton,
Cumbria CA8 1TR
Tel: 01697 73589 Fax: 01697 73211
e-mail: winged-heart@freeuk.com
website: www.winged-heart.com

Winged Heart Stained Glass is located in the small North Cumbria market town of Brampton, in a sandstone former brewery on the B6413 leading south towards Talkin Tarn and Castle Carrock. Winged Heart specialises in a very wide variety of hand-made and hand-painted glass gifts.

The range includes pretty window decorations, photo frames, jewel boxes and clocks, and there are many styles, from Celtic and Charles Rennie Mackintosh influenced designs to beautiful florals and wildlife, and even dramatically colourful cathedral stained glass reproductions.

Mara Eagle and Drew Landsborough started up Winged Heart in 1995 as escapees from London, turning a hobby into their way of earning a living in a part of the country they loved. The business grew rapidly and now supplies the gift shops of several cathedrals and many heritage outlets. Visitors are welcome in the studio/workshop, which is open from 9 to 5 Monday to Friday.

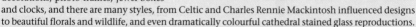

NEW MILLS TROUT FARM

Brampton, Cumbria CA8 2QS
Tel: 01697 72384

New Mills Trout Farm offers fly and worm fishing, from the lakeside or a boat, and the beautiful location makes it a delight even for visitors who don't want to fish. Rods and all equipment can be hired on the spot, and fishers can take their catch or leave it to be sold in the retail outlet, where visitors come to buy the delicious trout and salmon. Ice creams and light refreshments are available, and Ian Scott and his family, who run the business, plan to open a tea room and Bed & Breakfast accommodation.

the siege of Carlisle and it was here, on November 17, 1745 that the Mayor and Aldermen presented him with the keys to the city. A few months later, following the Prince's defeat, six of his supporters were hanged on the Capon Tree on the south side of the town and in sight of the Scottish hills.

The tree survived until the last century and in its place there now stands a monument commemorating the event.

Just off the Market Place is **St Martin's Church**, which was built anew in 1874 and contains one of the undiscovered secrets of the area - some magnificent stained glass windows designed by one of the founder members of the pre-Raphaelite brotherhood, Edward Burne-Jones. It was his fellow-member of the

CRACROP FARM BED & BREAKFAST

Kirkcambeck, Nr Brampton, Cumbria CA8 2BW
AA 5 Diamonds ♦ ♦ ♦ ♦
Tel: 01697 748245 Fax: 01697 748333
e-mail: cracrop@aol.com

Personally run by owners Marjorie and David Stobart, **Cracrop Farm** is a traditional farmhouse of distinction with lovely gardens and breathtaking views. Space, comfort and relaxation are guaranteed in this unbeatable setting, and the four individually designed en suite bedrooms are equipped with many thoughtful extras that contribute to a memorable stay. Guests have their own keep-fit room, a spa bath and sauna. The lounge is a perfect spot to catch up with the news, meet the other guests or browse through the plentiful supply of books and magazines, while the gardens - Marjorie's pride and joy - provide not only peaceful walks but plenty of seats to pause to take in the wonderful views.

The day at Cracrop Farm (for 20 years a working farm specialising in prize winning pedigree cattle) begins with a good hearty breakfast that caters for all tastes and includes bread and preserves made by Marjorie. The farm has its own marked trail for walkers, and among the local facilities are horse riding, sailing and boating on Talkin Tarn, golf, swimming and walking for all energy levels. It is also a convenient base for visiting Hadrians Wall, Carlisle, the Lake District and the Scottish Borders. Cracrop Farm is a non-smoking establishment.

BORDER HERITAGE TRAIL

Contact: Tourist Information Centres at:
The Moot Hall, Brampton CA8 1RA Tel: 016977 3433
Old Town Hall, Carlisle CA3 8JH Tel: 01228 625600
3 High Street, Longtown CA6 5UA Tel: 01228 792835

The vast rural landscape around Carlisle, combines rich pasture land, gentle meadows and natural woodland with meandering rivers, dramatic moorland and wild fells. From Hadrian's Wall to the Scottish Border, here is a captivating area containing numerous small villages and hamlets connected by a network of quiet roads lined with old hedgerows and wild flowers. The region offers a variety of outdoor activities including fishing, sailing, golf, horse riing, nature walks and cycle routes to suit all tastes The Border Heritage Trail gives you the opportunity to access all of these.

As well as the scenery, the route will take you past an assortment of historical buildings and sites, including castles, churches, bridges, Roman forts and, of course, Hadrian's Wall.

The trail can be accessed at many points and walks can be made as long or as short as you want. Cycle routes and farm trails are also available. Contact the Tourist Information Centre for more information.

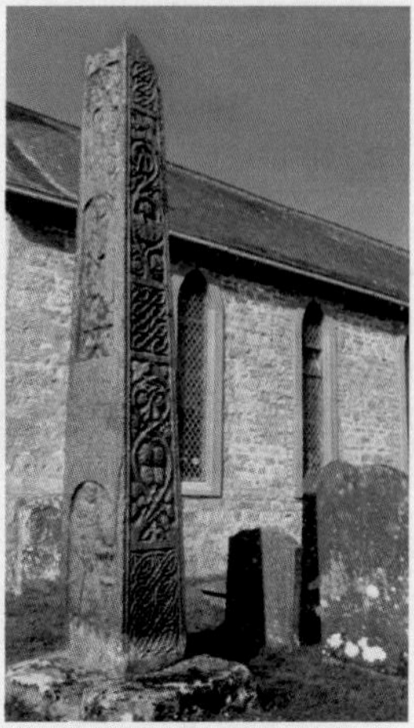

brotherhood, Philip Webb, William Morris's associate, who designed the church and insisted that contemporary stained glass should be installed.

AROUND BRAMPTON

LOW ROW
3 miles E of Brampton off the A69

Within easy reach of the town is Hadrian's Wall, just three miles to the north. If you've ever wondered where the Wall's missing masonry went to, look no further than the fabric of **Lanercost Priory** (English Heritage). An impressive red sandstone ruin set in secluded woodland, the priory was founded in 1166 by Robert de Vaux. Lanercost is well preserved and its scale is a reminder that it was a grand complex in its heyday. However, the priory suffered greatly in the border raids of the 13th and 14th centuries. One such raid is known to have been led by William Wallace, an early campaigner for Scottish independence from English rule. When

the Priory was closed in 1536, the sandstone blocks were recycled once again for houses in the town. But much of the Priory's great north aisle remains intact, set in a romantic and hauntingly beautiful position in the valley of the River Irthing. The Priory is well signposted and lies only three miles off the A69 (leave at Brampton).

Also most impressive is **Naworth Castle**, built around 1335 in its present form by Lord Dacre as an important border stronghold. The Castle's supreme glory is the Great Hall, hung with French tapestries and guarded by four unique heraldic beasts holding aloft their family pennants. The Long Gallery extends for 116 feet and was used as a guardroom.

The area around Brampton had good reason to be grateful to the Dacres of Naworth, who as Wardens of the Northern Marches protected it against marauding Scots. However, the townspeople of Brampton in Victorian times must have had mixed feelings about a later descendant, Rosalind, wife of the 9th Earl of Carlisle. An

enthusiastic supporter of total abstinence, she contrived to get most of the small town's 40 public houses and drinking rooms closed.

South of Brampton are **Gelt Woods**, lying in a deep sandstone ravine carved by the fast-flowing River Gelt. By the river is an inscribed rock called **Written Rock** which is thought to have been carved by a Roman standard bearer in AD207.

TALKIN

2 miles S of Brampton off the B6413

Talkin Tarn, now the focus of a 120-acre country park, has been a popular place for watersports for over 100 years. Glacial in origin, the Tarn was formed some 10,000 years ago and is continually replenished by underground springs. Modern day visitors can sail, windsurf, canoe or hire one of the original wooden rowing boats. Talkin Tarn Rowing Club

has been rowing on the tarn for 130 years and holds its annual regatta in July. Fishing licences are available, and there's a nature trail and an orienteering course, a play area for children under 8, a tea room and a gift shop; guided walks with a warden are also available for organised groups.

GILSLAND

7 miles E of Brampton on the B6318

Hadrians wall was built between AD 122 and 128 as a great military barrier across the narrowest part of Britain, from the mouth of the River Tyne, in the east, to Bowness-on-Solway, in the west. The wall was finally abandoned in the late 4th century, and in later centuries many of the stones were used for local buildings and field walls. There are many ways of exploring the Wall (including the bus number AD122!), and for those with the energy to walk from end to end the

---

BIRDOSWALD ROMAN FORT

Gilsland, Carlisle, Cumbria CA8 7DD
Tel: 016977 47602 Fax: 016877 47605
e-mail: birdoswald@dial.pipex.com

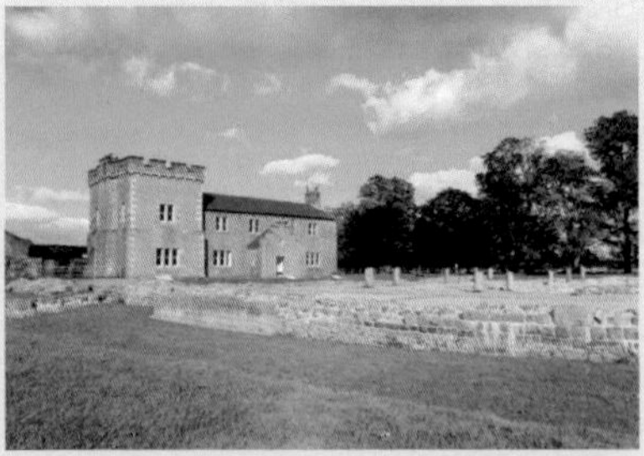

Located in one of the most picturesque setting along the whole length of Hadrian's Wall and overlooking the River Irthing, **Birdoswald Roman Fort** is one of the best preserved mile-castles along the Wall and unique in that all the components of the Roman frontier system can be found here. This World Heritage Site is set high on a plateau with magnificent views over the surrounding countryside. The early turf wall, built in AD122, can be seen along with the fort, and a superb stretch of the Wall stretches from the fort for a third of a mile. Originally, this fort would have covered five acres and it may have been the base for up to 1000 soldiers. During its 300-year occupation, the fort underwent substantial alterations and the turf wall, the stone wall, Harrow's Scar Milecastle, and the fort itself are all visible reminders of the occupation.

Between April and October, history comes to life at Birdoswald with a wide variety of events - battle re-enactments, music and drama, and the site also has an interactive Visitor Centre, a gift and tea shop, and a picnic area. In 1999, a residential study centre with a range of excellent study facilities as well as accommodation was added to the site's amenities.

It is thanks to Henry Norman, a Victorian romantic and owner of the land on which the fort stands, that today's visitors can see these wonderful remains. An enthusiastic archaeologist, Norman extended the farmhouse, built the tower, and carried out the major excavation work to the fort, walls, and gates.

newly opened Hadrian's Wall National Trail passes some of the country's greatest archaeological monuments.

Located in one of the most picturesque settings along the whole length of Hadrian's Wall and overlooking the River Irthing, **Birdoswald Roman Fort** (see panel opposite)is one of the best preserved mile-castles along the Wall and unique in that all the components of the Roman frontier system can be found here. Set high on a plateau with magnificent views over the surrounding countryside, the early turf wall, built in AD122, can be seen along with the fort.

Originally, this fort would have covered five acres and it may have been the base for up to 500 cavalry and 1,000 foot soldiers. Gilsland village is also known for its sulphur spring and there was once a convalescent home for miners and shipyard workers here. It is now owned by the Co-operative Society and people still drink the waters as a cure for arthritis and rheumatism. Near the spring is the **Popping Stone**, traditionally the place where a man 'popped the question' to his lover. It was here that Sir Walter Scott successfully popped to Charlotte Carpenter.

TOURIST INFORMATION CENTRES

CHESHIRE

ALTRINCHAM

20 Stamford New Road
Altrincham
Cheshire
WA14 1EJ
Tel: 0161 912 5931
Fax: 0161 941 7089
e-mail: tic@trafford.gov.uk

CHESTER NORTHGATE STREET

Town Hall
Northgate Street
Chester
Cheshire
CH1 2HJ
Tel: 01244 402111
Fax: 01244 400420
e-mail: tis@chestercc.gov.uk
web: www.chestercc.gov.uk

CHESTER VICARS LANE

Chester Visitor Centre
Vicars Lane
Chester
Cheshire
CH1 1QX
Tel: 01244 402111
Fax: 01244 403188
e-mail: tis@chestercc.gov.uk

CONGLETON

Town Hall
High Street
Congleton
Cheshire
CW12 1BN
Tel: 01260 271095
Fax: 01260 298243
e-mail:
     tourism@congleton.gov.uk
web: www.congletonasea.com

KNUTSFORD

Council Offices
Toft Road
Knutsford
Cheshire
WA16 6TA
Tel: 01565 632611
Fax: 01565 652367
e-mail:
     whats_on@macclesfield.gov.uk
web: www.macclesfield.gov.uk

MACCLESFIELD

Macclesfield
Town Hall
Macclesfield
Cheshire
SK10 1DX
Tel: 01625 504114
Fax: 01625 504116
e-mail: Informationcentre
     @macclesfield.gov.uk
web: www.macclesfield.gov.uk

NANTWICH

Church House
Church Walk
Nantwich
Cheshire
CW5 5RG
Tel: 01270 610983
Fax: 01270 610880
e-mail:
     touristi@netcentral.co.uk

NORTHWICH

1 The Arcade
Northwich
Cheshire
CW9 5AS
Tel: 01606 353534
Fax: 01606 353516
e-mail: cberesford
     @valeroyal.gov.uk

RUNCORN

6 Church Street
Runcorn
Cheshire
WA7 1LT
Tel: 01928 576776
Fax: 01928 569656
e-mail: tourist.info
     @halton-borough.gov.uk
web: www.halton.gov.uk

STOCKPORT

Graylaw House
Chestergate
Stockport
Cheshire
SK1 1NH
Tel: 0161 474 4444
Fax: 0161 429 6348
e-mail: tourist.information
     @stockport.gov.uk
web: www.stockport.gov.uk

WARRINGTON

The Market Hall
Academy Way
Warrington
Cheshire
WA1 2EN
Tel: 01925 632571
Fax: 01925 574735
e-mail: informationcentre
     @warrington.gov.uk

CUMBRIA

ALSTON MOOR

Town Hall
Front Street
Alston
Cumbria
CA9 3RF
Tel: 01434 382244
Fax: 01434 382255
e-mail:
alston.tic@eden.gov.uk
web: www.visiteden.co.uk

AMBLESIDE

Central Buildings
Market Cross
Ambleside
Cumbria
LA22 9BS
Tel: 015394 32582
Fax: 015394 34901
e-mail: amblesidetic
@southlakeland.gov.uk
web:
www.amblesideonline.co.uk/

APPLEBY-IN-WESTMORLAND

Moot Hall
Boroughgate
Appleby-in-Westmorland
Cumbria
CA16 6XD
Tel: 017683 51177
Fax: 017683 51090
e-mail: tic@appleby
towncouncil.fsnet.co.uk

BARROW-IN-FURNESS

Forum 28
Duke Street
Barrow-in-Furness
Cumbria
LA14 1HU
Tel: 01229 894784
Fax: 01229 894703

e-mail: touristinfo
@barrowbc.gov.uk
web:
www.barrowtourism.co.uk/

BOWNESS

Glebe Road
Bowness-on-Windermere
Cumbria
LA23 3HJ
Tel: 015394 42895
Fax: 015394 88005
e-mail: bownesstic
@lakedistrict.gov.uk
web: www.lakedistrict.gov.uk
Seasonal

BRAMPTON

Moot Hall
Market Place
Brampton
Cumbria
CA8 1RW
Tel: 016977 3433
Fax: 016977 3433
e-mail: ElisabethB
@CarlisleCity.gov.uk
Seasonal

BROUGHTON-IN-FURNESS

Town Hall
The Square
Broughton-in-Furness
Cumbria
LA20 6JF
Tel: 01229 716115
Fax: 01229 716115
e-mail: email
@broughton-tic.fsnet.co.uk

CARLISLE

Old Town Hall
Green Market
Carlisle
Cumbria
CA3 8JH
Tel: 01228 625600
Fax: 01228 625604

e-mail: tourism
@carlisle-city.gov.uk

COCKERMOUTH

Town Hall
Market Street
Cockermouth
Cumbria
CA13 9NP
Tel: 01900 822634
Fax: 01900 822603
e-mail: email@cockermouth-tic.fsnet.co.uk
web: www.gocumbria.co.uk/

CONISTON

Ruskin Avenue
Coniston
Cumbria
LA21 8EH
Tel: 015394 41533
Fax: 015394 41802
e-mail:
conistonic@lakedistrict.gov.uk
web:
www.lakedistrict.gov.uk/

EGREMONT

12 Main Street
Egremont
Cumbria
CA22 2DW
Tel: 01946 820693
e-mail: email@egremont-tic.fsnet.co.uk
Seasonal

GRANGE-OVER-SANDS

Victoria Hall
Main Street
Grange-over-Sands
Cumbria
LA11 6DP
Tel: 015395 34026
Fax: 015395 34331
e-mail: grangetic
@southlakeland.gov.uk
web: www.grange-over-sands.com/

GRASMERE

Redbank Road
Grasmere
Cumbria
LA22 9SW
Tel: 015394 35245
Fax: 015394 35057
e-mail: Grasmeretic
@lake-district.gov.uk
Seasonal

HAWKSHEAD

Main Car Park
Hawkshead
Cumbria
LA22 0NT
Tel: 015394 36525
Fax: 015394 36349
e-mail: hawksheadtic
@lake-district.gov.uk
Seasonal

KENDAL

Town Hall
Highgate
Kendal
Cumbria
LA9 4DL
Tel: 01539 725758
Fax: 01539 734457
e-mail: kendaltic
@southlakeland.gov.uk
web:
www.southlakeland.co.uk

KESWICK

Moot Hall
Market Square
Keswick
Cumbria
CA12 5JR
Tel: 017687 72645
Fax: 017687 75043
e-mail: keswicktic
@lake-district.gov.uk
web: www.keswick.org/

KILLINGTON LAKE

Killington Lake Services
M6 South
Nr Kendal
Cumbria
LA8 0NW
Tel: 015396 20138
Fax: 015396 21071
e-mail:
killingtonlaketic@hotmail.com
Seasonal

KIRBY LONSDALE

24 Main Street
Kirby Lonsdale
Cumbria
LA6 2AE
Tel: 01524 271437
e-mail:
kitic@southlakeland.gov.uk
www.kirkbylonsdale.co.uk

KIRKBY STEPHEN

Market Street
Kirkby Stephen
Cumbria
CA17 4QN
Tel: 017683 71199
Fax: 017683 72728
e-mail: ks.tic@eden.gov.uk
Seasonal

LONGTOWN

3 High Street
Longtown
Carlisle
Cumbria
CA6 5PU
Tel: 01228 792835
Fax: 01228 792835
e-mail: ElisabethB
@Carlisle-City.gov.uk

MARYPORT

1 Senhouse Street
Maryport
Cumbria
CA15 6AB

Tel: 01900 813738
Fax: 01900 819496
e-mail: maryporttic
@allerdale.gov.uk

PENRITH

Robinsons School
Middlegate
Penrith
Cumbria
CA11 7PT
Tel: 01768 867466
Fax: 01768 891754
e-mail: pen_tic@eden.gov.uk
web: www.visiteden.co.uk/

POOLEY BRIDGE

Finkle Street
Pooley Bridge
Cumbria
CA10 2NW
Tel: 017684 86530
Fax: 017684 86530
Seasonal

RHEGED

Rheged TIC
Redhills
Nr Penrith
Cumbria
CA11 0DQ
Tel. 01768 860034
Fax. 01768 868002
e-mail: tic@rheged.com

SEATOLLER

Seatoller Barn
Borrowdale
Keswick
Cumbria
CA12 5XN
Tel: 017687 77294
Fax: 017687 77294
e-mail: Seatollertic
@lake-district.gov.uk
web:
www.lake-district.gov.uk

SEDBERGH

72 Main Street
Sedbergh
Cumbria
LA10 5AD
Tel: 015396 20125
Fax: 015396 21732
e-mail: sedbergh
@yorkshiredales.org.uk
web:
www.yorkshiredales.org.uk/

SELLAFIELD

Sellafield Visitors Centre
Seascale
Cumbria
CA20 1PG
Tel: 019467 76510
Fax: 019467 27021
e-mail:
julia.s.watson@bnfl.com

SILLOTH

10 Criffel Street
Silloth-on-Solway
Cumbria
CA5 4BT
Tel: 016973 31944
Fax: 016973 31944
e-mail:
sillothtic@allerdale.gov.uk

SOUTHWAITE

M6 Service Area
"Southwaite, Carlisle"
Cumbria
CA4 ONS
Tel: 016974 73445
Fax: 016974 73445
e-mail: southwaite
@scot-borders.co.uk

ULLSWATER

Main Car Park
Glenridding
Penrith
Cumbria
CA11 0PA

Tel: 017684 82414
Fax: 017684 82414

ULVERSTON

Coronation Hall
County Square
Ulverston
Cumbria
LA12 7LZ
Tel: 01229 587120
Fax: 01229 582626
e-mail: ulverstontic
@southlakeland.gov.uk

WATERHEAD

Main Car Park
Waterhead
Ambleside
Cumbria
LA22 0EN
Tel: 015394 32729
Fax: 015394 31728
e-mail: waterheadtic
@lake-district.gov.uk

WHITEHAVEN

Market Hall
Market Place
Whitehaven
Cumbria
CA28 7JG
Tel: 01946 852939
e-mail:
tic@copelandbc.gov.uk

WINDERMERE

Victoria Street
Windermere
Cumbria
LA23 1AD
Tel: 015394 46499
Fax: 015394 47439
e-mail: windermeretic
@southlakeland.gov.uk

WORKINGTON

21 Finkle Street
Workington
Cumbria
CA14 3BE
Tel: 01900 606699
Fax: 01900 606699
e-mail: workingtontic
@allerdale.gov.uk

ISLE OF MAN

DOUGLAS

Sea Terminal Buildings
Douglas
Isle of Man
IM1 2RG
Tel: 01624 686801
Fax: +01624 686800
e-mail: tourism@gov.im
web: www.gov.im/tourism

LANCASHIRE

ACCRINGTON

Town Hall
Blackburn Road
Accrington
Lancashire
BB5 1LA
Tel: 01254 872595
Fax: 01254 380291
e-mail: infopoint
@acc11.fsnet.co.uk

ASHTON-UNDER-LYNE

32 Market Street
Ashton-Under-Lyne
Lancashire
OL6 6ER
Tel: 0161 343 4343
Fax: 0161 343 7225
e-mail: tourist.information
@mail.tameside.gov.uk

BARNOLDSWICK

The Council Shop
Fernlea Avenue
Barnoldswick
Lancashire
BB18 5DL
Tel: 01282 666704
Fax: 01282 666704

BENTHAM

26 Main St
High Bentham
Via Lancaster
Lancashire
LA2 7HL
Tel: 015242 62549
Fax: 015242 61030
e-mail: post
   @benthamdt.demon.co.uk

BLACKBURN

15-17 Railway Road
Blackburn
Lancashire
BB1 5AX
Tel: 01254 53277
Fax: 01254 683536
e-mail: paulin.whittaker
   @blackburn.gov.uk
web: www.blackburn.gov.uk

BLACKPOOL CLIFTON STREET

1 Clifton Street
Blackpool
Lancashire
FY1 1LY
Tel: 01253 478222
Fax: 01253 478210
e-mail: tic
   @blackpool.gov.uk

BLACKPOOL PLEASURE BEACH

Blackpool Pleasure Beach
Unit 25
Ocean Boulevard
Blackpool

Lancashire
FY4 1PL
Tel: 01253 403223
Fax: 01253 408718
e-mail: andrew.carruthers
   @bpbltd.com

BURNLEY

Burnley Mechanics
Manchester Road
Burnley
Lancashire
BB11 1JA
Tel: 01282 664421
Fax: 01282 664431
e-mail: tic@burnley.gov.uk
web: www.burnley.gov.uk

CLEVELEYS

Victoria Square
Thornton
Cleveleys
Lancashire
FY5 1AU
Tel: 01253 853378
Fax: 01253 866124

CLITHEROE

12-14 Market Place
Clitheroe
Lancashire
BB7 2DA
Tel: 01200 425566
Fax: 01200 414488
e-mail: tourism
   @ribblevalley-gov.uk

FLEETWOOD

Old Ferry Office
The Esplanade
Fleetwood
Lancashire
FY7 6DL
Tel: 01253 773953
Fax: 01253 876656

GARSTANG

Discovery Centre
High Street
Garstang
Lancashire
PR3 1FU
Tel: 01995 602125
Fax: 01253 604325

LANCASTER CUMBRIA GATEWAY

Lancaster Services
M6 North
White Carr Lane,
Bay Horse
Lancaster
Lancashire
LA2 9DU
Tel: 01524 792181
Fax: 01524 792676

LANCASTER

29 Castle Hill
Lancaster
Lancashire
LA1 1YN
Tel: 01524 32878
Fax: 01524 847472
e-mail: athomas
   @lancaster.gov.uk

LYTHAM ST ANNES

67 St Annes Road West
Lytham St Annes
Lancashire
FY8 1SH
Tel: 0906 680 0033
Fax: 01253 640708
e-mail: touristinformation
   @fylde.gov.uk

MORECAMBE

Old Station Buildings
Marine Road Central
Morecambe
Lancashire
LA4 4DB

Tel: 01524 582808
Fax: 01524 832549
e-mail: tourism
@lancaster.gov.uk

OLDHAM

12 Albion Street
Oldham
Lancashire
OL1 3BD
Tel: 0161 627 1024
Fax: 0161 911 3064
e-mail: els.tourist
@oldham.gov.uk

PENDLE HERITAGE
CENTRE

Park Hill
Barrowford
Nelson
Lancashire
BB9 6JQ
Tel: 01282 661701
Fax: 01282 661701
e-mail: tic@htnw.co.uk

PRESTON

The Guildhall
Lancaster Road
Preston
Lancashire
PR1 1HT
Tel: 01772 253731
Fax: 01772 563850
e-mail: tourism
@preston.gov.uk

RAWTENSTALL

41-45 Kay Street
Rawtenstall
Rossendale
Lancashire
BB4 7LS
Tel: 01706 226590
Fax: 01706 226590
e-mail: rossendale_leisure
@compuserve.com

ROCHDALE

The Clock Tower
Town Hall
Rochdale
Lancashire
OL16 1AB
Tel: 01706 356592
Fax: 01706 864215
e-mail: tic@rochdale.gov.uk

GREATER MANCHESTER

BOLTON

Town Hall
Victoria Square
Bolton
Greater Manchester
BL1 1RU
Tel: 01204 334400
Fax: 01204 398101
e-mail: touristinfo
@bolton.gov.uk

BURY

The Met Arts Centre
Market Street
Bury
Greater Manchester
BL9 0BN
Tel: 0161 253 5111
Fax: 0161 253 5919
e-mail: touristinformation
@bury.gov.uk

ENGLAND'S NORTH WEST
VISITOR CENTRE

Portland Street
Manchester
Greater Manchester
Tel: 0845 600 6040

MANCHESTER TOWN
HALL

Manchester Visitor Centre
Town Hall Extension

Lloyd St
Manchester
Greater Manchester
M60 2LA
Tel: 0161 234 3157
Fax: 0161 236 9900
e-mail:
manchester-visitor-centre
@notes.manchester.gov.uk

MANCHESTER AIRPORT
TRM 2

International Arrivals Hall
Terminal 2
Manchester Airport
Manchester
Greater Manchester
M90 4TU
Tel: 0161 489 6412
Fax: 0161 489 6413
e-mail: miat2
@nwtb2.u-net.com

MANCHESTER AIRPORT
TRM 1

International Arrivals Hall
Terminal 1
Manchester Airport
Manchester
Greater Manchester
M90 3NY
Tel: 0161 436 3344
Fax: 0161 489 8831
e-mail: miat1
@nwtb2.u-net.com

SADDLEWORTH

Saddleworth Museum
High Street
Uppermill
Saddleworth
Oldham
Greater Manchester
OL3 6HS
Tel: 01457 870336
Fax: 01457 870336
e-mail: ecs.saddleworthtic
@oldham.gov.uk

SALFORD

1 The Quays
Salford
Greater Manchester
M5 2SQ
Tel: 0161 848 8601
Fax: 0161 872 3848
e-mail: christine.ellis
    @salford.gov.uk

WIGAN

Trencherfield Mill
Wallgate
Wigan
Greater Manchester
WN3 4EL
Tel: 01942 825677
Fax: 01942 825677
e-mail: infounit
    @wiganmbc.gov.uk

MERSEYSIDE

BIRKENHEAD

Woodside Ferry Terminal
Birkenhead
Merseyside
CH41 6DU
Tel: 0151 647 6780
Fax: 0151 666 2448
e-mail: touristinfo
    @wirral.gov.uk
web: www.wirral.gov.uk

LIVERPOOL

Queen Square Building
Roe Street
Liverpool
Merseyside
L1 1RG
Tel: 0151 707 0986
e-mail: askme
    @visit-liverpool.com
web: www.visitliverpool.com

LIVERPOOL

Unit 4
Atlantic Pavilion
Albert Dock
Liverpool
Merseyside
L3 4AE
Tel: 0151 709 3350
e-mail: askme
    @visitliverpool.com
web: www.visitliverpool.com

LIVERPOOL JOHN LENNON AIRPORT "ARRIVALS HALL, SOUTH TERMINAL

Liverpool John Lennon
    Airport, Speke Hall
    Avenue"
Liverpool
Merseyside
L24 1YD

SOUTHPORT

112 Lord Street
Southport
Merseyside
PR8 1NY
Tel: 01704 533333
Fax: 01704 500175
e-mail: sue
    @visitsouthport.org.uk
web:
    www.visitsouthport.com

INDEX OF ADVERTISERS

Jarrold
Pathfinder Guides

- Ordnance Survey mapping

- 28 walk routes, graded easy, moderate and challenging

- Introduces you to the area and highlights the most scenic routes

- Details useful organisations, refreshment stops and places to leave your car

- Series covers all of the UK

15 *pathfinder guide*
Yorkshire Dales
WALKS

JARROLD

34 *pathfinder*
Pembrokesh
and Gov
W A
JARROLD

pathfinder guide
Somerset, Wiltshire and the Mendips
WALKS

JARROLD

Take the fuss out of planning a walk

Available at tourist outlets, bookshops and specialist walking outlets

Foreword

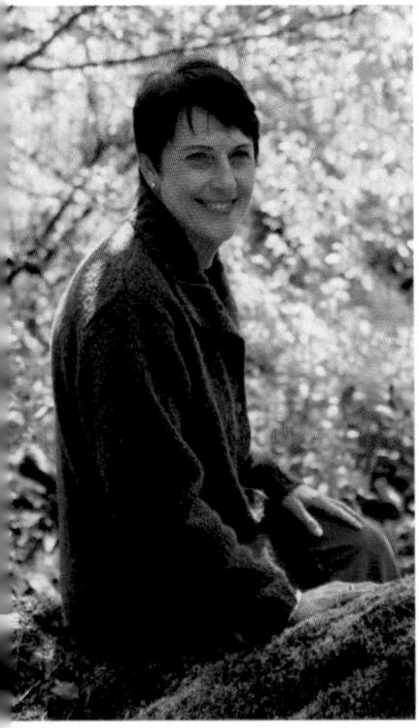

Britain is an explorer's paradise – the variety of landscape, wildlife and cultural attractions promises days of energetic walking and breathtaking sights, or quiet contemplation amid awe-inspiring nature.

Each month, *Country Living Magazine* celebrates the richness and diversity of our countryside with features on rural Britain and the traditions that have their roots there. So it is with great pleasure that I introduce you to the *Country Living Magazine Guide to Rural England* series. Packed with information about unusual and unique aspects of our countryside, the guides aim to point both fair-weather and intrepid travellers in the right direction.

This book provides a fascinating tour of the North West of England, from the sandstone villages of the Eden Valley in Cumbria to the rugged and varied terrain of the Forest of Bowland in Lancashire. One of the main attractions of this area is the Lake District. Venture out on one of the walking trails or explore the area by mountain bike. To take things at a more leisurely pace, enjoy a boat ride on one of the beautiful lakes or visit the historic houses and castles.

Each chapter also provides insights into local heritage and history, and easy-to-read facts about places to visit, stay, eat, drink and shop.

I hope this guide will help make your visit a rewarding experience and that you will return inspired, refreshed and ready to head off on your next countryside adventure.

Susy Smith

Susy Smith
Editor, Country Living magazine

PS To subscribe to *Country Living Magazine* each month, call 01858 438844

Introduction

Peter Long, the editor of this guide, is an experienced travel writer who spent many years with Egon Ronay's Hotels and Restaurant Guides before joining the Travel Publishing team. Peter has already used this experience to good effect on three other *Country Living* Rural Guides covering East Anglia, the South of England and Wales all of which have built up an enthusiastic readership. Readers will find the North West edition of *The Country Living Magazine Rural Guide to England* packed with vivid descriptions, historical stories, amusing anecdotes and interesting facts on hundreds of places in Cheshire, Lancashire, Merseyside, the Isle of Man, Greater Manchester and Cumbria.

Cumbria of course includes the Lake District famous for its impressive mountain scenery, green rolling hills, fast flowing rivers, deep lush forests and of course the enchanting lakes themselves. Readers who wish to explore the rural retreats of the North West however should definitely not ignore the hundreds of scenic attractions and interesting places to be found in the rest of this region.

The coloured advertising panels within each chapter provide further information on places to see, stay, eat, drink, shop and even exercise! We have also selected a number of walks from *Jarrold's Pathfinder Guides* which we highly recommend if you wish to appreciate fully the beauty and charm of the varied rural landscapes of the North West of England.

The guide however is not simply an "armchair tour". Its prime aim is to encourage the reader to visit the places described and discover much more about the wonderful towns, villages and countryside of the North West. In this respect we would like to thank all the Tourist Information Centres who helped us to provide you with up to date information. Whether you decide to explore this region by wheeled transport or by foot we are sure you will find it a very uplifting experience.

We are always interested in receiving comments on places covered (or not covered) in our guides so please do not hesitate to use the reader reaction form provided at the rear of this guide to give us your considered comments. This will help us refine and improve the content of the next edition. We also welcome any general comments which will help improve the overall presentation of the guides themselves.

Finally, for more information on the full range of travel guides published by Travel Publishing please refer to the details and order form at the rear of this guide or log on to our website at www.travelpublishing.co.uk

Travel Publishing

Locator Map

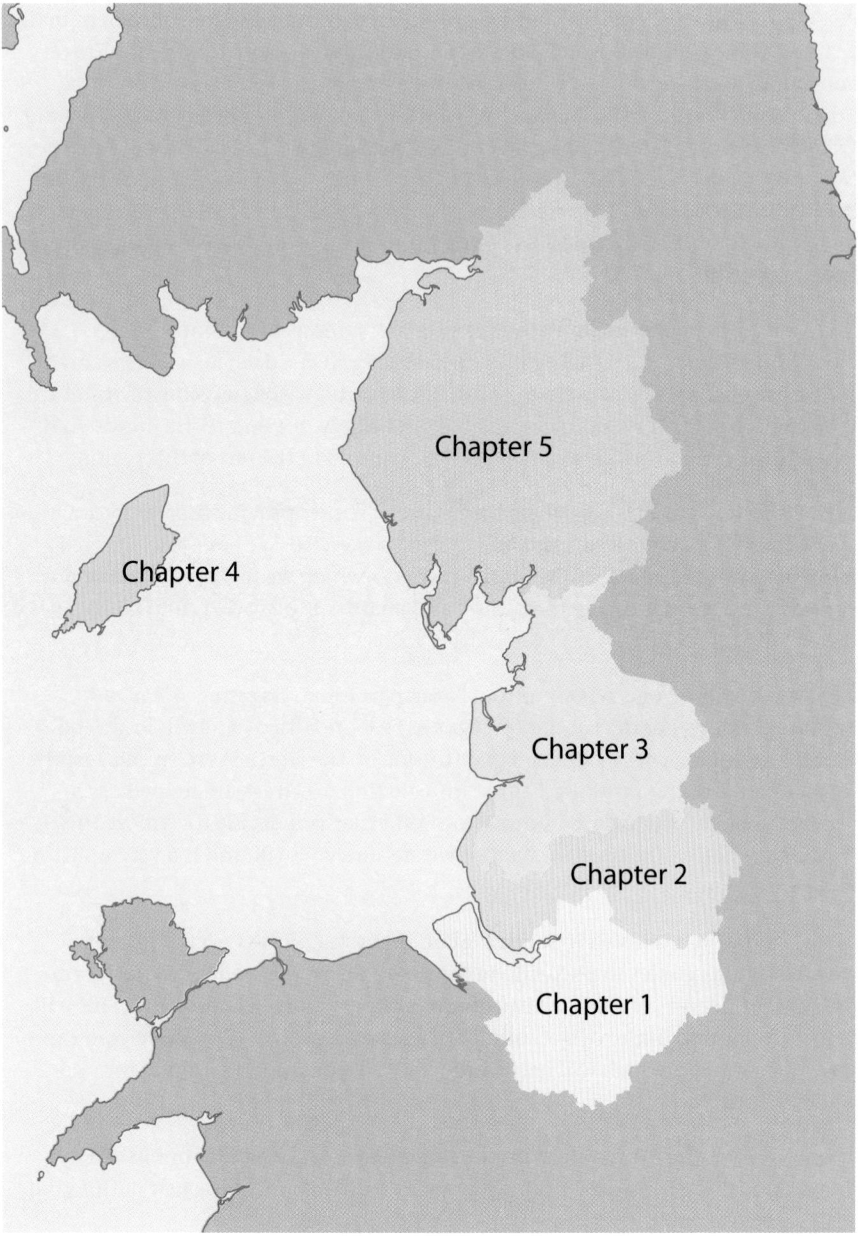
Chapter 5
Chapter 4
Chapter 3
Chapter 2
Chapter 1